PUBLICATION NUMBER 18

Duke University Commonwealth-Studies Center

*Administration and Economic
Development in India*

Duke University Commonwealth-Studies Center Publications

Administration and Economic Development in India

Ralph Braibanti, S. P. Jagota, Hugh Tinker, Richard L. Park,
Wilfred Malenbaum, Robert O. Tilman, Joseph J.
Spengler, N. V. Sovani, Ashok Mitra

Edited by
Ralph Braibanti
and
Joseph J. Spengler

PUBLISHED FOR THE
Duke University Commonwealth-Studies Center
DUKE UNIVERSITY PRESS, DURHAM, N. C.
CAMBRIDGE UNIVERSITY PRESS, LONDON
1963

Library of Congress Catalogue Card number 63-9006
Cambridge University Press, London N.W. 1, England

PRINTED IN THE UNITED STATES OF AMERICA
BY THE SEEMAN PRINTERY, INC., DURHAM, N. C.

INTRODUCTORY STATEMENT

THE DEVELOPMENT of growth economics as an autonomy which in the abstract can be detached from the tissue of culture has been much more rapid than similar developments in administration. Economic development has been blocked to a large extent precisely because its implementation depends on a structure and disposition of bureaucracy, neither of which can be jarred out of the larger societal whole.

In the spring of 1960 a group of social scientists presented papers on the manifold relationships of economic development and administration in India at sessions of the joint seminar of the Duke University Commonwealth-Studies Center. The papers presented in the seminar by Professors Mitra, Malenbaum, Sovani, and Park appear in this volume. Shri S. B. Bapat, Director of the United Nations Technical Assistance Program and Dr. I. G. Patel, of the International Monetary Fund, participated informally in the seminar. Six additional papers, written during months following the seminar by Professors Braibanti, Jagota, Tilman, Spengler, and Tinker also appear in this volume. While each paper is a separately conceived essay with no particular unity as to methodology, all focus on the problem of development in both its economic and administrative dimensions.

The range of experience from which the authors can draw their observations includes study and teaching in India, Burma, Malaya, Israel, Pakistan, Ethiopia, Japan, Okinawa, Thailand, Vietnam, Singapore, and Taiwan. The essays fall roughly into two groups: the first primarily concerned with administrative problems are, with one exception, written by political scientists. Ralph Braibanti, Professor of Political Science at Duke University, who was in Pakistan from 1960 to 1962 as Chief Advisor of the Civil Service Academy, analyzes the total structure of administrative reform, surveys the potential dangers which India avoided constructing this program, and reviews the transformation of the Indian Administrative Service as the successor to the Indian Civil Service. S. P. Jagota, Professor of Constitutional Law and Political Theory at the National Academy of Administration of India, describes the training of government officials in a paper which was a prize winning essay in a competition sponsored by the Indian Institute of Public Administration. It is published for the first time in this volume. Its publication has been approved by the director of the Indian Institute. Hugh Tinker, Reader in Politics and Government at the School of Oriental and African Studies of the University of London, analyzes the attempts to mobilize village society for economic development. Richard L. Park, Associate Professor of Political Science at the University of Michigan, on leave for 1962-64 as Representative in India of the Asia Foundation, writes of the dilemmas in transforming authoritarian district leadership into true self-government. Wilfred Malenbaum, Professor of Economics at the Wharton School of the University of Pennsylvania, explores the difficulties involved in political leadership of India's economic development. Professor Jagota in a second paper explores the constitutional aspects of national planning in India. Robert O. Tilman, Assistant Professor of Political Science at Tulane University, surveys various studies made of caste and assesses its influence on economic development.

The second group of essays is directed more specifically to economic problems. J. J. Spengler, James B. Duke Professor of Economics at Duke University, explores the concepts in Kauṭilya's *Arthaśāstra,* a classic work on statecraft written presumably in the fourth century B.C. N. V. Sovani, Joint Director of the Gokhale Institute of Politics and Economics, Poona, analyzes from an economist's point of view the non-economic factors affecting India's economy. Ashok Mitra, of the faculty of the Economic Development Institute of the International Bank for Reconstruction and Development, appraises the tax burden on agriculture and its relation to economic development.

Since the Commonwealth-Studies Center is concerned exclusively with the encouragement of research, specific theories or interpretations of Commonwealth affairs appearing in these publications do not constitute an expression of the view of the Center nor of the Carnegie Corporation, which has furnished financial support to the Center. The respective authors of the several essays are responsible for the conclusions expressed in them.

THE EDITORS

CONTENTS

CONTENTS

LIST OF TABLES

*Administration and Economic
Development in India*

Reflections on Bureaucratic Reform in India

Ralph Braibanti

THE DIRECTION TAKEN by reforms in the organization of the public bureaucracy is predetermined to a large extent by the quality of order with which a society can direct and thereby control change. In India the influence which traditionally molded the attitudes and structure of the entire bureaucracy was the Indian Civil Service (ICS), a relatively small elite cadre, consisting of 1,157 officers at the time of independence in 1947.[1] This small group of officers, 52 per cent of whom were British, constituted a mere .7 per cent of the total number of employees of the central government in India, which the Das Commission estimated at 156,912 in 1948 (excluding railways and post and telegraph employees, and defense ministry civilians).[2] When an undetermined number of employees of the fifteen states is added to this total, the number of ICS officers appears all the more insignificant. Yet whether the object of envy or respect, of hatred or admiration, the ICS, holding key posts throughout the bureaucracy, determined the policy of administration and molded the bureaucratic pattern.

In this essay the proposition is submitted that the program of administrative reform in India since 1947 has been unusually well conceived and has been marked by a firm sense of order, balance,

[1] This figure is derived from the *Combined Civil List for India and Burma, No. 158, Jan.-Mar. 1947* (Lahore, 1947). It includes officers of the Indian Political Service (IPS) who were chosen from the ICS and from the Indian Army, but it excludes officers serving in the Persian Gulf and in Burma.

[2] Government of India, Ministry of Finance, *Commission of Enquiry on Emoluments and Conditions of Service of Central Government Employees: 1957-59 Report* (Delhi, 1959), pp. 8-11. (Shri Justice Jagannadha Das, of the Supreme Court of India, was chairman; hence the designation Das Commission.)

and allocation of priorities. Part I of the essay reviews in cursory fashion administrative developments which appear to justify this hypothesis. This relatively orderly and rational adjustment to administrative needs was made possible in large measure by the strong tradition of intellectuality, independent spirit, and pride found in the Indian Civil Service. The first of these qualities, derived from Hindu society and sustained by the British Raj, was of singular importance in the evolution of the post-1947 higher bureaucracy. Part II of the essay seeks to array evidence demonstrating the existence of the quality here described as intellectuality in the ICS tradition. Part III is an effort to indicate, by constructing a hypothetical contrast, the relevance of a sophisticated bureaucratic intellectual apparatus to the problem of bureaucratic reform. It is assumed here that the acceptance of foreign aid and advice is a major factor in inducing change in the bureaucracies of developing states. There then follows an extended analysis of the dilemmas faced by nations accepting massive doses of such foreign governmental assistance. This analysis is meant to suggest the very pitfalls which India has avoided. This avoidance has been possible because of a venerable tradition of intellectuality and order which, involuntarily resisting wasteful change, accepted change which was compatible with strong intellectual predilections. India, not participating as a recipient of large-scale technical assistance in public administration from any foreign government, was able to control and direct her own bureaucratic destiny.

Part IV seeks to study one aspect of bureaucratic change, namely the transformation of the Indian Civil Service. The proposition advanced is that such transformation, largely because of its capacity to discriminate in selecting modes of change, was able to avoid the extremes of public administration fads. Its evolution into the Indian Administrative Service was unspectacular but orderly; marked by Indian domination and control, it was able to reject ephemeral modernisms and to adjust to the peculiar traditions and demands of Indian society.

I

To extract meaningful generalizations relating to the macrocosmic pattern of administrative change in India since 1947 is to court disagreement as to selection of factors. The description given here is necessarily cursory and highly impressionistic. It is based not on changes actually made, but rather on the totality of plans for change. Doubtless there is a yawning gap between well-intentioned planning and implementation. Certainly India continues to be faced with formidable administrative problems, not the least of which are corruption and inefficiency, rural uplift, and the administrative containment of disruptive cultural forces. But the actual condition of administration is beyond the scope of this paper. Concern here is for the intellectual edifice of bureaucratic change: the scaffolding which India has constructed for the change which she hopes will occur. It may well be that the edifice can never withstand the onslaughts of actual behavior. Certainly it would be naïve to suggest that mere administrative apparatus means sound administration or even good government. With respect to the actual state of administration, Appleby was able to say with justification (and certainly with consummate tact and finesse) that he had "come gradually to a general judgment that now would rate the government of India among the dozen or so most advanced governments of the world."[3] The intervening decade has demonstrated the reasonableness of this evaluation. With respect to the total blueprint for change, developments in public administration in India in terms of coherence, intellectual content, awareness of realities, balance between tradition and modernization are probably unequaled in Asia and deserve a high place when compared with similar developments in older nations of the West.[4] Certainly there is now little evidence that change in the government of India is premised exclusively on ancient Hindu political theory, which held that devices, forms, and systems of statecraft were of little consequence so long as the rulers had personal integrity and the citizenry moral sense. The pattern of administrative change (probably enhanced by two centuries of British emphasis on procedural means of attaining equity and probity) seems more related to the statecraft enjoined in Kauṭilya's *Arthaśāstra*[5] than the emphasis on kingly morality of the *Manusaṁhita*.

[3] Government of India, Cabinet Secretariat, *Public Administration in India: Report of a Survey*, by Paul H. Appleby (Delhi, 1953), p. 8.

[4] For an excellent review of administrative reform policies of the Government of India see Organization and Methods Division, Cabinet Secretariat, *Papers on Measures for Strengthening of Administration* (New Delhi, August 24, 1961).

[5] See Spengler's essay in this volume, especially pp. 233-239 ff.

For expository convenience, the ensuing commentary on the edifice of administrative change is divided into twelve characteristics supporting the favorable view taken of India's pattern of administrative change.

1. *Minimal reliance on foreign governmental advice and assistance.* The independence of India from United States technical assistance programs and other international and foreign governmental agencies is one of the most startling facts in her administrative development. Much of the change, particularly that in the organization and training of the Indian Administrative Service (successor to the ICS) was started even before contacts with foreign assistance programs were made. Although most of the administrative change in Asian states was generated by the United States Agency for International Development (USAID, formerly ICA), in India the influence of this organization (called Technical Cooperation Mission —TCM—in the field) was slight. A comparison of the USAID total budgets for the fiscal years 1959, 1960, and 1961 in certain selected countries of Asia and the Middle East and the proportion of such budgets allocated for public administration is shown in Table I.

Table I: USAID Project Obligations in Selected Countries for FY 1959, 1960, 1961

(in thousands of dollars)

Country	*Total* USAID *budget for 3-year period*	*For Public Administration* Amount	Per cent
Indonesia	23,462	4,999	21.3
Vietnam	44,398	7,319	16.4
Philippines	10,095	1,146	11.4
Pakistan	20,382	3,490	10.6
Thailand	17,987	1,900	10.6
China	24,952	2,597	10.4
Iran	15,677	2,624	10.3
Korea	40,863	3,117	7.4
Afghanistan	25,784	1,136	4.4
Laos	22,922	758	3.3
India	18,070	255	1.4

Sources: Tabulated from data in International Cooperation Administration, *Review of Mutual Cooperation in Public Administration for 1959* (Washington, 1959); *Operations Report for 1960* (Washington, 1960); *Operations Report for 1961* (Washington, 1961).

The total amount allocated to public administration projects by TCM in India from 1957 through 1962 is $395,000. Even the relatively small amounts spent in India on public administration have not gone into the major training institutions: National Academy of Administration, Institute of Public Administration, and Administrative Staff College. American help started at the Institute of Public Administration at Lucknow University in 1955 with a grant of $28,166 for books and provisions for a consultant for three months and the training of four Indians in the United States. In the next two years it concentrated primarily on furnishing advisors to the Indian Statistical Institute and in assisting the Ministry of Finance in conducting training programs. The TCM program in public administration has no subcontracts; hence the personnel dealing with administration are limited to four or five employees of TCM. When this is contrasted with the large contract groups of from twenty to sixty advisors operating in countries (such as Iran, Vietnam and Korea) far smaller than India, the limitations of TCM's influence become obvious.

Nor did India persist in depending on England for continued invigoration of the administrative system which had been developed under the British Raj. Ties with England were severed rather abruptly after 1947. Fewer than thirty British officers of the ICS remained in India and, presumably for reasons of economy, probationers in the successor IAS were not sent to England for training after 1940 as they had been for more than a century. There have been no large programs for sending Indian administrators abroad for administrative training, although there have been scattered fellowships under Ford, Rockefeller, Fulbright, and other auspices.

The major source of foreign aid came from the Ford Foundation, which, from the beginning of its operations in India in 1951 until January 15, 1962, allocated $2,047,000 to grants for public administration projects.[6] This was 4.3 per cent of the $46,698,316 given by the Foundation in the form of grants for various activities in India during the same period. The amount spent on public administration was allocated as follows:

[6] *The Ford Foundation and Foundation-Supported Activities in India, Summary of Grants from 1951 to January 15, 1962* (mimeographed) (New Delhi; Ford Foundation, Jan. 15, 1962), pp. 21 ff.

Indian Institute of Public Administration	$1,050,000
Administrative Staff College	134,500
Support for Master Plan for Calcutta	800,000
National Academy of Administration	62,500
Total:	$2,047,000

The impact of reforms generated by Ford Foundation support has been far greater than the small sum of about two million dollars might suggest. Probably few technical assistance programs can show as many direct and concomitant beneficial results from so small an investment. The first visit of Paul H. Appleby in September, 1952, and subsequent visits were sponsored by the Foundation. These visits generated many correlative changes, not the least of which was the creation of the Institute of Public Administration and a strong organization and methods agency in the central government. Ford Foundation support was largely initial stimulation of change rather than continuing, large-scale foreign advisory services. Assistance consisted largely of assessing the needs, indicating the direction of change, and assisting in library acquisitions and building construction. No permanent resident advisors or counterparts were used in the assistance program. The impetus for change came mainly from Indian leadership, once the over-all program had been formulated.

2. *Avoidance of ethnocentric reform and the adaptation of the traditional system evolved under the British Raj.* While it is true that connections with Britain were severed as regards training of administrative personnel, this does not imply a corresponding abandonment of administrative structure or attitudes. On the contrary, there was no revolutionary departure from the past in these matters. The parliamentary system and separate cadres including the IAS assured a high degree of continuity, and changes made were of an evolutionary character. Appleby set the tone for change rooted in unique cultural needs, rather than in a doctrinaire program based either on ideology or indiscriminate imitation. The tenor of his reports was reflected in his statement that the government of India was essentially different from all others, that it was an outgrowth of its own culture, and that the value of comparisons "is in stimulating some development which had nowhere before existed in precisely

the same form or manner."[7]   It is not unlikely that this genuine
understanding and respect for the administrative heritage of India
did much to establish respect for public administration as a discipline
and for foreign advisors in administration.   Both Appleby and others
were frank to point out, however, that what existed was not necessarily best merely because it existed.   The British had devised a
structure to meet colonial needs, and it was not necessarily the structure best suited to conditions of sovereignty.   Nevertheless, reform
in administration has been based on modifying the system rather than
abandoning it.   The basic structure of the services remains, with
divisions into cadres of varying degrees of esteem.   The reservation
of crucial posts in both state and Union governments for members
of the IAS continues.   The familiar pattern remained unchanged:
recruitment at an early age followed by successive postings in district
administration, central or provincial secretariats and in varying substantive fields.   The shadow of an omnicompetent generalism cast
by Macaulay, Wellesley, and the whole ICS tradition, while perhaps
not lengthening, is fading slowly.   Yet in some matters, such as
admitting women into the IAS, India seems innovative to the point
of daring.

3. *Early association of officials of superior talent with administrative reform.*   It is clear that from the outset the government of
India did not regard administrative reform or training assignments
as sinecure posts for the incompetent or as "transportation for life"
postings for officials who had fallen out of bureaucratic favor.   On
the contrary, from the beginning administrative reform received
the sustained personal attention of Prime Minister Nehru and the
executive direction of the most distinguished administrative talent
of India.   The fact that the Prime Minister is chairman of the
Planning Commission and is president of the Institute of Public
Administration not only conditions the status of these activities, but
puts him in a position of giving active direction to major policy.   It
was C. D. Deshmukh, now vice-chancellor of the University of
Delhi who, as finance minister, arranged for Appleby's visits to
India.[8]   S. B. Bapat, who was later to become director of the United

[7] Appleby *Report*, cited in n. 3 above, p. 5.
[8] C. D. Deshmukh, "The Role of the Central Services in Economic Development,"
Indian Journal of Public Administration, VII (1961), 127; and "The State of the
Administration," *Journal of the National Academy of Administration*, V (1960), 13.

Nations Technical Assistance Program, was first director of the Institute of Public Administration and before that was first director of the Organization and Methods Division of the Government of India.   A. N. Jha, a distinguished Sanskritist and former vice-chancellor of the Varanasi Sanskrit University, is director of the National Academy of Administration and Secretary to the Government of India for administrative training.   The first principal of the IAS Training School was M. J. Desai, a senior member of the ICS who in 1947 had nineteen years of government service and who is now secretary of the Ministry of External Affairs.   A. D. Gorwala, a distinguished officer of the ICS, was associated with administrative reform from the beginning.   It was Gorwala who wrote the first report on administration for the Planning Commission and who subsequently wrote a report on Mysore administration.[9]   One of the results of this identification of talented officials with administrative reform was ready acceptance of not only the concepts of administration but the very term "public administration," which was virtually unknown in India before independence.   Instead of becoming a term of opprobrium, it became a term of intellectual respectability.   This is the more remarkable because of the intellectual incompatibility of the literary-generalist concepts of statecraft implicit in the British Raj and the more technical empirical disposition of American public administration.   The intellectual gulf was bridged without great discomfort.

4. *Rapid erosion of the exclusivity and secrecy of administration as an activity reserved for the few and the association of the public with the problems of administrative reform.*   There was little paranoic secretiveness regarding reform and no classification of reports thus shielding deficiencies from public scrutiny.   This may be due in large measure to the vigorous political process of the Lok Sabha with its committees of oversight and question periods.   Whatever the reasons, both the first Appleby report and the second[10] were

[9] A. D. Gorwala, *Report on Public Administration* (Planning Commission, Delhi, 1951); *The Mysore Administration: Some Observations and Recommendations* (Bangalore, 1958).

[10] Paul H. Appleby, *Re-examination of India's Administrative System with Special Reference to Administration of Government's Industrial and Commercial Enterprises* (Delhi, 1956).

reprinted, widely distributed, and extensively discussed in both press and the Lok Sabha.[11] The reports of the Estimates Committee of the Lok Sabha on such issues as secretariat reorganization, public undertakings in general, and particular government corporations reveal at least the beginnings of a system of parliamentary supervision over administration. While perhaps the supervision is too petty and deals too little with general policy formulation, such a symmetrical relationship between legislature and administration is not easily achieved in any constitutional system in the early years of its growth.

The monopoly on administrative knowledge possessed exclusively by the bureaucracy has been broken further by the teaching of public administration in universities, organization of public administration societies throughout India, public seminars, and publications of the Indian Institute of Public Administration.

5. *Fairly sophisticated conceptual and eclectic approach to administration.* The training programs at the various institutions have been distinguished by a respectable intellectual leavening. The Institute in Delhi concentrated from the beginning on a useful research library, and it is now one of the most complete and most convenient in Asia. The staff at both the Institute and its affiliated School is drawn more from the academic realm than from the practicing bureaucracy. While this has been deplored by Appleby in an evaluation report of the Institute, it may not be as serious as supposed; in any case, there are strong signs that the "practitioner" point of view will be more strongly represented. Neither the Institute nor the School has concentrated excessively on any one aspect of administration to the exclusion of others. There has been a broad-based attack on the problems of administration, which is reflected also in the approaches of foreign scholars who have served as visiting professors at the Institute: Arthur Macmahon, A. H. Hanson, W. A. Robson, Wallace Sayre. At the National Academy in Mussoorie, a distinguished faculty, five of whom hold foreign doctorates, and an able research staff have been engaged in productive scholarship.

[11] See the Lok Sabha secretariat's compilation of press and other comments on Appleby's first report, *Report on India's Administrative System by Dr. Paul H. Appleby: Comments and Reactions* (New Delhi, Sept., 1956).

The *Indian Journal of Public Administration*, now in its eighth year, and the *Journal of the National Academy of Administration*, which has been published since 1955, are both creditable journals; and the number of research studies based on hard empirical data seems to increase as the publication of short speeches given by visitors seems to become less frequent.

6. *Ordering of basic research data.* The most essential primary task confronting the scholar in a developing state is the collation, classification, and evaluation of data. Without such basic bibliographic and statistical spadework, no research can proceed in a systematic, meaningful fashion. India has made noteworthy advances in this respect and the level of analysis and sorting of data compares favorably with the research circumstances in many Western countries. The British proclivity towards extensive public record issuance (from the scholar's point of view one of the greatest blessings of the British Raj) continues, augmented by Lok Sabha reports. The first pay commission report[12] and the report of the second pay commission[13] are exhaustive analyses prepared in the best tradition of government reporting. So elemental a research need as well-prepared, authentic organization charts of government, careful description of constitutional arrangements and functions of ministries has been adequately met in one of the first publications of the Institute.[14] Such indispensable tools as abstracting and indexing articles and printing current news of administrative developments in India and elsewhere have been provided. The former need has been met since 1946 by the Institute of Public Administration's *Abstracts and Index of Articles* and the latter by its monthly *Newsletter*. With respect to hard empirical data, a major problem in most developing states is the collation of data on the size of the public services, backgrounds of members of the higher civil service, descriptions of training programs, organization of government, and relationship of judiciary to bureaucracy. All of these issues have been dealt with, at least in a preliminary manner, which will make possible further more ad-

[12] *Report of the Central Pay Commission 1946-47* (Varadachariar Commission) (Delhi, 1947).
[13] Das Commission *Report*, cited in n. 2 above.
[14] Indian Institute of Public Administration, *The Organisation of the Government of India* (Bombay, 1958).

vanced research. Professors D. N. Rao, S. P. Jagota, and Mr. R. K. Trivedi, all of the National Academy of Administration, have done pioneering work of exceptional quality on the question of the size, composition, and training of the bureaucracy.[15] A good beginning has been made by Professor A. N. Khosla in compiling some forty-three decisions of the Supreme Court dealing with service matters.[16] Case law, a badly neglected field of study in Indian administration, is one of the principal sources of insight into the operations of government. Further, the problems of judicial control over administrative discretion and of judicial redress of internal bureaucratic grievances under articles 226 and 311 of the Constitution of India, both significant studies in comparative jurisprudence, have been given attention.

Case materials are still badly needed in Indian administration, but the prospects of remedying this deficiency in a few years are very good. The Institute is collaborating with the Inter-University Case Study Program in the United States and first drafts of some twenty cases have already been completed.

In sum, substantial progress has been made in the collation of empirical data for further analysis. There is a perceptible movement away from impressionistic, literary accounts of administration toward more sophisticated empirical research. Certain major deficiencies remain, however. First, the empirical research is not rigorous enough. The use of statistics is somewhat careless and results in distorted conclusions. Secondly, the analytical and interpretative elements in most of the research are deficient. This is due in part to relative inexperience in rigorous analytical scholarship and in part to the serious limitations implicit in the fact that scholars are, in the final analysis, employees of the government. The absolute freedom to do research on any subject and publish results whatever they may be, as is known in the United States, is absent in India. The prestige of the scholar in relation to the bureaucrat is such that the scholar must invariably seek approval of an administrative officer before

[16] See R. K. Trivedi and D. N. Rao, "Growth of Personnel and Civil Expenditure in the Government of India" *Journal of the National Academy of Administration*, VI (1961), 31-86. See analysis of Trivedi-Rao study in this essay, pp. 51 ff. below. See also Jagota's essay on training in this volume.

[16] A. N. Khosla, compiler, *Government Servants' Cases*, Vols. I and II (Bombay, n.d., probably 1953 and 1960).

publication is possible. Dispassionate, objective analysis which may be sharply critical of established government policy is still not common in India. There are also some important areas of research which have been badly neglected. For example, no carefully documented, rigidly controlled empirical study of district administration has appeared. Nor has the work of the Union Public Service Commission been carefully studied.

7. *Early acceptance of the concept and practices of state planning.* The socialist ideology on which the government of India is premised precluded the possibility of hesitation over the philosophy of planning. By early 1950 India decided to embark on a six-year (later changed to five-year) plan. The major advisory assistance on its formulation came from the Colombo Plan, with whose blueprint the First Five Year Plan 1951-1956 was integrated. The Second Five Year Plan covered the period from 1956 to 1961 and the Third Five Year Plan covers the 1961-1966 period. Considerable attention was given to administrative problems particularly in the First Plan, and the public management studies section of the planning commission was established to deal especially with government corporations and *panchāyats*. Not only was there no resistance to planning, but the Planning Commission was well organized from the beginning with the Prime Minister as chairman, a cabinet minister as vice-chairman, and with strong coordinative links with the Lok Sabha, state planning agencies, and advisory bodies. The stability and effectiveness of the Commission results in large measure from the soundness of its organization and the assignment of able officers to the Commission.[17]

8. *Rapid development of the public corporation as a means of infusing selected government operations with new vigor, speed, and dynamism.*[18] The growth of government corporations in India has

[17] For further analysis of planning, see a special issue of the *Indian Journal of Public Administration*, VII (1961) on administration and the Third Plan; see also Jagota's essay "Some Constitutional Aspects of Planning" in this volume and Indian Institute of Public Administration, *Planning in India* (mimeographed) (Delhi, 1961).

[18] Terminology relating to corporations is carelessly used in the literature on them. The terms public undertakings, public (government) enterprises, statutory bodies, state enterprises, and national industrial undertakings, and mixtures thereof, are usually used interchangeably, although there are technical differences between them. The Lok Sabha secretariat uses the generic term "public undertakings,"

been one of the outstanding developments in government. They have so increased in number and in scope of operation that the problem is no longer their creation but rather their control and co-ordination to insure that achievements optimistically expected of them will eventuate. The nature of the administrative problems which have arisen was well forecast by both Appleby and Gorwala.[19] The scandals which rocked the Life Insurance Corporation of India focused attention on problems of parliamentary supervision, reporting, and management. Reports of the estimates committee of the Lok Sabha have shown sharp awareness of the implications of these problems.[20] Reports of such large enterprises as the Damodar Valley Corporation and the Life Insurance Corporation reflect a sophisticated comprehension of the problems. Decisions taken, for example, not to split up the LIC and not to create a special management cadre for the corporations (as recommended by the Estimates Committee of the Lok Sabha in its ninth report) were taken after considerable exchange of views both in public, government, and legislative circles.[21]

9. *Appreciation of the value of empirical analysis of administrative work as a means of increasing efficiency.* One of the results of

---

which are then classified into nine types. The number of central government undertakings in each class is shown below: statutory corporations, 10; joint stock companies, 37; commissions, 6; boards, 31; committees, 23; councils, 36; universities, 4; institutes, 12; others, 21. (Lok Sabha, *Classified List of Public Undertakings and Other Bodies in India* [New Delhi, Oct., 1958].)

[19] Paul H. Appleby, *Re-examination of India's Administrative System with Special Reference to Administration of Government's Industrial and Commercial Enterprises* (Government of India: New Delhi, 1959); A. D. Gorwala, *Report on the Efficient Conduct of State Enterprises* (Government of India: New Delhi, 1951).

[20] The general dimensions of the problem of public corporate enterprises in developing states are analyzed in a United Nations report on a seminar held in Delhi in 1959, *Public Industrial Management in Asia and the Far East* (New York, 1960) and in a earlier United Nations report, *Some Problems in the Organization and Administration of Public Enterprises in the Industrial Field* (New York, 1954). See also A. H. Hanson, *Public Enterprise and Economic Development* (London, 1959). See also note 46 in Jagota's essay, "Some Constitutional Aspects of Planning," in this volume.

[21] See, for example, a lively exchange of views in the *Statesman*, Sept. 6, 1961, p. 8; Sept. 12, 1961, p. 6; Oct. 26, 1961, p. 8; Oct. 27, 1961, p. 1; Oct. 29, 1961, p. 8. See also H. C. Dasappa, "Parliamentary Control and Accountability in Public Undertakings," *Indian Journal of Public Administration*, VII (1961), 136; M. V. Pylee, "Government Enterprises in the Indian Economy," *Asian Survey*, I (1961), 16; Indian Institute of Public Administration, *State Undertakings* (New Delhi, Aug., 1960, mimeo.); *A Bibliography on Public Enterprises in India* (New Delhi, Aug., 1961, mimeo.); Lok Sabha Secretariat, *Hundred and Thirty-fourth Report: Life Insurance Corporation of India* (New Delhi, April, 1961); *Eighth Report, Damodar Valley Corporation* (New Delhi, May, 1954).

the Appleby *Report* was the creation of the Organization and Methods division in March, 1954, with S. B. Bapat, who had been Establishment Officer to the Government of India as its first head. There was disagreement as to whether the O & M function should be located in the finance ministry or the establishment division. This was reconciled by the wise decision to locate it in the cabinet secretariat where it would have the status essential to secure compliance.[22] Strengthened by this decision, O & M work has moved ahead with considerable vigor and speed. The concept of scientific analysis of work has been favorably received. This is somewhat surprising, since the extremely generalist bias of the ICS tradition would seem to mitigate against this kind of empirical investigation. The success of the O & M concept is due in no small measure to the assignment of Shri Bapat as O & M head, who, as establishment officer, had commanded the citadel of the orthodox ICS bureaucracy. This effectively transferred the prestige and esteem of the orthodox system to the newer, unfamiliar activity. Indeed, the strategic use of able officials who were immersed in the ethos of the orthodox bureaucracy to the newer, suspect administrative activities probably accounts for much of the success in constructing an apparatus of administrative reform. The fairly high level of sophistication of the O & M activity is indicated by the contents of its journal, *Work Improvement*, which started publication with the September-October issue in 1961.

10. *International acceptance of Indian administrative developments in the mainstreams of research, publication, and professionalization.* Within somewhat more than a decade, Indian administrative developments have commanded the attention and respect of other nations and have entered the stream of international scholarship in full parity with other sources for the study of comparative government. In part this is due to the interest shown in India by foreign (particularly American) scholars since 1947. But more fundamentally it is due to the emergence of an intellectual tradition and values in which the foreign scholar feels at home and in which research can be effectively pursued. The Institute of Public Administration has become somewhat of a model for Southeast Asia and, indeed, for other countries in the world. The journals have earned a decent reputa-

[22] S. B. Bapat, "O & M in the Government of India," *Indian Journal of Public Administration*, I (1955), 61-80.

tion for intellectual respectability, and the two-way flow of scholars is rather impressive. Publications, reports, and other materials are slowly reaching the desks of Western scholarship and the full weight of Indian experience in the grist of comparative experience will be felt probably in less than a generation. This has already been enhanced by Indian participation in international conferences, the preparation of case studies which will immediately have international recognition, and by advisory services of the Ford Foundation whose facilities are multinational.

11. *Evolution of an administrative structure for effectively transferring sovereignty to the people and reducing public dependence on bureaucracy as a source of impetus.* While this is probably the greatest unsolved administrative problem confronting India, significant conceptual advances have been made, however inadequate the implementation. The pattern of Union-state relations was determined by the constitution, and a solution to the vexing problem of stimulating the villager to new levels of initiative has been sought under the general rubric of "democratic decentralization." This rubric embraces the *panchāyati raj,* first started in Rajasthan in 1959, community development, and co-operatives, all of which have deep roots in Indian history. The dilemmas and literature of this problem have been analyzed elsewhere.[23] One of the key problems is the essential incompatibility of the shirt-sleeve (or, to put it in the proper cultural frame—*lunghī* or *dhōtī*) attitudes and techniques of the community development dynamic with the collar and tie (*achkan* and *churidār*) attitude of orthodox district administration. Certainly the problem has not been solved. Yet much has been done, as a later portion of this essay describes, to break the arrogance of the IAS, to destroy the *pakkā sāhib* attitude which characterized the worst part of colonial rule. Quite apart from change in composition of the IAS, it is significant that the community development idea (structurally, at least) is given high status and that if it does not command respect and attention, certainly it cannot be ignored or circumvented as an important aspect of bureaucratic life. Intellectually, the community development concept is not isolated as a phenomenon to be dealt with only when one thinks of the village. There is significant interpenetra-

[23] See the essays by Tinker and Park in this volume.

tion of community development and orthodox bureaucratic thinking in journals[24] and in the various training institutions.

12. *Reinvigoration of the orthodox bureaucracy and gradual transformation of its role in society without rejecting its historic role of administrative leadership.* India might have chosen to abandon the ICS structure or to allow it to wither away by surrounding it with more dynamic administrative institutions. There does not seem to be any serious move to abolish the IAS as a separate cadre or to amalgamate all cadres into one common service. The latter suggestion was made by Appleby in a public address in 1961, but has not thus far been considered with favor by the government. Since the Das Commission refrained from making recommendations relating to the IAS, what its view on this matter might have been is not known. It recommended unequivocally the abolition of existing service divisions of Class I, II, III, and IV, a distinction started by the Islington Report recommendations in 1917. It deplored the practice of the use of service designations such as IAS, IPS, IFS after names on the ground that this did not promote unity and the feeling of belonging to a common civil service. But its recommendations otherwise were based on the continued existence of separate cadres of services, including, of course, the Indian Administrative Service.

Nor has the reconstructed fortress of the orthodox bureaucracy, the National Academy of Administration in Mussoorie, been allowed to exist merely as an antiquarian shadow of the old ICS. On the contrary, it flourishes with a staff in size and competence matched by few if any institutions in India. The quality and volume of research in administrative problems done at the Academy matches that done elsewhere. It has a distinct advantage over other institutions in research through its intimate connection with the operating agencies of government, and by virtue of its status as lineal descendant of the Indian Civil Service. The close identification of the Academy with all administrative developments through appointment of its director as director of training for the central government, asserts its preeminence. The composition of the IAS has changed, its ethos has

[24] Note, for example, that in the special issue of the *Indian Journal of Public Administration*, VII (1961) on administration and the Third Plan, about one-third of the contents concerns "democratic decentralization." This one-third reflects a commendable integration of bureaucratic, economic, and "democratic decentralization" thought.

been modified, its functions are undergoing transformation. The eventual effective implementation of separation of the judicial from executive functions, the rise of local self-government, the increased role of the state civil services in district administration: these are long range developments which have been fomented by decisions already taken. In the abstract, an elite corps of high civil servants should evolve, divested of much of the petty power it formerly wielded, capable of administering the more demanding problems of a complex, modern state.

II

Within the short span of a decade and a half, India seems to have developed a sound institutional base for the diffusion of information about government, the training of non-officials in the study of government, the education of government officials in statecraft, and for mechanical efficiency and democratic control. Such uneventful, sophisticated absorption of a pattern of government reform and of the training of officials raises the question as to what made this possible.

The relatively felicitous adaptation of modern administrative reforms was enhanced by several conditions. First was the confrontation of reformist concepts by an integrated tradition of Brahminical intellectual life which sustained a respect for learning. This esteem for intellect had become part of an ICS ethos derived from Hailey-bury tradition. Karve has pointed out that the continuity of Hindu society is greater than that of Christianity and Islam because Hindu historical experience has never been separated into pre-Christian or pre-Islamic epochs whose symbols and beliefs have nothing more than antiquarian interest to the new religious eras.[25] While this is a fundamental aspect of the continuity of Hindu culture in its historical dimension, there is a spatial dimension which has crucial significance: the fabric of Hindu intellectual life has never been irreparably torn into segments separated from the sources of political power. Even the temporary displacement of Indian power by the British Raj accelerated and deepened the intellectualization of the Indian Hindu

[25] Iravati Karve, "Some Aspects of the Caste-Society of the Hindus," in N. V. Sovani and V. M. Dandekar, eds., *Changing India* (Bombay, 1961), p. 163.

bureaucracy, for Indianization occurred only when formal educational requirements of a high order could be met.

This fortunate circumstance is not to be found in all developing societies. In most developing states three elites are among prime determinants of the pace and direction of cultural change. They are (1) the tradition-minded religious elite, (2) the secular-minded public bureaucracy (military, civil, or both), and (3) the non-bureaucratic intellectual elite. The latter group may comprise the professions (especially law), politicians, scholars of the leisured classes, or a charismatic secular sainthood (such as manifest in Tagore and Gandhi in India). In some societies, where there is little effective interaction among these three elites, membership in one does not confer membership in another and may even preclude it. Where the spheres of influence of each elite are rather rigidly separated, there is very little interpenetration of values and dispositions. Where there is no conjunction of these three elites, the dispositions of intellectuality which may prevail in the other two have minimal influence on the bureaucratic power which controls the transition to a modern political system. There was, for example, such a fortunate convergence of elites in Japan, and the modernization of the Meiji era was thereby immensely facilitated. Buddhist and Confucian scholarship had penetrated not only the civil bureaucracy but influenced the military bureaucracy as well. No better illustration of interpenetration of religion and military values can be found than in the emergence of the highly disciplined austerity of Zen Buddhism. The application of the Japanese title *sensei* to both teachers and those government officers deemed to have scholarly qualities is symbolic of a convergence of scholarly and bureaucratic values in Japan seldom found in modern society. Only such fusion of power and intellect would have made possible the study tour of Ito Hirobumi's committee in Europe, its absorption of the teaching of von Stein and others, and its integration of these lessons with fundamentals of Japanese tradition. In societies less fortunate in this respect, the religious elite remains outside the threshold of bureaucratic power, cannot bring the discipline and order of its own intellectual tradition to bear on secular civil problems, is often overly resistant to bureaucratic power, and consequently, as in the case of the *ulema* in Egypt, may be dealt with harshly.

Pakistan, for example, has been less fortunate than either India or

Japan in this respect; hence her problems of political development are far greater. In Pakistan the Muslim religious elite embodied in the *maulānās* and *mullahs* is in every sense divorced from the secular-minded public bureaucracy. The intellectual tradition which, in the higher reaches, was both venerable and sophisticated, rejected Western secular learning and was oriented almost exclusively to Qur'anic and Persian scholarship. The efforts of Sir Syed Ahmed Khan which, through the Aligarh movement, sought to provide a second (Western) dimension to the Muslim intellectual heritage were started in the 1860's, too late to permit the same harmonious confluence of traditions which had developed for centuries in Hinduism. The penetration of the Indian Civil Service by Muslims was minimal. By 1947 only 9 per cent of the total ICS cadre of 1,157 officers was Muslim, as contrasted with 39 per cent Hindu and others, and 52 per cent British.[26] But even the Muslims entering were not themselves the religious elite, as were the Hindus. The Muslim's regard for the traditionalistic *maulānā* was of a different order from that of the Hindu's regard for the Brahminical tradition. The Qur'anic, Persian orientation of Muslim scholarship did not, therefore, converge with bureaucratic power, but was, on the contrary, in a separate compartment. Hence the intellectuality characterizing the Muslim component of the ICS and the later bureaucracy of Pakistan derived its strength from more recent British tradition, unsustained by the venerable, scholarly achievements of Islam, which continued to flow in a separate stream. The few *maulānā* or *maulvī* types found in the bureaucracy were in the lower clerical reaches or among superintendents and assistants. The very terms *maulānā* and *maulvī*, while respected in a curiously diffident way as symbols of a traditional way of life detached from the realities of an Anglo-oriented bureaucracy, certainly did not command the same eminence of respectability and esteem among the Western-oriented elite as the term *pandit* among Hindus or *sensei* among Japanese. India, like Japan, has had the advantage of a convergence of these three elites. The ancient tradition of Sanskritic scholarship molded the Brahmin mind, penetrated the civil bureaucracy, and constituted the secular, non-bureaucratic intelligentsia as well. The extent of Brahmin participation in the bureaucracy is indicated by the

[26] Computed from *Combined Civil List for India and Burma, No. 158, Jan.- Mar. 1947* (Lahore, 1947).

fact that in 1913, 40 per cent of the posts carrying salaries of Rs. 200 a month and over held by non-British officials, were held by Brahmins.[27]   Even today it is not uncommon to find an officer of the Indian Civil Service, learned in or at least respectful of Sanskritic learning, Brahmin by caste, wielding bureaucratic power, and acknowledged as a leader among the non-bureaucratic intelligentsia. This is not to say that the substance of traditional religious learning did not change or that the substance was even partially comprehended by the bureaucratic elite.   What is relevant is the cumulative development of attitudes toward learning and their unbroken continuity and permeation among the other elites.   Substance as such must, of course, undergo change and can be only marginally comprehended by large numbers who may, nevertheless, espouse its values and embrace its attitudes.   Spengler has elsewhere stated that the "content of men's minds" is crucial to politico-economic development.[28]   The frame upon which the content is arrayed is at least of equal importance, for the frame of attitudes is a residue of stiffening which may exist with little positive relationship to the substance of knowledge.   The latter may never fully have entered the mind or, entering, may have been eroded.   In this respect it is not crucially significant that the predominant affinity of the Indian intellectual has been, as Shils so well describes,[29] for British literary and other cultural values.   These may have displaced other values temporarily, but the attitude towards learning has not necessarily been thereby diminished.   Indeed, the likelihood is that it has been enhanced and that the apparatus for intellectual exercise has been at least rendered more versatile if not more refined.

It is appropriate now to list the attributes of what is here called the intellectual tradition which have relevance to the problem of introducing administrative reform.   The first of these is the disposition to read, not exclusively for liturgical or emotional satisfaction, but for the purpose of obtaining specific knowledge.   The second

[27] Report of the Royal Commission on Public Service August 14, 1915, Cd. 8382 (London, 1917), 20 vols. (Islington Report), I, 31.
[28] Joseph J. Spengler, "Theory, Ideology, Non-Economic Values, and Politico-Economic Development," in Ralph Braibanti and Joseph J. Spengler, eds., Tradition, Values, and Socio-Economic Development (Durham, N. C., 1961), pp. 1-56.
[29] Edward Shils, "The Culture of the Indian Intellectual," Sewanee Review, LXVII (1959), 231-261, 401-421. See also his "The Intellectuals and the Powers: Some Perspectives for Comparative Analysis," Comparative Studies in Society and History, I (1958), 5-22. See also Shanti S. Tangri, "Intellectuals and Society in Nineteenth-Century India," ibid., III (1961), 368-395.

is the respect for ordered data and the emotional discipline essential for the collection, appraisal, and classification of data within a rational scheme from which conclusions may be reached. The third is acute sensitivity to observed phenomena and the relating of such to reality as studied. Fourth is refinement of concepts by skilled disputation, both silent and oral, and by the application of critical and imaginative faculties to problems of reality. Fifth is awareness of the immense complexity of problems of cultural change, the humility which such awareness should induce, and appreciation of the role of critical imagination and wisdom to give meaning to empirical data. Implicit in these attributes is the transcendent requisite, i.e., respect for learning and commitment to the application of the methods of scholarship as an effective means of solving real problems. These are attributes of mind easily lost, but neither quickly nor easily acquired in the development of any society. These attributes are encompassed by the subsequent use of the term "intellectuality."[30] It may be that the net effect of Brahminical learning was marked reliance on intuition rather than empiricism as a mode of reasoning— a point of view well developed by Northrop.[31] Even though this may be true and may adversely affect the intellectual attitudes requisite for rational political development, there is, nevertheless, a substantial advantage in the mere posture of veneration for learning and for the profession of scholarship. To put it another way, the mere existence of a tradition of scholarship, even though intuitively disposed, is better for directing and controlling change than its absence.

The intellectual apparatus with which India was able to confront the problems of independence was strengthened by certain characteristics of the ICS tradition which dominated the ethos of the public bureaucracy. Foremost was the assumption that the Platonic

[30] Barzun's definition of what he calls the House of Intellect "embraces at least three groups of subjects: the persons who consciously and methodically employ the mind; the forms and habits governing the activities in which the mind is so employed: and the conditions under which these people and activities exist." Jacques Barzun, *The House of Intellect* (New York, 1959), p. 3. While this definition has stimulated my thinking in this essay, I find it necessary to add the first and fifth characteristics given in the five listed above and convenient to explicate the others. Without the first and fifth characteristics, intellectuality could too easily be defined as merely the process of scientific method as conceived by radical positivism. The burden of my argument here is for an intellectuality which includes rigid scientific method but is not limited to it.

[31] F. S. C. Northrop, *The Meeting of East and West* (New York, 1946).

guardians were men of superior virtue. But, as in the Platonic and Confucian concepts, the abstract determination of the locus of virtue by the possession of certain externals of behavior—i.e., propriety, calligraphy, knowledge, social relations, forensics, games, became contorted by the notion that the development of such external characteristics would conduce to virtue. Such contortion was environmental determinism par excellence. In both the Confucian and the ICS traditions, this reliance on externals as means of developing the spirit rather than as evidences of the inner presence of virtue resulted in a healthy respect for mental and physical training. Since the virtuous man was a man of inner harmony and outer tranquillity, the evidences of this perfection were thought to be as many and varied as the qualities thus harmonized. When the evidences became instruments, they had to be applied in the same proportion which appeared in their outward manifestations. Hence the intellectual tradition of the ICS was no mean obscurantism or sterile pedantry; at its worst it was dilettantism but at its best it was marked by an eclectic quality, an imagination, and a vision worthy of the greatest respect.

There are two major bodies of evidence to support the contention that the ICS tradition was leavened by intellectuality. First is the scholarly work of certain individuals of the Indian Civil Service, such as Denzil Ibbetson, F. L. Brayne, C. F. Strickland, Malcolm Darling, F. Nicholson, S. S. Thorburn, and James M. Douie. To name these seven is to omit many more whose craftsmanship and devotion to learning was reflected not only in prescribed census and settlement reports but in "extra-curricular" enterprises as well. In the work of these men, there was attention to meticulous classification of data,[32] integrated social and economic studies which would satisfy the canons of rigorous empiricism,[33] earthy humanitarian scholarship attuned to the homely requisites of village uplift, yet guided by uncommon missionary dedication,[34] and meticulous compilations (like Douie's

[32] Sir Denzil Ibbetson's *Punjab Castes* (Lahore: Government Printing Press, Punjab, 1916) reprinted from the 1883 *Report on the Census of the Panjab*, is an example.

[33] As, for example, S. S. Thorburn, *Mussalmans and Moneylenders in the Punjab* (London, 1886) and Sir Malcolm Darling, *The Punjab Peasant in Prosperity and Debt* (London, 1925).

[34] As in F. L. Brayne's work. See his *Better Villages* (Oxford, 1937) and *Socrates in an Indian Village* (Oxford, 1929). To those unfamiliar with the problems of village India, these small books and others by Brayne may appear to

manuals) of such precision that they remain today documents of legal standing for local administration.[35] The tradition of such scholarship characterized the work of institutions created by these men to carry on—institutions like the Board of Economic Enquiry established in the 1920's by Malcolm Darling in the Punjab. The work of many other officers was of scholarly significance even though it may not have been related to immediate, practical problems of administration. No one can read Philip Woodruff's two volumes,[36] Sir J. W. Kaye's *Lives of Indian Officers*,[37] or H. T. Lambrick's two biographies[38] without being impressed by such scholarly work. Sir John Malcolm, for example, author of the famous *Minute* of June 28, 1821, a set of idealistic injunctions on relations between Indians and British, entered the service as a boy of thirteen and became an eminent scholar of Persian language and history.[39] Nor were the British alone in scholarly proclivity. Romesh Chunder Dutt, one of the three Indians (all Hindu Bengalis) who were the first to enter the Indian Civil Service in 1869, had a brilliant career as administrator and scholar. His Bengali translation of the *Rig Vēda* and his English metrical condensations of the *Ramāyana* and the *Mahābhārata* as well as his *Economic History of India under Early British Rule*[40] and *Economic History of India in the Victorian Age*[41] amply attest his scholarship. This is not to say that ICS officers were in-

---

be too simple to merit serious consideration. This characteristic is disarming, for they deal with problems of village life with a simplicity based on profound understanding and insight. It is curious that they are not used even now as basic texts for the community development movement in India. It is difficult to imagine anything superior even with the current popularity of modern "communications theory" which dominates much of community development thinking. Indeed, this author would risk the wrath of professional community development planners by suggesting that a return to Brayne and the approach of his *Socrates in an Indian Village* would yield better and faster results in rural uplift than modern developments based on communications and sociological theory detached from the simple truths of village life.

[35] Sir James M. Douie, *Punjab Settlement Manual* (Lahore, 1908) and *Punjab Land Administration Manual* (Lahore, 1908). The Douie manuals have their counterparts in other provinces of India. For Bombay, for example, there is Sir Frederic S. P. Lely's *Assistant Collector's Manual* (Bombay: Government of Bombay Press, 1938) (revised by K. F. Knight). None, however, is quite the equal of the Douie volumes.

[36] See n. 58 below.
[37] London, 1889.
[38] See n. 58 below.
[39] See Malcolm's *The Government of India* (London, 1833); *The Political History of India* (London, 1811); *History of Persia* (London, 1815).
[40] 4th ed., Edinburgh, 1916.
[41] London, 1916.

variably scholars. Clearly the men here named were in a minority among colleagues who were perhaps more interested in pig-sticking and gymkhana activities than in compiling and interpreting masses of data. But the minority was a significant one, respected, decorated by the Crown, epitomizing values to which the whole system was attached. Moreover, such scholarly values went beyond the ICS. They penetrated the agricultural service and the archaeological service, to mention but two of many. The experiments in organic gardening of Sir Albert Howard and the excavations of Dr. Mortimer Wheeler and Sir John Marshall hardly need be mentioned as instances.[42]

The second body of evidence is the detailed written analysis of all aspects of Indian life which is one of the greatest legacies of the British Raj. Voluminous reports of commissions of inquiry, gazetteers, and settlement reports constitute a body of public record issuance probably unsurpassed in the history of colonial rule. The district, provincial, and imperial gazetteers are a monumental work of careful scholarship, embracing not only immense encyclopedic knowledge of the subcontinent but analysis and interpretation of a high order. Written for every district in India, their existence corroborates the observation that intellectual values were not espoused merely by an eccentric few but were diffused, though perhaps unevenly, throughout the bureaucracy. Settlement reports are in many respects microcosmic models of economic reporting and planning not only because of the skill, precision, and energy with which they were prepared, but also because the starkness of the empirical data was enriched by cultural analysis of penetrating insight and maturity. Some settlement reports, such as that of Sir Denzil Ibbetson for Karnal District in East Punjab, would, in our own time, be difficult to equal for wisdom and precision.[43] Such reports continue to be quoted, extracted, and reproduced nearly a century after their first appearance. The many massive reports on agriculture, famine, justice, police, and other issues cannot be mentioned within the limitations of this essay, even though the scholarly method employed, if not the substance, directly influenced bureaucratic attitudes towards

[42] See some of their written works, such as Sir Albert Howard, *An Agricultural Testament* (Oxford, 1940); Sir John Marshall, *Taxila* (3 vols., Cambridge, 1951); R. E. M. Wheeler, *Five Thousand Years of Pakistan* (London, 1950).

[43] Sir Denzil Ibbetson, *Settlement Report for Karnal 1873-1879* (Lahore: Superintendent, Government Printing, Punjab, 1879).

research and learning. Two groups of reports directly concerning, or closely related to administration must, however, be mentioned. For expository convenience, I have labeled them the "Great Five" and the "Little Seven" of Indian administrative history. The "Great Five," totaling some fifty published volumes appearing from 1887 to 1930, were not planned as an integrated series of administrative studies; on the contrary they emerged as *ad hoc* responses to the need for re-evaluation of the civil public bureaucracy. Surveyed in retrospect, they can be regarded as a group of closely related analyses, for each attempts to integrate the reasoning of the previous study with its own and there is a conscious effort to reinterpret former premises rather than to depart from them. The "Great Five" are similar in format: the first volume of each is really the substance of the findings and the remaining volumes are made up of appendices and annexures of questionnaires, interviews, statistics, and tour itineraries. These are important if for no reason other than the training and example they furnished to subsequent generations in methods of assessing opinion, arraying and analyzing data. It would serve no useful purpose here to summarize the substance of the "Great Five" except in the most cursory way. The first, the report of the Aitchison Commission,[44] determined the structure and the divisions of the services into imperial and provincial services. The report of the Islington Commission[45] abandoned exclusive reliance on the ICS-provincial services distinction as a formula for equalizing opportunity between Indians and British in the services, and formulated division of services by levels of work. The Montagu-Chelmsford Reforms,[46] which, Mr. Montagu told the House of Commons, was "the most momentous utterance ever made in India's chequered history," introduced the dyarchy which was to remain until 1937. The Lee Report[47] somewhat refined the bureaucratic pattern, adding public service commissions and revising the pay structure. The last massive effort to reassess conditions of British rule in India came in 1930 with the Simon Commission, whose report[48] is the most compre-

[44] *Report of the Public Service Commission 1886-87*, C. 5327, 8 vols. Superintendent of Government Printing, India, Calcutta, 1888.

[45] *Report of the Royal Commission on Public Services*, cited above, n. 7.

[46] *Report on Indian Constitutional Reforms*, Cd. 9109 (1918).

[47] *Report of the Royal Commission on the Superior Civil Services in India*, Cmd. 2128 (1924).

[48] *Report of the Indian Statutory Commission*, Cmd. 3568, 17 vols. (London, 1930).

hensive of the five. These five analyses, three of which deal exclusively with the public bureaucracy, constitute the bedrock of the Indian administrative system. They were an impressive effort to survey the Indian culture milieu, to adjust to emerging independence sentiments, and to introduce certain imperatives of constitutionalism without relinquishing ultimate control. Above all, they created and sustained a public bureaucracy whose structure and internal distribution of power shifted with the times but whose central philosophy was unyielding and whose shadow, though shrinking, is seen in the bureaucratic pattern of contemporary India.

There were seven other reports of significance to Indian administration. These are grouped together here because they are all concerned primarily with technical problems of administration rather than with broader aspects of bureaucratic structure and power. The crucial issue of spatial diffusion of power among districts, divisions, provinces, and the center was the concern of the Hobhouse Commission, whose report[49] is a comprehensive study of district administration and local government. The problems of internal administrative procedure and efficiency were dealt with first by the Llewellyn-Smith Committee and, after the demise of dyarchy, again by the Wheeler Committee.[50] Probably the best empirical analysis of district administration in print is the Chapman Report,[51] which avoids the usual nostalgia and sentimentality that characterize most of the writing on district administration. It is almost matched by Sir Archibald Rowland's study[52] immediately before independence and by the 447-page forerunner of India's five-year plans prepared under the chairmanship of A. Ahmad.[53] Finally, Sir Richard Tottenham's study[54] of the central government in which he urged the vigorous pursuit by government of welfare objectives and pressed for the "section officer" scheme which, after independence, was adopted by the Government

[49] Report of the Royal Commission upon Decentralisation in India, Cd. 4360, 10 vols. (London, 1909).

[50] Report of the Government of India Secretariat Procedure Committee (H. Llewellyn-Smith, chairman) (New Delhi, 1919); Report of the Government of India Secretariat Committee (Sir Henry Wheeler, chairman) (New Delhi, 1937).

[51] L. A. Chapman, I.C.S., Report Regarding the Establishments of Commissioners, Districts and Subdivisional Offices (Alipore, 1938).

[52] Archibald Rowland, Report of the Bengal Administration Enquiry Committee, 1944-45 (Alipore, 1945).

[53] Postwar Reconstruction, Bengal Government's Plan (Alipore, 1945).

[54] Report on the Reorganisation of the Central Government, 1945-46 (New Delhi, 1946).

of India, completes the body of administrative analysis which I have here called the "Little Seven." These twelve reports relating to administrative development are merely the major documents; they do not include studies made for princely states or for provinces in South India. Their existence as scholarly efforts of the highest quality amply attests to the extended experience in administrative analysis and the scientific temper and respect for learning which this experience represented. This tradition, converging with the un-broken tradition of learning which was already in Indian intellectual life, made possible an intellectual apparatus of considerable sophisti-cation with which India could approach her problems of administra-tive reform when she was free in 1947 to solve them alone.

The foregoing analysis is not meant to convey the impression that every ICS officer was, to use Brayne's felicitous expression, a "Socrates in the Village" or even a Plato in the secretariat. There was also a strong anti-intellectual disposition in the ICS which, one might effectively argue, overwhelmed the intellectual tradition. It is true that there was a good deal of pride among some ICS officers in their "ability" to dispatch their work in one hour a day, thus im-proving themselves and India during the rest of the time by early morning riding, afternoon tennis, evening bridge, and week-end *shikār*. This was presumably accomplished by skill in delegation—a concept accorded canonical status by many an ICS officer and even today sanctified by some. But the true purpose of delegation was perverted. Delegation to develop responsibility and to elicit latent talents in subordinates and to release time and energy for planning, policy formulation, and executive direction is a valid objective. But this ICS "*shikār* school" believed that the sloughing off of work on subordinates provided greater leisure for unending sport in which lay the answer to complex administrative problems. There is the true story which has become ICS legend of the deputy commissioner in North India who heard cases in a boat on a river. Posted about in other boats were lookouts who were to raise a red flag when alli-gators were sighted. At such a moment, court was hastily adjourned, and the magistrate raised rifle and took aim. Court was resumed when the alligator floated on his back. The "*shikār* school" took pride in never having read a book and in being men of action un-spoiled by the obfuscating influence of bookish learning. Good ad-ministration, according to the "*shikār* school," required only ability to judge men and quickness of decision. An officer who could not clear his desk in an hour was regarded as deficient in intelligence, cleverness, and wit. The worst disparagements such an officer could make of a colleague were that he "worked too hard" and "read everything he signed." Thus the ideal of the competent officer keeping himself physically fit and mentally fresh by a varied, balanced life of intelligent, uncluttered administration degenerated into the dilettantism of pig-sticking and tiger-shooting. The Indian Civil Service offered unparalleled opportunity for the play-boy mentality and the opportunity was seized by many. The swashbuckler may have commanded more attention and provoked more gossip at the gymkhana than did Douie quietly writing his manuals or Brayne inspecting his compost pits in Gurgaon, but such dilettantism was not the value held in highest esteem nor was it the dominant attribute of the ICS tradition. As early as the 1860's Trevelyan complained that young men who were then joining the service in India lacked the "physical dash and the athletic habits that are so essential in India" because they were not sufficiently addicted to field sports.[55]

The mode by which India accepted administrative reform was influenced by other factors within a bureaucratic tradition dominated by the ICS. Administration of the district in India was a major influence in shaping administrative attitudes of the higher civil service. It was in the district that ICS officers spent at least ten of the most impressionable years of their lives, and the fond nostalgia with which they recall those days indicates how strong the impression was. "I came up to Limbo," said Catullus, in charge of a district in North India in Aubrey Menen's novel, *The Prevalence of Witches*,[56] "because I had always wanted to possess a country of my own." This sentiment perhaps better expresses the appeal of district work than any formalized, technical description. District work was essentially autocratic, involving very little consultation among equals and equally little complex staff work.[57] A premium was placed on

[55] G. O. Trevelyan, *The Competition Wallah* (London, 1864), pp. 10-11.

[56] London, 1947.

[57] Descriptions of district administration can be found in the reports of the Aitchison, Islington, Montagu-Chelmsford, the Simon and Hobhouse Commissions and the Chapman and Rowland reports cited in notes 44, 45, 46, 48, 49 above. See also various state reports on administration, e.g., chap. ix on district administration of the *Report of the Administrative Enquiry Committee* (Bombay, 1948); *District Administration in Bombay Province* (Bombay, 1950); A. D. Gorwala, *The Mysore Administration: Some Observations and Recommendations* (Bangalore,

quick decision, independent and firm action, not unlike the attributes of field military administration. Such habits and attitudes toward consultation, democratic planning, and clientele were necessarily transferred to secretariat work, where, as Sir Richard Tottenham noted in 1946,[58] the needs may have been quite different. The relative autonomy and character of personal rule in the district has not been easy for either Americans or Britons to comprehend. Macaulay found need a century ago to explain to the House of Commons: "Such a power as that which collectors of India have over the people in India is not found in any other part of the world possessed by any class of functionaries."[59] The net result of district experience was often a marked independence sometimes bordering, as Woodruff has described in *The Guardians,* on not unpleasant eccentricity, a tough-minded sense of reality, a pragmatic approach to problems, and the courage to disagree with superiors and to write sharp notes of dissent to secretariat colleagues who were not always regarded with the greatest respect. These were not qualities of the British alone, they were qualities encouraged in the young Indian collector through close association with his district superiors—a relationship described so well by Gorwala[60] and other senior ICS officers. The independence of ICS officers was enhanced by security carefully safeguarded and by a remarkably highly developed corporate sense

---

1958); *Report of the Administration Reforms Committee, 1958* (Trivandrum, 1958). Two recent works are S. S. Khera, *District Administration in India* (New Delhi, 1960) and K. N. V. Sastri, *Principles of District Administration in India* (Delhi, 1957). See also notes in this essay and notes in Park's essay in this volume.

The fascination of district work has captured the imagination of more than one novelist. See, for example, Philip Woodruff, *The Wild Sweet Witch* (London, 1947) and *Call the Next Witness* (London, 1945). While all of John Masters' novels on India touch on district administration, his *Lotus and the Wind* (New York, 1953) and *Far, Far the Mountain Peak* (New York, 1957) are especially illuminating. Jim Corbett's incomparably sensitive novels are valuable, especially *My India* (Oxford, 1952) and *Man Eaters of Kumaon* (Oxford, 1944). Philip Woodruff's two volumes *The Men Who Ruled India*, Vol. I, *The Founders*, Vol. II, *The Guardians* (New York, 1954) include perhaps the most revealing quasi-biographical accounts of district life. See also H. T. Lambrick's historical biographies, *Sir Charles Napier and Sind* (Oxford, 1952) and *John Jacob of Jacobabad* (London, 1960). Other accounts are: G. W. Whish, *A District Officer in Northern India* (Calcutta, 1892); C. H. Birck, *The Assistant Commissioner's Notebook* (London, 1906); C. A. Kincaid, *Forty Years A Public Servant* (London, 1934); R. D. Macleod, *Impressions of an Indian Civil Servant* (London, 1938); Bernard Houghton, *Bureaucratic Government* (London, 1913).

[58] Tottenham *Report* cited in note 54 above.

[59] *Parliamentary Debates*, 3rd series, CXXVIII, June 24, 1853, cols. 745-746.

[60] A. D. Gorwala, *The Role of the Administrator: Past, Present and Future* (Poona, 1952).

derived from common training. Such corporate feeling was engendered for half a century by the excellent education given at
Haileybury College, which operated from 1806 to 1857. Trevelyan
deplored the passing of the "old days" when a writer "came out in
company with a score of men who had passed the last two years of
their English life in the same quadrangle as himself." Haileybury
formed a tie which the "vicissitudes of official life could never break.
In the swamps of Dacca, in the deserts of Rajputana, amidst the ra-
vines and jungles where the Khoond and the Santhal offer an inter-
mittent but spirited opposition to the advance of civilization and the
permanent settlement, wherever two Haileybury men met they had
at least one set of associations in common."[61]   Even with gradual
Indianization of the ICS (29 per cent of whose officers were Indian
in 1929) and the closing of Haileybury, the sense of cohesion remained. Its source became not so exclusively that of common education as Anglicization, which divorced the ICS Indian officers from
their own people and pushed them into a self-contained social group
not quite on a par with their British colleagues yet not at home with
their Indian compatriots.

A correlative attribute, resulting in part from the confluence of
the Indian intellectual tradition and the intellectuality and independence of the ICS spirit at the center of bureaucratic power, was
immense and formidable pride in Indian culture with which the
nation confronted the problems of independence in 1947. Indeed,
the existence of what is perhaps the nation's greatest problem, namely, the arresting of centrifugal forces leading to cultural and political
disintegration, is in itself a manifestation of that cultural pride—even
though it is pride often focused on regional or linguistic bases rather
than on the national being. There was little need to create *de novo*
a cultural image or to reassemble from a fragmented past and dis-
integrated present the essential ingredients to endow that image with
meaning. The Gandhian ethic, perhaps now slowly fading, has been
a vital force in sustaining the image, and the pride in national dress
shown by the political leaders who have partially inherited the
Gandhian charisma is as much a manifestation of unconcern for
differentness which flows only from inner pride as it is the deliberate
means to maintain popular appeal, which has been alleged by India's
detractors. It may be true that this national pride is disappearing in

[61] Trevelyan, *op. cit.*, pp. 7-8.

the face of a rather massive infusion of Western technique and values whose assault is affecting especially the generation which did not know the British Raj and the independence movement. On the other hand, it may be simply that national pride among the younger generation is assuming a different external form whose outward signs are less idiosyncratic, but whose inner pride in the new India is just as formidable. In either case, the important point here is that during the formative decade following independence, such pride did exist and was a formidable influence of iceberg-like dimensions in tempering the faddism of change by the restraints of conservatism.

III

Of what significance is the confrontation of ideas of administrative reform by a strong intellectual tradition, marked by independence and pride residing in the public bureaucracy? Simply this: that such a bureaucracy is better able to select its own form of change, to integrate such forms with its own traditions and values, and to resist or reject the glittering temptations of foreign aid generated by massive financial power but often dominated by philistinism and non-intellectualized ethnocentrism. A developing state which cannot bring to bear a resisting force equal to or greater than the penetrating force of foreign technical assistance must accept the bad with the good, and in so doing, jeopardize the mastery of the direction of its own social change. In a fundamental sense this is the significance of the wearisome cliché "aid without strings." The transmitting nation, having reached a level of fiscal and bureaucratic probity higher than that of the receiving nation, is justifiably concerned about the ultimate effectiveness of its help. The receiving nation, uneasy in the knowledge that the transmitting culture is unaware of its historical development and cognizant that technical assistance programs generate their own force by the natural laws of bureaucratic expansion accelerated (in the case of the United States) by the relentless aggression of the behaviors of commerce and public relations, fears that certain values it holds dear may be overwhelmed by reforms which appear otherwise innocent. The two nations may then become engaged in the silent combat of sparring, jostling, rhetoric, camouflage, and delay, usually in an arena highly charged by non-rational bureaucratic and political rivalries rather than by carefully routinized intellectual processes.[62]

The adoption of administrative reform by any nation requires the greatest caution. The more so because the package labeled "administration" seems to contain a special mana alleged to possess almost instantaneous curative powers. It is probably true that an important sector of administrative knowledge, mainly in procedure, is relatively autonomous, may be fairly quickly introduced into a system, and may produce fairly rapid beneficial results. Even so, the autonomy is not complete, for there is some dependence upon cultural, historical, and political factors. For example, the introduction of the section officer system in the secretariat is a relatively autonomous change yet its success is dependent upon delegation, which in turn depends on competence and experience, whose existence is determined by historical and economic circumstances. Other forms of administrative change, particularly as regards the use of executive leadership and the training of executives, are enmeshed in cultural forces in a much more complicated and inextricable way. Ideally the acceptance of notions of administrative reform requires the prior sorting out of two categories of data and the further refinement of each category into two subgroups. The first category consists of ideas and institutions found in a foreign source which appear to be attractive to the developing nation engaged in reforming its administration. These ideas and institutions must then be separated into acculturated phenomena and universally applicable imperatives. The first group would probably be rejected and the second group more favorably considered for adaptation. Thus such institutions as the French concept of administrative tribunals or the training system of the *École Nationale d'Administration*, the American structure of a unified civil service, the American pattern of relying on private universities for educating policy officials, and the British device of the Whitley Council would have to be assessed in terms of their uniqueness to the nation of origin or their indispensability for all nations aspiring to administrative efficiency. The second category consists of those ideas and institutions of the receiving society whose preservation is deemed essential and those which can be dispensed with in the interests of

---

[62] Further elaboration of this point can be found in Ralph Braibanti, "The Relevance of Political Science to the Study of Underdeveloped Areas," in Braibanti and Spengler, eds., *op. cit.*, pp. 160 ff.

beneficial change. Noting and minuting, appeal and classification rules, the use of the writ-petition in the high courts to seek redress of grievance, the existence of cadres of services and the training of cadres at an early age, the roles of the public service commissions and the establishment divisions in the Union and state governments— those are elements which must be so assessed. The assessment of both categories must then be compared. For example, the possible disappearance of the historic role of the high courts as the peoples' champion of justice with the introduction of administrative tribunals would have to be considered. The profundity of each institution, its political implications, and its possible effect on other activities would have to be weighed. It is not meant to be suggested by the few examples given above that this is a simple process. On the contrary, the process by which this synthesis would be worked out calls for the highest possible degree of historical knowledge, cultural insight, creative imagination, and wisdom. Moreover, it is a process that cannot easily be detached from political and emotional sensibilities. It is, indeed, a process so difficult to implement that it raises doubt as to the possibility of its utility, except as an abstraction to serve as a guide. However imperfectly it may be carried out, it is a process involving learning and intellect rather than politics and salesmanship. What is of greater importance: it is a process of selecting cultural change which is much more likely to operate, at least informally and implicitly, when scholarly values motivate those involved. Conversely, it is, except for accident, a process which will not at all come into play if the participants are activated primarily by non-rational factors and by political opportunism. It is for this reason that, especially in periods of rapid social change, the public bureaucracy inducing its own reforms holds in its hands not only the nation's destiny but the fate of the nation's historical experience. The dictum that statecraft must be influenced if not dominated by men of culture, whatever its validity may be for the internal affairs of the state, has crucial significance in times of rapid social change and transnational trade in ideas and institutions. Under such circumstances, the public bureaucracy becomes the guardian of the inner genius of its own civilization as well as the guide for orderly innovation essential for the existence of all organisms. Should, for example, the public bureaucracy allow change to be introduced which would destroy the generalist competence of the ICS tradition (now perhaps only dimly reflected in the IAS) and substitute the technical competence of certain Western bureaucracies, only to find a decade or less hence that it has lost a priceless heritage and must recreate it synthetically?

The problem is the more complicated by the probability that the innovators who represent the nation generating technical assistance may not have submitted the pattern of their own contribution to the purging exercise of separating imperatives from cultural phenomena. This is especially true in the instance of nations giving aid, whose public bureaucracy has not traditionally attracted the best minds or whose dispositions have been un- or even anti-intellectual. This difficulty is compounded by the likelihood that a substantial hiatus may exist between what the foreign innovators seek to impose and what intellectual reflection in the innovators' own nation deems to be best. This hiatus or lag has often characterized the process of change induced artificially by foreign experience. It is quite natural that reformers turned loose, or almost loose, in a nation hospitable to foreign reforms will suggest what was dominant in their own ex- perience of two decades or more ago. This is essentially the problem raised by what German sociology called "conflict of generations," which here assumes dimensions of cross-cultural significance. In other instances, the very reverse of lag may characterize the circum- stance of reform. That is, when the nation from which the reformist ideas emanate possesses an unusual quality of dynamism which puts a premium on change for its own sake, the reform ideas may be in the nature of fads of the moment unseasoned by the test of time and un- restrained by the humility of a traditionalistic disposition. If such restraints are absent and if there is no commitment to a rational intellectual appraisal of the content and mode of change and its manifold implications, and if the change is propelled by the aggres- siveness of commercial and merchandising techniques coupled with the lure of money, there can only be minimal rationalization of the process of change. These characteristics are especially true of the United States, which is probably, of all the Western nations engaged in technical assistance, the nation of greatest dynamism and skill in persuasion. Neither the hiatus nor the opportunistic attachment to fads characterize transfer of ideas in the pure sciences or the more rigorous technologies, for these seem to be restrained by the demands of empirical laboratory proof. But they are markedly characteristic of the less precise social sciences imbedded as they are in non-rationality. They are even more characteristic of public administration which as a discipline has not yet found itself intellectually and which, infatuated by the notion of an administrative science, is quick to wed itself to whatever appears scientific. This ambivalence in the status of public administration is encouraged by its natural affinity to commercial science and business administration. Both of these activities manifest the same opportunistic eagerness for rapid change and adaptation as does corporate enterprise, which is their clientele and model. This natural affinity is, of course, not deterred by the equally natural estrangement which public administration feels for the better established, more intellectually disposed disciplines of the university.

It is difficult to assess which of these two dangers—hiatus or faddism—is the greater. They often occur in tandem and must be dealt with at the same time. As for the problem of hiatus, any intellect must wage relentless battle against the inclination to espouse the known comforts of obsolescent phenomena. When there is little contact with the intellectual currents of one's own culture, there is little hope for meaningful discrimination and the likelihood of introducing doubtful or even discredited reforms is very great. Two illustrations of the effect of hiatus and faddism will suffice: (1) In India somewhat less than in other nations of Asia, much has been heard of the alleged inadequacy of a carefully trained generalist cadre of government executives. There has been advocacy of its elimination and of the filling of certain policy-making posts by technically oriented officials. The elimination or crippling of a carefully trained generalist cadre and the domination of bureaucracy by technically trained executives is in reality a distorted reflection of a situation which partially existed in the United States thirty years ago. Since then the need for intellectually oriented executives has been apparent in both commerce and statecraft. It was strongly urged by the Hoover Commission, it has characterized the training for public affairs at Harvard, Princeton, and other universities, and it underlies the various movements to educate or re-educate business executives in "great issues" or the "classics." Moreover, it has been the theme of a considerable volume of writing and rumination, not the least of which are Dewey's lectures at Kenyon College in 1926, Lippmann's essay, and Kissinger's more recent assessment of the role of the intellectual in policy-making.[63]   (2) The second illustration is closely

[63] John Dewey, *The Public and Its Problems* (3d. ed., New York, 1957);

allied to the first in that it focuses on the role of intellectuality and creativity as related to social relations. For some two decades the concept of "the organization man" whose individuality was to be compressed into the rounded personality of a neutral integer dominated training for executives both in business and government in the United States. Concepts of the human relations clinic, sensitivity training, and social adjustment were regnant. The emphasis on an organization product gave rise to the equally distorted practice of "barnstorming" or "brainstorming"—a pattern of group behavior designed to encourage breaking the shackles of conformity and encouraging originality. This psychologically oriented approach, which is in reality an academically garbed composite of Dale Carnegie-ism and social adjustment theories of education, occupies an important place in much of the public administration reform fomented by the United States in technical assistance programs abroad. Yet in the United States a transformation has occurred in business attitude towards the bland extrovert as a source of creative thought. Corporate life is becoming disenchanted with the conformist executive and places new stress on individuality and originality, even at the risk of disturbing the outward tranquillity of corporate harmony and uniformity of view. The emphasis on "human relations" as a "science" is disappearing in the wake of the realization that, as one business executive put it, people can't be taught human relations after the age of six.[64] The introduction of a behavioristically oriented administration in a developing state like India may actually be introducing a pattern of thought which is obsolescent in the nation of origin. This phenomenon of intellectual lag, however, is not easily dealt with, for obsolescent practices cannot be dismissed merely by pronouncing them to be out of date. Innovators inducing reform in a developing state may be deeply committed to an obsolescent point of view and may not view it as obsolescent at all. Or, viewing the developing of trends by sheer chronology they may assert their views as being more "modern," hence "better" than older views. For example, in some

Walter Lippmann, *Essays in the Public Philosophy* (Boston, 1955); Henry A. Kissinger, *The Necessity for Choice* (New York, 1960), pp. 340-358.

[64] See a brief review of these developments in the *Wall Street Journal*, Nov. 22, 1961, p. 1, and in John J. Corson, "Innovation Challenges Conformity," *Harvard Business Review*, XL (1962), 67-74. See also the sympathetic analysis of caste-structured, highly individualistic corporate management in Europe in David Granick, *The European Executive* (New York, 1962).

public administration circles the concepts of Chester Barnard, or Mary Parker Follette, may be viewed as "old-fashioned" or outmoded by a "newer" human relations approach. A further complication is that posed by different stages of political growth in various countries. Thus what is obsolescent in a nation in x stage of growth may be needed in a nation in q stage. This implies a precision as to "stages" and prescriptions for each "stage" not now found in the study of political development. Such disagreement as to what concepts of administration are valid and up to date or invalid and out of date can be resolved only by thorough comprehension of the theory and practice of government rather than by reliance on chronology or popularity.

An important segment of American administrative thought is dominated by a corruption of the democratic dogma of consensus. Consensus, participation, and procedure have become a trinity worshiped on the altar of the committee. Each of these in its proper place is important. Consensus as a guide in making wise and just decisions is of considerable value, and consensus arrived at by the "circular behavior" of Mary Parker Follette is probably one of the best means of decision-making. But a consensus achieved merely by counting noses on the erroneous assumption of the inevitability of majoritarian wisdom is a contortion. Participation in judgments is part of the corollary of democracy that the responsibility and creativity of each person must be given maximum opportunity to develop. Participation genuinely used to attain these ends partakes of nobility. But participation as a contrivance for manipulating human beings, of providing them with a chance for "blowing off steam" without genuine concern for their development, approaches immorality. The executive who smugly burns the unread contents of the suggestion box is a caricature of its immoral use. Procedure, as Kissinger has so aptly pointed out, can easily be corrupted into an end. Certainly, developing states need not submit to such aberrations of democratic theory merely because they are not recognized as aberrations by the purveyors of technical assistance who offer them as pliofilm-wrapped gadgets guaranteed to banish administrative rheumatism.

If judgment can be made from written government policy, India has not fallen prey to the "organization man" absurdity.[65] Bureauc-

---

[65] See, for example, the policy statement, "Resort to Committees, groups, conferences, etc. should be reduced drastically. Full responsibility should be given to

racy must be dominated by an ethos of courageous, independent thought. Most bureaucracies do not have such disposition, but India is remarkably fortunate in this respect for the ICS tradition elevated the quality of independent judgment high above the retreat behind anonymity which results from carrying the concept of committee or group decision to the *reductio ad absurdum*. This disposition was enforced by the pragmatism of the British Raj in which independence, courage, and, in many cases, eccentricity of officials dominated the disposition of the bureaucracy. A bureaucracy without such a disposition is likely, under the guise of group co-ordination, to have courage replaced by a psychological and spiritual compulsion to be popular with the majority. There results, also, an emphasis on procedure which excludes values and on consensus as an end instead of one of several modes of ascertaining truth and achieving justice. Innovation in any society can spring only from creative imagination, which in turn is derived from according high esteem to independent and dissenting judgment. The weight of conformity rests heavy on the shoulders of all bureaucratic systems. Unless it is lifted, society cannot tap the genius of creativity and innovation which are vital to any organism.

Thus it is essential to preserve the existing quality of independence within the Indian bureaucracy. In so doing, a dilemma is confronted. It is probably true that Indian administration has been excessively affected by compartmentalization and an absence of co-ordinative effort, particularly at middle and lower levels. If this is so, then there may be some need for the leavening influence of some consultative behavior. But this is best accomplished by structural changes inducing consultation where needed rather than by behavioral changes which seek to eliminate independence and courage.

Ideally the responsibility for controlling the lag between reform recommended for one nation and its obsolescence in the nation from which it is being borrowed should reside in the process by which foreign advice is transmitted to the receiving nation. For reasons already discussed this is not often the case; indeed, it appears to be

agencies and to individuals and, with it, the necessary measure of support and trust" (*Papers on Measures for Strengthening of Administration*, cited in n. 4 above, (p. 5). The need for what the Government of India calls "creativity in administration" is explicitly recognized by the proposal of the O & M Division to establish a "brains trust on administration of the future" in which a group can continually plan for future articulation of administrative needs and economic growth (*ibid.*, p. 41).

rarely so in administrative reform simply because the agents of such reform are seldom a comfortable part of the major intellectual developments of their own civilization. What may then result is a curious contortion in which the bureaucracy of the receiving nation may be in a better position to evaluate the nature of the ideas and institutions sought to be introduced by the donor nation than are the donor's agents. But that evaluation is possible only when a sense of discrimination has been developed by erudition, reflection, and a disciplined intellect, or when those qualities transmitted in the bureaucracy are allowed to be put into play. In India such evaluation was enhanced also by an independent spirit combined with cultural pride, both products of unbroken Indian intellectual tradition and enhanced by the Haileybury spirit of the ICS. Pride and the courage to stand alone are necessary counters to the irrational tendency to imitate reforms when generated by a society whose political power, zeal, sales efficiency, and prestige tend to smother and overwhelm. It has not been uncommon in past instances of acceptance of foreign ideas of administrative reform for the receiving society to manifest distaste and shame of its own institutions and to accept without discrimination what appeared new merely because of its appearance. When such indiscriminate reform prevails, the receiving nation runs the risk of disordered retreat to the security of its cultural base when pride has been regained, and this upsets the orderly process of change. The nation from which the reforms were received runs an equal risk of being repudiated as chauvinistic and guilty of cultural imperialism. It also risks the probability that changes it helped introduce may be rejected merely on the ground of angry national pride. On the other hand, excessive national pride can be as much an obstruction to orderly change as can absence of pride. In such case, sensitivity is usually so acute that the rationalization of change becomes impossible; it is superseded by an extravaganza of quixotic actions highly charged with emotion.

The other possibility, namely, the indiscriminate acceptance of fads, is even more difficult to deal with. Fads always hold forth the hope of quick and dramatic solutions and the glitter of modernity. There is always the risk that their ephemeral quality is not recognized by those who support them, and they may be pushed with false but contagious confidence bordering on messianic zeal. Once again the best counter to such a circumstance is an intellectually based sense of discrimination on the part of the receiving bureaucracy which is undergoing reform.

The alternative means from which a developing state may choose help in administrative reform have been of three types: (1) international assistance programs such as the Colombo Plan and United Nations technical assistance; (2) private philanthropies such as the Rockefeller, Ford, and Asia foundations; and (3) national assistance programs, the largest of which is the United States Agency for International Development, whose field mission in India is known as the Technical Cooperation Mission (TCM). In the last category, other nations are beginning to play a more significant role, although not as yet in the problem of administrative reform. The mere fact of the existence of three types of alternatives and several sources of help within each type poses serious problems for the nation which seeks help yet insists on preserving certain values of its own bureaucratic system which it feels may not be fully understood by agencies willing to foment reform. Foremost is the responsibility for coordinating such help when received from multiple sources and for adapting the peculiar national and cultural characteristics of such help to whatever reforms appear suited to them. Since there is no formal international mechanism wherein the total pattern of help can be wrought in a rational pattern and in which the imperatives and acculturated phenomena of both categories of ideas and institutions can be separated, the responsibility for rationalization of the process of transmission and acceptance of reforms rests almost exclusively with the receiving bureaucracy. It can be stated as a hypothesis that the greater the range of alternatives of foreign help, the more complicated the process of ordering change in the receiving nation, and the greater the need for intellectualizing that process. A correlative hypothesis is that once a nation has mastered the means of controlling and integrating the manifold sources of foreign reform, the possibility of achieving rational change is greater than if the source of reform is limited to one nation. The selection of alternatives cannot be made under circumstances of equal competition, for not all sources are interested in administrative reform and the fiscal support offered by some may not be of the desired magnitude. The operating range of alternatives, therefore, is usually reduced to (1) the United States Agency for International Development (2) or certain private American philanthropies, notably the Ford and Asia foundations.

The Colombo Plan and the United Nations Technical Assistance Program have been involved more in training administrative officials abroad than in large-scale administrative reform in nations receiving help. Each alternative presents certain difficulties of choice. The private philanthropies are necessarily less bureaucratically rigid than the large government foreign aid operations, and they may be somewhat more responsive to whims of the receiving government, which may not be necessarily integrated into a comprehensive national program. It may appear that the looser organization of private philanthropic aid mitigates against a careful, rational assessment of a nation's priority of needs. But this is only a superficial impression, for the complicated assessment allegedly inherent in United States programs is less rational than commonly supposed. The absence of bureaucratic rigidity in the private philanthropic activity may be a distinct advantage. In the first place, the process of scrutiny and integration of separate projects into a country program, presumably accomplished by the "programming" function of the United States Agency for International Development is more often based on technical criteria than on substantive issues firmly rooted in intellectual comprehension of the problems which may be of almost overwhelming magnitude. Hence the contrast between the complex "programming" mechanism of the USAID activity and the simple scrutiny of the private philanthropy is a contrast based on the magnitude of procedure rather than on actual substantive merit. The private philanthropic agency has the further advantage of being able to recruit technical experts from countries other than the United States, whereas the official operation is obliged to limit its employment to United States citizens. This is a serious handicap to administrative reform in nations like India where the British tradition is remarkably strong. The intellectual component of that tradition is little understood or appreciated in administrative circles in the United States; indeed in many respects the intellectualism which dominates the Indian Civil Service and the British tradition is antagonistic to the technical bias which characterizes an important part of American public administration. But perhaps the greatest handicap of the United States Government operation is its difficulty in recruiting technical advisors who can command the respect of well-educated civil servants of nations like India. The government agency itself is limited by the relatively low esteem of government service as a profession in the United States and by the absence of a cadre of international administrators carefully selected and rigidly trained and with multi-national experience. To be sure, a body of American international administrators has emerged on an *ad hoc* basis since the American experience in the occupation of Japan which began in 1945. During these fifteen years a number of officials have moved in overseas assignments from Japan to Okinawa, thence with UNRRA to Korea and thence with the various foreign aid programs starting in Greece and gradually extending to other parts of the globe. As individuals they have developed immense experience in foreign aid activity, but the lacuna in the system is their estrangement from serious intellectual activity either before embarking on or during the course of such careers. The United States Agency for International Development has not been unaware of this problem, and the creation of courses of study at Vanderbilt, Johns Hopkins, Boston, and other universities was a move to introduce an element of intellectual perspective to a cadre of experienced officials otherwise pragmatically well trained. There is an anomaly in the fact that it is thus implicitly conceded by the United States Government that it is itself deficient in this very quality of rigorous intellectuality, and yet its foreign programs cannot always appreciate (and even sometimes imperceptibly destroy) this very quality in bureaucracies which they seek to render more efficient. This anomalous situation appears almost inevitable even when there is great reliance on university or other groups as contractors. University groups as contractors to carry out specified programs of technical assistance have been used by the United States Agency for International Development with increasing frequency. In 1953 twenty-two contracts were being administered by twenty universities; in 1961 one hundred contracts were administered by fifty-eight universities operating in thirty-seven countries.[66] In almost all countries in which USAID-sponsored public administration programs operate, the university contract group is the principal mechanism used. For the most part, the universities willing to undertake this sort of international responsibility are in the land-grant college tradition and are pragmatically rather than theoretically oriented. Thus to the already pragmatic bias of American public administration there is wedded the limitation of tradition and the commitment of the institution itself.

[66] International Cooperation Administration, *Operation Report: Data as of June 30, 1961* (Washington, 1961), pp. 26, 129.

Moreover, the contracting institution finds it exceedingly difficult to recruit staff from among theoretically oriented experts in administration, in part because the esteem of government service (even once removed by contract) remains below that of first-rate academic positions, in part because service of this kind abroad does not fit into the career pattern of the professional scholar, in part because the academic environment in which the scholar flourishes cannot be re-created within the bureaucracy overseas, whose restrictions and ethos are fundamentally antagonistic to conditions of rumination and creativity essential to intellectual life. In this regard another anomaly should be noted. One of the prime reasons such national assistance programs as those of the United States Agency for International Development contract with universities to carry on specific functions is to permit a greater degree of flexibility of operation than would normally be possible by the government operation itself. In this respect a contracting university stands in relation to the USAID much as a government corporation stands in relation to a department of government, i.e., part of it, yet quasi-autonomous and free from many of its restraints. Yet the university cannot be as free as may appear in the abstract. The bureaucratic restrictions of the government operation inevitably penetrate the university contract operation and, combining with the restrictions imposed by its operation as a subbureaucracy, create a pattern of rigidity which may equal or exceed the very limitations of the government bureaucracy which were sought to be avoided.

The net effect of these deficiencies in technical assistance is a curious scrambling of roles played in the process of inducing administrative reform with foreign aid. First, there is the possibility that the foreign advisor may have the uneasy feeling that his own intellectual training is inferior to that of the officials whom he seeks to advise. The foreign advisor, filled with a sense of inadequacy and inferiority, withdraws from intellectual contact with the host bureaucracy and retreats behind the routine of internal business within his own agency. This reduces further his understanding of the host bureaucracy and engenders a rationalization which quickly develops into hostility. Thus, sympathetic contact of the foreign advisory program and the receiving bureaucracy are effectively sealed off, and there ensues a frenetic skirmishing about the edges of problems of reform which is often taken for meaningful, rational, technical assistance. When this is also sensed by the indigenous bureaucracy, there is a consequent loss of esteem for the foreign advice. The indigenous bureaucracy may then control the relationship, and the foreign advisory function, overawed by its host bureaucracy, may acquiesce when it should resist and, vaguely aware that something is wrong, resist when it should acquiesce. Thus, the normal roles by which reform may be introduced with a maximum degree of rationality and ecological sensitivity may become juxtaposed. Again, this places a heavy burden of responsibility on the receiving bureaucracy, which is forced by this juxtaposition of roles not only to interpret its own cultural heritage but to evaluate the relevance of reforms sought to be introduced. This dual role is possible in a country like India where the qualities described above permit a sophisticated process of selectivity to take place. But in nations lacking the strength of a reasonably proud bureaucracy capable of conceptualizing its own reform, the results obtained from the introduction of administrative change may ultimately lead to greater disarticulation rather than to improved administrative efficiency.

There is another difficulty common to both official and private technical assistance in public administration, namely, the highly pragmatic orientation of public administration as an academic discipline. Here we are confronted by a major dilemma. The greatest administrative need of developing states like India is for technical and mechanical efficiency in administrative procedure. This is a need which can efficiently be met by Western management consultant firms, which have developed organization and methods work (now called administrative analysis) to a remarkable level of scientific precision. Yet, the common pattern in providing technical assistance in administrative reform is to utilize not commercial management consultant agencies, but rather universities, which have developed the discipline of public administration in a manner ostensibly related to the intellectual dispositions of the greater university, but which, in reality, are oriented predominantly towards management organization. The university cannot by its very nature limit itself to reforms in procedure alone, for it is committed to the proposition that administrative reform necessarily involves associating the public and the universities in the nation seeking reform generally with the hitherto closed preserves of administration. It must, therefore, go far beyond procedural technique; it must create elaborate training programs, research centers and other institutions for associating the public with its bureaucracy. This activity is important, for the public bureaucracies of developing states cannot remain the detached, arrogant agencies which they presumably had to be to fulfil the requirements of colonial rule. The relocation of the locus of sovereignty in the public demands a new relationship between public and government, and this relationship is best achieved when the art of statecraft is not the exclusive possession of its practitioners but is dispersed in other power centers of society. The dilemma is that the fomentation of these necessary activities may so dominate the pattern of administrative reform that the leavening of intellectuality already prevalent in the indigenous bureaucracy may be eclipsed and perhaps pushed aside by the sheer pressure of size and permeative energy of the new reform activity. This is especially a risk when foreign administrative reforms suggested are behavioristically oriented by emphasis on such activities as "human relations," "sensitivity training," and "leadership methods." Whatever merit there may be in such emphasis, it is highly ethnocentric and has only minimal value in societies in different social and economic circumstances from those of the United States. A further limitation is the fact that such foreign aid programs usually have provision for training administrators in the United States, and the inclination is invariably to train such administrators almost exclusively in the university whose services have been contracted for. In some instances it may be that university demand for graduate students compels this introversion or it may be simply that the university contractual operation cannot resist the doubtful distinction of appearing to be responsible for improving the administration of an entire nation. Either is a snare and delusion, for no university can manifest the resources or energy for such a vast accomplishment. Indeed, what has often happened is that the failure of the administrative reform program to meet the expectations of the host country often turns the nation both against the university and the whole concept of Western-fomented administrative reform. There then ensues bitter repudiation and retaliatory denunciation which can have only unfortunate consequences. It is to be expected that universities which contract for inducing administrative reform in developing states will reflect their own institutional ethos, or the ethos of the staff engaged to carry on this activity. Indeed, the stronger the commitment to a particular point of view, the greater will be the pressures to have this point of view dominate administrative reform.

On the other hand, private philanthropy as a source of technical assistance can avoid many of these deficiencies. In the first place, the nature of its contacts with the host government are detached almost completely from the diplomatic restrictions of official agencies yet are usually attuned to the broader philosophical objectives of the nation of which they are part. This is a fine but crucial distinction. There is great difference between broadly reflecting a nation's culture and aims by virtue of unarticulated inner conviction and, on the other hand, carrying out a nation's specific and perhaps ill-conceived interpretation of its objectives through the formal restraints of bureaucracy. The difference is as subtle as that between the inner spirit and empty forms of ritual.

There is still another distinction to be made between government and private technical assistance. Private philanthropic advisors, lacking diplomatic privileges, commissary and Army postal facilities, are compelled to "live off the land." This circumstance, unimportant though it may seem, is really a fundamental determinant of the distinction between private foundation and governmental foreign aid. It compels members of the private activity to immerse themselves in the indigenous society and thereby to sharpen the acuteness of their insight; it may give their judgments a quality of realism and cultural understanding. When this is coupled with freedom from the restraints of official status, it is likely to produce a kind of technical assistance of very high quality and imagination. Moreover, since private philanthropic technical assistance is not attached to a university, it has little or no institutional point of view either to pursue deliberately or to be reflected unwittingly in its overseas operations. It is able to recruit, for reasons some of which have been alluded to, specialists of generally high ability and intellectual disposition who are attracted by the flexibility of an operation which closely parallels academic conditions and values conducing to creative originality in the United States.

Private philanthropic foreign aid which operates multinationally (as do the Ford and Asia foundations) is better able to make quick use of comparative national experience simply because it does not suffer the handicap of immense size, which delays the collating and application of such experience. Related to this is the closer relationship to the main currents of intellectual life maintained by the private philanthropies whose advisors are drawn from university circles and whose staff are what sociologists would call "academic types" rather than "bureaucratic types" found in government service. This makes possible the easier application of comparative experience. For in the final analysis, the intellectual exercise of enriching one experience by relating similar and dissimilar experience occurs in single human minds. While such integration may be assisted by collation of collective experience, its operative significance is limited by the extent to which it is applied by individuals comprehending the integration. The agency giving technical assistance which is staffed by persons understanding such comparability or at least aware of its implications is the agency likely to earn the greatest respect from an indigenous bureaucracy with strong intellectual predilections. Consequently, it is likely to achieve the most rational results.

Finally, neither private philanthropic nor multinational foreign aid is victimized by identification with the vagaries of national policy. When the relations between nations are subject to barometric deviations over national attitudes on such issues as Kashmir, Goa, Hungary, or non-alignment, technical assistance postures unwittingly respond accordingly.[67] The nation giving aid easily becomes the scapegoat for a variety of vague dissatisfactions. While these feelings are rarely manifested in such drastic action as severance of aid, strong undercurrents of hostility are commonly generated and may be profoundly felt in program implementation. Where there is distrust of the political intentions of the donor nation, polite, external, seeming acquiescence may conceal inner resentment and petty harassment. On the other hand, distrust of the receiving nation or revulsion at the foreign policy may result in an abdication of responsibility by the donor.

There is a final aspect of administrative reform induced by foreign aid in which an intellectual tradition converging with bureaucratic power plays a crucial role. Of the two modes of inducing reform, (1) changing the attitude of government and people towards each other and (2) increasing technical efficiency by improving procedures, foreign help would appear to be more suitable for the latter. Foreign

[67] See, for example, Mahesh Chandra's statement that national revulsion at criticisms of the Goa invasion in the West might cause deviations in Indian foreign policy and that if speeches like those of Lord Home and Adlai Stevenson are repeated, there might well be "a hardening of Indian attitude" and difficulty in keeping Indian policy "as detached in some respects as at past Afro-Asian conferences and seminars" (*The Statesman*, Delhi, Jan. 6, 1962, p. 4).

aid programs which rely heavily on changing attitudes by training abroad in the expectation that this changed attitude will eventually affect indigenous procedure for the better are placing more confidence than is warranted in the inevitability of a causal relationship between the shock of foreign training and indigenous institutional change. The effect may often be one of frustration in the face of what appears to be the impenetrable maze of traditional procedure. The typical foreign devices of training in conference leadership and human relations have too little compatibility with patterns of behavior generally found in highly caste-structured, quasi-feudal societies. As for attitudes on the philosophical level, such as belief in constitutional democracy, equality of opportunity, and the like, they have already been implanted in many developing states and in India have taken root. Their subsequent development might better be left to the ferment taking place in Indian intellectual life. Certainly there is a rich base for the evolution of indigenous democratic theory which can be evoked to sustain a democratic structure. The development of an Indian attitude which will utilize Western political thought to refurbish and strengthen the latency in Indian thought and to refine the democratic institutions which have already been borrowed from Western experience seems to me to be a responsibility peculiarly suited to the Indian intelligentsia and the Indian bureaucracy rather than to foreign sources. In practical terms, this would simply mean that an intellectually disposed bureaucracy should assume the role of fomenting behavioral change among its own members. It is hardly likely that any bureaucracy will willingly perform this function, for the forces against such change are particularly great. But in a reasonably viable democracy like that of India, a strong Parliament and a vigorous political life can eventually compel a change in the attitude of officials towards the public and towards each other. Intra-bureaucratic behaviors of democratic consultation, leader-subordinate relations, and the like can be more effectively generated from within the system. This is not to say that there is no relationship between administrative procedure and attitude; on the contrary, each affects the other. But the deliberate, purposeful evocation of change in attitude is better left to Indian inspiration and impetus.

IV

The background and training of new officers taken into the Indian Administrative Service is of considerable significance. In a bureaucracy in which there is great discretionary power and little or no institutional or public means of restraining such power, the predispositions which mold the values held by men making bureaucratic decisions may be crucial to the nature of the decision. In India this situation is not as serious as in other countries, for an effective legislative system, political parties, and a mature judiciary function as restraints on bureaucratic power, although perhaps not with the degree of effectiveness hoped for as the ideal.

The social and academic background of new officers entering the IAS has probably changed significantly from the ICS pattern. The study Trivedi and Rao made of all 615 probationers who entered the service from 1948 through 1960 shows the direction of departures from the traditional pattern.[68] Unfortunately a scientifically precise contrast between the background of ICS officers before 1947 and IAS officers after that period cannot be made, since carefully ordered data are not available for the former group. Even with this limitation, a contrast, half of which is impressionistically derived, may not necessarily be inaccurate, since the pattern of training and background of ICS officers is quite generally known and agreed upon.

The rigid exclusivity of the ICS which made it a tightly knit body of men recruited at a uniform age and exposed to a common education is no longer characteristic of the new IAS. Recruitment to the ICS was based on direct entry (by competitive examination) of men between the ages of twenty-one and twenty-four years. There was no significant deviation from this by way of lateral entry. By 1960 the composition of the IAS had lost this characteristic of homogeneity. This is indicated both by the Trivedi-Rao data and subsequent statistics of Srinivasavaradan.[69] By 1960 out of 1,830 officers appointed

[68] R. K. Trivedi and D. N. Rao, "Regular Recruits to the IAS—A Study," *Indian Journal of Public Administration*, V (1960), 50-80. While the Trivedi-Rao data are used in this section of this essay, the conclusions deduced from them are those of the present writer.

[69] T. C. A. Srinivasavaradan, "Some Aspects of the Indian Administrative Service," *Indian Journal of Public Administration*, VII (1961), 26-31. There appears to be an unreconciled discrepancy of 141 officers in the figures given by Trivedi and Rao and those used by Srinivasavaradan. Here, the breakdown of cadre strength as given by Srinivasavaradan is followed. Both sets of data agree on the

in the IAS, 216 (11.8 per cent) were from the ICS, 91 (4.9 per cent) were war service officers from the defence forces, 198 (10.8 per cent) were men from public or non-public life recruited in two special recruitments in 1949-51 and 1956-57, 598 (32.6 per cent) were direct recruits by the traditional method of competitive examination, 472 (25.7 per cent) were promoted from the state civil services, and 255 (13.8 per cent) were recruited from the state services by emergency recruitment. This egalitarian leavening of the IAS has also been a major factor in dissipating much of the antagonism directed towards its predecessor service, the ICS. The views of Jawaharlal Nehru[70] on the ICS were not at all unusual; on the contrary they were views generally shared by India's intelligentsia. Had the IAS retained the rigid exclusivity of the ICS and continued its close attachment to British colonial educational values, it might have alienated other professional groups as well as politicians who have resented what they regarded as its position of privilege. Although some feeling against the IAS continues, smoldering envy and resentment of other cadres and of the state services towards the IAS is certainly not a major problem in India. Members of state services and older members of professions outside of government had ample opportunity to enter the IAS. The door for some time was partly opened, and banging against it made less noise. The IAS has not become the scapegoat for India's frustrations, and in the legislature and the press and among the public there is no more irresponsible criticism directed against the IAS than against other aspects of Indian political life. In this respect the IAS seems to have accomplished the difficult feat of transformation from the elitist cadre of the British Raj to a higher civil service with some elitist attributes not violently incongruous with the total pattern of the nation's political needs. Opening the ranks of the IAS has had another important effect: it has weakened the grip of the ICS tradition and permitted the emergence of a somewhat new point of view. The heterogeneous source of recruitment means that fewer than half (44.4 per cent) of the IAS cadre in 1960 came in direct contact with the traditions of the ICS. The infusion of officers of various ages and varying backgrounds to the extent of more

---

figure 615 as the number of officers entering the IAS by competitive examination. In subsequent analysis of the background of these 615, the data of Trivedi and Rao are relied upon since Srinivasavaradan does not present equivalent data.

[70] Jawaharlal Nehru, *Toward Freedom* (New York, 1941), p. 282. See also Nehru's *The Discovery of India* (Calcutta, 1946), pp. 309-310.

than half the cadre may be expected to contribute much to softening the elitist fraternal bonds which had been a hallmark of the ICS since Haileybury College opened its doors in 1806.[71] The recruitment of young men all of the same impressionable age, detaching them from the maelstrom of life, subjecting them to common discipline and conditions of close corporate living and immersing them in common studies—such is the tested, traditional formula for creating a corporate body espousing common values. This mark of the ICS, while it has not disappeared, has been submersed by the heterogeneity of the new IAS and is clearly no longer the dominant attribute it was two decades ago. The ethos of a tightly knit group cannot long maintain its exclusiveness when subjected to the challenge of admitting to its ranks more than half of its membership from diverse sources. This change in the disposition of the new IAS is in marked contrast to what occurred in Pakistan, where, due to many circumstances not found in India, the CSP—lineal descendant of the ICS—remained a tightly knit cadre adhering closely to the ICS traditions and dispositions. In Pakistan, of a total cadre strength of 362, 20 per cent were ICS officers, and 5 per cent were war service recruits or promoted from the provincial services; the remaining 75 per cent were recruited directly by ICS-type examination.

Unfortunately, data on the background of slightly more than half the strength of the new IAS are not available. The Trivedi-Rao study presents data only for the 31.2 per cent who entered service from 1948-61 by direct recruitment. These data are the most significant because they relate to the largest single group in the IAS. Moreover, since direct recruitment will probably be the chief means of entry into the service in the future, there may be some predictive value in the data. Srinivasavaradan presents some limited data on the 13.8 per cent who entered by emergency recruitment from the states. Thus, if we exclude the 11.8 per cent who were ICS officers (whose pattern of education is known in a general way), data are lacking for 54 per cent of the total cadre strength.

Data on the 615 new entrants selected for the IAS are relatively complete. The new IAS "competition wallahs," to borrow Trevelyan's apt term, are predominantly Hindu, and thus reflect more or

[71] See p. 32, and n. 55 above and Bernard S. Cohn, "The British in Benares: A Nineteenth Century Colonial Society," *Comparative Studies in Society and History*, IV (1962), 169-199, esp. 181, 199.

less the religious composition of the nation. Nearly 90 per cent of
the recruits taken from 1948 to 1960 are Hindu; 4.4 per cent are
Sikh, 2.9 per cent Christian, and 1.9 per cent are Muslim. Social
background of the ICS was an important factor, for the sons of landed
families or families with other forms of wealth were the usual source
for the cadre. This seems to be changing perceptibly, but not sharply: 44.5 per cent of the IAS recruits since 1948 come from families
already in government service. The fathers of the remainder are
teachers (14.3 per cent), lawyers (10.6 per cent), businessmen (9.9
per cent), agriculturalists (8.0 per cent) and physicians (4.9 per
cent). The data assembled by Trivedi and Rao show no perceptible
trends in family occupations except that the number of sons of "agriculturists" seems to be slowly increasing. If this means that sons of
small landowners are entering the service, this is probably an egalitarian tendency. There is, on the other hand, a perceptible trend
with regard to the wealth of the families from which the new entrants
come. Although about one-half the entrants come from middle-class
families whose monthly income is Rs. 300-800, there appears to be
a decrease in the number of such entrants. On the other hand,
entrants from families with incomes less than Rs. 300 have increased
markedly, so that in 1960 they constituted 23.6 per cent of the total
batch although for the decade before the number exceeded 10 per
cent only once (in 1959 when it was 11.1 per cent). The number of
entrants whose monthly family incomes are more than Rs. 800 is
relatively stable—averaging about 32 per cent. These statistics on
family income related to the new IAS are perhaps the most significant
of the Trivedi-Rao findings. They indicate clearly a perceptible
change in the social background of the IAS in the direction of a fairly
rapid egalitarian leveling. This may eventually have a significant
effect in changing the power and prestige relationship of the public
bureaucracy with other sectors of society. In a caste-structured society in which the bureaucracy has commanded esteem so high that
other professions and activities are denigrated, a major problem is to
reconstruct the value system so that other sectors can successfully
challenge the power of bureaucracy. The development of technical,
industrial, academic, and other elites which attract men of ability is
one means of righting the imbalance. In a society in which family
background still plays an important, even though diminishing, role
a bureaucracy to which officials of low-income groups are recruited is

not likely to command the power which a bureaucracy of sons of zamīndārs, industrialists, and an aristocracy educated at Oxbridge might command. To put it in specific terms, a deputy commissioner from a low-income family dealing with a local industrialist from a traditional upper stratum of society is involved in a different power relationship from that which would exist if the roles were reversed. It is this changed factor in the composition of the IAS which has the greatest potential for affecting the ultimate power of bureaucracy and its controllability by social forces.

The excessively generalist orientation of the Indian Civil Service had a classical literary disposition which repelled empirical and en- trepreneurial values. This problem was aggravated by the low esteem of science, commerce, and technical studies. It is, accordingly, pertinent to inquire into the character of pre-entry university educa- tion of the new IAS entrants. While it must be admitted that at- titudes towards an empirical methodology cannot be determined solely from type of degrees held by the probationers, some crude observations might be ventured. The Trivedi-Rao study shows that 32.7 per cent of the IAS entrants had science degrees and the re- maining 67.3 per cent held arts degrees. Trivedi and Rao imply that this may be desirable since it shows that scarce scientific and technical talent has not been uneconomically diverted to administra- tion. Further analysis by Srinivasavaradan of the subjects offered by the entrants for examination shows no marked disposition against sciences and other empirical disciplines.[72] Only about 15 per cent of the total took degrees in classics or languages. This fact may be of some significance in changing the disposition of the cadre from one of excessive literary-generalism to a more empirical orientation.

Nearly 95 per cent of the entrants have master's degrees, and from this fact Trivedi and Rao suggest that a master's degree might as well be made a prerequisite for taking the entrance examination. About 56 per cent had first-class degrees, but the data do not show whether only one of the degrees was first class, or both. Notwith- standing this deficiency in the data, it can be said that certainly half of the entrants are from among the university graduates with the best academic records. The egalitarian leavening already alluded to is

[72] This is not quite the same situation as that found in the other lineal descendant of the ICS—the Civil Service of Pakistan. See statistical data in Ralph Braibanti, "The Civil Service of Pakistan: A Theoretical Analysis," *South Atlantic Quarterly*, LVIII (1959), 278.

reinforced by the fact that only 10 per cent of the entrants were educated in expensive Indian public schools and foreign universities. Madras University ranks first as a source of IAS entrants, furnishing 27 per cent of the recruits. Thus the numerical strength of Madrasi Brahmans continues to be significant in the IAS as it was in the ICS. Delhi and Allahabad rank second and third. Nearly 80 per cent of the recruits come from urban background, although only 25 per cent of India's population live in cities. Perhaps the most startling change is that 3.1 per cent of the recruits are women—a drastic departure from the ICS pattern. Recruits from scheduled castes and tribes form 3.6 per cent of the entrants.

The significance of the Trivedi-Rao data is that the homogeneity of the ICS corps has been seriously disturbed and an egalitarian leavening has occurred. Snowiss[73] has indicated that the new IAS has not developed a new tradition but continues to draw strength from the ICS tradition, which is not suitable to the administrative needs of modern India. It is true that no drastic, clearly defined break with the past has occurred, but the composition of the new cadre indicates that a new tradition is being forged. The resilience and permeative strength of the ICS tradition of classical-generalist, oligarchic guardianship has been seriously reduced by the overwhelming numbers of new entrants who may have a vague sense of pride in the tradition but who are not emotionally or intellectually committed to it. Moreover, there is no conscious, systematic effort either in recruitment or in subsequent training to invigorate the ethos of the new IAS with the spirit of the old ICS. On the contrary, the pragmatism of economic development, technical efficiency, and political modernization seem to have captured the imagination of the new IAS and the traditions of the ICS seem to have been pushed to the background of historical, almost antiquarian interest. This is a commendable tendency if the tradition can be kept as a meaningful source of cadre pride and continuity rather than as a baffle of obfuscation to intelligent change in the administrative order.

The method of recruitment of the 31.2 per cent of the IAS who entered in the "regular" competitive manner has not changed substantially from the ICS pattern.[74] The age limits remain the same

[73] Leo M. Snowiss, "The Education and Role of the Superior Civil Service in India," *Indian Journal of Public Administration*, VII (1961), 1-25.

[74] See N. S. Mani, "Public Service Examinations—A Peep behind the Scenes," *Indian Journal of Public Administration*, I (1955), 318-327; A. A. A. Fyzee,

21 to 24 years, and the examination is administered annually by the Union Public Service Commission. The large number of students taking the examination has increased each year, reaching more than 11,000 in 1960. Since the total number of degrees awarded by Indian universities is not known, the percentage of university graduates taking the examinations cannot be determined. It is fair to conclude, however, that the IAS still has much of the attraction of the ICS. It is probable that its glamor is somewhat diminishing, but this cannot be demonstrated without analyzing how many university graduates of equal or greater merit than those taking the IAS examination have entered other activities such as business. It would be revealing, also, if it could be determined how many sons of ICS or IAS officers are entering other fields of activity such as commerce, where remuneration is higher. In any case, the data on continued popularity of the civil service examination must be interpreted with care. They do not mean that of several alternative means of livelihood of parity of esteem and income, university graduates prefer government service. Such alternatives do not exist. University teaching has little appeal in prestige, working conditions, or income; neither law nor medicine has the esteem or security of government service. The IAS inherits the power, prestige, and security of British colonial society. Hence it continues to attract many young men of non-bureaucratic inclinations who, if other avenues were open, might be Sanskrit scholars, poets, artists, scientists, or successful men of commerce. From this writer's observations and talks with probationers at the National Academy, the guess might be ventured that a large number of IAS entrants, like their ICS forebears, enter government service because it is a respectable means of livelihood rather than because they have a strong liking for administrative work. Many continue poetry, writing, or painting as avocations. Whether this has the effect of saving them from the fate of becoming sterile, philistine functionaries found typically in bureaucracies or of siphoning their full attention and energies from the problems of administration, I would not venture to say.

In the preceding section I have attempted to show that the com-

"On Interviews," *ibid.*, II (1956), 201-207; R. C. Dutt, "Principles of Selection in Public Services," *ibid.*, I (1955), 204-211; W. T. V. Adiseshiah, "Selection Interviewing: The Need for a Scientific Basis," publication scheduled for *ibid.*, VIII (1962); Leo Snowiss, *op. cit.*; Indian Institute of Public Administration, *Recruitment and Training for Public Services* (New Delhi, 1957).

position of the Indian Administrative Service has changed, even though the mechanism of recruitment has remained the same as that of the ICS. It remains to be seen whether or not the perceptible egalitarian leavening characterizing recruitment is arrested, enhanced, or unchanged by the subsequent training of the young IAS entrants. There is no need to describe the course of training in detail, as this has been done adequately elsewhere.[75] I shall try to indicate that the course of study enhances the egalitarian leavening of recruitment and is hence a substantial departure, although perhaps not a clean break, from the ICS pattern which had been dominant for a century and a half.

The first marked distinction that startles anyone acquainted with the pre-1947 ICS pattern is the abrupt termination of training in English universities. The old ICS pattern for Indian officers recruited in India required a two-year probationary period at either Oxford, Cambridge, London, or Dublin (the latter being rarely chosen). During this period a special program of study was followed by the probationer. While this was not a degree program, many pursued other courses in addition and took a degree. Some probationers even read law at one of the Inns of Court. In any case, two years of British university training was common to all entrants. This was probably more responsible than any other single factor in conditioning the attitude of the ICS. It put them in intimate contact with English intellectual and social life, perfected their use of the English language, and enhanced their self-confidence, poise, and command presence. It forged a bond of common experience between themselves and their British ICS colleagues. If it served also to detach the Indian officers from the realities of Indian life, it could also be said that it severed them from the corrupting web of tribal, communal, and familial obligations which so strained the impartiality of Indian members of the service. Above all, it immersed them in the stream of British life and thus made them aware of a society in

---

[75] Observations in this section of the essay are based on three periods of study at the National Academy in 1960, 1961, and 1962 and a visit to Metcalfe House in Delhi in 1959. For detailed descriptions of the IAS course of training, see Jagota's essay "Training of Public Servants in India," in this volume; S. B. Bapat, "The Training of the Indian Administrative Service," *Metcalfe House Journal*, I (1956), 39-65; A. N. Jha, "National Academy of Administration," *Journal of the National Academy of Administration*, V (1960), 1-8. See also N. K. Bhojwani, "Training of Public Servants in a Developing Economy," *Indian Journal of Public Administration*, VII (1961), 447-474.

which a high degree of rationality had been achieved and in which Western concepts of the rule of law had effectively permeated the fabric. At its worst, this training conduced to a quality of arrogance exasperating to many Indians and a kind of disdain for Indian customs which bordered on snobbery. Few Indian political leaders were more contemptuous of this ICS attitude than Jawaharlal Nehru, who, referring to them as an expensive luxury and as kept classes, asserted that they lived in a circumscribed world of their own—an Anglo-India—surrounded by sycophants and unaware of the dynamics of the Indian social scene.[76] At its best, however, it forged a vision of good administration, a set of values emphasizing quality of intellect, and it provided a glimpse of the order and progress possible under a government of high discipline and dedication.

Recruitment into the ICS was suspended in 1943 under the pressure of war, and when it was resumed in 1946 on an emergency basis and in 1947 on a regular competitive basis, the probationary period in England which had been stopped in 1940 did not reappear. This sharp break with one of the dominant characteristics of the ICS system was evidence of a maturity in administration as well as a self-confidence which few newly independent states have enjoyed. It threw the burden and responsibility for developing a new tradition entirely on Indian shoulders. The source of cultural radiation from which the ethos of the ICS absorbed its strength was closed. Nor was it possible for this ethos to be effectively generated by the old Indian ICS officers who remained in service, for, as has already been shown, they were a mere 10 per cent of the cadre, overwhelmed by the heterogeneous new entrants into the service. This break with the traditional source of the ICS spirit left almost a clean slate on which a new training program could be chalked out. While it is a distinct advantage to thus be free of the encumbrances of an intellectual tradition not entirely suitable to contemporary needs, certain problems were thereby created. Chief among them was the difficulty of finding within India a training system of intellectual respectability and discipline capable of replacing the probationary training at England's venerable seats of learning.

Several temporary expedients were devised before the establishment of the National Academy of Administration in Mussoorie

---

[76] See n. 70 above.

in 1959. From 1941 to 1944 a camp training school was operated in Dehra Dun, and in 1947 the IAS Training School was opened in Metcalfe House at Delhi. But it was at the new National Academy, opened in August, 1959, in the Charleville Hotel in Mussoorie, that the curriculum took shape and a point of view of the new IAS began to emerge. Almost simultaneously with the opening of the new Academy, a second major departure from the ICS tradition took place. This was the inauguration in November, 1959, of the foundational course in which probationers from all non-technical Union Class I services[77] participated. The significance of this decision to train probationers of ten different services in the same institution, at the same time, and in the same course of study cannot be appreciated without some awareness of the opposite ICS tradition which the foundational course destroyed. That tradition was one which assumed that the ICS was the elite service, clearly superior to all others. At no time in the career of an ICS officer from his entrance at 21-24 years of age to retirement did he compete with a non-ICS officer or did he participate in training with anyone but his own cadre fellows. The exclusiveness of the ICS cadre was remarkably rigid and the ICS officer could not help but view members of other cadres as somewhat inferior or, at least, very unlucky. This remoteness has been effectively broken. For four months IAS probationers take classes with other cadres, compete with others for grades, and measure each other's intellectual stature and character. Of perhaps even greater importance is the fact that rooming assignments are deliberately made to mix the members of all ten cadres. Over a period of time the foundational course is bound to dissolve the artificial barriers between services which previously existed and to engender attitudes of mutual respect which will subsequently affect patterns of co-ordination in Indian government. Moreover, this exclusiveness has been further eroded by the fact that nearly half of the total IAS cadre itself is composed of older recruits drawn from state and other services. It might be argued that the foundational course is not as effective in diminishing this exclusiveness as might be imagined, because the course is only four months long, and attitudes

[77] These services are: (1) Administrative Service (2) Police Service, (3) Foreign Service, (4) Frontier Administrative Service, (5) Audit and Accounts Service, (6) Income Tax Service, (7) Defense Accounts Service, (8) Customs and Excise Service, (9) Postal Service, and (10) Military Lands and Cantonments Service.

of cadre clannishness seem to develop during that time.   These attitudes are barely perceptible but are not serious.   To this writer, at least, it appears clear that the old attitude of one former ICS officer who expressed the futility of training mules and thoroughbreds together has been superseded by an attitude of mutual respect and tolerance.

The most impressive organizational development with respect to the National Academy at Mussoorie is the fact that it as well as the IAS cadre which it represents has not been eclipsed by other administrative training reforms.   Had the IAS not adapted to changed conditions, it might easily have been by-passed by a more dynamic Institute of Public Administration in Delhi or Administrative Staff College in Hyderabad.   But, in fact, the contrary has occurred.   The Academy and the IAS have assumed their rightful, historic position of leadership in administrative training and research.   This is evident by the fact that the Academy director, A. N. Jha, is also director of administrative training for the Union Government.   The pre-eminence of the Academy as the nerve center of training is enhanced also by the director's distinguished reputation and career as a Sanskrit scholar and as a civil servant of twenty-six years service. The competent, highly trained faculty at the Academy, the research associates on the staff, and the Academy journal create conditions which have enabled the Academy to play its role of leadership with confidence.

It is significant also that the Academy has no foreign national on the staff and has received no formal foreign aid of overwhelming magnitude, except for study trips abroad for faculty members financed by the Ford Foundation or other agencies.   The huge million-dollar projects which, under United States technical assistance projects, established similar centers in Korea, Vietnam, the Philippines, Iran, Turkey, Pakistan and other nations, played no role in the establishment or strengthening of the Academy.   The result is an institution which is articulated to the traditions and needs of Indian administration and which has not been buffeted by the high gales of administrative reform in the image of the United States or any single country.   This intellectual independence of the Academy has resulted in an approach to public administration which is somewhat eclectic and avoids the fads and extremes of various American schools.   There is, for example, virtually no attention given to such ethnocentric oddities as "human relations" or "leadership training." Public administration is conceived more as both the art and the science of statecraft. The curriculum and the staff reflect an intellectual approach which seeks to examine the problems of Indian government—broadly conceived—not merely the problems of organization and management. Of the nearly ten full-time professional scholars on the teaching staff, five have doctor of philosophy degrees from American universities in such disciplines as law, social administration, economics, linguistics, and history. There is no scholar trained specifically in public administration, yet impressive research in matters relating to administration is carried on at the Academy.

The National Academy places some emphasis on the cultural and artistic heritage of India. This is in large measure due to the artistic interests of the director, an interest reflected in his donation to the Academy of several pieces of religious sculpture. The lounge and dining room are used as display areas for works of art, both contemporary and ancient, and several lectures on cultural subjects, including music, are included in the curriculum. This inclusion of such seemingly irrelevant, non-administrative matters may shock those accustomed to the philistine, sterile content of many American and European public administration training programs. Indeed, although it might be impatiently dismissed as a vestige of the literary-generalist traditions of Macaulay and an anachronism in the face of the Academy's program, it can be amply justified as an essential part of administrative training. First, an understanding and appreciation of national cultural heritage is the soundest and most sophisticated way of developing a sense of nationalism and pride—both of which are attitudes crucial to the development of new states. Secondly, in a nation as heterogeneous as India the need to enhance mutual respect for internal cultural differences is an urgent one. Thirdly, the breadth of cultural understanding brought to bear on problems of administration is of direct relevance to the development of Indian political values.

The broadly based program in law, history, and other traditional disciplines can also be defended. In India the power and prestige of government is not yet counterbalanced by the influence of other sectors of life, such as universities, commerce, religion, political parties, professions, and special interest groups. This uneven development in the competitive and balancing strength of the segments of society results in what might be called an asymmetry of power diffusion. Although the contours of the spheres of power are changing rapidly in India, it is doubtful if symmetry will be achieved within a generation. The public bureaucracy remains more highly developed than other sectors, hence the predisposition or ethos of the bureaucracy is of immense importance. Even though in India a strong Parliament and other institutions are fast matching the power of bureaucracy, the scope of administrative discretion is likely to continue to expand rather than shrink. This can be assumed simply because the total range of governmental power, particularly through the expression of the statutory corporation, is itself expanding. Further, both the judiciary and the legislature are likely to become more and more generalizers of basic policy rather than supervisors of administrative detail. Thus even though the strength, sophistication, competence, and efficiency of the legislature increases, the changing nature of its relationship with the bureaucracy will probably result in an absolute increase of bureaucratic power. Rapid technological change now occurring in India will vastly increase the technical and intellectual complexity of administrative tasks. While technical administrative skills conducing to rational, efficient, speedy execution of the business of government are of immense importance, technical competence in administrative science is not sufficient. Certainly for district administration, the personal qualities of humane, vigorous leadership remain important, as does pride in cultural heritage.[78] It might be effectively argued that the needs of district administration, whatever they might be, are of diminishing significance for the IAS since fewer district and division posts are filled by IAS officers than in ICS days. It does appear to be true that the dominant interest of the IAS has shifted rather sharply away from district administration to corporate management and economic planning. Srinivasavaradan shows that in 1960 only 41.2 per cent of IAS posts in the states were those of collectors as compared with 75 per cent in 1912. The present writer's random interviews at the Academy in 1959, 1961, and 1962 revealed that every probationer interviewed stated without hesitation that the assignment desired more than any other is one in corporate management, secretariat, or economic planning. The state services seem to have taken over district adminis-

[78] On the latter point, see J. C. Mathur, "The Administrator as a Man of Culture," *Journal of the National Academy of Administration*, V (1960), 45-49.

tration and the old glamor of district work has diminished. It may be assumed, therefore, that the scope of IAS work will increasingly be the administration of Union level activities rather than local administration. This requirement may change somewhat the emphasis on training needed by administrators, but the quality would remain essentially that of broad humanism. The policy questions with which a quasi-elitist cadre like the IAS must deal embrace the most complex issues of administration, economics, technical assistance and social change. In the last quarter century an immense body of literature and experimentation on these questions has developed. An acquaintance with this scientific knowledge is an essential quality of the generalist administrator. The Indian Administrative Service, if it is to maintain its status as a truly superior service in the face of diffusion of administrative knowledge in society, must be equipped intellectually for the task.

The foundational course at the Academy includes the following subjects: Constitution of India, Indian History, Public Administration, the Indian Economy, Social Welfare in India, Science and Government, Statistics, Population Problems, Indian Culture, Linguistics, Law, and Hindi. These subjects are covered largely in daily lectures from ten o'clock in the morning to four o'clock in the afternoon, six days a week. Some courses are taught by permanent staff members; others are given by means of lectures by visiting ministers, government officials, and scholars. Syndicates are held in the afternoon, during which the probationers are assigned research topics. The papers resulting are sometimes of fairly high quality and often are published in the *Journal of the National Academy of Administration*.

At the end of the four-month foundational course, probationers of the various services leave the National Academy for further training in other institutions of their respective services. For the IAS, this additional training is of seven months' duration and is given at the National Academy. Three months are devoted to extensive touring of India arranged for and supervised by the Academy. This is deemed to be of major importance in giving probationers an appreciation of cultural regions other than their own and in impressing them with the major industrial and power developments, such as the Damodar Valley Authority. The remaining four months at the Academy are devoted to additional study of some of the subjects covered in the foundational course, especially law. After this eleven-month period under Academy jurisdiction probationers are sent to the states for practical training, which varies in length from ten months to two years. Jagota describes the program of Madras as "being an inspiring example of extensive on the job practical training."[79] Although there is variation in the quality of training from state to state, the emphasis is on practical work, which is patterned after the meticulous field training of the prepartition ICS officer.

While this essay reflects the view that the transformation of the Indian Administrative Service has proceeded on a sound basis, consistent with the best of its intellectual traditions, avoiding the pitfalls of excessive foreign influence, at least two major problems remain unsolved. The first of these is that the course of training at the Academy attempts to combine two objectives which probably cannot be successfully mixed. The first objective is to remedy the deficiencies of the university system in which the probationers have been trained. That system[80] is characterized by a lack of discipline, spasmodic work, a high degree of tension and frustration culminating in student strikes and other overt resistance to authority, and by desire for a degree rather than the substance of education. The reasons for this condition are many and cannot be analyzed here. In this writer's opinion the condition springs primarily from the transplantation of a British university structure without the social conditions which prevail in Britain and sustain the system. The British system of higher education with its dependence on a high degree of student responsibility and ever greater faculty responsibility and scholarship is ill-adapted to the educational needs of a developing state. The Indian system, revolving around the sanctity of a final examination, makes possible months of leisure and dilettantish coffee-house carousing, capped by a month of frenetic cramming from simple outline books. The psychology of the advocate dominates the classroom, the lecturer defending a point of view the demolition of which with sophistry, rhetoric, and sheer confusion is the aim of the student audience of inquisitors. Regular attendance at classes, systematic daily preparation of assignments, careful reading and research, frequent internal quizzes and examinations and equally frequent dis-

[79] Jagota's essay, "Training of Public Servants in India," in this volume.
[80] See Edward Shils, "Indian Students," *Encounter*, Sept., 1961, pp. 12-20 for a lucid impressionistic account of conditions in Indian universities.

missal of students not submitting to these essential disciplines: these attributes are missing in most Indian universities with the possible exception, as Shils points out, of Madras. Moreover, it is probable that the average Indian student has never had to submit to the routine of a strict time schedule for a long unbroken period in his life. The program at the Academy is designed to remedy these defects. There is a kind of softened, para-military discipline requiring regular and prompt attendance at classes during the entire course. Early morning rising is assured by placing physical training or riding under the supervision of army officers during the early morning periods. For the remainder of the day unbroken periods of lectures follow. This routine, rather carefully enforced, does at least compel the probationer to submit to regimentation of the clock for two periods of four months each, and this is probably the most severe discipline to which he was ever subjected. Since the probationer is a member of the IAS and subject to its rules there is no question of protest, strike, or resistance; indeed, morale being fairly high, the question does not really arise. While such a regimen solves one deficient legacy of the university system, it does not solve the question of intellectual rigor. The probationer has very little time to immerse himself in research or to pursue any subject deeply. The method of instruction perpetuates the evils of the university system: it is based almost entirely on lectures and student repetition of their contents. The only difference is that the professional competence of the lecturers is high and the standard of instruction better than in most Indian universities. The syndicate system is an effort to remedy this deficiency, and judging from some of the syndicate reports, the effort sometimes meets with moderate success. But they are, by and large, too superficial and not at all comparable to graduate seminar standards in the better American universities. If a system could be devised wherein probationers had enough time for careful daily preparation of assignments, the rigor of the course would be improved. This would have to be coupled with an internal examining system by which probationers are released from service if their grades fall below a specified standard. No such internal examining system exists now. Instead the Academy duplicates the university system by relying almost exclusively on a final examination administered by the Union Public Service Commission. Papers in criminal and civil procedure and evidence, political theory and constitution of India, economic development, and general administrative knowledge count 400 points. The Academy director is empowered to assess each probationer using a maximum of 250 additional points. On the basis of these ratings, the probationers' position on the seniority list is determined. The net result of this system is an absence of competition among probationers and a complacency which results from the certainty that a secure berth in life has been achieved by admission into the service and that hard work is not essential. Only the generally high native ability of the probationers and a climate of intellectuality which, if not contagious, is nevertheless of some influence, prevents the training from being that of consummate smugness. Yet an outside foreign observer cannot help speculating on what rigorous intellectual discipline would eventually produce at the Academy with its annual intake of the best students from Indian universities.

V

The Indian Administrative Service appears to have manifested impressive adaptability and resilience. Without departing from the essential concept underlying the Indian Civil Service, it has changed its composition, disposition, and to a lesser degree, the character of its activity. The changes were made without serious hesitation and with considerable self-confidence. It has not engendered hostility on the part of the public or the other services. It has retained its pre-eminence as an elite corps serving all of India yet has been able to eliminate many of the objectionable qualities of an extreme exclusiveness incompatible with democratic values. The content of training in the National Academy of Administration, while not as thorough or as rigorous as that of certain Western nations such as France, is eclectic rather than doctrinaire. It is neither excessively legalistic, technical, nor philosophic in its approach. Its approach is that which recognizes scientific administration as merely one segment of the education of executives. It arrives at such a pattern not so much as a result of careful discriminating selection of the possible training patterns, but rather by adapting the deeply ingrained concept of a classical-generalist statecraft to the urgencies of a democratic state.

The development of training for the IAS was part of a larger unfolding of administrative changes in India which were generally not doctrinaire but pragmatic and sensible. The major problems of administration were approached with candor and a structure of reform built, well balanced, and involving the public, the legislature, and the bureaucracy itself. This gradual evolution of the structure of the British Raj was made possible by the relatively peaceful, uneventful transition from colonial rule to independence. A strong apparatus of government was inherited intact. It was facilitated further by a vigorous intellectual tradition which permitted meaningful discrimination in selecting modes and elements of change consistent with national ideals. India was one of the few Asian nations, indeed was the only major state in Asia, which accomplished its administrative reforms without massive financial or advisory assistance from foreign governmental sources. India was able thereby to avoid facing perplexing dilemmas and excruciating decisions which might otherwise have arisen.

2

Training of Public Servants in India

S. P. Jagota

I

THE FIRST CRUCIAL political decisions of independent India related
to framing a constitution, integration of British India and the five
hundred and fifty-five princely states into one nation, planning for
rapid economic development and social progress, and the formulation
of an independent foreign policy. The Constitution established India
as a sovereign democratic republic, organized in the form of a federation, operating as a parliamentary democracy of the British pattern,
and wedded to the concept of a welfare state. The administrative
consolidation of the nation eliminated the distinction between former
British India and the princely states, thus ending dynastic and personal rule. The regrouping of areas into fifteen major states, most
of which possess a measure of linguistic and cultural homogeneity,
converted the dream of political unity into reality. With the attainment of political unity the Union Government and the state governments prepared plans for the economic and social development of the
country on a national basis within a framework laid down by the
Constitution.

To secure expert assistance in the formulation of the policies of
free India and to assure their efficient implementation, decisions had
to be made regarding the quality and size of the public service establishment. These matters have been undergoing continuous examination. Thus, new services or cadres have been established in technical
and scientific fields and for the management of industry. Suitable
training programs have also evolved for the education, training, and
orientation of scientific and technical personnel (as in Sindri, Dhan-

bad, Bhopal, and Perambur), for the generalist administrator at the National Academy of Administration in Mussoorie as well as for tax services, audit and accounts, postal and other non-technical Union services at several other institutions. The Central Secretariat Service and subordinate services have their training school in Delhi. The states have extensive training programs for their administrative and subordinate personnel. The Administrative Staff College at Hyderabad offers a high-level course in the problems of management in business, industry, and government. The Ministry of Community Development has organized a network of institutions throughout the country for training officials and non-officials in community development. The Co-operative Training College at Poona and its thirteen affiliated institutions train intermediate and block-level personnel. Finally, the Indian Institute of Public Administration in Delhi provides facilities for training at various levels in short-term specialized courses and for training administrators of industrial undertakings. Its affiliated School offers a diploma course in public administration.

This paper, confined to the training of public servants, has limitations which must be pointed out. Although a comprehensive study of this subject should include an examination of the training programs of all groups of public personnel—technical and scientific, administrative and subordinate, both at the Union level and in the states— this study is confined to the administrative services. Such a limitation results from the fact that details of the training programs of technical and scientific cadres have not been readily available. Nor have the training programs of the administrative services in the states been studied in detail, again for the reason that the training programs vary in details from state to state. By and large, however, the pattern is the same and will be referred to in this paper at the appropriate place. Training of defense personnel has also not been included here. Thus the present study examines mainly training programs of the administrative services, with special reference to the training of the Indian Administrative Service (IAS), successor to the famed Indian Civil Service (ICS).

Recruitment and training for public services were the subjects discussed in a seminar at the Indian Institute of Public Administration in March, 1957. The precise subject of this essay was a topic for another seminar conducted by the Institute in April, 1960, and was further discussed by the members of the Institute at their annual conference in August, 1960. Background papers for this conference, along with the proceedings of the seminars, have been published. Again, in November, 1960, a Conference on Public Service Management, attended by an Indian delegation, was sponsored by the governments of Australia and New Zealand. One of the subjects discussed at the conference was education and training in public service.

Reports of the Central Institute of Community Development, Mussoorie, and the prospectus of the Administrative Staff College, Hyderabad, survey the work done at these institutions. In regard to the training of recruits to the Indian Administrative Service from 1947 to 1959, and of all the non-technical Union services from 1959 onwards, ample information was available from articles in the journals of the IAS Training School and the National Academy of Administration and in the annual reports of these institutions, copies of which are available in the library of the Lok Sabha and summaries of which are included in the annual reports of the Ministry of Home Affairs. The evolution of the training policy and curricula at the IAS Training School and the National Academy of Administration will be described below. Against this background of a fairly large body of information available, this study examines the adequacy of the present training programs for the requirements of a developing economy.

As stated at the outset of this paper, the Constitution sought to establish a welfare state. The preamble and the directive principles of state policy elaborated the concept in its various aspects—economic development, social services, social welfare, including welfare of the backward classes, and economic equality. The underlying principles of economic development were described as follows:

The State shall strive to promote the welfare of the people by securing and protecting as effectively as it may a social order in which justice, social, economic and political, shall inform all the institutions of the national life.[1] The State shall, in particular, direct its policy towards securing . . .

   (b) that the ownership and control of the material resources of the community are so distributed as best to subserve the common good;
   (c) that the operation of the economic system does not result in the concentration of wealth and means of production to the common detriment.[2]

[1] The Constitution of India, Article 38.
[2] Ibid., Article 39.

Economic development was also to take place within a democratic (parliamentary) and federal political structure. The method of implementing these constitutional directives was outlined by the government in its industrial policy resolutions of 1948 and 1956, which indicate the spheres of state control of industry and services.

The two five-year plans prepared a comprehensive program of economic development, aiming at the growth of both human and material resources. With the completion of the Second Plan, more than Rs. 10,000 crores (including private sector investment) should have been invested in the fields of agriculture and community development, irrigation and power, industry, transport and communications, and social services. During the Third Plan the tempo of development will increase, for the Plan envisages an outlay of the order of Rs. 10,400 crores (including the private sector) during the next five years.

This spurt of economic activity since 1950 had many consequences, among which were these:

(1) There has been a sudden transformation in the nature of the state and the scope of its activity. Though the traditional functions of the state (such as the maintenance of law and order, collection of revenue, defense and internal security, administration of justice) continue to be important, greater emphasis is now being placed on economic and social functions of the state relating to development, land reform, management of public undertakings, community development, and social services.

(2) The requirement that planning for economic development must be democratic and within the political framework and social policy outlined in the Constitution has resulted in certain strengths and weaknesses. Such planning is better rooted in public need and is more responsible and responsive to public opinion, but it also slows the pace of economic growth, generates political pressures not always conducive to growth on economic principles, raises complex problems of the relationship of enterprises with the legislatures, complicates Union-state and interstate relations, creates difficulties for uniform and efficient implementation of the plans, and delays evaluation.

(3) The increase of state activity in the new fields has raised other vexing issues, solutions of which in most cases have been attempted piecemeal and pragmatically. To mention a few, the attendant increase in the volume of legislation has raised problems re-

lating to permissible delegated legislation. The considerations of expeditious implementation of policy and cheap and quick justice have armed the administration with power of adjudication and yet the whole system of administrative tribunals has grown with virtually no plan, and the relations of these tribunals with the courts are still vague to the administrator. The question of public undertakings—industrial, commercial, promotional or others—has raised problems of structure, organization, relations with the government, and responsibility to the legislatures, apart from the problems created by shortage of higher management personnel of requisite quality and experience. The role of the administrator in the emerging *panchāyati rāj* has raised problems of attitudinal adjustment and acquisition of new techniques of administration. The administrator in his new capacity has to act as a planner, promoter, organizer, co-ordinator and evaluator—all in one.

In the changed context of state activity and in the wake of the problems raised thereby, what sort of public personnel will be needed for India? The First Five Year Plan mentioned the following as one of the essential conditions for successful planning: "an efficient administrative set-up, with personnel of requisite capacity and quality."[3] This may be expanded to imply that the higher civil service must have basic knowledge of what is happening in the country, of the theory and working of the contemporary social revolution, and of the history of comparable revolutions elsewhere, and that they must have the right outlook and the right attitude to fulfil the many demands of public service. Basic knowledge does not imply cramming of the mind with facts of all sorts, mostly unrelated to one another. It implies the development of the capacity of the mind to collect, analyze, and relate facts, to draw correct inferences, to encompass the total range of a problem, and to be methodical and skilful. With such a mind, one could go in any field of activity, however varied and new, and perform with confidence and success.

The right outlook and attitude include qualities of integrity, humility, purposeful zeal for public service, and adaptability to the demands of each function a public servant may be called upon to perform. The attempts being made to produce personnel of such capacity and quality under the existing arrangements for training administrative personnel will now be examined.

[3] Government of India, Planning Commission, *The First Five Year Plan* (Delhi, 1951), p. 9.

II

Before India attained independence the key administrative posts in the country, including those in fields requiring specialized knowledge of commerce and finance, where held by the members of the Indian Civil Service (ICS), popularly understood as the steel frame of British administration in India. Recruitment to the ICS had been stopped in 1943, because of war conditions. With agreement on the Cabinet Mission Plan of May, 1946, and the establishment of the Interim National Government in September of the same year, a conference was called by the Home Minister, Sardar Patel, in October, 1946, to consider the question of the establishment of an Indian Administrative Service and an Indian Police Service as successor services to the ICS and the IP, to which all the provinces of India, with the exception of Punjab, Sind, and Bengal, agreed. This agreement was subsequently incorporated in Article 312 of the Constitution. The All-India Services Act, adopted in 1951, authorized the Union Government to frame rules, after consultation with the state governments, regarding recruitment and conditions of service of persons appointed to the services.

With the attainment of independence and the partition of the subcontinent, the strength of the ICS was depleted by the departure of European and Muslim officers. Out of a total of 1,064 ICS officers in 1947, only 451 stayed in position immediately after the partition. Quick IAS recruitment had therefore to be made, between 1946 and 1949, from war-service candidates and from the open market, in addition to the regular recruitment by open competitive examination which was started in 1947. Emergency recruitment was again resorted to in 1956-57. From 1950 to 1960 the size of the service doubled; the authorized strength of the IAS on November 1, 1960, was 2,010, and the number of officers in position was 1,830.[4]

Although recruited by the Union Government and trained at a central place, IAS officers actually work in the states. The Union also draws on the IAS to manage its higher administrative posts, although for short tenures. The service has also contributed to the Industrial Management Pool, a cadre for management of industrial and other public undertakings.

[4] T. C. A. Srinivasavaradan, "Some Aspects of the Indian Administrative Service," *Indian Journal of Public Administration*, VII (1961), 26.

The training period of an entrant to the IAS comprises about twenty-eight months, before he is given independent charge of a subdivision in a state. The period of training is divided into (*a*) institutional training and (*b*) training in the state to which he is assigned.

Probationers of the ICS were trained in British universities for a period varying from one to two years, depending on the place of their selection. Those selected in England pursued a one-year course; those selected in India took a two-year course. The courses given at Oxford, Cambridge, or London comprised a study of Indian criminal law, Indian history, an Indian language, and riding.[5] Training in England was stopped in 1940, primarily because of war conditions and economy, and a camp training school located at Dehra Dun trained the entrants to the ICS from 1941 to 1944.

With the decision to establish the IAS as successor to the ICS in October, 1946, and with recruitment to the service from war service candidates, the IAS Training School was established at Delhi and started functioning in March, 1947.

The evolution of the training program at the IAS Training School, redesignated the National Academy of Administration in September, 1959, passed through three distinct stages: (1) March, 1947, to April, 1955, (2) April, 1955, to July, 1959, and (3) July, 1959, to the present.

The period from March, 1947, to April, 1955, was one of germinal evolution for the National Academy. The IAS Training School was called upon to conduct short-term courses for all categories of entrants to the service—war-service candidates, emergency recruits, and regular recruits. These early tasks were greatly complicated by the disparate ages and experience of the new officials and by the urgent requirements of the states. For example, trainees of the first course in 1947 had to be sent on active duty to East Punjab and Delhi immediately after partition, and special orientation courses for officers from the former princely states had to be quickly established. Such disrupting factors prevented the school from functioning in more than an emergency fashion. From 1952 on the School operated on less of an emergency basis; trainees were now regular

[5] For details of the training of the ICS, see Asok Chanda, *Indian Administration* (London, 1958), pp. 119-120 and Braibanti's essay in the present volume.

recruits to the IAS, the period of training became one year, and the training conformed to a pattern carefully formulated in 1951.

The curriculum of training had actually been prepared by the first principal, M. J. Desai, after consulting the states. The course comprised two parts, (a) subjects of professional interest and importance, including Indian criminal law and procedure and the law of evidence, Hindustani, regional languages, and riding and (b) general subjects to develop the background of the new civil servants. The latter included a broad understanding of Indian history in its cultural, political, administrative, and constitutional aspects, the stress being on "the effect of historical events on the mind, character and conditions of the people," general principles of economics with special stress on current economic developments in India, and general principles of public administration, with emphasis on the organization, functions, and ideals of a modern civil service.[6]

During 1951-55 this core program was further developed and supplemented. The subject of district administration, including special study of community projects and the five-year plan, was added to the professional subjects; and public administration was modified in 1949 to include a study of the essential features of parliamentary democracy, Constitution of India, principles of general administration and organization, including a general survey of departmental organization and rules and standards of conduct expected of IAS officers. Economics was made very comprehensive and included general principles, economic history, special studies of co-operation, food production, cottage industries, state management of industrial enterprises, and a comprehensive study of public finance.[7] The curriculum as modified in 1955 became (and continues to be) the basis of the IAS Probationers Final Examination conducted by the Union Public Service Commission (UPSC) for Academy trainees.[8]

[6] The curriculum of training of the School in this period is given in the appendix to a pamphlet, *Indian Administrative Service Training School* (Delhi, 1948), published by the Ministry of Home Affairs.

[7] For detailed description of courses of training in 1955, see the *Metcalfe House Journal*, I (1956), 43-46.

[8] See I.A.S. (Probationers Final Examination) Regulations, 1955, *Handbook of Rules and Regulations for the All-India Services*, I (1960), 79-82. In accordance with the new regulations (amended 1961), the UPSC examination will comprise four papers of 75 marks each on (1) Indian Criminal Law and Procedure, Civil Procedure and the Law of Evidence, (2) Political Theory and the Constitution of India (3) Principles of Economics and the Five Year Plans, and (4) General Administrative Knowledge. The first examination on this basis was held in May, 1962.

By 1955, although emphasis on professional subjects remained, about a third of the instruction time was still spent on general subjects. The emphasis in the training program was on providing the probationer with the basic professional and background knowledge and on molding and developing his personality. Participating in a symposium on the Indian Administrative Service Training School, S. B. Bapat, the second principal of the School, described the philosophy of training as follows:

Finally, and in what is perhaps the most important sense, training implies what the good gardener does to the growing sapling—pruning off the unwanted bits, supporting the weaker limbs, generally giving shape and direction but otherwise leaving the plant free to grow to its full natural stature. While all other aspects of training were duly allowed for, it was this last named aspect which has been most emphasised in the pattern evolved for the basic training of the IAS probationers.[9]

In addition to the regular curriculum, outside lecturers, including foreign visitors and senior officers, were invited to the School to give talks on their specialties. In 1953-54, for instance, talks were given by such guest lecturers as Sir C. P. Ramaswamy Mudaliar, Professors Paul Appleby and William Robson, Sir V. T. Krishnamachari, Dr. Ambedkar, Mr. M. C. Setalvad, Justice G. D. Khosla, Dr. K. N. Katju, and Professor Anjaria. Probationers also visited a number of places for field study, including study of a community development block. Even a short study tour provided a welcome break from lecture routine and gave an empirical dimension to academic discussion.

The Planning Commission in its First Five Year Plan had suggested, by way of administrative reforms, the appointment of a full-time principal at the IAS Training School, who was also to be designated director of training, with official responsibility for seeing that all states had adequate training programs for their administrative services. The Commission also recommended the development of the School into a center of studies in public administration generally and the organization of refresher courses for senior administrative officers.[10] Accordingly, the first full-time principal appointed in February, 1955, was also designated the Director of Training to the

---

[9] S. B. Bapat, "The Training of the Indian Administrative Service," *Metcalfe House Journal*, I (1956), 40. For full record of the symposium, see pp. 39-65.

[10] *The First Five Year Plan*, pp. 121-122.

Government of India. For the purpose of training emergency recruits to the IAS (1956-57) and for organizing refresher courses, the IAS Staff College, Simla, was established in July, 1957. No important refresher courses, however, were organized during this period.

At the IAS Training School the content of training was further modified and broadened by the inclusion of new studies. Thus, talks were delivered on the cultural, religious, and philosophic heritage of India in 1955, and in 1956 the School arranged for a long series of lectures on social welfare, a broad coverage of Indian history, and a number of talks on development, planning, and co-operation. Since 1957 the subject of Gandhian philosophy has been dealt with in all its aspects by persons like Shriman Narayan, Pyarelal, and Kaka Saheb Kalelkar; and since 1958 a course in Indian socialism has been included.

Along with attempts to make the content more comprehensive, proposals for the integration of training programs of the various services and for a central training institution to provide all services a common training in basic subjects were also examined during this period. As early as 1955, Asok Chanda, then the Comptroller and Auditor-General of India, proposed the establishment of such a common training institution. He said:

The best training in any Service is provided by the actual doing of the job for which the Service exists. Much time and wastage can, however, be saved by providing a certain amount of basic training to shorten and facilitate the process of learning by doing. Such basic training has to be both "general" (i.e. applicable to all higher public servants) and "special" (i.e. relevant to the needs of particular Services). The "general" part comprises the basic knowledge which all higher public servants should possess, e.g. the main principles of the Constitution, the role of public servants in a Parliamentary Democracy, the organisation of the machinery of Government at the Centre and the States, the principles of Public Administration and personnel management and the techniques of public relations. It should also include a knowledge of Economics in general and Indian Economics in particular, and an appreciation of India's social and economic problems.

The "special" part of the basic training would cover studying the Acts and Rules relating to the particular Service, departmental procedures, etc. The course of training in the IAS Training School covers both the general and the special parts of the basic training needed by the IAS officers. Arrangements for training of the Audit Service Officer, Income-Tax, Railways, etc., have been made by the Ministries concerned, but these are confined largely to the "special" part of the training. It would be of great advantage if, each year, the recruits to the higher services are brought together in some Central establishment for about six months to receive the "general" part of the basic training. This will also enable officers coming from different parts of India to benefit by close contact with each other and lead to elimination of Service consciousness. It may also help in re-allotting the few officers, who, by temperamental or other reasons, prove unsuitable for the Service to which they were originally assigned.[11]

This proposal for a common training institution was accepted by the Government of India. Details regarding the services to be included, syllabus of training, requirement of staff, and finance were worked out in 1958, and it was decided to designate the new training institution the National Academy of Administration. The Home Minister to the Government of India made the following statement in the Lok Sabha on April 15, 1958:

We also feel, and we are giving thought to this matter, that training in foundational and fundamental subjects should be given to all those who are recruited for senior grades of service. So, instead of our Indian Administrative Training School, we propose to set up a National Academy of Training so that the Services, wherever they may function, whether as Administrative Officers or as Accountants or as Revenue Officers, might imbibe the true spirit and discharge their duties in a manner which will raise their efficiency and establish concord between them and the public completely.[12]

The other improvement in the training program, up to July, 1959, related to study and cultural tours, which were made fairly extensive from 1957 on. They included a visit to the principal development projects and plants and the main cultural and historical places in the country; they involved an extensive tour of South India by probationers from North India, and vice versa.

Pending the establishment of the National Academy of Administration at Mussoorie, a hill station in Uttar Pradesh, but in pursuance of their policy decisions of 1958, the government decided to start a four-month foundational course of combined training for the probationers of the IAS, the Indian Foreign Service, and the non-technical Class I Union Services on July 13, 1959, at the IAS Training

[11] Quoted from unpublished files by A. N. Jha, "National Academy of Administration," *Journal of the National Academy of Administration*, V (1960), 2-3.
[12] *Ibid.*, p. 5.

School in Metcalfe House, Delhi.   Late in August, 1959, the School was moved to Mussoorie along with the IAS Staff College, Simla, and both were merged to constitute the National Academy of Administration, officially created September 1, 1959.

The National Academy had completed the first foundational course, started in Delhi, by November, 1959.   The next year a second foundational course was organized for a period of five months from May to October.   The third foundational course began early in June, 1961.   The prescribed course of training for the foundational courses comprises the sum total of the training programs in general subjects evolved at the IAS Training School from 1947-59.   Thus, the study of criminal law and procedure and the law of evidence and district administration is excluded.   However, a few other subjects have been added, such as the evolution of modern India as a democratic, secular, and welfare state; the impact of science and technology; population trends; phonetics and linguistics; and the basic principles of law.   The detailed syllabus is as follows:

(1) The evolution of the modern Indian State as a democratic, secular and welfare state.   Survey of main currents of Indian history: political, economic, and social.   Interplay of world forces, Asian and European.

(2) The Constitution of India: its evolution, basic principles and main provisions.   Parliamentary democracy, its postulates and implications; Central and state governments, their inter-relationships.

(3) Public Administration principles, organization and procedure. Machinery of Government—Central Ministries and Departments, public corporations, and other semi-autonomous bodies.   The public services—ideals, attitudes, and code of conduct.

(4) Indian Economy: economic policy, development and administration; Public Finance: policy, budgeting, fiscal legislation and administration; public enterprises.

(5) State and the social services: Sarvodaya, Gandhian philosophy, welfare state; socialism, social services, social security and social welfare; industrial relations, trade unions.

(6) Science and technology: impact on economy, administration and social institutions in general, with particular reference to Indian conditions.

(7) Statistics.

(8) Population trends in India.

(9) Indian Culture and recent history of progress in science, arts, and literature.

(10) Phonetics and linguistics along with the common features of the various languages in India.

(11) Basic principles of law, including personal law, equity and jurisprudence.

(12) Hindi.[13]

The course is thus highly concentrated and is covered by a resident faculty, whose number has been increased to eleven teaching members, and by guest lecturers.

A significant development relating to courses of study was the conference of heads of training institutions in the various participating services convened in June, 1960, by the director of the National Academy of Administration (as the Director of Training to the Government of India) to examine the syllabus of foundational training and to suggest modifications in the training programs of their respective institutions. The foundational course was approved by the conference and consequent modifications in the training programs are expected to be made.

A further development in the National Academy of Administration is the adoption of the syndicate method of study, in which emphasis is laid on intense, original, co-operative research in a specified subject. Discussion of the report before the entire body of the Academy (which in 1961 comprised 270 probationers) develops critical faculties, powers of argumentation, effective public speaking, and forceful debate. Some of the syndicate studies are units of a larger series of related studies. Examples of such serial studies are (1) the study of land utilization patterns in the various states and (2) the study of various aspects of planning. Selected syndicate reports are subsequently published in the *Journal of the National Academy of Administration*. Another aspect of development relates to research, both in relation to the syndicate studies and on independent subjects. Departmental bulletins surveying the latest development in the various subjects are distributed to the trainees and are also published in the *Journal*, which became a quarterly in January, 1960, replacing the *Metcalfe House Journal*, which had been published since 1956.

Thus, with the establishment of the National Academy of Administration, the emphasis on background subjects has increased not only for the IAS but for all higher administrative personnel partici-

[13] *Ibid.*, pp. 6-7.

pating in the training program. With a common knowledge of the political, economic, and social framework within which the administration functions and acquaintance with the machinery of government, a knowledge of Indian history and culture, and an experience of community living, the higher administrative personnel are expected to have the required attitudes and motivation for public service.

The National Academy of Administration conducts three separate but related programs: (1) the foundational course, (2) training of IAS probationers, including emergency recruits to the service, and (3) refresher courses or special seminars for senior personnel of all services.

The training of IAS probationers continues to be for a year and has now been divided into the period of foundational training, and a subsequent seven months' course exclusively for the IAS. Although the training program of the first period concentrates on general subjects, courses in criminal law and district administration are conducted for the IAS even during that period. About three months of the remaining period are spent on extensive study tours, following the pattern developed in 1957. The remaining four months are spent on detailed study of subjects which, although covered in the foundational course, are of crucial professional interest to the IAS. The Union Public Service Commission final examination still continues to be conducted at the end of the training period, although the material covered is by and large covered in the foundation course. Changes in the IAS (Probationer's Final Examination) Regulations, 1955, were adopted in 1961 which have divided the paper on the Constitution and the Five Year Plans into two separate papers and increased their value. They have also added political theory to the paper on the Constitution.[14]

The National Academy of Administration has also conducted short-term courses for IAS special recruits, and organized special refresher courses and symposiums. The most recent refresher course (February-April, 1961), related to a basic study of the problems and prospects of public undertakings and was attended by experienced officers both of the IAS and of other services. A new refresher course, confining its study to the question of pricing policy in public

[14] See n. 8 above. Political theory at the Academy includes (1) theory of political organization, (2) major political philosophies, (3) evolution of the modern state in India, (4) Indian foreign policy.

undertakings will be conducted in April-May, 1962. These courses also enable the participants to refresh their understanding of the latest developments in the various aspects of the nation's activity. A symposium on social justice attended by, among others, N. V. Gadgil, governor of the Punjab, S. K. Dey, minister of community development and co-operation, Government of India, U. N. Dhebar, former congress president, Shriman Narayan, member of the planning commission, and a number of senior civil servants, was held at the Academy in September, 1961. A record of the symposium will be published by the *Journal* of the Academy shortly.

After completing their training at the National Academy of Administration, entrants to the IAS whose probation has recently been extended to a period of two years, report to the states of allotment and undergo an extensive practical training for a period varying from ten months to two years. The Indian princely states, recognized between 1950 and 1956 as part "B" states, had no training programs of their own and sent their officers for training to the adjoining part "A" states.[15] Since the reorganization and integration of princely states, however, all the states have adequate training programs both for their own services and for their IAS cadres.

The states' training programs are of two types: (1) those providing a detailed and extensive on-the-job training and (2) those providing a combination of field and institutional training. An inspiring example of the first type is the training program followed by the state of Madras. The training period of fifteen months is organized as follows:

Work with the collector	One month
Training as a *karnam*	One month
Training as a revenue inspector	Six weeks
Training with a *Tahsīldār*	One month
Training with a revenue divisional officer	Five weeks
Training with district magistrate (judicial)	One week
Training in maintenance of revenue records and registration and advanced survey	Two weeks
Treasury training	One month
Secretariat training	Ten days
Training in labor department	Ten days
Settlement training	Four weeks
Training in the collector's office	One month

[15] The standard work on the problems of the states is V. P. Menon, *The Story of the Integration of the Indian States* (New York, 1956).

Training with minor irrigation supervisor or overseer	Two weeks
Training with an executive engineer	Two weeks
Training with district superintendent of police	Two weeks
Training in the cooperative department	Two weeks
Training with district forest officer	Two weeks
Training with district agricultural officer	Four weeks
Training with block development officer	Four weeks
Jamabandhi training	One week
Training with the commissioner of a muncipality	One week
Training with the secretary of the district board	One week
Taking charge of *tāluk* as revenue divisional officer under the general control of the revenue divisional officer.[16]	Two weeks

The IAS trainee in Madras is also required to prepare an economic report on a village, with the assistance of a very comprehensive questionnaire supplied by the government. The state lays great emphasis on the quality of this report.

Examples of the second type of training program are those followed by Uttar Pradesh, Punjab, and Rajasthan. In these states the training programs are extensively planned, but the periods of field training are separated by attachment to a training institution for six and a half months (Punjab) to six weeks (Rajasthan). The training program in Uttar Pradesh is very comprehensive and includes training at an orientation and study center for six weeks and a tour of the state.

As will be observed, the emphasis of the state training programs is justifiably on the practical aspects of work and different states may have different programs with varying emphases. Such training could not be done effectively at a central institution like the National Academy of Administration. However, with the appointment of the director of the National Academy of Administration as the Director of Training to the Government of India, increased integration or at least co-ordination of state training programs is not unlikely.

III

The Indian Police Service, the second all-India Service, was established along with the IAS. The probationers of the IPS also

[16] Government of Madras, *G.O. No. 307, Public (Special) Department,* dated January 28, 1956, p. 10.

undergo an elaborate one-year training program at a central institution (Central Police Training College, Mount Abu) and in the states. The emphasis in training is obviously on the subjects of professional importance, such as drill, criminal detection, scientific criminology, investigation, arrest and prosecution, maintenance of law and order, and internal security. Police history, police organization and administration, and the role of police in modern India are also studied. The study of the Constitution of India, with emphasis on provisions relating to fundamental rights, powers and privileges of members of the legislatures, the Supreme Court, the High Courts, and the Services is also provided in the course of training at Mount Abu. Since May, 1960, probationers of the IPS have joined the National Academy of Administration for a five-month foundational course before joining the Mount Abu Central Police Training College.

Probationers of the Indian Foreign Service have been trained at the IAS Training School since its inception. The period of training was six months. They attended, with the IAS probationers, the courses in general subjects and also underwent special training in Indian history and culture, Asian history, geography, and international law and aspects of diplomacy. Since May, 1960, they have also participated in the foundational course at the National Academy of Administration. Their post-Academy training comprises field observation in districts, study tours, training in the Ministry of External Affairs, and training in the country of their assignment.

Probationers of the Indian Frontier Administrative Service, a new service, also attend the foundational course at the National Academy of Administration and have special training programs in anthropology and tribal regulations and customs both at the Academy and in the secretariats of the states.

Recruitment for the non-technical Class I Union Services (such as the Indian Income-tax Service, the Indian Customs and Excise, Audit and Accounts Service, and the Indian Postal Service) is combined with recruitment for the All-India Services and the IFS. Almost all of these services have their specialized training institutions emphasizing professional matters. With the exception of the Railway Service and the Central Secretariat Service, all of them have participated in the foundational training program at the National Academy of Administration since July, 1959, and the Railway Service started its participation in the foundation course in July, 1961; and their own training programs have been revised to avoid unnecessary duplication. For example, the Income-tax Training College at Nagpur has reduced its training period from eighteen to thirteen months and no longer teaches Indian economic conditions and the Constitution of India.

Among the institutions organizing special courses for experienced higher personnel are the following: (1) the Administrative Staff College of India, Hyderabad, (2) the Institute of Study and Research in Community Development, Mussoorie, and (3) the Indian Institute of Public Administration, New Delhi.

The Staff College was established in May, 1957, to organize programs of studies in higher management, based on the report of an expert committee of the All-India Council for Technical Education. It offers three courses a year, each of twelve weeks' duration, Participants are between thirty-five and forty-five years of age. The objects and aims of the College are officially described as follows:

The College seeks to bring together experienced executives of proved administrative capacity and give them an opportunity of examining different administrative practices in order to prepare them for still higher responsibilities in the future. With the increasing complexity of administration, whether in Government or industry, it is felt that those who would be entrusted with top management should have an opportunity of discussing their problem with others having different but comparable experience, and training to the end that an awareness and thinking on the objectives of their own work and the methods which they have been following may be created.[17]

Accordingly, each course is attended by a balanced proportion of senior administrators from the Union and state governments, and higher executive or managerial staff from the nationalized industries and the private sector. In the composition of each class there is also a balance of experience in industrial production, marketing, finance, banking, accountancy, personnel work, research, and general administration. The composition of each session is thus "representative of the entire managerial community in the country." The number of participants in each course was initially thirty but has been increased to fifty. The College, which is modeled on the British Administrative Staff College at Henley-on-Thames, follows the syndicate meth-

[17] *Prospectus of the Administrative Staff College of India* (Hyderabad, Nov., 1960), p. 2.

od of study. Some thirty lectures by outstanding experts throughout India are also arranged for each course.

The course of study comprises the following six divisions: (1) comparative administrative structures; (2) structure and interrelationships of departments of government; delegation, control and accountability, and personnel management; (3) specialized functions, such as production management, research, and development, office services, sales and supply management, and industrial finance; (4) relations between the Union and state governments, the role of government in economic development, organized labor and local administration; (5) administrative adaptation to economic and technological change; and (6) the role of directing authorities.[18] The College is also developing a research wing and publishes a bi-annual journal. The reports of the syndicate studies, however, are not published. Up to March 31, 1961, the College had conducted ten courses, with 60 per cent of the participants in the courses from the private sector. Out of the total trained group of 430, as many as 157 senior officers from the central government, state governments, and nationalized industries, participated in the programs.

Another place for specialized study by higher administrative personnel is the Central Institute of Community Development, which is at the apex of a network of training institutions throughout India. The Institute was established in June, 1958, and was originally designed to run short-term courses of one week to a month's duration for training key administrative and technical personnel as well as non-officials in the theory and methods of community development. The objectives of the course are described as follows:

One of the basic objectives is to ensure through Orientation Courses of 25 days each, that the participants by living and working together are enabled to interchange ideas and experiences; imbibe the past history and the latest developments of the movement, both in its theoretical and practical aspects; get a better understanding of the inter-relationship between the C.D. programme and the over-all national Plan; appreciate how the respective official and non-official roles complement each other in the achievement of the common national objectives; thereby balance and synthesise their approach to Community Development, and in the process throw up possible suggestions for program improvement.[19]

[18] Ibid., pp. 4-5.
[19] Government of India, Central Institute of Community Development, Report 1960, p. 3.

Like the Administrative Staff College, the Institute conducts courses by the syndicate method. The syllabus for the orientation course is broad-based and practical and covers the following aspects: philosophy, concepts and objectives of community development; techniques of community development; evolution of socialist society and welfare state and the community development program; reorientation towards a welfare state attitude; and agriculture, co-operation and allied subjects.[20] Since 1960 the Institute has vigorously developed its activities in many directions. A clearing house of information on community development has been established and a research wing has been organized to conduct research and to co-ordinate the studies done at training centers and in the universities. The Instructors' Training School, Dehra Dun, was merged with the Institute on April 1, 1962. When these developments mature, the Institute is likely to be redesignated the National Institute of Community Development. Through December, 1960, the Institute had offered seventeen courses, attended by 385 officials, 120 non-officials (including 12 members of Parliament and 88 members of state legislative assemblies), and 15 participants from other countries. Of these, 233 attended the course in 1960, 96 of whom were general administrators, including 52 collectors.[21] These figures indicate the extent to which the higher bureaucracy is being oriented to the demands of a very important aspect of national development.

Another major administrative training establishment is the Indian Institute of Public Administration in New Delhi. Established in March, 1954, the Institute has become the principal center of research and study in all problems of public administration—general, economic, financial, and social. The Institute has conducted a number of special courses, seminars, and conferences for senior administrators, including those relating to recruitment and training for public services (March, 1957), planning (August, 1959), budgeting (September, 1959), state undertakings (December, 1959), and co-ordination in social welfare administration (March, 1960).[22] The Indian School of Public Administration, a part of the Institute, also trains officers of the state services in diploma and short-term courses and toward the end of November, 1960, sponsored a four-month course for junior officers of

[20] For detailed description of syllabus, see *Ibid.*, Appendix I.

[21] *Ibid.*, p. 4.

[22] For details regarding these courses, see the Indian Institute of Public Administration, *Sixth Annual Report, 1960* (Delhi, 1960), pp. 9-12.

the Hindustan Steel Corporation, Ltd., one of the thirty-seven joint stock companies run by the Government of India.

IV

Although there may be shortcomings and scope for further improvement and innovation, the training programs surveyed above appear to be adequate for the requirements of India. The growth of the programs has kept pace with the increasingly complex needs of the economy. New institutions have developed with new, highly specialized programs, adjusted to the requirements of the changing conditions in the country. One need not, therefore, be unduly skeptical of their adequacy and over-critical. As to the National Academy of Administration, a few comments may be made. The large number of trainees (340 for the 1962 course), the short period of training (five months), and the highly concentrated nature of the foundational course create several problems—the most important being how to make the training useful and effective. Although adequate staff, adequate accommodation, and suitable methods of training can solve many problems and promote greater contacts among trainees and with the staff, the desired length of training is a controversial problem. The trainees come from diverse academic backgrounds; it would be very difficult to bring the level of each group from basic understanding to more advanced competence in each subject. Certainly every effort is made to do this but the results may not be satisfactory to all concerned.

This raises a problem particularly for the IAS probationers. Since the course in general subjects is largely completed in the foundational course and is the prescribed course for the final UPSC examination at the end of training, the content of the remaining seven months' training is open to question. If the courses are repeated, it is an admission of inadequate coverage or inadequate results of the foundational course. If new subjects are dealt with or new depths probed during this remaining period, perhaps personnel of the other services should also participate. A remedy might be extension of the period of foundational training to one year. This is possible only if all the training institutions are located at one place, as was planned in 1958. The foundational course could be organized for the mornings at the

Academy, and the evenings could be utilized for professional training at the respective institutions. An alternative would be to utilize the seven-month period of IAS training for increased emphasis on field observation and training related to general subjects. Even now, the trainees go on an extensive tour for a period of about three months. Attachment to institutions for professional training might be continued. But the rest of the program might be modified so that the trainee or a small group of trainees would be deputed to various institutions, such as a public undertaking, the Planning Commission, or the Lok Sabha. The places of deputation might be so selected as to give the trainees from North India an opportunity to visit South India, and vice versa, a practice which is already followed on the study tours. Short cultural study tours in the area of deputation might also be arranged for the trainees. On their return the reports of the trainees might be critically discussed by the entire group at the Academy.

By and large, the training programs for the IAS in the states are adequate. To orient the entrant to the IAS to the practical demands of the policy of democratic decentralization, it would be highly desirable to commend the system followed by the state of Rajasthan, where IAS personnel are appointed as block development officers for short periods. To integrate the states' program with the program at the National Academy of Administration the latter might organize short-term review courses for IAS officers at the termination of their state training. In such courses the participants might discuss their field experiences and subjects of professional interest. A very brief course covering the latest developments in the various fields of the nation's activity might also be given. The different periods of training in the states might make it difficult for the course to be conducted at the same time for all the officers of a batch. It is understood that Sir V. T. Krishnamachari is preparing a comprehensive study of the state training programs with a view to increased standardization. Pending these developments, the timing of review courses might be scheduled to enable all officers of the same batch to participate in the program together. Such review courses are being conducted at present at the Administrative Staff College, Hyderabad, for participants who have been out of the college for fifteen months.

With regard to the training of experienced personnel, the existing opportunities are not inadequate and are generally satisfactory. An improvement in the existing programs could be the provision of opportunity for all higher administrative personnel, after a service experience of five or six years, to go abroad on study leave with transportation provided by government.

The views of Asok Chanda with respect to administrative training are significant. Dealing with the executive in his *Indian Administration*, he made a forceful plea for the establishment of a single civil service of India and the abolition of the various Union services as they are organized at present. After reviewing the system of training in the École Nationale d'Administration, he urged the adoption of a similar system for India. The French school conducts a three-year course of training, the first year being spent on field training in the office of the departmental *préfet*. The second year is spent on theoretical training at the École where the trainee selects his field of specialization, i.e., general administration, economic, financial, or social administration. Training is imparted both in general subjects and in the field of specialization. In the third year, for part of the time, the trainee is deputed to business firms or public undertakings and on his return is given an intensive course in the field of his specialization.[23]

Asok Chanda's argument for adopting the French system of training in India is this:

There are distinct advantages in the adoption of a similarly comprehensive training scheme in India. It is necessary, for considerations mentioned earlier, to give all the superior civil service officers a basic training in a primary unit of administration, which will bring them into touch with the problems of the common man, with the way the welfare measures are being executed and administered and with the extent to which these fulfil their purpose. It may be urged that without a working knowledge of the legal and the revenue system of the country, the probationers will not derive any benefit in the course of a year's attachment to a district; that they will be unable to follow or participate in its administrative processes; that the French system works because of the inclusion of law and politics as compulsory subjects in the entrance examination. This difficulty can be readily met by attaching the probationers, in the first instance, to the school for a period of three to six months, to give them a grounding in the legal and revenue systems of the country before they are sent out to the districts for training. It is equally necessary to give these officers an insight

[23] For details of the system of training at the French School, see Asok Chanda, *op. cit.*, pp. 124-126; Brian Chapman, *The Profession of Government* (New York, 1959), pp. 115-124.

into the organization and management of industrial and business enterprises—even more so, since the public sector in India is being rapidly developed to embrace economic activities previously left entirely to private initiative. It would also add to administrative competence if theoretical training were enlarged and intensified to cover both general and specialized functions of government, which it is hardly possible to bring within the compass of a year's course prescribed for the Indian Administrative Service. Such a scheme would also largely remove the deficiencies of present-day university education and enable recruitment to be made in larger numbers without detriment to the efficiency of the administration.[24]

In this scheme members of the higher civil service would be attached to the districts following a short course at a common training institution. They will also be deputed for study at a public undertaking. The suggestion of this training program presupposes the establishment of a single civil service with allotment to the various activities made after district training and training at the central institution.

The feasibility and utility of a unified civil service for India cannot be discussed in this paper because of limitations of space. It is pertinent to note, however, that the idea of a unified service has been recommended by Paul Appleby[25] as well as by Asok Chanda.[26] Given the existing system of separate cadres of services, the present training programs of the IAS and the other services are fairly comprehensive and adequate. The training of the IAS probationer continues on an average for twenty-eight months and is evenly balanced between theoretical training at the National Academy of Administration and field training in the states. In the case of the other services, the period of training varies, but the balance between training in general subjects and training in professional subjects has been developed in the same proportion. The deputation of an IAS probationer to a public undertaking is desirable and has already been recommended above. Acceptance of the proposal to organize review courses would integrate the field training programs for the IAS with the initial program at the National Academy of Administration. The desirability of providing intensive district training for probationers of the Union services is open to argument. It would not be of much professional importance to the other services, whether they are part of

[24] Asok Chanda, op. cit., p. 127.
[25] See Appleby's statement in the Sunday Statesman, April 16, 1961, p. 4.
[26] Asok Chanda, op. cit., 127. See Braibanti's essay in this volume, p. 18, for comment on the position of the Das Commission on services.

a single service or are organized separately as at present. With the location of all training institutions at one place, the effectiveness of the foundational training will increase and inter-service amity will be promoted. Common training programs might emerge, for example, in regard to deputation to a public undertaking. If the existing programs with modifications are found adequate, these which have been developed in other nations need not necessarily be adopted for India.

3

The Village in the Framework of Development

Hugh Tinker

THE APPROACH of this essay (as with every other study of the Indian village) is external to the subject. The writer has had practical experience of local government institutions in India and in Britain, but his view of village life is inevitably that of a spectator: one, moreover, who views the 500,000 villages of India as somehow amenable to the artificial description of "the Indian village." In other words, his outlook is that of a historian or political scientist, attempting to deduce a general hypothesis from a wide area of evidence, rather than the observation of the anthropologist, building up his conclusions from a detailed knowledge of a limited area. In this essay we shall consider the attempts (largely by government agencies) to mobilize village society for economic, social, and political activities whose ultimate purpose is national. Of course, these attempts to put government policy into practice hinge entirely upon the response of the village folk. All the government activity of the last fifty years or so in this direction has been based on persuasion rather than compulsion (the line of demarcation is sometimes a little hazy) and has therefore succeeded or failed only so far as it has won the co-operation of the villagers. But the initiative for all these efforts has been external. There has been nothing to compare (for example) to movements during the last century in Britain, originating entirely among the people, such as the Sunday School movement for adult education, the co-operative movement, or the trades union movement. The twentieth-century Indian village has yet to produce its own panacea for its own needs: even *Bhoodan* is an external force.

However, most observers will agree that Community Development is a massive attempt to enable the ordinary people of India "to want what they need, and do what they want."[1]   This essay tries to assess the impact of this program upon village India.

During the last ten years the Indian village has been the subject of three main types of investigation.   There have been anthropological studies—pure research enterprises—which have deepened our understanding of relationships between different social groups within the village and have explored extra-village ties.   There has been work (it may be described as "social engineering") by political scientists and others who have developed theories of community behavior by means of the application of certain values to actual experience; in this field the name of the American town-planner, Albert Mayer, is pre-eminent.   Finally, there has been the activity of administrators, politicians, and social workers, concerned largely in an *ad hoc* manner with the practical task of building a new India.   These three groups have been almost exclusively concerned with analyzing and evaluating the Indian village as it is today.   They have almost all begun by accepting a certain model of the village—the village as it has emerged from the ages—as axiomatic.   It is agreed that the Indian village throughout the ages has been a corporate body, guided and guarded by a council, the *panchāyat*.   There is tacit agreement that the functioning of the *panchāyat* provided a kind of prelude to democracy, even if almost all are careful to qualify their words.   Sooner or later Charles Metcalfe's celebrated phrase about the "little republics" comes out, endowed with overtones that would astonish Metcalfe himself.   Many go on to suggest that these republics were destroyed by the British; some assert that this was a deliberate policy of extermination.[2]   The conclusion which generally follows is that the village republic must be revived as the foundation of the new India; here, it is said, is a living tradition from which will grow a grass-roots democracy that is native to Indian soil.

This modern Indian belief in the special political genius of the people, stemming from times long past and drawing its strength from local associations, had a parallel in nineteenth-century England. Toulmin Smith, and those of his school, in urging the importance of

[1] J. S. Furnivall, *Colonial Policy and Practice* (London, 1948), p. 470.
[2] Thus, V. B. Raju, in *Kurukshetra*, Oct., 1958 (p. 57), writes, "Panchayats have been in existence from the Vedic Age. . . . They continued to be live bodies . . . till about 1800 A.D. when they were mercilessly destroyed by the British."

local self-government went back to the Anglo-Saxons and saw in their Moots and Hundreds the origins of parliamentary democracy.[3] They affirmed that this community spirit had been passed on to their descendants, so that Victorian Britons possessed as their birthright an innate talent for local organization. Out of this political mysticism came the spate of late Victorian local government legislation; but few nowadays would rate the achievement of British local government in the twentieth century as fulfilling the faith of the nineteenth.

Present-day Indian belief in the village as the political bedrock stems, of course, largely from the preaching of Gandhi. Forty years ago Indian political theorists, looking back to their past, considered the village only as the base of royal authority; today, they view the ancient village as a self-governing community.[4] Gandhi had a semi-mystical vision of the village and ascribed to his ageless (and perhaps idealized) community the qualities he sought to inspire in the India of his dreams. His philosophy, drawn from Tolstoy and Kropotkin, rejected the modern state as a foreign accretion upon the true India which he regarded as a federation of village republics, Panchāyat Rāj. "That state will be best which is governed least," declared Gandhi, and "Society based on non-violence can only consist of groups settled in villages in which voluntary co-operation is the condition of dignified and peaceful existence. . . . The nearest approach to civilisation based on non-violence is the erstwhile village republic of India."[5] Gandhi's teaching has become the accepted doctrine of India's public men. Very few are bold enough to stand up against this idealized concept of village society. During the debates upon India's constitution, Gandhian speakers constantly reiterated the necessity to base the new Indian system of government

---

[3] "It is forgotten that Parishes and our other Local Institutions do not owe their origin to Parliament; but that, quite the reverse, Parliament itself is a result derived from out of the pre-existing action of these institutions." Toulmin Smith, *The Parish* (2nd. ed.; London, 1857), p. 10.

[4] As a factual illustration of the change, compare the treatment given to a passage from the *Sukraniti*, a medieval political treatise. In the standard translation by B. K. Sarkar (Allahabad, 1914) the six chief local officials are clearly shown as servants of the king (p. 76). In 1954 a Congress committee which included scholars of repute could refer to these officials as examples of "composite leadership for management of village affairs." See *Report of the Congress Village Panchayat Committee* (New Delhi, 1954), p. 19.

[5] Cited in S. N. Agarwal, *Gandhian Constitution for Free India* (Allahabad, 1946), pp. 39, 58.

in "the old plan of Panchayat Raj or decentralised democracy."[6] Only Dr. Ambedkar, leader of the *harijans*, was bold enough to call these arguments obscurantist: he declared, "The love of the intellectual Indian for the village community is of course infinite if not pathetic. . . . I hold that these village republics have been the ruination of India. . . . What is the village but a sink of localism, a den of ignorance, narrow-mindedness and communalism? I am glad that the Draft Constitution has discarded the village and adopted the individual as its unit."[7]

However, Dr. Ambedkar found few supporters in the Constitutional Assembly, and the belief in "the self-sufficient village community" remains an article of faith with most Indian intellectuals.[8]

Recent American anthropological work has sought to revise that oft-accepted view of the village as a self-sufficient unit. The multiplicity of ties (social, economic, and religious) which have made the village part of the "great society" have been elaborated. Yet, two of the most perceptive of such studies agree that an Indian village is "a living thing . . . a system," with "a well-defined separate entity and an individual quality."[9] Most Indians are subject to a whole series of interlocking community ties, but the only *territorial* tie that is really compulsive is the village. The district, the state (now that this is everywhere based upon linguistic grouping) are both important, it is true; but the village is the sheet-anchor of a man's sense of place, of home. This becomes sharply clear with regard to those who appear to have cut loose from the village. The professional man, cosmopolitan and urbane, clings to his piece of ancestral village land, although it yields him nothing but trouble and expense, because it is his link with home. The factory worker in the distant city still calls himself a member of X village.[10] The prosperous Mar-

[6] *Indian Legislative Assembly, Debates,* XI, 690.
[7] *Indian Legislative Assembly, Debates,* VII, 39.
[8] See, for example, A. H. Desai, *Social Background of Indian Nationalism* (3rd ed.; Bombay, 1959), p. 7. "The Self-sufficient village as the basic economic unit had existed for centuries in India." Desai cites, in support of his belief, Metcalfe's Minute: it is typical of this cogent, forceful, but slipshod book that he does not cite the Minute accurately.
[9] McKim Marriott, ed., *Village India: Studies in the Little Community* (Chicago, 1955), p. 176; and Morris E. Opler, "The Extensions of an Indian Village," *Journal of Asian Studies,* XVI, no. 1 (1956), 5.
[10] A Christian missionary, working among industrial laborers in suburban Calcutta spoke of his difficulties in welding the Christians into a real congregation: "None of them regard this as their church," he said. "*Their* church is somewhere

wari banker or industrialist maintains his connections with his ancestral village in Rajasthan.

There is no space here to trace out the remote origins of this intense loyalty to one particular huddle of houses and patch of ground (this loyalty, we may note, is in sharp contrast to the much looser village ties of Burma and Malaya). Certainly this loyalty was intensified by the eighteenth-century Time of Troubles (the *Gardī-kā-Wakht*) when central authority collapsed and local communities had to fend for themselves against marauders and the exactions of local tyrants. This factor is identified by a modern British anthropologist with regard to Malwa. Quoting accounts he was given of intervillage relations, he says, "Formerly, it seems, villages were separate units, linked only by the ties of kinship between their inhabitants of the same sub-caste. In the unsettled days of the early nineteenth century, villages were maintained by the courage and acumen of their headmen who had to defend the place from marauders."[11]

This quotation brings us back to the question of village leadership. In matters requiring immediate action and decision a committee cannot lead; in the Indian village today there is usually one outstanding individual who leads, because of hereditary status or personal ability.[12] And so it was in the *Gardī-kā-Wakht*, from the evidence of contemporary writers such as Sir William Sleeman. The headman is sometimes represented as a creature of the British administrative system, but there was an older type of headman (the *paṭēl, chaudhurī, dēsai*) who corresponded more to the English squire, or perhaps the Burmese *myothugyi*. Such men the villagers recognized as *their* leaders. But what of the *panchāyat?* Here we must attempt to disentangle legend from historical evidence. There is a clear record of the village *panchāyat* in ancient India, but it is far from certain that it was found everywhere.[13] In south India there is some evi-

---

in Bihar or U.P., even though some of them have lived all their lives here in Calcutta."

[11] Adrian Mayer, "Local Government Elections in a Malwa Village," *Eastern Anthropologist*, XI (1958), 193. Mayer stresses the separateness of individual villages.

[12] Cf. J. T. Hitchcock, "Leadership in a North Indian Village," in *Leadership and Political Institutions in India*, ed. Richard L. Park and Irene Tinker (Princeton, 1959), pp. 395-414.

[13] Even such a careful historian as A. L. Basham can write, "The village council is rarely referred to in most sources, though it certainly existed all over India. . . .

dence that the *panchāyat* was composed of the representatives of the different castes.[14] During the Middle Ages the *panchāyat* virtually disappears from the record. The Muslim historians who portrayed the Indian scene in such careful detail give it no mention. Indeed, for this long period references to village life are scanty; among these few is the picture of Bengali rural life depicted by Mukunda Ram.[15] The absence of evidence has not prevented historians from assuming that "village committees" were functioning throughout the Mughul period. The first really firm references to the *panchāyat* were made by British administrators like Munro and Elphinstone at the beginning of the nineteenth century. Perhaps too much has been adduced from what they said. Englishmen (and Americans) look at the world through political spectacles; in their society any kind of organized activity tends to be a reflection of the town meeting or the parish council. It seems possible that the British pioneers in describing the *panchāyat* saw it first as a reflection of their own accustomed municipal institutions. Certainly, mistaken assumptions were made.[16]

For what it is worth, the following formulation is suggested. The word *panchāyat* describes form, not purpose—a technique of seeking agreement through consultation, hallowed, according to tradition, by divine sanction: *panch men paramēśwar*. This technique was mainly employed in social or economic organisms (the closest Western parallels are the medieval trade guild or the Victorian friendly society) but it was also extensively used for the arbitration of both caste and village disputes.[17] With possible reservations re-

---

We have no record of the composition of the village council in the North." *The Wonder That Was India* (London, 1954), pp. 105-106.

[14] Cf. H. Tinker, *The Foundations of Local Self-Government in India, Pakistan and Burma* (London, 1954), p. 19. It may be significant that the same practice is followed in south India in modern times (*op. cit.*, p. 198); see also Park and Tinker, *op. cit.*, p. 430.

[15] See J. N. Das Gupta, *Bengal in the Sixteenth Century* (Calcutta, 1914), based upon Mukunda Ram and other contemporary writers. Das Gupta produces no evidence for the existence of the village *panchāyat*; he does not even mention it.

[16] In Bengal the early British administrators concluded that the "village" watchman they found must be the servant of the village; he was actually the agent of the absentee landlord. See W. W. Hunter, *Annals of Rural Bengal* (London, 1868), p. 334. One of the best accounts of north India in the early nineteenth century is the narrative of *A Journey through the Kingdom of Oude in 1849-1850*, by Sir W. H. Sleeman (2 vols; London, 1858). Sleeman, a master of observation, makes one reference to a judicial *panchāyat*. He constantly produces evidence to show that the Oude peasants followed their landlords' orders without any kind of village consultation: see I, 253-254.

[17] One Indian writer, at least, has reached the same conclusions. K. S. V.

garding south India, the *panchāyat* was not an administrative body in the usually accepted sense, but it was sometimes employed to apportion the village land revenue assessment and may have had a role in regulating the duties of the village servants. Most probably, when its members assumed this quasi-administrative role, they belonged to the dominant *zamīndār* or proprietor group, descendants of the putative founder of the village.

If the *panchāyat* first found a place in the records of administration thanks to the field-work of pioneer British officials, such as Munro and Elphinstone, their successors turned their attention elsewhere. For a quarter of a century the British in India were imbued with a belief in reform and the beneficent influence of Western ideas and institutions: Indian law and custom were regarded as superannuated. This movement largely came to an end with the Mutiny. Thereafter, British policy was conservative. From believing that India could be changed within a generation, the British came to believe in "the unchanging East." Matthew Arnold wrote at this time:

> The East bow'd low before the blast,
> In patient, deep disdain.
> She let the legions thunder past,
> And plunged in thought again.[18]

The British administration was, as it were, a dome over the life of India. Traditional Indian institutions were permitted to function; but an aloof, laissez-faire philosophy did little to stimulate activity. An excellent illustration of contemporary policy is Lord Lawrence's Resolution on Local Self-Government of 1864: "The people of this country are perfectly capable of administering their own local affairs. The municipal feeling is deeply rooted in them. The village communities . . . are the most abiding of Indian institutions. . . . Holding the position we do in India, every view of duty and policy should induce us to leave as much as possible of the business of the country to be done by the people."[19] Yet, while

Raman, in *Kurukshetra*, Jan. 26, 1961, p. 26, writes: "There seems to be hardly sufficient ground to maintain that Panchayats as institutions of self-government for an area, are indigenous to India. A few public works committees organised in the South, and a few *Janapadas* in the North may have worked in the past. Otherwise Panchayats seem to have been organisations mainly for adjudication of disputes of a particular profession or class, sometimes distributed over fairly large areas."

[18] From "Obermann Once More."

[19] Tinker, *op. cit.*, p. 36.

this was the declared policy, the forces which the British had set in motion (what Lord Dalhousie called "the engines of progress") were sapping ancient institutions and ways of life. A recent Indian survey observes, not unjustly, that "While on the one hand the Britishers created tier upon tier of courts of law they also tried to revive in their peculiar half-hearted manner the panchayat system of judicial administration."[20] Throughout the nineteenth century there were spasmodic efforts to succor the *panchāyat* and relate it to the structure of government. In the 1880's Lord Ripon sought to raise his new system of local self-government upon the ancient village system; typical of the legislation which followed was the Madras Village Courts Act of 1888. During the parliamentary debates upon the Indian Councils Act of 1892 (the measure which introduced elected members into the Indian legislatures), Sir W. Plowden moved that the new legislators be selected throughout India by *panchāyats*.[21] But there was no sustained support for the *panchāyats*, and every trend of the times served to complete the disintegration of traditional custom and influence. The pressure of the courts of law, the railways, new patterns of trade, and the shift of power to new classes all had their effect on traditional village society. Tarlok Singh, out of the breadth of his knowledge, sums up thus:

For several decades, as a well-knit social organisation the village community has been slowly but steadily declining. As the pursuit of individual interest within and outside the village has become more common, the influence of the community over its members has diminished. The growth of inequality in the ownership of land, land transfers to non-cultivators and migration to towns are evidence of these trends. . . . The old leadership in the village has been losing its position and influence without substantial signs of a new leadership stepping into its place. The institution of caste has less of social incidence, but it may well be that the economic incidence of caste . . . is being accentuated. . . . In this situation conflicts of interest within the village community have sharpened and the process continues. There are now few values which can be said to be common to the whole community, and certainly there is no common purpose which inspires all sections equally.[22]

[20] G. S. Chooramani, *Nyaya Panchayats and Panchayati Adalats in Uttar Pradesh* (Bureau of Agricultural Information, Lucknow, n.d.), pp. 2-3.

[21] *House of Commons Debates*, London, April 25, 1892. His amendment was defeated, 94 to 47.

[22] Tarlok Singh, *The Village Panchayat and the Pattern of Village Development* (mimeographed, 1955), pp. 2-3.

This historical sketch has attempted to establish that, while the *panchāyat* is an ancient institution of unique prestige, it provides no precedent for the village council of today. During the greater part of recorded time *panchāyats* were ignored by officials and official chroniclers until after the arrival of the British. Thereafter, attempts to endow the *panchāyat* with some kind of formal status failed, partly because the British had no firm policy, but mainly because the *panchāyat* could not resist the assaults of the modern age. These points have been made at some length as a reminder that the assumptions that the present-day village council has a historical antecedent, and that village solidarity exists as a social force ready to be tapped, are both without foundation.

From the early 1900's the role of government in India began to be diversified. The old style of village contacts with the machinery of government—and the kind of leaders which it had brought forward—can be glimpsed in this cameo of village leadership in Punjab, delineated by a reforming British district officer: "Socrates came into the village and found the patwari and the kanungo and the zaildar and sufedposh sitting with the lambadars, discussing the new jamabandi. . . . 'Good morning' said Socrates. . . . 'Silence' said the patwari. 'Can't you see the hakims are taking counsel together? Who are you, old man, to interfere with your croaking?' "[23] Who are these folk? They are the petty revenue officials (petty in their superiors' eyes, but all-important to the villagers) and the village bigwigs who are responsible for insuring that the land revenue is paid, and that law and order are maintained. Their discussion is concerned with the revenue record (*jamābandī*: literally, "binding and tightening") and if any outsider dares to interrupt their grave counsels he is peremptorily repulsed. This was the old order, but as the twentieth century opened, social welfare and political education received higher priority. The Decentralisation Commission, reporting in 1909, insisted that a whole-hearted attempt must be made to build up village councils: "the foundation of any stable edifice which shall associate the people with the administration must be the village." *Panchāyats* must be constituted, with petty civil and criminal jurisdiction, and responsibility for village sanitation, education, and minor

[23] F. L. Brayne, *Socrates in an Indian Village* (3rd. ed.; London, 1937), p. 47. Socrates is, of course, the author. *Patwari* is the village accountant, *kanungo*, the (superior) circle revenue officer. The others are "squires" or yeomen, presented in order of diminishing importance.

public works.[24]   In the following years legislation was passed to implement these reforms, such as the Punjab Panchāyats Act of 1912; but it was not until after World War I that this legislation became effective, so far as it was effective.   The period bears the same relation to the present that an overture does to an opera.   Every problem that has exercised Indian opinion since independence was first sounded during the Dyarchy years.[25]   Perhaps the dominant problem was the uneasy balance between established autocracy and immature democracy in a time of transition.   Is it possible for the high official to hand over power to elected representatives of the public while at the same time retaining a measure of residuary power and responsibility in the expectation that the elected leaders will conform to the same code that he follows?   A tall order, but it might be done, given good will on both sides.   During Dyarchy the Congress was dedicated to the principle that there could be no co-operation with the British administration; so the only contribution of the chief political party to local government was to further its disruption.   But, leaving aside politics, there was an inescapable ambivalence in this transitional situation.   The traditional attitude to the administration was aptly summarized by an experienced Pakistani official:

In one important respect the British regime bore a strong resemblance to the regimes that had preceded it.   It was essentially a *Mai-Bap* [Mother-Father] regime.   The King-Emperor was not averse to be viewed as a benign and kindly being who had replaced the Grand Moghal and had been ordained to look after the interests of his subjects.   A certain psychological atmosphere was created.   A belief was assiduously fostered that the Government was capable of doing everything under the sun. . . . A school wall is cracking up in the rural area; well, the Government will set it right.   A small bund is needed to save the people from seasonal floods; why not address a representation to the Government?   That will do the trick. . . .   Such an attitude killed initiative.[26]

The newly constituted *panchāyats* functioned against this background—and also against a barrage of adverse propaganda from the Congress.   Despite certain good work (particularly in the traditional sphere of judicial arbitration), they disappointed expectations; especially, they failed to create a sense of belonging to the village.[27]

[24] Tinker, *op. cit.*, p. 85.
[25] Tinker, *op. cit.*, pp. 116-118 and 197-213.
[26] *Village Aid in West Pakistan* (Village Aid Administration, Lahore, 1957), pp. 20-21.
[27] When in 1958 the writer visited villages which (according to the records)

Because the villagers thought of themselves as separated from an aloof and beneficent government, they were exceedingly reluctant to introduce new taxes or to collect taxes actually introduced: "Government will provide." With absurdly small financial resources they were able to accomplish little.

In the 1930's emphasis was transferred to rural construction or rural uplift, the precursor of Community Development. This idea was first launched by individuals, of whom F. L. Brayne and M. L. Darling are the best known. In the early days, their activity "was regarded [by higher authority] as a heresy practiced by crazy district officers,"[28] but in time these ideas became official orthodoxy. Brayne, in arid, parched Gurgaon, tried to awaken the villagers to possibilities of agricultural and domestic betterment; he devised a scheme of Village Guides, as a kind of bridgehead whereby the activities of the "nation building" departments might be more effectively brought into touch with the villagers. Brayne's approach was empirical. He intended that in each individual village, the people should work out their own solution to social and economic problems. But Gurgaon District was an especially difficult area in which to make progress. Partly because of its appalling climatic uncertainty, partly because of its long history of invasion and disturbance, the people were suspicious and unresponsive. Brayne found himself in a dilemma familiar to the social reformer: he had to win over a hostile audience. Among his official colleagues there were many who cast doubt on his motives and denied the validity of his theories, while among the people of the district there was an equal disbelief in the new ideas. He had to show results; and that meant forcing the pace. Brayne probably tried to push through too much too quickly; he himself realized that his approach relied to a dangerous degree upon his own personal leadership and example. His detractors (of whom there was no shortage) alleged that the "Gurgaon Experiment" left no permanent legacy, and unfortunately for students of Community Development it is to no one's interest to attempt an objective assessment of Brayne's work.[29] The

had set up *panchāyats* in the 1920's, he was sometimes met with denials that a *panchāyat* had ever existed there, perhaps because it had been so ineffective or perhaps because, to the villagers, it had never been "their" *panchāyat*.

[28] *Village Aid in West Pakistan*, p. 56.

[29] Cf. Brayne, *op. cit.*, pp. 116-119; see also Albert Mayer and associates, *Pilot Project, India* (Berkeley, 1958), p. 19: "Brayne's work, it seemed, had not in any

rural reconstruction program did achieve a distinct measure of success, but mainly in material terms: new wells, drains, paved lanes. All this depended heavily on higher direction.[30]

Following independence, Congress's plans for regenerating local administration began from two main premises. There was the Gandhian doctrine which led to including among the Directive Principles of the Constitution a provision for the formation of village *panchāyats* as "units of self government" (Article 40). There was also a conviction that autocratic administration and public passivity were exclusively derived from British rule and would now disappear with independence.[31] There was renewed activity in devising a legislative framework for administrative *panchāyats*.[32] One important consideration was the size of the proposed administrative unit: should this be the nucleated village (the actual village community, which might comprise a small market town of three thousand or a hamlet of fifty souls) or should it be manufactured out of combinations of villages and hamlets to make an area which would be viable in terms of competent leadership and adequate financial resources? This question had been debated through the Dyarchy period, and both solutions had been found to have disadvantages. In Uttar Pradesh under the 1947 Act, the countryside was divided into *Gaon Sabhā* (administrative) circles, containing a population of about a thousand and comprising an average of three or four villages; the executive committee of the *Sabhā* was the elected *Gaon Panchāyat*. Three or four *Gaon Sabhā* circles formed a *Panchayati Adālat* (local court). With the abolition of landlordism in Uttar Pradesh village management committees (*Gaon Samāj*) were formed in every village, leading to "chaotic conditions" of conflicting jurisdiction.[33] Subsequently, the area of the administrative *panchāyat* was narrowed so that each

permanent way affected village well-being, life, or outlook." No evidence is offered that Mr. Mayer actually visited Brayne's Gurgaon villages.

[30] In visiting villages where development work is flourishing today, the writer was impressed with the number which had been prominent in the program of the 1930's. But the "sample" was too small to show whether this correlation was significant.

[31] Cf. Albert Mayer, *op. cit.*, p. 8. Nehru wrote in 1946 to Mayer, "Our people have naturally developed a number of complexes during these past generations of foreign rule and foreign exploitation. But we can get over them. . . ."

[32] See *Report of the Congress Panchayat Committee*, Appendix B (Panchayat Organisation in India).

[33] *Report of the U. P. Panchayat Raj Amendment Act Committee* (Lucknow, 1954), p. 14.

village with a minimum population of 250 had its own *panchāyat*. The other states can be divided into a "big *panchāyat*" group (Madras, Andhra, Orissa, Bihar, Rajasthan, Kerala, and Himachal Pradesh) and a "small *panchāyat*" group (Bombay, Madhya Pradesh, Punjab).[34] The trend towards a larger unit appears to predominate.[35] This is applauded in what is probably the most influential survey of local administration which has appeared since independence —the Mehta *Report*:

Little panchayats constituted for small villages are generally swayed by narrower considerations and sometimes dominated by caste interests which are toned down in a bigger body, comprising a number of villages inhabited by practically all castes. Membership of such a body infuses a wider outlook and a sense of responsibility which transcends narrow and parochial considerations.[36]

In general, the *panchāyat* experiment showed the same discouraging refusal to "get off the ground" as before independence. Reporting in November, 1957, the Mehta team declared that "the available information indicates that possibly not more than 10 per cent of the total number of panchayats are functioning effectively."[37] Their poor performance stems directly from the circumstances of rural life. Faction dominates most Indian villages, and "the number of panchayats which are torn by factions or in which squabbles are rampant is large. In fact in some States they are in a majority."[38] "Panchayat elections have resulted in creating or aggravating factional rivalries in about one-third of the villages in which there was a contest."[39] Also, "separatism arising out of caste distinction" is said to be on the increase, and "caste becomes a political division of society at the same time it is losing its position as a ritual division."[40] The remedy often urged is a return to the ancient tradition of choosing village leaders by general agreement.

[34] West Bengal, Mysore, and Assam "have not made any appreciable progress" in establishing *panchayats;* see *Fifth Evaluation Report*, Programme Evaluation Organisation, Planning Commission (New Delhi, 1958), p. 17.

[35] According to the *Fifth Evaluation Report*, the average population of each *panchāyat* circle in a sample survey was 2,600.

[36] *Report of the Team for the Study of Community Projects and National Extension Service* (Balvantray G. Mehta, Leader) (New Delhi: Committee on Plan Projects, Government of India, 1957). Vols. I and II (Nov., 1957); Vol. III (Parts I and II) (Dec., 1957), II, 3.

[37] *Ibid.*, II, 1.

[38] *Ibid.*, II, 7.

[39] *Ibid.*, I, 18.

[40] *Ibid.*, I, 18; and Adrian Mayer, *op. cit.*, p. 202.

"It is this principle of unanimity which was the soul of Panchayats in ancient India, and it . . . requires revivification."[41]   Many committees are formed with an appearance of unanimous support, but frequently the absence of an election merely "indicates lack of interest in the community."[42]   Committees are usually dominated by the conservative, upper-caste, prosperous elements in the village; one survey reported that, on an average, 60 per cent of members were over forty years old, and 90 per cent were landowners.[43]   "The economically weaker sections have as yet little voice in the affairs of the panchayat."[44]

The Minister for Local Self-Government in Uttar Pradesh observed (in 1954) that "the *panchayats* and district boards alike suffered more from poverty than from any other evil or disease."[45] Of course Indian villages are desperately poor, but the poverty of the *panchāyats* is at least partially self-inflicted. They have been given powers to impose taxes, but do not apply them; taxes in force are not collected; average collections are less than 50 per cent and in some states less than 30 per cent. *Panchāyat* members are themselves frequent defaulters.[46]   The majority of *panchāyats* have a total annual income, inclusive of grants, of less than Rs. 500 ($100). Of the funds collected, at least half is absorbed by administrative costs.[47] A large proportion of the *panchāyats* fail to render an account of their financial stewardship to the general body of the *Gaon Sabhā* as required by law.[48]   It is not surprising that their over-all record is unfavorable. A survey of sixty *panchāyats* at work revealed that only about twenty made provision for lighting and sweeping the streets, while "their role in economic development is negligible."[49]

Reports of this kind began to mount up in the early 1950's, but attention had already shifted to another sphere (Community Development) reproducing almost exactly the sequence of the 1920's and 1930's. During the first decade of independence there was an in-

[41] *Report of the Congress Village Panchayat Committee*, p. 22.
[42] *Fifth Evaluation Report*, p. 18. Six of the eight *panchāyats* investigated by Adrian Mayer in Malwa were constituted by unanimous choice of the villagers. Mayer, *op. cit.*, p. 201.
[43] *Fifth Evaluation Report*, p. 18.
[44] Mehta, *Report*, II, 2.
[45] *Report of the U. P. Panchayat Raj Amendment Act Committee*, p. 18.
[46] Mehta, *Report*, II, 7; and *Fifth Evaluation Report*, p. 20.
[47] *Report of the Congress . . . Committee*, p. 47.
[48] *Report of the U. P. . . . . Committee*, p. 28.
[49] *Fifth Evaluation Report*, p. 23.

creasing degree of official and centralized control throughout the whole range of local affairs. The Mehta *Report* speaks of "the gradual eclipse of district boards from the social polity."[50] In many states the boards were relieved of their main functions, such as education, the highways, and medical care. All over India, individual boards and municipalities were superseded and their functions vested in appointed government officials. The new constitutions drafted for such major municipalities as Greater Poona and Greater Delhi transferred the actual powers of management to a Municipal Commissioner, a senior administrator. In consonance with this national trend, rural reconstruction was placed almost exclusively in the hands of government officials. The purpose of the Community Development Programme is thus defined by V. T. Krishnamachari:

To create in the millions of rural families a burning desire to change their old-time outlook and arouse enthusiasm in them for new knowledge and new ways of life. This "will to live better" is to be brought about by ensuring that *every* family has a programme for increased employment and production for which it is assisted: that *every* family is represented on at least one multi-purpose cooperative society in its own right: that *every* family makes its voluntary contribution to works of benefit to the community as a whole.[51]

The new movement was set in motion in 1952, and in conception and organization drew heavily upon the Etawah Pilot Project. Albert Mayer, the overseer of this project, had laid great emphasis upon assisting the village folk to realize "felt needs"—to attain ends which they themselves desired rather than what the government thought was good for them; to create a co-operative effort, with villagers and government technicians pulling together as a team, dissolving the age-old division between aloof officials and docile villagers. Mayer made no claim to have discovered new principles but did claim to have "systematized" previous methods and to have enrolled all concerned in a sense of shared decision and effort.[52]

The Etawah Project started with the advantages of consistent support from the highest in the land, a hand-picked team of workers, and an area that was manageable and had a tradition of local initiative. Great emphasis was laid on the role of the Village Level

[50] Mehta, *Report*, II, 12.
[51] V. T. Krishnamachari, "The National Extension Movement and Community Projects," *Sainik Samachar*, Jan. 1957.
[52] Albert Mayer, *op. cit.*, p. 65.

Worker (*Grām Sēvak*) as a "multi-purpose worker and friend of the village people."[53] The aim was to establish a new kind of relationship between the *Grām Sēvak* and the small group of villages with which he was linked—that of a social worker rather than of a minor government servant. The success of the Etawah Project was undoubted, but this was due (more than Mayer and his colleagues cared to admit) to their own single-minded leadership. And as the scope of the project was enlarged, the "felt needs" of the people became submerged in the larger plans of the government. The autonomy of the development organization and staff, to which Mayer attached great value, was increasingly sapped away; the control of the administrators was extended until, in 1954, the District Officer became directly responsible for development work in his district.

However, long before this, the Etawah Project had become merged in a national program. In 1952 fifteen pilot projects were inaugurated in different states on the Etawah model of a "block" of 60 to 100 villages, the block being divided into circles of 5 or 6 villages under the *Grām Sēvak*. By the end of 1958 there were 2,361 blocks, covering about 300,000 villages with a population of 162 million (about three-fifths of rural India). Yet this immense achievement was accompanied by an ever-increasing volume of criticism. The Mehta *Report*, which appeared in November, 1957, brought this to a head, insisting that the program was right off its course; it had been meant to kindle a new sense of community and assist in launching the "take-off" in economic development, but instead it had been diverted into an officially controlled "bricks and mortar" program of public works, devoid of almost any popular dynamic.[54] The Govind Sahay Committee, appointed by the government of Uttar Pradesh, came to a similar conclusion: it reported "The whole programme has suffered from a lack of vitality and is tending to degenerate into a number of material benefits for a limited few. In the absence of a proper perspective and an ideological bias, the programme has not so far developed into a people's movement with a purpose. It is mostly spoon-fed, and lacks a purpose."[55] A review prepared by the Development and Planning Division of the Reserve

[53] *Ibid.*, p. 82.
[54] Cf. *Kurukshetra*, April 1959, p. 11: "Successive evaluation reports have have pointed out that community development programme in India is Government's programme carried out with people's participation and not people's programme."
[55] Quoted in *Kurukshetra*, March 1961, pp. 17-18.

Bank of India estimated that the contribution made by the people, during the period of the First Five Year Plan, came to 34.9 per cent of total expenditure; it rose in 1956-57 to 40.8 per cent of the total, and then steadily declined to 28.4 per cent in 1959-60. The Bank review adds: "there is also a tendency to overvalue this contribution. Anyway, it seems the programme has lost its original attraction."[56] What were the reasons, in detail, why the "government programme" failed to evolve into a "people's programme," as the publicists insisted it would? The following is offered as a very tentative analysis.

The block has been the working unit for development, but the level of effective administrative decision has been that of the state or district. The First Five Year Plan forecast that the "first effect ... of development will be to increase the district officer's work and responsibility still further."[57] The district officer is the bottleneck of the government process: loaded with new duties, compelled to fulfil a quasi-political role (like the French prefect) yet still burdened with all his former responsibilities, he is now expected to coordinate and inspire development. He is supposed to share this task with a district advisory committee but everywhere this committee has been little more than a formality. The First Plan urged that the district boards should have "a vital part to play" but "in practise these recommendations have not been carried out to any great extent."[58] The district officer remains the keystone of the development structure but has been unable to make this his principal concern. He has often to delegate his work to the district planning officer, and the departmental district-level officials resent the interposition of this officer (often their junior in service). They often persist in pursuing the policy laid down by their department. Block Development Officers (BDO's) find they are under a system of "duplicate control" and have to refer to two sets of superiors; some BDO's talk of "a Cold War among the higher ups. . . . Administrative coordination as it exists at present is only a pious word."[59]

The BDO is the actual supervisor of activities in the field.[60]

[56] Reserve Bank of India, *Bulletin*, Jan., 1961.
[57] *First Five Year Plan* (New Delhi, 1952), p. 131.
[58] *First Five Year Plan*, p. 131; and *Second Five Year Plan*, 1956, p. 160.
[59] Mehta, *Report*, II, 44.
[60] The block headquarters staff also includes assistant development officers, one for agriculture, one for social education, and one for *panchāyats* and co-operatives. There is usually an engineer, one or two health visitors, a veterinary officer, and others; see Mehta, *Report*, II, 38.

Sometimes he comes from the Agricultural or the Veterinary Department; some are directly recruited university graduates; a few are promoted *Grām Sēvaks;* and in several states all BDO's are appointed from the Revenue service. In Bihar and Bombay the *Tahsīldār* or *Māmlatdar* (subordinate revenue officers) has to run a block in addition to his regular duties. The block program (planning, budgeting, etc.) is supposed to be decided by the Block Advisory Committee, but this body has all too often had the same shadowy existence as its district counterpart. Membership of the committee is commonly sought and awarded purely for reasons of status and prestige.[61] In most blocks at least a year elapses—the most critical year—before a committee is constituted. In size they vary from over 150 in Uttar Pradesh down to 18 in Kerala. Where the committee is unwieldy it is difficult to get through the business, and where it is small the official component is too strong to permit an effective local voice to be heard.[62] Attendance of non-officials averages a little over 50 per cent.[63] To the village representative, attendance at block headquarters means a journey of many miles over rough roads, out of his familiar environment into an alien, official milieu. Most block headquarters are modest enough—bare brick buildings with no luxuries—but they are laid out in traditional official "cantonment" style, with the traditional office peon, symbol of petty extortion, at the door. At the meeting the villager is uneasily aware that he is not on his home ground but is dealing with officials, very much on their ground; his instinct is to defer, to "play it safe."[64] And so the officials make the decisions—for the good of the people, of course, but without their active participation. Instead of Community Development being built up out of rural needs, it is dispensed from

[61] [*Fourth*] *Evaluation Report,* 1957, p. 18.
[62] Of the 150-160 U. P. members, 138 on average are non-officials and 21 officials; in Madras there are twice as many official members as non-officials; in Bihar there is an average of 15 officials to 13 non-officials. Mehta, *Report,* II, 90.
[63] Where attendance figures of non-officials are worst (in U. P. with 40 per cent), the highest proportion (90 per cent) "felt they could effectively influence decisions." In Bihar, where the attendance record is the best (75 per cent) the proportion who thought they could influence decisions was lowest (30 per cent). This paradox seems to indicate that statistics based upon reported opinions should be accepted with caution. It is inconceivable that if the Bihar representatives thought they could do no good, they should continue to turn up in large numbers. See Mehta, *Report,* II, 93.
[64] The phrase comes from Evelyn Wood, "Patterns of Influence in Rural India," in Park and Tinker, *op. cit.,* pp. 372-390. This study of peasant psychology should be required reading for all concerned in Community Development.

above, often concentrated into a few major projects which are easier to plan and administer and yield concrete results. Of course it is practical policy not to scatter the never plentiful funds around in penny packets—a few rupees in this village, a few in that, and nothing permanent to show for it anywhere. But an unduly large share has gone into bricks and mortar, sometimes into office buildings; "apart from being waste, [this] has an unfavourable effect upon the people's minds and widens the gulf between the people" and administrators.[65] That gulf has remained in the mind of the village folk, and the original intention of development, whereby the administrator's role would be to "prime the pump"—to insure that a venture was fairly launched and then transfer authority to the people—has been disappointed. In many areas, when the impulse from above has weakened, the people's contribution has dwindled away.[66]

The originators of Community Development envisaged the Village Level Worker (*Grām Sēvak*) as the vital link between government and people, the means whereby popular initiative might be awakened and sustained; but the *Grām Sēvak* has not always been able to fulfil these expectations. To a highly status-conscious society, his status remains peculiarly ambivalent.[67] Is he on the side of the villagers or that of the government? He is not received as a social worker, as the Gandhian village workers were; but it is entirely correct to assume that the *Grām Sēvak* "earning less than Rs. 100 a month is a new bureaucrat whether he likes it or not."[68] His role is such a novelty that he is often able to create his own *persona*. This partially depends upon the number of villages for which he is made responsible; the greater his area, the less of a "villager" he will be. His jurisdiction has varied widely, but the average appears to fall between 10 and 17 villages, with a population of 8,000 to 14,000.[69]

In the Etawah scheme the *Grām Sēvak* had been responsible for only four villages. It seems that most of his time is spent in the headquarters village; those more distant (45 per cent of the total) are visited less than once a month.[70] However, the *Grām Sēvak* is the most frequent visitor among the village level govern-

[65] Mehta, *Report*, I, 117.
[66] Mehta, *Report*, I, 115.
[67] For a detailed analysis of his position, see S. C. Dube, *India's Changing Villages* (London, 1958), p. 177.
[68] Park and Tinker, *op. cit.*, p. 385.
[69] Mehta, *Report*, III, Pt. II, 105.
[70] *Fifth Evaluation Report*, p. 12.

ment agents.[71]   Another important element influencing his position is, of course, his caste. Official reports are silent on this matter, and one can only surmise that many *Grām Sēvaks* are *brāhmans* or members of the higher agricultural caste (such as *rajputs* and *jats*); non-agriculturalists (such as *kayasthas* or *banias*) will be few and *harijans* even fewer.[72] In this situation the *Grām Sēvak* will tend to work with upper-caste, conservative village leaders, leaving the "have-nots" outside. But his personality will be of greatest consequence: what does he himself make of the job? His list of duties is Herculean: it includes agriculture, animal husbandry, and irrigation; "human development" or welfare activities; help to youth, women, and sections of the community needing special assistance; and in general "he should function as the *sēvak*, or servant of the village and help individual villagers."[73] But it is reported that many *Grām Sēvaks* acquired a place in village esteem not so much for acting as a universal Mr. Fixit but because, when the programs were first launched, ample government funds became available and the *Grām Sēvaks* were able to arrange for subventions, supplies, and credits for their villagers.[74] When this "give away" phase tapered off, some *Grām Sēvaks* found their position had altered and their role in village society became nebulous.

Some reacted by "getting more 'official' in their behaviour" and acquiring a tendency "to prefer desk work to field work."[75] The *Grām Sēvaks* began to "expect the villagers to come to their 'offices' for their requirements," but they in turn were put in their place by their superiors: "at the least provocation, the *Gram Sevak* was required to visit the Block headquarters for small odds and ends in which the BDO and his extension staff were interested."[76] There was an almost total eclipse of the "team" concept of development by the traditional "hierarchic" bureaucratic relationship. The *Grām Sēvak* is not treated as the key pioneer in a new adventure of nation-building but as the lowliest figure in yet another branch of administration, to fetch and carry for official or political bosses.

The diminution of the status of the *Grām Sēvak* is related to the

---

[71] Mehta, *Report*, III, Pt. II, 102.
[72] See Dube, *op. cit.*, p. 159.
[73] [*Fourth*] *Evaluation Report*, p. 27.
[74] [*Fourth*] *Evaluation Report*, p. 28.
[75] [*Fourth*] *Evaluation Report*, p. 26-27; and Mehta, *Report*, I, 120.
[76] Mehta, *Report*, II, 172.

minor role assigned to village leaders in Community Development. It is scarcely credible that, after all the talk about *panchāyats* and village democracy, they were given no effective place in the new enterprise; yet such was the case. Despite long passages in both the First and the Second Five Year Plans on "Village Planning and Village Panchayats" it was still necessary in 1957 to acknowledge that "they have not come into the [development] field to any appreciable extent."[77] Instead of incorporating the already established *panchāyats*, in most areas *ad hoc* development committees (*Vikās Maṇḍal*) were set up, bringing a fourth committee into the village to be set alongside the administrative *panchāyat*, the co-operative, and the land management committee. In some states, the development staff are linked with the *Panchāyat Rāj*, and elsewhere the work of the two parallel departments is brought into some sort of alliance, but in many areas the *panchāyats* were entirely by-passed by those in charge of Community Development on the grounds that they were "dormant, inactive and ineffective."[78] The situation is analagous to that which elicited F. W. Maitland's celebrated aphorism concerning the old unreformed English boroughs: "untrusted because untrustworthy, untrustworthy became untrusted." One survey, designed to assess village responsiveness, declared that:

Suggestions for raising income and for increasing taxes are forthcoming much more readily from those blocks where the *panchayats* have levied taxes, mobilised resources and shown some activity. On the other hand, in blocks where the *panchayats* are not active, or the resources mobilised by them are meagre, the response is poor. The correlation is by no means perfect but the trend does suggest that the very fact of effective functioning of the *panchayats* for some time might prove a stimulus for further progress.[79]

In the same vein, while the Mehta team's members found in general "excessive dependence on continued Government initiative," they report that a "few *panchayats* have been successful in a small measure in mobilising voluntary labour for community work.

[77] *Ibid.*, I, 5.
[78] *Kurukshetra*, April, 1959, p. 13. See also *Sixth Evaluation Report*, (June, 1959), pp. 16-18. A sample survey of 190 villages situated in 38 blocks, scattered all over India, revealed that 37 villages had no *panchāyat*; the remaining 153 villages were covered by 145 *panchāyats*. Of these, only 13 are reported to have undertaken some planning and execution of programs. In 24 out of the 36 blocks in which *panchāyats* exist, they have failed to levy taxes.
[79] *Fifth Evaluation Report*, p. 24.

In such villages a new leadership is emerging, indicative of a new attitude to local welfare and local development and a realisation of the value of local institutions."[80]

On the basis of this faith in local leadership, Balvantray G. Mehta and his colleagues recommended broad measures of "democratic decentralization." The main responsibility for development should be transferred to a local representative body at the block level, the *Panchāyat Samiti*, to be composed of members indirectly elected, by the village *panchāyats* and certain other bodies. The *samiti* is to take over "the development of agriculture, improvement of cattle, promotion of local industries, public health, welfare work, administration of primary schools," and "other functions." Its income is to include a proportion of the land revenue. The staff is to be strengthened; BDO's are to be put on the junior administrative cadre, and all junior revenue officers are to be posted as BDO's after their initial training, before they are imbued with the "revenue bureaucratic spirit." *Grām Sēvaks* are to be increased in numbers, and the area of the circle limited to cover a population of four thousand: they should establish closer links with village *panchāyats*, for whom they will serve as development secretaries.[81]

The Mehta *Report* was endorsed by a National Conference on Community Development, which met at Mount Abu in May, 1958, and subsequently by the Conference of Local Self-Government Ministers of all the states meeting at Hyderabad in October, 1959; but perhaps of greater significance than this support by politicians and officials was the appearance of a similar proposal for local community action evolved by Jayaprakash Narayan. His draft *Plea for Reconstruction of Indian Polity* is a restatement of Gandhian principles which, as he says, has "much in common" with the Mehta *Report*: Jayaprakash Narayan, one-time revolutionary Marxist, and now *jīvan-dānī*, "life devotee" and leader of the *Bhoodan* movement and exponent of *Sarvōdaya*, or "ideal harmony," finds himself alongside the hard-headed Gujerati businessman and Chairman of the Estimates Committee of the Union Parliament, Balvantray G. Mehta. This merging of the philosophies of the idealist and visionary, and the practical man of affairs, in a mutual insistence upon the necessity

[80] Mehta, *Report*, I, 44.
[81] The full list of recommendations is given in Mehta, *Report*, I, 125-161.

for genuine local self-government may be one of the seminal influences in the emergence of Indian democracy.

Jayaprakash sees this as a "problem of social reconstruction," to be attained by means of a co-operative or "communitarian" society. He insists that neither society nor the state can be an aggregation of individuals: the community remains the foundation-stone of India. His goal is *grām dharma*: the function of *dharma* is law rooted in social custom, or social ethics. Jayaprakash contrasts his communitarian society with the present regime: democracy in name, but centralized bureaucracy in practice. His solution draws heavily on Gandhian teaching, but he insists that the community must be wider than the village. He builds his polity around what he calls the "regional community," i.e., a group of associated villages. This regional community would be the basic unit for planning and for joint activity and even for agricultural and industrial production. The whole of his argument is directed against what he describes as "the divisive influence of the existing atomistic policy." The villagers merge into the village, the village merges into the regional community, and the regional community into the district, the state, and the nation.[82]

Both Balvantray Mehta and Jayaprakash Narayan have discarded the hoary myth of the "self-sufficient Indian village," which Gandhians have nurtured right to the present day. And their ideas have been taken up and have become the orthodoxy of Community Development. The Minister, S. K. Dey, in his somewhat orotund way, has preached the new doctrine many times. For example:

A self-sufficient village republic, even regionally, is a myth in the sputnik age where the world has already shrunk to the virtual size of a peanut and life is springing forward for a leap into the wider cosmos. . . . The revolution already under way in the means and processes of production makes it quite obvious that self-sufficient village republic can at best be a dream.[83]

To symbolize the transformation, in place of the phrase used so often by Gandhi, *Panchāyat Rāj*, the usage *Panchāyatī Rāj* has supervened. It is, perhaps, not just an exercise in semantics to suggest that "Village Council Government," and "Government of the Village Councils" are subtly differentiated.

[82] Quotations from the "draft for private circulation" of *Plea for Reconstruction of Indian Policy*, Banaras, Sept., 1959.
[83] S. K. Dey, *Community Development: A Movement Is Born* (Allahabad, 1960), p. 173.

The new system has been introduced in a number of states. The procedure varies. In some states, enabling legislation has been followed immediately by the inauguration of the new councils. In others, the legislation was implemented at leisure, elections preceding the actual constitution of the councils by many months. In Mysore, *Panchāyatī Rāj* was introduced by phases; the Madras method was similar. The inauguration of *Panchāyatī Rāj* in Assam did not result in any early change of note. Subject to these variations, which affected the progress of the new system, the following states were the pioneers of *Panchāyatī Rāj*: Rajasthan brought the new scheme into operation on October 2, 1959; Andhra followed on November 8, 1959. In 1960 Madras formally inaugurated the scheme on October 2 and Mysore on December 21. During 1961 *Panchāyatī Rāj* came into being in Orissa on January 26 and in Punjab on October 2. The pattern is roughly the same. The old district boards are abolished, and a new structure arises. At the base are *Grām Panchāyats* for each large village or for a group of small villages or hamlets. Above are the *Panchāyat Samitis*, coterminous with the Community Development Block, or the revenue Taluka, and forming the main executive unit, the focus of activity. Over all is a district council, termed the *Zilā Pariṣad* in north India and the District Development Council in the south. Its functions are least well-defined; it is intended to act as a co-ordinating body. Only one state, Gujerat, has signified that it intends to continue to utilize the district as the main unit of administration.

At the time of writing (August, 1961) any assessment of the trend of *Panchāyatī Rāj* is premature. Two evaluation reports have indeed appeared. A parliamentary study team, led by Raghubir Sahai, M.P., was asked by the Congress party to assess the working of the new system in the two pioneer provinces of Rajasthan and Andhra. The team spent nine days in Rajasthan in October, 1960, and ten days in Andhra in December, 1960. Their conclusions (necessarily limited to surface impressions) were published soon after.[84] A second survey was made under the auspices of a private venture known as the Association of Voluntary Agencies for Rural Development (AVARD); their team visited Rajasthan in November, 1960.[85] In the main, both reports present a similar picture. On the

[84] Summarized in *Kurukshetra*, and *Panchayat Raj* (formerly *Grām Sevak*), March, 1961.
[85] Summarized in *Kurukshetra*, April, 1961.

credit side they pronounce that the new elected chairmen, endowed with executive authority, are working well with their chief officers, formerly their leaders and now their coadjutors. The AVARD report has some reservations and notes a "mild tussle for power" between the block development officer (now called *Vikās Adhikārī*) and the *Pradhān*, the chairman; the Raghubir Sahai team detected only a small amount of friction between the official and the elected heads—mainly attributable to the misconduct of a small minority of the *Pradhāns*. Both reports state that the *Panchāyat Samiti* is the principal center of activity. The role of the *Zilā Parīṣad* in Rajasthan is only vaguely defined, while in Andhra the continuing presence of the District Officer as chairman inhibits non-official enterprise, though the Andhra District Councils have inherited most of the powers of the old District Boards.

Concerning the village *panchāyats* the AVARD team found that the success of the *Panchāyat Samiti* had been achieved at the expense of village-level institutions. The village *panchāyats* are inclined to look up to the *Panchāyat Samiti* as the fount of power (a new variant of the old *Ma-Bāp* attitude?). The village councils have failed to attempt any extension of economic activities. They have also failed to exploit the resources within their grasp by levying the taxes which they are empowered to introduce. The Raghubir Sahai team noted that "general meetings of the *Grām Sabhā* [the assembly of the whole village] were not called, and therefore the village people as a whole were not apprised of the activities of the *Grām Panchayat*." Both reports emphasized that, because of *Panchāyatī Rāj*, faction and division within village life had been intensified. Most *panchāyats* were split into factions, some on political party lines. In the same way, caste conflict had been intensified: in Rajasthan, the principal struggle appears to be that of *jat* cultivators and *rajput* traditional leaders; in Andhra, the new system served to define the gulf which lay between *harijans* and caste Hindus. On the credit side, the village *panchāyats* had lessened the power of petty officials to exact petty levies from their village "clients," even if this petty corruption had to some extent been appropriated by the *arrivistes*, the elected bosses.

It would be unwise to deduce from this evidence that the pattern of village power and leadership has been transformed by *Panchāyatī Rāj*. Past experience, both in the Rural Reconstruction and Community Development movements, provides warnings of the false impression of change which the first impact of a new movement seems to portend. The novelty of the new activities—even the novelty for the village folk of being suddenly promoted from the back row of the audience to the front row of the show—generates a temporary dynamic, which can appear quite impressive. In the past this dynamism has evaporated when the outside interest has dwindled and the village folk have been left to themselves again. The time to form a balanced estimate of the new system may not arrive for another five years. However, it may be worth attempting to examine some of the trends which appear to be emerging. First, there is the widespread decision to make the block the principal unit for development. On practical grounds much can be said in its favor. In the view of the Mehta team, "The block . . . offers an area large enough for functions which the village panchayat cannot perform and yet small enough to attract the interest and service of its residents."[86] But the average block has a population of sixty to eighty thousand and contains from twenty to a hundred villages. Experience has demonstrated that between the village or neighborhood and the district there is no intermediate area that provides a basis for a sense of community. The object of local government planners from the time of Ripon onward has been to get away from the district down to a more cohesive area, such as the subdivision or the *tahsīl;* but the pressure of local circumstances has always frustrated such intentions. The administrative district, merely through having functioned for a hundred years or more, has acquired a certain meaning. At district headquarters are the Law Courts and the lawyers; here is located the only decent hospital, the government high school, perhaps an intermediate college; here is all the mechanism of commerce and exchange. The administrative center has taken on the character of a social center, at any rate for the middle classes. The *tahsīl* headquarters is nothing—a treasury, a police station, a dispensary, and that is about all. A block headquarters is even less a potential nucleus of the local community, except where by chance it is situated in a market town serving the surrounding villages. As the center of the principal unit of the new local administration, block headquarters will not only be artificial, but will actually have a negative quality. Social, political, and administrative pressures will

[86] Mehta, *Report,* I, 9.

combine to make district headquarters the focus of Community Development—at any rate until middle-class leadership gives way to a broader democracy which includes the underprivileged classes, when an area evolved out of a neighborhood (perhaps coterminous with the *Grām Sēvak*'s circle) may become the local unit. In this regard the proposals of Jayaprakash Narayan to constitute "regional communities" of neighboring villages in an "integral" community is more in keeping with the nature of Indian village society. Marriage ties and economic connections do often provide a neighborly nexus which could provide the basis of intervillage co-operation, which the block can never hope to emulate.

Of course, it is artificial to consider the balance of rural leadership and influence except in relation to the over-all pattern of power. The initiative in planning and programming still comes from above; the rural folk still look up to government, or to the new block councils as the emanation of government for purposes of fund-raising. Moreover, the pull of the central government, the state governments, and even the pull of the district administration, still insures that the "center of gravity" of politics is at high level. So long as this government from above persists, the attempt to build up *Panchāyatī Rāj* as a counter-attraction will not prevail against the general political trend. The forces of centralization have been actually increasing, as S. K. Dey has made clear: "In administration, despite the provisions of our Constitution demarcating the relative spheres of States' and Central subjects, there is a tendency of more and more powers concentrating in the Centre. The States, in their anxiety not to be left behind, are dealing in the same way with the local bodies. Though the panchayats remain, they are being used mainly as organisations for offering receptions to V. I. P.'s and ministers. The people in India . . . are doing just the opposite of what ideals the Mahatma stood for all his life, viz. that the village should be treated as the base for the democratic structure in this country."[87] The budget debates in Parliament in April, 1961, revealed anxiety at the mounting control over local activity. Thus Kamal Singh, M.P.: "The sense of dependence and helplessness is increasing in our villages. Villagers look to the government for every little thing. There is also lack of co-operation. The result is that constructive work is hampered. Village factions and power

[87] *Kurukshetra*, Jan., 1961, p. 4.

politics add to the problem." Similar qualms were expressed by Munishawar Dutt Upadhyay, M.P., among others: "Regarding *Panchayati Raj*, we have to see whether decentralisation has really taken place or not. One still feels that nothing can be done without orders from above. It was seen at one or two places that the local people collected some money for certain schemes. Yet approval from above came after years."[88] The retention of political power in the hands of the few was the keynote of the presidential speech which Jayaprakash Narayan delivered to the All-India Panchayat Parishad which convened at Jaipur in May, 1961. He likened Indian democracy to "an inverted pyramid that stands on its head," as opposed to the broad-based pyramid of a genuine democracy. In assessing the potentialities of Community Development for broadening the base in India and creating what Jayaprakash called "participating democracy," he pointed to the cramping effect upon the program of its initially limited purpose, which he defined as "a procedural reform of the administration at the lower levels." It would be necessary, he intimated, to introduce "a real devolution of power, and not a make-belief." To implement this radical change, Jayaprakash wanted the District Magistrate to "disappear or remain only as a representative in the district of the State Government. . . . *Panchayati Raj* even in Rajasthan, where it began, is yet a far cry from this consummation."[89] Of the three tiers of the new structure, the *Grām Panchāyat* must be the solid foundation; and the village community must be the source of the authority of the *Grām Panchāyat*. The *Grām Sabhā* of the whole village must become a reality: at present Jayaprakash declared, *Grām Sabhās* "do not function, and the panchayats, or some times only their presidents, usurp all authority, naturally inducing a sense of indifference among the people. . . . The gram sabha should meet as often as possible, say, quarterly. . . . Then it would be that the people would awaken to their responsibilities and opportunities, and the gram panchayats cease to be convenient tools in the hands of officers of the State or the vested and selfish interests in the village communities themselves."

If under the new order, the public services are to become advisers and supervisors instead of direct administrators, a change of attitude will become more than ever necessary. Today it is probably true to

[88] *Ibid.*, May, 1961, pp. 11, 12.
[89] *Panchayati Raj*, June, 1961, pp. 3-8.

say that the senior district official is more aloof and out of touch with the general public than was his British predecessor. The old-style British District Officer spent anything up to half the year in camp, from September to May. It is easy to ridicule the almost Mughal style in which he moved: the elaborate camp, the ceremonial entry into a village on horseback, surrounded by a posse of notables; the inspection of village accounts and the hearing of disputes under the banyan tree. The snipe shooting, the memsahib's dispensary—how dilatory, how pompous it all was! But in 1850 or 1900 this was often what the villager wanted. He was able to receive the *hakīm* on his own native ground, he could speak to the great man face to face; he was able to make proposals or register grievances and expect an answer. If all this has become an anachronism, it has not been replaced by anything new; there is just a vacuum.

Today, few District Officers go out on lengthy tours. Certainly, they are tied to headquarters by all the reports they have to compile and the ministers and other visitors whom they have to please. So today's inspections are perfunctory and unsatisfactory.[90] There is no leisurely entry into the village demesne on horseback, giving time for the village folk to absorb their visitor into their own environment. He arrives, in a storm of dust in a jeep, a visitor from another world, and he keeps his other-world aura with him. There is a hasty walk around, a conference with the leaders, a propaganda speech, a cup of tea, and he is off—to another village, and another.[91] It is unheard of to stay more than one day in one village. A District Officer said to the writer, "I am trained to find out all I need to know in one day," and another younger official said, "Frankly I do not like to spend a night in a village. I have nothing to say to the villagers, nor have they to me."

Much of the British Indian Civil Service tradition has been adopted by the Indian administrators of today, but the legendary British District Officers have bred no Indian successors. A few Indian officials cling to a still older tradition: they take with them the aura of Mughal *Mansabdārs*; men of power, men of rank, they still see rural society in terms of rulers and ruled. But the younger

[90] Mehta, *Report*, I, 40-41.
[91] The Mehta *Report* recommended that jeeps be withdrawn from use by BDO's. Because the jeep can go so fast and so far, "The result [has been] that visits to the villages, even for the junior-most officers, become affairs of a few minutes, rather than the work of a few days."

Indian administrator sees government in terms understood at the London School of Economics and Political Science, or the University of California. He is something of an economist, statistician, and political scientist; he readily finds his way about the Secretariat or the Planning Commission in New Delhi where his accomplishments will stand comparison with any. But Houghton Street or Berkeley have not prepared him for the district world of Indian peasant and landlord. Perhaps the old British idea of the father of the people (who toiled and sweated to give them justice and prosperity, whose memorial was an equitable revenue assessment, an irrigation canal, a hospital, and a reputation for fair dealing) was always more of an ideal than a reality; anyhow it was fast becoming an anachronism, and one need not have lamented its disappearance too much if it had given way to something better. The young Indian Administrative Service probationer still has to learn to ride a horse; but this is little more than a gesture to tradition, like the Latin grace said in hall before dinner in a Cambridge college. The old gear, the saddle, the gun, tent, medicine-chest are brought out no more. But a new technique of face-to-face encounter has still to be created. The young Indian administrator is well endowed with a sense of public service, but in an abstract rather than a personal sense. His approach is inclined to be clinical; the villagers appear as suitable material for analysis by means of I.B.M. cards. He rejects the relationship of squire and villein which many British officials seemed to cultivate, but he has no new pattern to adopt. One recalls the spectacled, stooping pilgrim who trudged patiently from village to village, lodging where he could, quietly listening and talking with the village folk. Is not this perhaps the pattern for India?

It seems that in the future IAS probationers appointed to Rajasthan will begin work on BDO's. This echoes the former practice of making the fledgling ICS officer spend his first year carrying out the work of subordinate officials, from the level of the *Paṭwāri* or *Lēkhpāl* (the village accountant) upward. It is to be hoped that these young IAS men will, like their ICS predecessors, live away from headquarters in touch with rural life, learning the rustic speech and thought, and developing a philosophy that is not just handed down by their seniors.

Desirable though it is that today's officials should evolve a new relationship of confidence and understanding with the country-dweller, this does not mean that their role as leaders is finished, despite the forthcoming "democratic decentralization." The new situation will not be democracy but another, more positive, attempt to bridge the awkward transitional period when autocracy and democracy are trotting along in dual harness. It will be years before the present administrative framework (still essentially that created by the Mughals) is finally dismantled. The administrators now beginning their service must try to succeed where their British and Indian predecessors did not, in creating a new image of government and its relation with the people. It was somewhat in this spirit that Raghubir Sahai addressed the Lok Sabha during the April 1961 budget debate: "We found that the District Collector was a non-voting member of the *Zila Parishad* in Rajasthan; in Andhra he presided over all the standing committees of the *Zila Parishad*. In Madras and Mysore he presided over the *Zila Parishad* directly. I think the time has come when his role should be defined. I personally feel that the best role for the District Collector would be that of a friend, philosopher, and guide. He should remain away from these institutions, but still near them."[92] If the younger generation of civil servants can rise to this challenge they will have an invaluable part to play.

But of course they can only do so much: the interested onlooker will be looking most for signs of a change in the heart of village India. The refurbished *panchāyats*, despite enlarged powers and better finances, will still depend heavily upon the voluntary co-operation of all their village brethren. The *panchāyat* has to do so much more than village councils in other lands—to run schools and repair roads; it has to expend the wealth of the community, for only so can India attain higher living standards. It is difficult to know how the community spirit can be wholeheartedly awakened under the existing system of agriculture in which there are marked inequalities. It is arguable that the result of the first phase of the Community Development program was to accentuate these inequalities. "Caste and class distinctions are so acute that the feeling of belonging to one community has not yet come. Self-help, therefore, has amounted to helping certain sections or individuals only."[93] The *harijans* especially feel that they have had little benefit from Com-

---

[92] *Kurukshetra*, May, 1961, p. 8.
[93] *Kurukshetra*, April, 1959, p. 12.

munity Development, though they are compelled to give their labor for Shramdān.[94] Within a neighborhood, development funds are likely to have been applied to one village only. The program has tried to encourage self-help, and the only villages capable of showing initiative are those which are reasonably prosperous. The poorer villages and hamlets see funds and benefits going into perhaps the one village which was already prosperous. Is there an escape from this impasse? Tarlok Singh believes in a total solution:

Village society has to be transformed so that, on the one hand it offers equality of status and opportunity to all its members and, on the other, it offers gainful employment to individual workers. . . . The village panchayat must take upon itself the responsibility for creating and maintaining sufficient work opportunities, in other words, for development of resources and employment. . . . The concept of joint or cooperative village management is important for the further development of the rural economy. It means that the land and all the resources of the village are to be managed and developed in the interest of the entire village community. That is to say, the village as a whole is an economic unit in which agriculture and other occupations are organised by or on behalf of the community.[95]

It is possible to agree wholeheartedly with this analysis and yet to doubt whether this total co-operation can ever become effective on a voluntary basis.

American sociologists, such as Carl C. Taylor, have been important advocates of group participation in development: yet American history offers interesting evidence of the limitations which voluntary community projects must accept. The small town in America offers one of the most striking examples of the community spirit anywhere. In the small country town, the wealthy lawyer, fifth-generation descendant of the original settlers, and the threadbare newly arrived Hungarian janitor are both united by this spirit in supporting new buildings for the high school or better amenities for the park; but even this close sense of community operates only over definite areas of common interest. It vanishes in other areas where religious or social divisions intervene, and in the economic sphere all experiments in total community development on a New Harmony

[94] A study of *harijan* response to Community Development found that 11 per cent felt they had definitely benefited; 53 per cent said "they were not exactly aware" of any benefit; and 36 per cent said they had definitely received no benefit. Mehta, *Report*, II, 88.

[95] Tarlok Singh, *op. cit.*, pp. 4-6.

model have sooner or later collapsed. The Mormons have provided an exception to the individualism of American life with their emphasis upon close community organization, but they, equally, have rejected communal economic effort.[96] When Americans have proved that the community as a voluntary economic unit does not work, it is difficult to understand why they should expect Indian experience to be different. If compulsory co-operative or collective farming is not accepted—and it would undoubtedly cause greater social and economic disruption in India than in the Russia of the 1920's—then there remains the slow way of social change. What are the prospects for a more unified village society?

The prevailing trend of opinion expects to find the key in the concept of unanimity, applied particularly to the process of choosing the members of the *panchāyats*. The people's choice, it is averred, must be unanimous, or when complete agreement is not possible then the choice must be left to fate—as signified in the drawing of lots. Many have argued the need for unanimity, but none so consistently as the proponents of Sarvōdaya, led by Jayaprakash Narayan.

The more I have thought over this question, the more I have discussed it with others and the more I have learnt of the workings of the village panchayats, the more convinced have I become that if *Panchayati Raj* is to succeed, contests at village elections must be avoided. . . . A community spirit must be created before there could be proper community development. To introduce electoral contests into the village is to throw a monkey-wrench into the works. . . . Self-government through faction fighting will not be self-government but self-ruination. . . . Electoral contests have already produced such tensions that there is a virtual stalemate in the affairs of the panchayats.[97]

The All-India Panchayat Parishad, meeting at Jaipur in May, 1961, with Jayaprakash in the chair, passed a resolution urging the holding of "unanimous elections." This being the climate of opinion, it is instructive to consider some of the actual results in the elections of *Grām Panchāyats*. Elections were held in Punjab in December, 1960, in preparation for *Panchāyati Rāj*. Out of 13,439 *panchāyats*, 3,779 were chosen by unanimous consent. The Punjab Government awarded grants-in-aid equivalent to one year's land revenue to all

[96] For example, the Orderville Mormon community collapsed from a combination of internal and external pressures; see R. B. West, *Kingdom of the Saints* (London, 1958), pp. 311-315.

[97] *Panchayati Raj*, June, 1961, pp. 9-10.

villages where the *Sarpanch* (chairman) and members were returned unopposed. Yet despite this notable inducement, only 29 per cent of the elections were unanimous. The villagers of Uttar Pradesh showed themselves less contumelious. Elections held at this same time included the unopposed return of 42 per cent of the *Pradhāns* (chairmen) and over 50 per cent of ordinary members. However, only in the case of the *Pradhāns* were these the result of elections by ballot.[98] *Panchāyat Samiti* elections in Orissa showed about 30 per cent of "unanimous elections."[99] Mr. Nehru has indicated that the All-India proportion of uncontested elections is also about 30 per cent; it therefore does not appear probable that the concept of unanimity through electoral agreement will quickly take hold in the villages. Nor is it obvious that this concept assures all the beneficent effects anticipated by Jayaprakash Narayan. In a characteristically perfervid passage, S. K. Dey has denounced unanimity as a synonym for apathy: "Heat and cold, light and darkness, saint and devil are opposites which make for life and its continuance. A self-sufficient village republic consisting of God-fearing people, thinking, believing and acting all alike, is a village dead before it is born. Life cannot spring from such an inanition. Democracy demands ideology and ideals in a perpetual but healthy clash. Only dead people do not compete." S. K. Dey goes on to argue that it is better to channel the "competitive instincts" into the service of the *Panchāyat*, rather than to leave them to fester in caste and class conflict.[100] It would be a travesty of the thesis of Jayaprakash Narayan to suggest that he expects to resolve conflict by pretending it does not exist: he clearly indicates the necessity for digging deep into the socio-economic causes of tension in order to eradicate them. But the popularizations of the "unanimity" idea do not recognize these root causes of tension: they insist that unanimity can work in the village as it exists today. In the present-day village it is more realistic to recognize the power of faction and caste and attempt to institutionalize conflict, to some extent, by means of local self-government, through properly constituted organs of procedure.

This article in its early pages insisted upon two apparently conflicting propositions: first, that the villager is uniquely aware of his

[98] *Kurukshetra*, May, 1961, 38.
[99] *Ibid.*, March, 1961, p. 28.
[100] Dey, *op. cit.*, p. 173.

village as his own place; second, that the village's capacity for leadership and its corporate sense have generally proved inadequate to make the village of today a better place. The two propositions are not irreconcilable. The villager is attached to his village because rural India is still, after centuries of change, a society dominated by tradition and, in an important sense, static. Villagers have a strong sense of antiquity, of the primordial origins of their community, which may go far beyond any historical basis.[101] The ancient bonds of caste are frequently forged out of local village custom.[102] In the present-day class struggles within village society, caste solidarity can be of greater advantage than individual enterprise. Most villages have their own godlings and local cults; religious custom (for example, veneration for certain beasts and birds) is one of the severest inhibitions upon agricultural improvements. So one could go on, demonstrating that village associations are powerful but mainly negative, working against corporate action and initiative.

Attempts to bring together the villagers for common purposes made during the past forty years have all been external, from above; this is just as true of the "democratic" *Panchāyatī Rāj* as of any other scheme. The traditional view of government as external has continued to apply to the new statutory *panchāyats*. Today, India's political leaders try to bring the rural population to realize that village and nation and government are all one. The casual visitor to a village involved in a development program may well be irritated by the amount of energy which is devoted to propaganda. Perhaps the first project in the village will be to build a Gandhi *chabutra* (a meeting platform)—what could be more superfluous? Yet this provides a symbolic link between the village and India's greatest leader. Playgrounds, wall newspapers, slogans, songs—all these often precede work of a really solid character. This may be right if it brings the epic of India's planning and development right down into the village.

But this dramatization of the national effort has to be mirrored by an effort within the village. It may be necessary to stimulate the process from outside, to shatter what Gandhi called the "pathetic contentment" of the villager; but this process must become self-

[101] Bernard S. Cohn reminded the writer that many Gangetic village settlements, which by their own traditions are a thousand years old, were actually founded in the sixteenth or seventeenth century.

[102] Adrian Mayer, *op cit.*, p. 193.

sustaining, if only because there are insufficient national resources to support an all-out program of rural reconstruction. Signs are not wanting that in some villages a new spirit of self-confidence is building up. Perhaps this is more striking to the visitor returning after a long absence than to those closely involved with events. To-day Indian women are taking part in village affairs to an extent unimaginable only fifteen years ago. Untouchables' children, if not their parents, are receiving a more equitable share of facilities; they are accepted in village schools without being penalized, so that they will be better equipped in the future to obtain that equality which is legally their right. In the small percentage of "developed" villages the visitor detects a new sense of self-confidence, a new awareness that change can be made where there is determination and sticking power. Of course, the visitor who strays away from the "developed" villages will discover, only a few dusty fields away, the age-old village world. There will be no school and no *panchāyat;* lanes are foul and homes are desolate; all is apathy and men can only await the will of God. India's plight would have broken the hearts of any people less forbearing, less patiently determined to go on.

It is easy to enumerate changes which would strengthen community feeling, but unfortunately the obstacles to such desirable changes are all too plain. Village leadership would be strengthened if the flight of the educated to the towns could be reversed. For fifty years a small minority of village boys have been going on to higher education, but as soon as these young men pass the matriculation or intermediate examination, the village sees them no more. If they could be retained, they could usefully contribute to fighting obscurantism, bringing order into the business of the *panchāyat,* speaking more equally to the agents of the government. But nothing about the village of today makes it any more attractive to the educated; it is still a place to get away from.[103] Village solidarity would be strengthened if the lower castes were recognized by the higher-born as having equal rights; if they really shared in the fruits of co-operative action, they would not grudge their share of the labor. Yet almost everywhere the attempts of the lower castes to raise their status are strenuously resisted. The civic sense of the

[103] "With the progressive spread of education, there can be seen emerging . . . a new class of educated youth, many of whose members are unemployed, not fully occupied or just not fit for absorption into village life." [*Fourth*] *Evaluation Report,* p. 66.

villagers would be strengthened if the rich would accept the obligation to utilize part of their wealth for the good of the community. In former days rich men made charitable contributions for religious purposes and for such quasi-religious objects as rest-houses, wells, or bridges. This tradition was somewhat strained during the British period when rich men were more or less compelled to contribute towards good works like hospitals and schools in order to remain in official esteem. Today, the ancient tradition of charity and selflessness has become faded, and the wealthy Indian (like his counterparts throughout southern Asia) is increasingly dazzled by the glittering gadgets of the West. Finally, there is the rising spirit of individualism which permeates the village, especially in the economic sphere. Despite the abolition of *zamīndāri* (in some ways, because of abolition) there has been no improvement in the lot of the small peasantry. The beneficiaries are the capitalist farmers, some drawn from the classes of absentee landlords, some from the more enterprising, prosperous peasantry. The activities of these farmers are quite separate from the rhythm and routine of traditional agriculture. They employ their own machinery and plan their crops for a definite market. Their technique is leading directly to the individualist farming of Northwest Europe or North American. A recent study of the agricultural co-operative movement throughout India emphasizes this division between the big farmers, the "village oligarchs" as the writer calls them, and the smallholders and laborers. The big farmers were able to manipulate the land reforms, and they also manipulate the co-operatives.

Control of the co-operatives tends to vest in the hands of a few of these landholding families. Often they do some informal money-lending, and sometimes they carry on trading as well. In a striking number of cases the members of these same families also serve as headmen in their villages, or hold other posts of local or district importance. The membership of the State legislatures and the State ministries is drawn largely from their ranks. In the village world, these families are the big people. . . . As against them, the ordinary people of the village are little folk, small people.[104]

It may well prove the paradox of the era of Community Development that, while all the forces of government authority have been directed to bringing together the mass of the village folk and im-

[104] Daniel Thorner, *Prospects for Cooperation in Indian Agriculture*, advance copy, mimeo., n.d., p. 24.

proving their general lot, economic forces have led to the elevation of *kulak* farmers and the liquidation of the marginal peasantry. If this hypothesis should unhappily prove correct, it will stimulate still further the flood of migrants into the cities. We have all become so used to thinking of "village India" as the bedrock of Indian society that we may be in danger of failing to appreciate the significance of Indian urbanization today. For a century the great metropolises were steadily expanding; but this new urbanization is upon an entirely different scale. For example: Delhi had a population of some 400,000 in 1947: it is now a city of nearly 2.5 million. This phenomenon is accompanied by a rootless squalor which is worse than that of the early industrial revolution in England. Here, if anywhere, communism will feed and flourish; as it has in the wretched suburbs of Calcutta. The Congress governments will be compelled to change their priorities, to focus attention upon the city slums which hitherto have been neglected by all: central, state, and municipal governments. Emphasis, both in politics and development, could shift from the countryside to the cities, leaving Community Development to die of neglect.

The list of factors which prejudice the success of village co-operation is seen to be formidable: the continuing counter-attraction of centralization, government from above, the divisive forces of caste and faction, the decay of the sense of community and the growth of individualism, and the gradual sapping of rural life by the drift to the cities. But village Community Development is by no means a lost cause. The village remains the most vital social factor in the India of today, as yesterday. One Indian writer of a pragmatic and practical sort, having honestly acknowledged the stresses of village disunity, is led to insist: "The common needs of environment and the sharing of problems of living are the essence of community development and the mechanical age in breaking through it. Our country has not yet gone as far as the West. Individual and social happiness with all the things it involves is the ultimate goal. Social desires will have to be created which will result in small self-managing communities. *It seems as though it could still be achieved in India and her 'backwardness' is one definite advantage from this point of view.*"[105] But a policy of village reconstruction must, necessarily, be accompanied by a deliberate policy of dismantling the whole super-

[105] K. S. V. Raman, *Kurukshetra*, Jan. 26, 1961, p. 26 (italics inserted).

132   ADMINISTRATION AND ECONOMIC DEVELOPMENT IN INDIA

structure of control. This same writer sees this clearly and adds: "The time seems to be getting ripe in our country for a shift of power from the State level to the Panchayat." This is also the view of the writer on co-operation previously cited: "the government must become the instrument of the ordinary people and must be considered as such by the ordinary people."[106] This, of course, is the essence of the philosophy of Gandhi and Jayaprakash Narayan: the need to make democracy a reality by bringing it into the lives of ordinary village folk. Hard-headed Balvantray G. Mehta came to the same conclusion:

It is not theory or dogma which is impelling us to make these recommendations but practical considerations. Democracy has to function through certain executive machinery but the democratic government operating over large areas through its executive machinery cannot adequately appreciate local needs and circumstances. It is, therefore, necessary that there should be a devolution of power and a decentralisation of machinery and that such power be exercised and such machinery directed by popular representatives of the local area.[107]

If the philosophy of village-level democracy is to succeed, then it is surely important that the Community Development movement itself should faithfully reflect the "leveling down" of the locus of power to the village level. Present evidence suggests that the trend is towards just that "inverted pyramid" which Jayaprakash condemned as the failing of parliamentary government in India. The issue of *Kurukshetra* for June, 1961, was a Special Training Number. It is virtually an unconscious indictment of present-day Community Development. Parkinson's Law has nowhere been applied with such assiduity as in independent India. The employees of the central government (excluding the "productive" servants of government, posts and telegraphs, railways, and the armed forces) increased from 49,000 in 1939 to 669,439 in 1956. Community Development has proved one of the most flourishing fields for bureaucratic empire building, and the June *Kurukshetra* gives us a big parade of its minions. Orientation and Study Centres, Reorientation Centres, the Central Institute of Study and Research, the Planning Research and Action Institute: these are a few of the rarer fields in which the Community Development experts happily graze. One article is

[106] Thorner, *op. cit.*, p. 27.
[107] Mehta, *Report*, I, 20.

significantly entitled "Training of the Trainers"; one feels that in a year or so, a sequel, "Training of the Trainers of the Trainers" will be required. All this froth might be dismissed as a sensible solution for India's problem of graduate unemployment (and a useful device for enabling Americans to visit India) were it not necessary to recall that this vast *papeterie* is all carried on the back of the peasant. He is the producer: all the rest are consumers. And the Indian peasant, like peasants everywhere, is no fool. He can figure out who is actually pitching in with him, and who is just getting a ride. One day he may protest. To alter the context of G. K. Chesterton's lines:

> We are the people of India; and we have not spoken yet.
> Smile at us, pay us, pass us.
> But do not quite forget.[108]

It would be irony indeed if the collapse of Community Development came about not from external causes but because of the increasingly Byzantine characteristics of the Community Development empire itself.

The concept of *Panchāyatī Rāj* runs counter to all the traditions of a thousand years of Indian government. India's principal inheritance from the British period was an administrative service of unrivaled integrity and efficiency. Is the tried and tested steel frame to be dismantled to give room to the mud and thatch of village democracy? The whole idea may appear to be a gamble; a gamble which deliberately discounts the known failures and disappointments in village reconstruction in the recent past. Yet, if India is to be true to her declared purpose of creating a society based upon consent, molded together by voluntary co-operation, with the ordinary people working together as equal citizens, then *Panchāyatī Rāj* is a major step forward upon this road.

[108] From *The Secret People.*

4

Administrative Co-ordination and Economic Development in the Districts of India

Richard L. Park

INDIA'S FIRST AND SECOND Five Year Plans have stressed the development of heavy industry, electric power, improved transportation and communications facilities, irrigation works, and other attributes of a modern industrialized society. That this priority has been given to the industrial sector and its related services was the natural outcome of a determination to reduce dependence upon raw materials' production and processing and to move towards the time when Indian manufactured goods would provide the bulk of the stock for an enormous internal consumers' market, and for a share in the world's markets as well. Vastly increased productivity, a favorable balance of trade, greater opportunities for employment, and a substantial and continuing rise in per capita income were among the goals that led India's planners to concentrate on the necessary and yet demanding preparatory stages for industrial development. The Third Five Year Plan continues and very greatly expands the industrializing trends established by the first two plans, while at the same time increasing allocations for agriculture.

It remains, however, that 80 per cent of India's people are resident in rural areas, and 70 per cent of the total population is dependent directly upon the soil for its livelihood. Rural-urban migration proceeds at a pace that is a matter of national concern, but the rate of migration affects only slightly the basically rural nature of India's occupational profile. The time has not yet come when industrial growth is adequate to provide urban employment for the larger portion of India's unemployed rural labor force. Indeed, unemployment is expected to rise under the Third Five Year Plan by three to four millions. And population increases at a steady 2 per cent plus (or about nine millions per year as of 1962), with most of this increase being added to rural areas. Thus, however much India's planners would like to concentrate even more of its limited resources on the industrializing process and on urban development, the countryside demands and receives what approximates fair shares. Food deficits being what they have been and are expected to be over the next decade, rural "fair shares" loom very large in the confines of a compressed budget.

Which brings us to the theme of this paper, namely, the organization of the governmental process of economic development in district India, including comments on recent legislation and formal proposals for reorganization at the village and district levels of administration.

It should be said at the outset that formal organization for development, as such, is substantively less crucial in importance than the quality of the economic plan itself, the character and skill of the people who do the work, and the will that embraces the people and encourages them to work. Ultimately, however, the implementation of national and state programs must funnel through particular channels and in accordance with given sets of procedures. This is as true for the upward thrust of ideas and demands from the individual peasant, his family, his group, his caste, or village, as for the downward filtration of grand plans translated into village or field-wide enactment. Unless one knows who is to do what, when, and how, and when and how supplies are to be obtained and from whom, and what patterns of political and administrative power are established, and where within these power centers rest the ultimate decision-makers, no amount of good planning can result in effective action. Administration and its organization, it must be agreed, are important ingredients in the process of economic development.

Before independence in 1947, and over the centuries from Mughal times to the height of British power in the nineteenth century, a system of district administration evolved in India that served the country well.[1] The Mughals, for purposes of land

[1] For a review of the traditional organization of the district administrative

revenue administration, for local taxation, and for the maintenance of law and order, divided their provinces into modest-sized administrative units, the rough equivalent of modern districts. The British adopted Mughal patterns, spread the system throughout the country, and adapted its operating mechanisms to suit the imperial need for tighter bonds between central, provincial, and local powers. By the latter part of the nineteenth century the pattern was perfected: the official heading the district was the Collector (or Deputy Commissioner) for land revenue purposes, and District Magistrate for the overseeing of law and order functions. In addition, as demands for economic and social reform increased, the Collector became the recognized local planner, financial expert, adviser without limit—in short, the Collector became the governor of local affairs. Beneath him, of course, were assistants, and they had their assistants, all spread regularly in a hierarchy within the district's boundaries. But the Collector decided. At least he decided most matters. There were (and are) district and regional field workers from various state government departments, such as agriculture, public works, and irrigation, who maintained liaison with the Collector, but who were not directly subordinate to him. Using technical and departmental lines of communications, these departments managed to escape co-ordination by the Collectorate. For rural development, these "unco-ordinated" departmental representatives have proved to be a blockage to effective and intermeshed planning, a blockage that has not been removed adequately to this day.

Municipal boards and district boards (union boards in Bengal) arose in due course to represent local opinion. But these boards hardly ever operated effectively, except perhaps the union boards of Bengal. Corruption and inefficiency often were the order of the day, and this situation of general ineffectiveness is almost as true today

system, see M. Ruthnaswamy, *Principles and Practice of Public Administration* (Allahabad, 1953), pp. 147-167, or G. N. Joshi, *Indian Administration* (London, 1953), pp. 281-292. A book that gives much greater detail, not always clear, on the workings of government at the local level in one state, Uttar Pradesh, is M. P. Sharma, *Evolution of the Rural Local Self-Government in the Uttar Pradesh* (Bombay, The All-India Institute of Local Self-Government, 1957). See also Albert Mayer and associates, in collaboration with McKim Marriott and Richard L. Park, *Pilot Project, India: The Story of Rural Development at Etawah, Uttar Pradesh* (Berkeley, 1958), pp. 56-86, and Richard L. Park, "District Administration and Local Self-Government," in Richard L. Park and Irene Tinker, eds., *Leadership and Political Institutions in India* (Princeton, 1959), pp. 337-344.

as it was thirty or forty years ago.[2] So it was the Collector, in the end, who disposed of problems, for he was the adviser upon whom all depended. Many British and Indian men of public life who later became high officials or politicians in Indian government gained their training in the districts. But the districts taught frustration and techniques of authoritarian government too. The district, indeed, was an image of total government writ small. The Collectorate model, however, was efficient and responsive to central control, if not so readily responsive to local needs. It is not surprising that independent India saw little reason in 1947 to develop a new organization. The old administrative pattern was accepted more or less intact.

Within the districts of India are the hundreds of thousands of villages, large and small, that contain the bulk of India's population: over half a million rural societies. These villages vary widely in their social organization and their patterns of leadership. They are differentiated by caste structure, economic resources, extent of personal holdings, and by such important characteristics as types of dwelling, food, language, clothing, religious belief, and social philosophy. In a sense each village in India is its own private world, connected in many cases only in an ephemeral way to neighboring villages, the state, and the nation. It is over such villages that the district Collector has presided, and the district plan of administration cannot become clear without taking a closer look at village organization itself.

Tradition holds that the basic political and administrative organization in Indian villages was, is, or at least should be the *panchāyat* (literally, council of five). The *panchāyat* theory that is held by many in India avers that in ages past, and in some parts of the country up to the present, a system of village democracy evolved wherein a group of village elders, the *panchāyat*—an elected body— decided questions in dispute in an orderly, judicious fashion. All could be heard, and, on the whole, justice would be done. On the basis of this theory and on some history as well, the Government of India has directed the development of *panchāyats* in all parts of India. But in encouraging their growth, the government has recognized them as statutory bodies with officers, duties, and sanctions. In effect, modern village *panchāyats* have become the lowest units

[2] M. P. Sharma, *ibid.*, esp. p. 233 ff.

of administration in India, and the heads of these *panchāyats*, while elected, are also recognized but unpaid agents of the state governments.

The literature on *panchāyats* in India is vast and highly controversial, and cannot be detailed here.[3] However, the evidence gathered by field workers in anthropology and related studies[4] demonstrates that the *panchāyat*, where it has operated with some effectiveness, has been an involved social system of decision-making and not a formal institution as such. It appears that many Indian village societies accept the view that intra-caste rivalries properly may be decided by a particular group of caste fellows, selected informally and without written rules, and in accordance with the nature of the case in dispute and of the individuals directly involved. Many intra-village disputes properly may come before a body of village elders (*panchāyat?*) who sit as a group for the particular case and are accepted as judges because of their peculiar qualifications for the given case only. Further, intra-village disputes are not decided abstractly by a group unmindful of the dominant caste's influence (especially if a member of this caste is involved in the dispute), or of the

[3] A few of the works on *panchāyats* may be listed. H. D. Malaviya, *Village Panchayats in India* (New Delhi: All India Congress Committee, 1956); *Kurukshetra: A Symposium on Community Development in India (1952-1955)* (New Delhi: The Publications Division, on behalf of The Community Projects Administration, 1955), Part VI, "Life and Work in Indian Villages," pp. 257-325; S. V. Samant, *Village Panchayats (with Special Reference to Bombay State)* (Bombay: The Local Self-Government Institute, 1957); A. V. Raman Rao, *Structure and Working of Village Panchayats: A Survey Based on Case Studies in Bombay and Madras* (Poona: Gokhale Institute of Politics and Economics, Publication No. 28, 1954); U. N. Dhebar, "Our Village Panchayats," *Kurukshetra*, IV, No. 6 (March, 1956), 22-25; R. P. Dhokalia, *Village Panchayats in Uttar Pradesh* (Allahabad, 1951). Those listed are only a sample. The literature on *panchāyats*, favorable and unfavorable, idealistic and based on empirical evidence, is indeed vast.

[4] Some of the general studies of village India that offer empirical evidence on the actual workings of the *panchāyat* system include: McKim Marriott, ed., *Village India: Studies in the Little Community* (Chicago, 1955); M. N. Srinivas, ed., *India's Villages* (Calcutta: West Bengal Government Press, 1955); Richard L. Park and Irene Tinker, eds., *Leadership and Political Institutions in India*, pp. 391-469; Oscar Lewis, *Village Life in Northern India* (Urbana, 1958); S. C. Dube, *Indian Village* (London, 1955). A multitude of articles exists on this subject. Two especially important studies by M. N. Srinivas are "Village Studies and Their Significance" (mimeographed), p. 10 (later published in *Eastern Anthropologist*, VIII, Nos. 3 and 4, March-Aug., 1955), and "The Concept of the Dominant Caste," (typescript), 20 pp., no notation as of Aug. 16, 1957 of publication.
One of the most incisive examinations of the nature of the *panchāyat* system in India, tied to a broad survey of the nature of administrative control and local self-government in contemporary India, is Hugh Tinker, "Authority and Community in Village India," *Pacific Affairs*, XXXII, No. 4 (Dec., 1959), 354-375.

powerful economic interests of one of the parties, or of the special prestige held by one party in terms of access to higher officials. On the contrary, the evidence suggests that the operative, informal *panchāyat* system has been effective because it has taken into account the power structure of the village and has tended to support existing strength and to disregard, when expedient, the claims of the weak.[5]

The statutory *panchāyats* that have been established by law since the 1930's, and increasingly since 1947, have not taken into account, at least until recently, the informal *panchāyat* system that has been relatively effective as a stabilizing element in village India's past. Officials may assume that the statutory body has supplanted the informal; but the facts seem to indicate that the two co-exist, with the statutory body more often than not being manipulated simply as the recording office for decisions actually made informally (and, incidentally, illegally) by the older, officially unrecognized, *panchāyat* system.

It is important to take the measure of the politics of village India, varied as it may be, not as an opening for unconstructive criticism, but to add a realistic note to the kind of optimism about village Indian government that has been all too prevalent in recent years. Plans for the reorganization of district India necessarily must be based upon certain assumptions concerning the organization and workings of the villages within. It is, perhaps, for this reason that new organizational plans have by-passed the village as the crucial level for the development of local self-government and economic planning in favor of a tier above that combines the interests of a good many constituent villages.[6]

In the past, the Collector and his field agents have provided the district's administrative co-ordination, including the supervision of affairs in all villages and municipalities within the district. The Collector has traveled periodically through his territory, listening to complaints, hearing appeals against previous local judgments, having an opportunity to anticipate social and economic crises. By becoming

[5] See Evelyn Wood, "Representative(?) Government in Rural India," *Thought* (Delhi), XII, No. 5 (Jan. 30, 1960), 12-13, being a review of Adrian C. Mayer, "Local Government Election in a Malwa Village," *Eastern Anthropologist*, XI, Nos. 3 and 4 (1958), 189-202.

[6] A corrective to the romantic view of the self-sufficiency of Indian villages will be found in M. N. Srinivas and A. M. Shah, "The Myth of Self-Sufficiency of the Indian Village," *Economic Weekly* (Bombay), XII, No. 37 (Sept. 10, 1960), 1375-1378.

aware of the patterns of leadership within the district, the more alert and sensitive Collectors have been able to bring to their sides by patronage those key villagers who would support official policy on crucial future occasions. The villages themselves, as social and economic units, were not seriously affected by the Collector's attentions, of course. But at least the worst outbreaks of disorder were checked, and there always was the right of appeal to the Collectorate. Such an administrative process was patronistic—almost feudal—in its conception and execution. But it did have the advantage of working effectively for a good many years, as far as law and order were concerned. Feuding and factional discord within and between villages remained largely unchecked. Yet the most gross cases of injustice came to the attention of the Collector at his periodic sessions at village *darbār*, and more often than not decisions were made that, if less than fully just, were at least quick.[7]

Independence, however, brought new challenges to district India. No longer was it considered adequate for Collectors and other district officers to administer benevolently—if strictly—over a *status quo* society and economy. As the welfare state got underway after 1947, the Collector was ordered to supervise and encourage the revitalization of the countryside: more food; new schools and more teachers; better seeds and more irrigation; sanitary wells and compost pits; improvement of the status of *Harijans*; the location of new sources of rural leadership; better roads and more of them; bridges, village community centers, adult education, women's involvement, animal husbandry, preventive medicine. The list of new plans and new programs grew, and the Collector was left responsible, as in the past, to see to the implementation of a multitude of higher policies, some of which were not even under his direct jurisdiction. Further, in the early years after independence little or no planning was instituted for the district as a whole. Plans, in bits and pieces, flew out of the state governments' offices like pips from a squeezed orange, and the Collector had his hands full passing out administrative orders and forms for completion by his subordinates. Co-ordination, if any existed, was left to the inner recesses of the Collector's mind.

[7] On the origins of the broad functions of the Collector, see Sir Percival Griffiths, *The British Impact on India* (London, 1952), esp. Section II, "The Administrative Impact." For a classic statement on the ubiquitous role of the Collector, see Philip Woodruff (Mason), *The Guardians* (Vol. 2 of "The Men Who Ruled India") (New York, 1954), esp. Part II, pp. 207 ff.

In 1952 a new and all-pervasive element entered the district picture, namely, the founding of a Community Development Program and National Extension Service to revitalize rural India, to increase agricultural productivity, to bring the benefits of national and state welfare legislation to the grass roots.[8]

Community Development has many antecedents in India: the meticulous and effective regular activities of British and Indian district officers going back for decades, and exemplified by the unusually fine work of F. L. Brayne in Gurgaon; the Gandhian constructive workers; Tagore's Sriniketan in Bengal; the Indian Village Service of the Wisers in Uttar Pradesh; the work of the Allahabad Agricultural Institute; and the experiments of Christian missionaries and individual patrons of rural betterment in several parts of India. Most important, however, was the pilot project in rural development at Etawah, established first in 1948 by the Government of Uttar Pradesh under the guidance of Albert Mayer and expanded through the years up to and beyond the establishment of a universal Indian system of rural extension in 1952.[9]

In the Etawah project it early was discovered that the regular district system of administration clashed with the more experimental— and perhaps troublesome—needs of the pilot project.[10] Extension plans called for a co-ordination of activities at the village level so that a number of social and economic changes could be effected there at the base of the social pyramid in an integrated fashion and simultaneously. Such activities were to be held together by the functioning of a multi-purpose agent of extension called a *Grām Sēvak*, or Village Level Worker. Likewise, as one went up the hierarchy of development, unity, co-ordination, and a close interlinking of working levels were essential, plus expeditious action at the top to assure the supply line to the villages under development. Whereas the Collectorate was calculated to operate effectively when the pace of movement and change was slow or routinely haphazard, the new developmental

---

[8] Community Development in India has an extensive literature. A few of the most important works are listed in "Community Development: A Working Bibliography" by Arthur Dunham and Rameshwar Nath Paul, in *Community Development Review* (Washington, International Cooperation Administration, IV, No. 1, March, 1959). For a simplified and exhortatory view of Community Development in India, see *Road to Welfare State* (New Delhi: Issued on Behalf of The Community Projects Administration, 2nd ed., 1955).

[9] *Pilot Project, India,* esp. pp. 5-55 and 311-330.

[10] *Ibid.,* pp. 56-86.

effort was dynamic, irregular in motion, often nervous, and called for hand-tailored, snappy attention, and thus was not adapted to the routines of file noting. The clash was partially resolved in Etawah by the personal involvement of the Collector in pilot project activities; partially the clash was left unresolved.

When Community Development and the National Extension Service were adopted for all-India purposes in 1952, a rapid expansion of activities began that by 1962 had resulted in over three quarters of India's villages being serviced by some form of extension arrangement. The conflict between routine and developmental systems of administration that had existed at Etawah then spread all over India. In an attempt to find a solution to this conflict, Collectors in 1955 were given charge of all developmental functions within their districts. It was hoped that by this change in policy Collectors would be encouraged to devote their best energies to economic and social change and would give less time to revenue and law and other functions. In some districts, because of the interests of individual Collectors, such a change in emphasis took place. But in others, the clash between systems remained—in mind and in action, if not in law. For a variety of reasons, the Block Development Officers have had to carry the burdens of planning in most districts.

At best, however, even had this top-level problem of administrative co-ordination been resolved, a larger and more significant difficulty lurked in every corner of Community Development, namely, the difficulty of involving the peasantry in the making of crucial decisions concerning their own betterment. At Etawah much success had been achieved in this direction.[11] With the passage of time and the leaving of many of the original stimulators of the project, even at Etawah peasant involvement became less vital and more apathetic. The national Ministry of Community Development (established in 1956 and now titled the Ministry of Community Development, Panchayati Raj, and Cooperation) and development commissioners in the several states have been concerned continuously with this problem of local co-operation—which, if successful and regularized, would signal the invigoration of rural India. And, of course, if peasant involvement grew, the dominant role of the Collector and his tradition of all-over administration within his district were bound to be challenged. If

[11] *Ibid.*, chaps. iii, iv, and v. See also R. C. Dwivedi, "Local Leadership in the Pilot Project, Etawah," in *Kurukshetra*, IV, No. 6 (March 1956), 45-47.

democratic forces from within village India were organized and their powers articulated, the essentially bureaucratic powers of the Collectorate could not remain untouched.[12]

It might be best at this point to review the several aspects of the dilemma of developmental administration in rural India. Productivity comes first. It has been deemed crucial to increase agricultural yields throughout the country, and to give some momentum as well to other forms of economic growth, such as cottage and small-scale industry. Economic betterment for the families of town and village India and economic growth for the country as a whole obviously are not to be ignored. Indeed, with food shortages continuing, few contest the high priority of the strictly economic aspect of development in the equation. Some might argue that the essential need of the times is to change the traditional structure of administration as little as possible; to bolster, rather, the powers of the Collectors; to provide more agricultural advisers, more improved seeds, better and more fertilizers; and more water for irrigation. In this view, the less one encourages local social and political forces to become entangled in the growth process, except as assisted workers, the better. Community Development, following this line of argument, would better devote its energies to agricultural extension activities as such, and leave administrative co-ordination and policy-making to the Collectors and higher authority. A case can be made for this proposition, and not a few experienced Collectors (and former Collectors)— and some economists—have so argued.

However, rural development in India is not meant to be only an economic effort: it is a multi-purpose effort. As the First Five Year Plan stated the proposition in 1952: "Community Development is the method and Rural Extension the agency through which the Five-Year Plan seeks to initiate a process of transformation of the social and economic life of the villages."[13] Sushil K. Dey, former Development Commissioner in West Bengal, put it more bluntly: "The purpose of Community Development is to improve the quality of living of the people who are involved."[14] Not only must rural

[12] A most provocative recent study that questions easy optimisms concerning rural "revitalization," and raises serious doubts about Community Development's theory, is Kusum Nair, *Blossoms in the Dust: The Human Element in Indian Development* (London, 1961).

[13] *The First Five Year Plan: A Summary*, Planning Commission (New Delhi, 1952), p. 63.

[14] See Sushil K. Dey, "Community Projects in Action in India," in *Leadership*

144 ADMINISTRATION AND ECONOMIC DEVELOPMENT IN INDIA

development improve village standards of living; it must also lead to the betterment of the quality of village life.

It is argued by exponents of this second position that quality in village life can be improved lastingly only if village people are brought organically into the process of planning for their own future. Village statutory *panchāyats*, and other local advisory bodies, after gaining experience under the guidance of Extension and Collectorate personnel, should be encouraged to make the hard decisions for themselves—in effect to take charge of a large segment of the growth process. Moreover, advocates of what might be called the "village democracy" plan would expand the functions of local bodies to include the collection of land revenues and the imposition of new local taxation. By such moves local governments would tend to supplant, in the administrative sphere, most of the functions hitherto performed by the Collectorate's hierarchy.

Between the "hard" proposition of bolstering Collectors' powers and the "soft" proposition of turning over to the *panchāyats* greater measures of power, there have been numerous middle positions. The basic conflict in views has stemmed from a different appraisal of the efficacy of village "democracy" under present social conditions, or at least a difference of opinion over the speed at which such self-government should be encouraged to develop, and the method of training for such self-government. Those favoring the continuation of the Collectors as co-ordinators of administration have had little faith in the efficiency or justice of current *panchāyat* operations, and they feel that the time is not ripe for experimentation. Those favoring greater measures of power being given to the *panchāyats* believe that the *panchāyats* can work well, often do work well, and in any event they represent India's best hope for rural self-rule. As a colony cannot exercise its political genius without freedom and power to operate, so it is argued the *panchāyat* without substantial functions and powers cannot prove itself.

One of the most significant recent surveys of the working of Community Development in India, the *Report of the Team for the Study of Community Projects and National Extension Service* (Bal-

and Political Institutions in India, p. 347. See also, S. C. Dube, *India's Changing Villages: Human Factors in Community Development* (Ithaca, 1958), and G. D. Parikh, "An Approach to Planning," *Radical Humanist* (Calcutta), XXIII, No. 43 (Oct. 25, 1959), 499 and 507.

vantray G. Mehta, Leader), reviewed the Indian rural scene critically, especially in terms of Community Development, and suggested a major administrative reorganization.[15] The *Report* emphasized the extensive by-passing of the *panchāyats* by rural extension in the past, and called this a "confession not merely of our lack of faith in democracy but of our failure to make the programme a genuine community development programme."[16] The *Report* goes on: "It [the program] can become genuine only by operating through the cooperatives on the one hand and the statutory elected representative bodies [*panchāyats*] on the other."[17]

Turning to the administration of development, the *Report* urged that a policy of "democratic decentralization" be adopted nationally, wherein the central and state governments (including the Collectorate as the district representative of the state) would divest themselves completely of certain responsibilities and devolve these to locally selected bodies for developmental planning. In more detail, the *Report* proposed a three-level system of local government. At the village (or small village group) level, a directly elected *panchāyat* would exist, among other things to direct programs for the village's development. Above the village, and within the boundaries of a developmental block, would be a *Panchāyat Samiti* (assembly), composed of the heads of each *panchāyat* within the block, and presided over by a chairman (*pradhān*) elected from among the *samiti's* membership. This *Panchāyat Samiti* would be the critical unit in the local governmental process. All of the resources of the block would be controlled by the *samiti*; the Block Development Officer, for example, would be responsible to it, technically as the secretary of the *samiti*. Above the *Panchāyat Samiti*, at the district level, would be the *Zilā Pariṣad* (or district committee) made up of all the chairmen (*pradhāns*) of the *samitis* within the district, and headed by a chairman (*pramukh*) elected from among the *pariṣad's* membership. At the levels of the *panchāyat*, the *samiti*, and the *pariṣad*, certain

[15] *Report of the Team for the Study of Community Projects and National Extension Service* (Balvantray G. Mehta, Leader) (New Delhi: Committee on Plan Projects, Government of India, 1957). Vols. I and II (Nov., 1957); Vol. III (Parts I and II) (Dec., 1957). See also Evelyn Wood, "Power to the Peasant," *Economic Weekly* (Bombay), Oct. 11, 1958.

[16] Mehta, *Report*, I, 3.

[17] *Ibid.*

co-opted members were to be invited to join in order to assure representation to groups such as the backward classes, women, etc.[18]

Although the Balvantray Mehta committee made many other recommendations, the administrative reordering is the one that concerns us directly.

There can be little doubt, as the full four volumes of the Mehta *Report* demonstrate so well, and as successive evaluation reports on Community Development issued by the Program Evaluation Organization (PEO) of the Planning Commission support, that as Community Development expanded rapidly in the late 1950's, touch seemed to have been lost with the villagers. The desire for improvement had been stimulated to some degree. But no adequate two-way communication system had been devised between the villagers and higher levels of administration.[19] It was natural, under the circumstances, that the Mehta committee concluded that radical change was needed to connect the villagers organically with their own self-improvement, and thus the three-tier system of government suggested by the *Report*.

The Mehta proposals were not relegated to academic wastebaskets. Indeed, Part II of Volume III of the *Report* contains the detailed views of the state governments and of the central government's ministries on the draft recommendations of the Mehta team. Later a national Conference on Community Development was held at Mount Abu to discuss all aspects of the *Report*. At least as a general proposition, the Mehta team's conclusions were accepted broadly by the state governments and as a matter of national policy.

The first state actually to adopt the new "democratic decentralization" scheme was Rajasthan, one of the more backward of the states

[18] *Ibid.*, pp. 5-23. See Arch Dotson, "Democratic Decentralization in Local Self-Government," *Indian Journal of Public Administration*, IV, No. 1 (1958), 39-50. For the details of this plan as brought into operation in Rajasthan, see Ralph H. Retzlaff, "Panchayati Raj in Rajasthan," *Indian Journal of Public Administration*, VI, No. 2 (1960), 141-158; and "Panchayats Today Promise Democracy Tomorrow," *Statesman* (New Delhi), June 29, 1960, p. 8.

[19] On problems of communications, see the following articles by Evelyn Wood: "Time for Transformation," *Economic Weekly* (Bombay), Aug. 9, 1958; "New Markets from Old—II," *Thought* (Delhi), Dec. 12, 1959; "Rural *Self* Government Needs Controlled Communications" (mimeographed), 14 pp., Sept., 1958. See also Evelyn Wood's "Patterns of Influence Within Rural India," in *Leadership and Political Institutions in India*, pp. 372-390. For an evaluation of the workings of *panchāyats* in recent years, see chap. iv, "Case Studies—Panchayats and Cooperatives," in *Seventh Evaluation Report on Community Development and Some Allied Fields* (New Delhi: Programme Evaluation Organisation, Planning Commission, Government of India, 1960), pp. 121-135.

in the Republic, with a good deal less experience in Community Development and local self-government than many other states, and thus perhaps a state where experimentation was a risk worth taking. The Rajasthan State Legislative Assembly passed the Rajasthan Panchayat Samiti and Zila Parishad Act, 1959, on September 3, 1959, and the new program went into operation on October 2, 1959, following an inaugural celebration at Nagaur, with Prime Minister Nehru as chief speaker. Although differing on minor points with the Mehta team's recommendations, the Rajasthan plan essentially is identical with it. Reports vary concerning the consequences of the Act.

One early observer[20] in Rajasthan reported enthusiastically the "tremendous potential" of the plan for "rooting democracy firmly in India, not only in the superstructure at the top—in state and national parliaments—but in the dust, dung, and irrigation ditches of the village and the blocks." According to this report, developmental activity at every level in the state had increased enormously. Town meetings (*gaon sabhās*) had been called often and regularly so that leaders could communicate plans with the people. The number of village *panchāyats* was expected to be expanded almost two-fold to meet new demands for a voice in local affairs by the village people. A new respect for the people is said to have been felt by the Block Development Officers (now called *vikās adhikārīs*, or development secretaries) as they have seen the ability of the elected local bodies in operation. If this report of success is accurate and is sustained in field operations over time, the Mehta team and the Government of Rajasthan can be proud of their accomplishments.

Another, perhaps unanticipated, aspect of the Rajasthan experience has been the fact that political parties have taken hold of the *samiti* and *parisad* elections because the parties recognized the new power that local bodies had gained in the total arena of all-India politics. The enthusiastic report from Rajasthan states that the Congress Party took a great many of the top posts in the *samitis* and *parisads* and put into office as chairmen a good many party men. It is interesting to note that the Congress Party gained many of its most important seats by the technique of "co-opted members." It is reported that many of the chairmen of the *samitis* and *parisads* were

[20] Anonymous, "Democracy Has Come to Rajasthan" (mimeographed), Jan. 15, 1960.

co-opted, rather than elected members.[21] Elections to the *Panchāyat Samitis* and *Zilā Pariṣads* in Rajasthan in 1961, however, often favored anti-Congress Party forces and contributed to the poor showing in Rajasthan of the Congress Party in the General Election of 1962.

But there are cooler voices, also, concerning the Rajasthan case. One, for example,[22] points out that at the village *panchāyat* level, a two-thirds majority of all members in that body must approve developmental decisions. Factionalism being what it is in most Indian villages, such a provision is likely to result in deadlock after deadlock in Rajasthani village affairs, and thus hold up, rather than expedite, development. The provision was included in an attempt to secure greater unity of purpose in Rajasthan's villages; but the result is likely to be quite the opposite. Our critic also underlines the provision in section 66 of the Act whereby the Government of Rajasthan is enabled to cancel any resolution or order passed by any *Panchāyat Samiti* if the state government feels that these acts are illegal or constitute an abuse of power. The Collector in the district, also, is empowered to suspend resolutions and orders if he believes that they are immediately harmful. For the plan to work, the critic feels, the government would have to control and direct and correct even more than it does at present. He sees such a development as a retreat rather than advance in local self-government—although this conclusion seems unrealistic, considering the generally non-existent force of local self-government previously in Rajasthan.

It is far too early to judge the success or failure of the Rajasthan experiment. New developments in Andhra, Madras, Orissa, Kerala, Assam and elsewhere have been (or are about to be) put into effect along the lines of the Mehta *Report*, with local adaptations.[23] We can expect to read over the coming months numerous reports on the

[21] For a brief report on some of the party politics involved in a more recent *panchāyat* election in Rajasthan, see the New York *Times*, Dec. 11, 1960, p. 32.

[22] P. K. Chaudhuri, "Decentralisation or Delegation of Power? The Rajasthan Panchayat Samiti and Zila Parishad Act, 1959," *Economic Weekly* (Bombay), Oct. 3, 1959.

[23] See *ibid.*, and "Democracy Has Come to Rajasthan," *loc. cit.*, "Panchayat Raj in Madras," *Hindu Weekly Review*, December 7, 1959, p. 13, and an additional article on Madras in the same *Review* for Oct. 10, 1960, p. 3. For some recent, cautious steps taken in West Bengal, see "Panchayats in West Bengal," *Hindu Weekly Review*, Nov. 28, 1960, p. 10. On Andhra, see "Panchayat Samitis—Andhra Government's Aid Scheme," *Hindu Weekly Review*, Feb. 22, 1960, p. 13, and "Panchayat Raj in Andhra," *Hindu Weekly Review*, Nov. 14, 1960, p. 6.

workings of this legislation. And it may be fair to anticipate that all of these reports of progress will not glow with optimism.[24]

Few will dispute the great need in India to involve the people, not only superficially but concretely and responsibly, in the developmental process and in the control of local government. What the Indian Parliament and the several state legislative assemblies provide for higher levels of government undoubtedly should be given parallel strength in the district and village jurisdictions of government. Administrative co-ordination and economic development could, more likely than not, gain realism and wider popular support were they fused to a regional and local system of truly democratic government. There is no reason, in the abstract, why Block Development Officers and Collectors could not function under the control of local bodies, as similar administrators before them have done in many parts of the world.

But it appears to be exceedingly risky, under Indian conditions, to rush into an administrative (really political) reorganization as radically different from the older patterns of district government before carefully thought-out pilot projects have been established to test and systematize the new plans. This is especially true because of what appear to be unusually broad administrative powers given to local legislative (*samitis*) bodies. There is no indication that such caution has been taken in Rajasthan, and the same rapid acceptance of the new scheme of things seems to be probable in most of the other states of India as well. It is significant, perhaps, that Maharashtra, possessing as it does one of the more conservative, capable, and cautious civil service traditions, has been slow in moving towards the Mehta team plan. And in West Bengal, it can be surmised that the government is skittish of programs of local administrative reorganization that might politically upset the precarious hold of the Congress party in that state. (Even for the Calcutta Corporation, the franchise remains strictly limited to the well-to-do and educated.)

[24] For a critical review, see P. K. Chaudhuri, "A Year of Panchayati Raj," *Economic Weekly (Bombay) Annual*, XIII, Nos. 4, 5, 6, Feb. 5, 1961, 137-142. Cf. the more optimistic views in the editorial by Sadiq Ali and the article by P. R. Chakravorty, "Panchayat Elections and Casteism," (The All India Congress Committee) *Economic Review* (New Delhi), XII, No. 13-14, Nov. 22, 1960, 3-5 and 39-41. Two excellent reports—critical but constructive—have been published by the Association of Voluntary Agencies for Rural Development: *Report of a Study Team on Democratic Decentralisation in Rajasthan* (New Delhi, 1961); *Report of a Study Team on Panchayati Raj in Andhra Pradesh* (New Delhi, 1961).

Most disturbing, to one observer at least, is the apparent indifference exhibited by the Mehta team and the state governments adopting the new organization to the plentiful evidence in the scholarly literature concerning the operating nature of village social structure and its rough, competitive dynamics. The social patterns of village India vary by state, region, and locality. Fortunately some local modifications by states are being incorporated in the new schemes as they are adopted throughout the country. But to assume that belief in the *panchāyat* must be a matter of faith, is asking too much. One should know by conducting controlled experiments and by examining with care the known data about local affairs in India before embarking upon uncharted administration and political waters. For example, the *Zilā Pariṣads* and *Panchāyat Samitis* have been quite willing to allocate within their jurisdictions such largesse as has been given to them by higher governmental authority; the same bodies have been reluctant to use their powers of taxation to raise new funds to support local planning and local projects. The first process is one of political patronage; the second calls for statesmanship. It is understandable that members of the legislative assemblies have insisted on their right to be co-opted members of *Zilā Pariṣads*, as long as such potent political patronage is to be dispensed at district levels. The forces of politics at work are elementary to students of local government in India, and they could easily have been predicted.

Now that the Mehta plan (with local variations) has been accepted without prior testing, an alternative check could be the addition to the program of a major effort in political and administrative education for the peasants and town residents who, supposedly, have become their own masters in local affairs. Carefully selected guides at every level desperately are called for, plus abundant availability of technical advisers and, perhaps more important, friendly, persuasive development personnel who have the ability to argue convincingly and responsibly before the new elected councils. Such educational guidance is a poor substitute for rigorous pre-investigation and trial. But even this substitute has not yet been provided, except on an irregular basis.

As the Mehta team *Report* moves from its form as a paper proposal into legislation and finally into state operations, it becomes clear that economic development in most of district India will depend for its administrative co-ordination not only upon the Collector, or upon

Extension personnel; the people now are asked to carry much of the lion's share themselves, subject, no doubt, to *ad hoc* checks and plenty of "informal" direction from top levels. Will this alteration of older patterns of administration really take hold, and will the *samitis* and *pariṣads* be able to integrate piecemeal plans into co-ordinated programs, or will the ubiquitous Collector, sure of his skills, simply manipulate the new bodies as he controlled district and municipal boards in the past? We do not know as yet, but the signs are strong that the Collectorate, as a system of administration, is being challenged fundamentally as the people try their hands at the co-ordinating tasks.

The risk involved in the change is great, for the decentralization and democratization of developmental planning and execution are, indeed, revolutionary steps to take. Under skilful and sensitive guidance, the plan has a chance of success. With even a reasonable level of achievement in releasing rural talents, India's economic growth and social change could be enhanced enormously. But "skilful and sensitive" guides are in short supply everywhere; routine-oriented bureaucrats and inexperienced youths will not do. This is the rub that cannot be ignored.

5

Leadership Tasks in India's Economy*

Wilfred Malenbaum

I

INDIA HAS JUST EMBARKED upon its Third Five Year Plan. Inevitably this is a time for hope and expectation. In the perspective of the decisive years ahead, the past decade is appropriately interpreted as years of preparation for the major achievements ahead. This interpretation encompasses the decade's record comprehensively; positive achievements are the stepping stones to greater accomplishments. Failures and lesser achievements are the results of the lack of experience—a situation which rapidly corrects itself; there are inevitable uncertainties in a dramatic new effort. Nonetheless, one should also look at the past record intensively, seeking a thorough understanding of any gaps between plan and performance. The rationale here is that the early experience can reveal the strength of traditional forces in the economy. Only from a careful analysis of this experience can there be any assurance that the knowledge is in hand for reducing the possibility of wide departures between plan and performance in the future.

In its official publications, the Government of India leans quite understandably toward the first of these two ways of appraising the record. Not that the lessons of the past can be ignored: India is obviously less far along the path to self-sustaining growth than the Second Plan had visualized. The Government recognizes that major impediments are to be overcome during the next decade if self-sustaining growth is in fact to be assured. The present paper pro-

* This paper was based on material analyzed while the author served as Director of the India Project, Center for International Studies, Massachusetts Institute of Technology. Revisions were made in the summer of 1961 with assistance from the Economic Research Center, University of Hawaii.

ceeds on the assumption that the gaps between past performance and plan can provide insights for the future, that their pattern permits a systematic explanation which characterizes relationships of the pre-industrialization stages of economic growth. So thin is the documentation of contemporary economic growth experience in any of today's economically underdeveloped areas—especially in countries which seek their economic goals in a free society—that the very availability of data for India demands full exploitation in the search for greater understanding of this important process.

Basic facts are readily presented, at least in summary form.[1] In 1955-56, the last year of the First Plan, national income was about 18 per cent above that of 1950-51, in contrast to the plan expectation of an 11-12 per cent increase. Recent government projections for 1960-61 also suggest an 18-19 per cent expansion above 1955-56, as against the 25 per cent of the Second Plan.[2] The favorable performance of the first program is attributable in considerable measure to the favorable monsoons and harvests of 1953 and 1954—an explanation which extends also to the impressive increase in national income in 1958-59 above the preceding year and again in 1960-61 over 1959-60. India's economy, so heavily based on agriculture, responds readily and clearly to important vagaries of climate and rainfall. What is more significant for comparing plans with performance is the insight to be found in the under-structure of the economy. Here, the relevant areas are first the level and pattern of savings and investment: a growing economy manifests systematic increases in the savings ratios and a shift in investment patterns to conform to the plan's objectives. Secondly, the economy must give evidence of increasing interconnections among its various sectors as these change in relative importance. Only a growing interdependence can assure reasonably efficient rates of utilization of old and new fixed capital, and indeed of other factors of production. On both of these basic points, the experience of the past decade in India prompts a cautious outlook for the future.

Domestic savings do not seem to reflect a steady upward movement on a relative basis, at least since sometime in 1956. Insofar

[1] See Government of India, *Appraisal and Prospects of the Second Five Year Plan*, May, 1958, pp. 1-37; *Third Five Year Plan, A Draft Outline*, June, 1960. See also my *East and West in India's Development* (Washington, 1959) and chaps. x-xii of my *Prospects for Indian Development* (London, 1962).

[2] The final estimates for the last year of the Second Plan may turn out to be closer to 20 per cent above 1955-56. For some analysis on this point, see K. N. Raj, in the *Economic Weekly*, Feb. 4, 1961.

as India did actually achieve investment targets during 1956-61, the large increase in resources originated abroad, partly from the liquidation of India's exchange balances and partly from a level of foreign assistance of one kind or another which was far beyond what had earlier been anticipated.

On the more subtle matter of sectoral interdependence, one need but note the growing level of unemployment despite significant rates of growth in national product and marked growth of modern industrial output. There seemed to be but limited spill-over from expanding industries to other industries and to other sectors of the economy. On the other side, even the bumper food crop of 1958 did not flow readily into more ample urban food supplies. Food prices in the urban markets tended to retain the very high levels reached with the poor crop of the previous year.

Underlying these illustrations are arguments which make the point that the gap between plan and performance will not simply go away, that performance will not just "catch up" in some sense. Rather, the gap of the Second Plan, and perhaps gaps in prospect for later plans molded in the same image, arise from a failure to formulate a program directed at the economic realities of India. Only a thorough attack on the problems of agriculture—an approach based upon hypotheses of changes in rural consumption, investment, and production as they actually seem to occur—offers the possibility of breaking down the urban-rural barriers which still inhibit full measures of successful industrial growth. A similar statement might be made with reference to programs for small-scale enterprise generally. In both cases one might even question whether the necessary studies have been initiated in India which permit the formulation of the hypotheses upon which to base such a program.

In addition to a significant shift in sectoral allocation of investment, both in the plan itself and through the mechanics of plan implementation, a realistic program for India needs assumptions about savings behavior which are again grounded in the reality of the economic and social relationships of that country. So long as plans proceed with estimates of monetized savings only, and with patterns of popular savings behavior derived from observations in the wealthier lands of the West, the systematic exploitation of actual savings for optimum investment will not be possible.

In sum, there is need for a plan which is grounded upon the ways of economic behavior of India (and of similar countries) or which is accompanied by a program directed specifically at changing existing behavior patterns in the society. When neither element is present in the plan, there may well continue to be important gaps between plan and performance.[3] Such a possibility should prompt concern on the part of India's leaders responsible for the launching of the Third Plan.

II

In this context, it is worth while to seek some generalized characterizations of India's governmental elites—in the Civil Service and in the top ranks of the Congress Party. Let us first look back upon the initial economic challenge which independence posed for the Government of India. Of itself the end of colonialism could not establish a new economic order in India, whatever responsibility the departing British had to bear for India's limited economic progress. However broad-based the hopes for rapid industrialization, this objective, along with land reform and land redistribution, had to be carried into independence as longer term achievements in the future. The leaders of the new nation were confronted from the start with formidable tasks of political, social, and cultural consolidation on the domestic scene and of establishment as a nation in the eyes and institutions of the world. At the same time these leaders had to face, almost anew, the major tasks of adapting India's economic heritage to the demands and opportunities of modernity. They had to create a dynamic economy which could spark and maintain steady persistent expansion. The very process of achieving independence had engendered visions—certainly on the part of the educated and of leaders of groups of people, if not on the part of the general public—of a better society and a more prosperous state; but this meant a *new* growth.

Prime Minister Nehru lost little time in taking positive action; the official machinery for economic planning was soon in place. A rapid series of major administrative actions assured the official availability of the basic tools needed for implementation of these new measures.[4] The Government moved rapidly toward the recruiting

[3] See my "The Role of Government in India's Third Plan," *Economic Development and Cultural Change*, VIII, No. 3 (1960), 225-236; also *Prospects for Indian Development*, chap. xv.

[4] Thus in April, 1948, the important Industrial Policy Resolution delineated new

and training of personnel with the types of skill appropriate for the new economic and administrative tasks of independence. So conscious was Government of new needs that procedures were adopted for altering traditional practice in the Civil Service. Seniority and salary considerations were not to impede the progress of persons with the ability to cope with the new challenges.

The Planning Commission itself assumed its formal existence in March, 1950. A tribute to even earlier beginnings is the fact that by September of that year the Government of India could present (to the first meeting of the Colombo Plan Consultative Committee in London) a six-year development program which contained the germ of subsequent plans. This was a major performance without parallel among the other nations represented in the Consultative Committee. Given India's own economic past and the limited knowledge available of the interrelations of various parts of its static economy, it was obvious that new programs had to rest upon actual growth experience elsewhere. Similarly, reliance was placed on growth theories which were developed elsewhere and upon the actual economic conditions and relationships found elsewhere.

Initially this was inevitable. But soon there were years of actual experience under India's own development program. New developments were "feeding back" onto the original assumptions and analysis of the current plan, onto the drafting tables of future plans. Given the extent of borrowing in the first efforts, one would anticipate a constant study of the record, either to confirm original hypotheses or to provide the basis for changes in them. In any event, the economic challenge for the leaders of independent India might be posed as a double one: the rapid formulation of a program of action aimed at jarring into systematic progress a long-static social and economic order; and a mechanism acutely attuned to the "feed-back," so that assumptions can be tested and changed with experience.[5] From a

---

areas of industrial activity for government and delimited parts of the private sector where standards of performance were of particular public concern. Implementation authority (licensing and takeover devices) were provided by the Industries (Development and Regulation) Act of 1951. Finally a Ministry of Production was established in the Central Government. Relevant also was the initiation of the Community Development program and the national extension service during 1952 and 1953 to help bring about change in rural areas.

[5] A third and later component might be implementation of the revised program: the administrative and other structures needed to convert the program into reality. See below, n. 29.

human viewpoint the combination required leadership which was at once bold and audacious while simultaneously graced with humility. The initial shock had to be strong—but the bold step of yesterday might well need redirecting tomorrow.

The record is clear on the formulation of the striking new programs of action. The record seems equally clear on the matter of changes in the original plans, presumably in response to actual experience. Thus, the realization in late 1953 of how great was the actual number of unemployed led to an expansion of the public plan, particular attention being given to programs with a high labor component.[6] One can note the very important changes in assumptions about the marginal savings rates and the capital-output ratio in the Second as against the First Plan.[7] Similarly new methods of analysis were applied in formulating allocation schemes.[8] With changing emphasis in the development effort, there were important modifications in basic policies of the past.[9] Governmental organization itself was adapted to the new stress which was to be given to public enterprise in steel and other heavy industry.[10] In response to needs in other directions, the Community Projects Administration was given ministerial status (and later assigned responsibility for co-operative activities) so that it could deal more effectively with the major co-ordinating functions of necessity involved in its operation. So also, with the recognition of the need to do more in the small-scale industrial field, a new complex of agencies and activities was established for these tasks.[11] And beyond organizational and structural change one can find full expression of government realization of the double challenge in the words of the Second Plan itself:

[6] Government of India, *Review of First Five Year Plan*, pp. 18-19.
[7] Government of India, *Second Five Year Plan*, pp. 8-11.
[8] P. C. Mahalanobis, "The Approach of Operational Research to Planning in India," *Sankhyā: The Indian Journal of Statistics*, Vol. XVI, Parts 1 and 2 (Dec., 1955).
[9] A notable illustration is found in the amendments of 1956 to the 1948 Industrial Policy Resolution.
[10] The Ministry of Production gave way in 1957 to expanded functions in three ministries: Steel, Mines and Fuel; Transportation and Communication; Commerce and Industry.
[11] A Small Scale Industries Board had been established in the Ministry of Commerce and Industry. Special financing institutions have been created. The National Small Industries Corporation is concerned with many aspects of the problem, but especially marketing. The new Regional Institutes undertake research investigations and the states themselves—the major link with the small operator himself—have a broad range of complementary offices and personnel.

Flexibility in working a five year plan is both a necessity and an advantage. In view of uncertainties inherent in imports of equipment and steel and in foreign exchange and changes in basic economic conditions, the working of the plan has to be reviewed periodically. To the extent a plan is flexible, it becomes possible to take advantage of new information and experience and to adopt new technological developments. . . It is proposed that beginning with 1956/57, following the annual budgets, there should be published specific and detailed plans for each year within the general framework of the five year plan. This would avoid undue rigidity in implementation and will permit changes to be made according to the developing needs of the economy.[12]

Here was explicit recognition from the highest counsels of government of the necessity for combining short-period flexibility with a total outlook that required the formulation of a ten- or fifteen-year program in some sectors. There was the double need to adhere to the bold over-all scheme for long period economic change and to temper this with specific steps adapted to developments over individual months and years.

Actually, however, these two needs were not meshed; there emerged the persistent gap between plan and actuality. If India's development outlook is to become a more favorable one, changes are needed in the type of plan or in the degree of accomplishment—perhaps both in some measure. The evidence seems less that there was inadequate implementation than that the plans were not real enough to be more implementable. Indeed a major reason for the gaps appears to lie in the limited extent to which program and theory have in fact been tempered with facts of actual experience. The basic underlying propositions—largely borrowed from experience elsewhere—do not seem to be modified as new insight becomes available. This would seem to be inconsistent with the official statement of intent quoted earlier.

It is true that India is and expects long to remain a mixed economy. Government officials and operations are but part of a total in which there is broad scope for individual freedom—in the consumer market for goods and services and in the producer market for factors and intermediate goods. This suggests the possibility that private actions may offset in some way the measures adopted by government. But it also points up how large an order was assumed by India's leaders at the time of independence. Government action was to provide

[12] Government of India, *Second Five Year Plan*, p. 140.

shocks, stimuli, guidance—and actual production—in order that the total mixed effort, private as well as public, might attain a new momentum. Again, it seems worthwhile to explore possible hypotheses explaining the actions taken by government. At least, some insights may be ventured on these matters.

III.[13]

India's development plans reflect the work of professional economists and other social scientists. It is not likely that there is any conceptual device, statistical tool, or theoretical argument known to economists anywhere which has not in some way been used, or mentioned, in the five-year plans. Not that all economists would agree with the specific assumptions or estimates that play a role in the Indian program. But the formulations make perfectly clear that consideration has been given to the elements which would be treated by the "best economists" in any land. Indeed, in *Sankhyā*, India's outstanding journal of statistics, Professor P. C. Mahalanobis has published what is perhaps as elegant an econometric underpinning for planning in India as exists for any other actual plan in operation. Yet, according to the Planning Commission: "The Plan which is now presented to Government for submission to Parliament is a result of the labours of large numbers of persons in the Central Government, in the States at various levels and leaders of thought and opinion in every part of the country. In its preparation, men and women in all walks of life have given generously of their time and experience. . . ."[14]

The time schedule available for preparing the First Plan permitted the roots to go down, in general, no farther than the state level. Work on the Second Plan, however, was formally initiated two years in advance and an even longer gestation period has attended the preparation of the Third Plan. With respect to the second, the Planning Commission requested the state governments in April, 1954, to arrange for district and even village plans, particu-

[13] This section draws heavily upon my "Who Does the Planning?" in Richard L. Park and Irene Tinker, eds., *Leadership and Political Institutions in India* (Princeton, 1959), pp. 301-13. For valuable insights of a scholar close to the plan-making process, see D. R. Gadgil, "Prospects for the Second Five-Year Plan Period," *India Quarterly*, XIII (1957), 5-23.

[14] Planning Commission, *The Second Five Year Plan* (New Delhi, 1956), p. 4.

larly with respect to agricultural production and rural industries—sectors where the Commission felt that local initiative in formulating plans should be stimulated to the maximum extent. This pattern was apparently adhered to generally in all the states; village plans and district plans were prepared and formed some basis for the draft plans presented by state governments. Even if the contribution from these lower levels was small, the entire procedure provided opportunity for some public participation. In any event here was valuable training for both the rural people and the rural officials associated with development.

Simultaneously, preparation was undertaken at state and central levels with the chief ministers and development commissioners appraising what needed to be done and, with the aid of the technical ministries, what could be done and what resources and procedures this would require. These meetings were paralleled by detailed discussions among senior technicians of the ministries and governments and, of course, the staff of the Planning Commission. Nor did agreement need to be achieved only between the sum of state "needs" and what the Centre could accept as a total; key functional reconciliations were also necessary.

The merger of planning which starts from both ends is never easy, no matter how carefully general principles and objectives are laid down to start. The reconciliation gives full play to technical argument: how much can the economy allocate to investment? How can it best be deployed? What will it yield? But at least as important is the interplay of various groups in the administrative chain of command, from village to district to state to the Centre, and in the various levels of the Congress Party, the political organization of the present government.

Moreover, into each of these channels and at various levels there is injected a large number of suggestions of outside groups: the plans of the smaller political parties, of religious and professional groups. For the Second Plan, these ranged from proposals for motivation by the organization of *sādhus* to the detailed programs carefully prepared by large business groups and their representatives. Thus, the proposals made through the *Eastern Economist* and by the Federation of Indian Chambers of Commerce impinge upon the official planners at all levels, but particularly at the state and Centre, and through all channels—the technical, governmental, and political—to which these groups have special access, given their wide and influential membership.

This entire panoply of popular planning is well revealed in India—clearly in 1955 and 1956 and again in 1960 and 1961. Issues are publicly aired and debated in the Parliament as well as in the full breadth of published materials. Eventually, there appeared in May, 1956, the Second Five Year Plan, and in 1961 the Third Five Year Plan, presumably the products on the one hand of these broad interchanges of a "people's plan" and on the other hand of the efforts of Indian economists, social scientists, and technicians— the essential contributors to a "professional's plan."

Perhaps a procedure which somehow combines the votes of the specially skilled and of the people will yield some "best plan." Whether or not it will, the process in India is still more apparent than real. Tremendous credit is due India for the structure of this multiple interchange, created in the candid hope that its educational benefit will bear fruit for future plans. Today, planning is essentially at the top for the bottom.

A significant flow from the bottom can scarcely exist in a land where some 80 per cent of the population is illiterate, where an even larger number may be only remotely concerned with the need for a development plan or program. The power of the Central Government on these matters is so great that at the planning stage agreement will be reached reasonably close to the Centre's position. In these circumstances, Indian plans can only be the product of a group very near the top of political and administrative life.

Does this concentration in an elite group promise a technically sound development program? Two points need to be raised here. First is the likelihood that the economist and social scientist will in fact espouse a technically meaningful program for India's development. Second, can these scientists be expected to assure, in discussions with other components of the nation's top leadership, that political requirements and objectives are realistically moderated by the technical and economic potentials? (There is no inference here that the ultimate program be anything but one which is politically meaningful. The query is only whether such political determinations in India can be confined to areas which are "possible" from an economic point of view.)

The experience of the past decade certainly prompts some doubts on both these points. Thus, there is ample evidence that the technical underpinnings of the Second Plan leave much to be desired. Moreover, the economists were apparently not in a strong enough position to assure that policy be confined to economically realistic realms.[15] Observations on the relative influence of political figures and administrators as compared to social scientists may of course be traceable to the specific individuals in the high command over the years. One can nonetheless question why Indian economists not in government service have failed to protest this course of developments. The Panel of Economists, officially constituted by the Planning Commission to advise with respect to the preparation of the plan, contains the leading economic figures of India. They had the opportunity to present policy proposals and to give their views on the general lines of action being considered by government. They were invited to make research contributions for the plan.[16] Indeed, through the Research Programmes Committee of the Planning Commission, social scientists, and especially economists, in the universities are given ample research resources by government with the precise objective of their pursuing studies that would help in this advisory function. Almost overnight the classic problem of the university professor—shortage of research funds—was replaced by a plethora of funds. (University professors were protesting against the pressures to take on more research; the faculties were becoming business administrators.)

All this notwithstanding, some basic problems of India's economy have yet to be assayed by the professionals—despite the resources already allocated to the Indian Statistical Institute, to government departments, and to the universities. Why? What deters the Indian social scientist from a pragmatic appraisal of his country?

[15] See Shigeto Tsuru, "Some Theoretical Doubts on India's Plan Frame," *Economic Weekly*, Annual Number, Jan., 1957, pp. 77-79; Ryutaro Komiya, "A Note on Professor Mahalanobis' Model," *Review of Economics and Statistics*, XLI (1959), 29-35, and chap. iv of my book, *Prospects for Indian Development*.

[16] Some of this work (in connection with the Second Plan) was released by the Planning Commission in October, 1955. See Panel of Economists, *Papers Relating to the Formulation of the Second Five Year Plan* (Delhi: Planning Commission, 1955). A few Indian economists did in fact reflect some disagreement with the plan formulations at an early stage. See in particular, the "Note of Dissent" written by Professor B. R. Shenoy of Gujarat University in April, 1955, and published in *The Second Five Year Plan: The Framework* (New Delhi: Ministry of Information and Broadcasting, 1955), and the article by B. K. Madan, "Some Aspects of the Draft of the Draft Plan-Frame," *Reserve Bank of India Bulletin*, Sept. 9, 1955, pp. 964-72.

True, the leading figures in this group are very busy. Top university men, because of their heavy academic and advisory responsibilities, have schedules which do not permit their own devotion to study and research on India's current problems. There is undoubtedly a great unwillingness to admit how limited is the basis of their understanding of India's own economic structure. For the most part, however, the reasons in the case of these social scientists—as indeed for other Indian intellectuals involved somehow at different stages of the planning process—seem to have rather general applicability among Indian elite groups.[17]

IV.

Efforts have been made to seek general, broad characterizations of the kind of leadership found in the Government of India. Three distinctions seem pertinent. The first centers about the fact, and the characteristics responsible for the fact, of the continuity of a single stable government in India since independence. This circumstance is noteworthy against the political developments in any new postwar nation. While this characterization frequently ends on the theme of ". . . but after Nehru, what?," there are great strengths in the *esprit* of government and the training of a Civil Service which achieved this phenomenon of stability over so eventful, and so dislocating, a series of years. On the whole, however, this type of characterization is not of itself overly relevant to the present examination.

A second group of characterizations concerns the non-Indian orientation of Indian elites, including the government in power and especially the civil servants. Reference is usually made of the extent to which governmental leadership is recruited from the 2 per cent of the population which speaks English, of the continuity of their contacts with the British in the course of their formal education and in governmental responsibilities before independence, and in negotiations and prison terms during the struggle for freedom. In some measure there is overlap here with the earlier characterization, for it was presumably this long and effective association with people from

[17] Including, one may observe, many of the "political figures and administrators" referred to immediately above (p. 162). The fact that they seem to have prevailed over the economists, say, in this instance need not mean any very different basic set of attributes.

outside India that contributed to the deep roots of parliamentary procedures and of British principles of freedom and justice in Indian leadership—all relevant to stability.[18]

Invariably, this category focuses upon the vast numbers in this group who were educated abroad or in India by professors and a discipline which stress the experience of more economically developed parts of the world. It is again clear that this association need not facilitate the conduct of India's affairs in the mid-twentieth century. It may contribute to "an insufficient appreciation and knowledge of conditions in the field on the part of those in ultimate authority. The extent of this may be best illustrated by the fact that it is possible for highly placed persons in Delhi to talk about a social revolution brought about in India by community projects. There are no signs of even an impending large change anywhere in the country. . . ."[19]

A third grouping goes beyond the second: the elite is not only Western oriented, it is also alienated from India, or rather, from the mass of Indians. Usually, and following from the Indian Prime Minister's own suggestions in this regard, these characterizations include reference to the two halves of the leaders.[20] Torn between the fact of being an Indian and the appeal of this Westernization, governmental elites find difficulty in applying themselves effectively in India.

It might be possible to elaborate these and perhaps other general descriptions of Indian leadership and to find in them some guides as to the root causes for the courses of action pointed out above. But

[18] Again, some writers go farther and argue that it is precisely this external association that can also explain the persistence of rationality and objectivity in the conduct of India's economic affairs. Here there is certainly considerable room for differences in interpretation. It would appear that these interpreters of the Indian scene have in some measure at least overrated program relative to action. For some recent references to the economic policy gains from Westernization, see Myron Weiner, "Changing Patterns of Political Leadership in West Bengal," *Pacific Affairs*, Sept., 1959, especially pp. 285-287; also Lloyd I. and Susanne H. Rudolph, "Toward Political Stability in Underdeveloped Countries: The Case of India," *Public Policy*, IX (Graduate School of Public Administration, Harvard University, 1959), especially pp. 158-59, 176-77.

[19] Gadgil, *op. cit.*, p. 17.

[20] "In consequence of this, (the Indian intellectual) is alleged to be neurotic, schizophrenic, ambivalent, suspended between two worlds and rooted to none." Edward Shils, "The Culture of the Indian Intellectual," *The Sewanee Review*, LXVII (1959), 6. Professor Shils takes strong objection to this type of interpretation of the elite, whether its source be foreigners or the Indian intellectual himself. See in particular Shils' references (*ibid.*, n. 2) on such characterization by Indians, including Mr. Nehru. But Shils may protest too much; his Indian intellectual does confront a major task of synthesis (*ibid.*, pp. 42-56).

this is a task of analysis somewhat removed from the present paper. A less rigorous exercise would be the examination of a few specific illustrations which are relevant to problems of planning and operation. While the evidence from such treatment cannot be definitive, it will be suggestive. And that is sufficient for present purposes.

Consider first the problem of housing. India's undersupply of housing was estimated at 1.84 million units by the Census Commissioner in 1951. Since then the position, at least in urban areas, seems to have deteriorated. A degree of overcrowding in the larger cities is patently obvious. Population in these large urban centers is now expanding at significantly higher rates than is total population. Housing is therefore a legitimate and indeed important concern for India's planners. The shortage aggravates health and social problems; in some areas there is an inadequate supply of houses for workers, which could mean a direct interference with growth in material output. Thus, in some urban centers, including the areas surrounding new industrial establishments, housing must be set up for the new workers. This usually means, as indeed it should, advance planning and construction.

What type of housing can the average workingman's family in urban India support? Even with government subsidies and loans, the average value of a minimum standard house of brick and plaster —and with minimum sanitary facilities—would entail monthly costs beyond what such a family could afford to pay.[21] If so, perhaps the plans might provide workers with a roof and frame, plus materials (or special access to materials through loans or price concessions) which would permit them to add to the basic structure as time, inclination, and energy permitted. This is a risky alternative. The workers' section might rapidly deteriorate[22]—unless the governmental authorities were prepared to apply the time and super-

[21] I have in mind a cost per house of about Rs. 3500, and a minimum monthly expenditure for housing of Rs. 20. This would usually exceed 10 per cent of family income, and is a multiple of current housing expenditures in urban areas.

[22] Some support for this comes from Chandigarh, the Le Corbusier-designed capital of the East Punjab. There, government is incurring costs for low-income housing well above receipts. Moreover, these low-income houses are depreciating more rapidly than was anticipated. This last is another consequence of putting families in houses where costs would normally be higher than the new family can afford to meet. Of course where people take satisfaction from living above their means in housing (as in the United States)—and therefore expend their own labor and ingenuity in maintenance—this need not be serious. A high psychic value for housing does not appear to prevail among low-income families in India.

vision that would more or less compel completion along lines agreed to in advance. Conceivably, as another alternative, some sort of temporary housing made of less durable material might be used. Again, this would require later expenditure of additional efforts by the house-dweller and additional supervision by housing authorities if the area was not to deteriorate quickly.

These are not pleasant alternatives. Unless government wants to expand the allocation it makes for such housing (at the expense of other investment, in the typical case) a country in India's economic condition cannot today afford on any significant scale what is generally considered as the minimum standard new house for that part of the world. But the Indian planner in the housing agency proceeds with the houses which meet this minimum standard.[23] There is little inclination to experiment in the substandard area, despite the reality of the cruel dilemma into which costs and needs place India. Adoption of any alternative route could constitute a patent index of India's status; India's new houses would be below standards applied for public housing by experts elsewhere.

A very different kind of illustration is cited at the central planning level. India plans investment programs for five-year periods, and indeed projects the orders of magnitude of the basic macro-measures, including investment, for several decades. Yet India does not publish actual investment data for the economy as a whole. At least, the major documents of the Planning Commission do not use actual figures at all; or they give orders of magnitudes which are not helpful.[24] This is all the more surprising since a branch of India's National Income Unit has long been making estimates of net and gross investment in the nation. These have appeared in non-official working papers published by the Planning Commission.[25] They have been released to private individuals and to research organizations in India.[26] It is of course true that these estimates, even though de-

[23] See Planning Commission, *First Five Year Plan*, chap. xxxv. Presumably such action might be his means of forcing government into a higher level of allocation for housing—and this may even be the correct alternative. The point in this event is whether this indirect route for achieving this goal is a desirable procedure.

[24] And these are not in line with such non-official data as are available. (See text.) Reference is made to the Government of India, *Review of the First Five Year Plan*, pp. 9-10; *The Second Five Year Plan*, p. 3; *Appraisal and Prospects of the Second Five Year Plan*, pp. 3-4.

[25] Government of India Panel of Economists, *Papers Relating to the Formulation of the Second Five Year Plan*, pp. 154-65.

[26] See, for example, V. Bhatt, "Savings and Capital Formation," *Economic*

rived with procedures broadly used in other countries, are necessarily in a preliminary stage. They may well be of somewhat lesser reliability than India's published national income estimates, which do encompass them. Be that as it may, so central are the orders of magnitude of actual investment, and their sectoral composition, to any planning or to any appraisal of actual performance that lack of precision is not a sufficient explanation for the failure to use them. Indeed, future planning—at least subsequent to that of the First Plan —is basically suspect unless it can be related to these all-important actual figures. Any argument that they are too imprecise for such use is an argument against any comprehensive forward projections which are in any way articulated by time and sector of the economy. One cannot help wondering why this situation is permitted to prevail. Since these arguments have been made to key members of the Planning Commission staff—many times, without doubt—and since in any case the non-official data have been used in publications, the decision to proceed along present lines would seem to be a deliberate one.

It is true that actual developments with respect to investment have not conformed well with projections. But this experience does not seem to be self-correcting, so that the eventual reconciliation may well be a more extreme one. Similarly, the present line of action stands in contrast to the objective of planning for the longer pull with greater reliance upon the actual record for immediate next steps. This objective does not seem to be supported by the record in investment.

The very nature of investment in India places considerable importance upon direct investment which occurs without benefit of transactions in money. Official plan projections have been made for monetized investment only. While this procedure does of course parallel treatment in the economically more advanced countries, it cannot be justified, either on data or analytic grounds, in an economy like India's where non-monetized transactions are of considerable quantitative significance. What is perhaps even more pertinent, only through a recognition of these actual structural characteristics of the Indian economy can an appreciation of the nature of savings behavior

Development and Cultural Change, VII (1959), 318-42; P. S. Lokanathan, "A Study of Saving in India," a paper read before the American Statistical Association Annual Meeting, Dec. 28, 1959; and my "Role of Government in India's Third Five Year Plan," Economic Development and Cultural Change, VIII (1960), 225-36.

be formulated. Without realistic hypotheses on this structure, the bases for projection of future domestic savings are impaired.

Greater reliance upon such factors in India's economic life does emphasize differences from the economic life in more advanced economies of the world. However—and perhaps compensating for these differences—there is the fact that only Indian experience to date provides a real opportunity for the development of theoretical concepts which may have greater relevance for the problem of growth in the poor lands than does presently accepted doctrine. Given the importance of the so-called "underdeveloped areas problem" in today's world, the study of India's actual savings and investment behavior may open a door to the major breakthrough in analysis which social scientists have long been seeking in the field of economic growth. To take this opportunity is important, however much it might seem to constitute a break from the respected procedures and relationships of the foreign, wealthier world.

Further illustrations can readily be presented. In the field of urban growth, for example, there are strong reasons to plan for a slower and different path of urbanization for India than has prevailed in the past developments in the now-richer nations. But official action to decelerate rapid urban expansion is not being taken. In the field of industry, India's obvious factor endowments—abundant labor and relatively scarce capital—call for a different allocation of investment between large and small industries from what seems to have been the case in past experience with economic growth. Indian economists have given the world an extensive literature on the theoretical problems of small- vs. large-scale industry—mostly based on assumptions which are grounded more in theory than in fact. And India persists in relative neglect of the small-scale industrial sector, at a cost not only to the national effort but to the big industry sector itself.

These illustrations do suggest the problems which confront India's governmental leadership as it shoulders the economic responsibilities and challenges of independence. They raise doubts about the rapid emergence of an objective sense of self-criticism, grounded upon extensive, original empirical analysis. Nor is the prospect favorable that the necessary insight will be imported from outside. Neither the attitude of India's elite groups nor indeed the analytic information available elsewhere offers this possibility as a solution.[27] Furthermore, these illustrations provide details which are consistent with the general picture of leadership attitudes revealed in studies by sociologists and psychologists. Thus, Professor Shils writes:

Even among scientists in these countries work seems to be done for an invisible jury of scientists in England, the United States and Germany. . . . This displacement of the intellectual center of gravity . . . arises out of xenophilia (and on that account it might harm the culture, science and economy of the underdeveloped country). . . . The real disadvantage of xenophilia is that it is associated with a severely deficient empathy for the states of mind of one's fellow-countrymen, by a lack of intimacy with the material environment and thus fundamentally a form of social blindness to the capacities and incapacities of one's fellow countrymen and their problems and their disposition to rouse themselves to do something about them. This 'social scotoma' is not in the first instance a product of Westernization; it is a product of hierarchical society in which the higher castes and classes had little feelings for those beneath them, and it is also a product of the religious tradition of non-attachment. Whatever its causes, the result is the existence of an educated class with little deeper understanding of the real state of mind, and the real problems of the country.

A common reaction against xenophilia is populistic nationalism. This beslavering of the uneducated, this praise of the 'wisdom of the humble' and of the sagacity of the ancestors is often hypocritical, but it is at least as often, sincere. Either way it brings no improvement in the situation. Where realism of perception and judgment is required, the creation of passionately espoused illusions is no better than indifference and disregard. From the point of view of the needs of a new society which would combine economic progress with democracy and individual liberty, xenophilia and nationalism are at least equal hindrances. Both are unrealistic and both apply vague clichés where differentiated and specific judgment and a feeling for the concrete situation are called for. Neither is capable of that patient, matter-of-fact scrutiny of situations in a mood free from the preconceptions and preoccupations connected with rigid and vague principles. Without that kind of scrutiny, the sober assessment of achievements which is indispensable both to the realistic formulation of policy, its sound administration and to constructive factual assessment of achievements and shortcomings is not very likely to develop.[28]

[27] Increasingly perhaps the experience of leadership on mainland China may be brought to bear. This observation, it should be stressed, does not imply an Indian shift to communist control or philosophies. See my "Political Ideology and Economic Progress" (with Wolfgang Stolper) in *World Politics*, XII, No. 3 (1960), 413-21.
[28] These quotations are from his "The Intellectual, Public Opinion and Economic Development," a mimeographed paper read in Feb., 1957, at the Tokyo meeting of the Committee for Cultural Freedom and subsequently published in *Economic Development and Cultural Change*, VI, No. 1 (1957), 55-62. For an

Shils thus points up "certain inherited obstacles [to] the adequacy [for economic development through planning] of quality and quantity of planning and administrative personnel." He then argues the importance of developing—inside the government, but especially outside, as in the press or in universities—those capacities for criticism and objective appraisal of national policies. This answer is certainly not an immediate one—especially since leadership attributes in these other areas may well have much in common with those in government.

Finally, Professor Gadgil has expressed himself as perhaps even less sanguine about this long-period type of solution. "It is obvious that the country requires personnel in the higher services recruited in much more diverse ways and from among many more diverse strata than is possible under the present system. Everybody agrees that without full understanding and conscious participation on the part of the people permanent results will not flow. However, it is impossible to expect a radical change in the pattern of officer behavior overnight and . . . there has been no overt and conscious effort made and no concrete example set to bring about such a change. . . ." While Professor Gadgil cites certain possibilities which might "generate pressures and lead to unexpected action" he feels the need is for the "hard and consistent effort . . . to eradicate the inadequacies of thinking in attitudes and approaches, and in instruments . . . the real obstacles of notable economic progress in India."[29]

V.

This formulation places the bottlenecks to India's progress squarely upon India's leadership. An expanded capital supply, even low-cost capital from abroad, cannot of itself eliminate the problem. It can always help—but its effectiveness (and indeed its very volume) depends upon prior domestic activity, and more specifically, activity

---

amazing endorsement of the views expressed above, see G. Morris Carstairs, *The Twice Born* (London, 1957), *passim*, but especially pp. 89-174. Dr. Carstairs is a professional psychologist.

[29] *Op. cit.*, pp. 16-17, 22-23. Mention might also be made here of Gadgil's concern on the administrative side—the third dimension of the challenge of independence, referred to in n. 5 above. He mentions "the tendency [of officials] to concentrate attention on the volume of total expenditure incurred rather than on the directions in which or the care with which it is incurred" (*ibid.*, pp. 19-20).

by India's elite groups. In some measure, the very fact of indifferent achievement will sooner or later stir some awakening. Thus, India's planning has long been in the world's limelight: middling performance will need some explanation. Communist China has provided a sharp reminder that rapid progress can in fact be made from the low level of economic welfare characteristic of poor, overcrowded countries. While the Indians might attribute some of the difference in performance to India's preference for a route which respects individual freedom, an objective appraisal would suggest that the key difference arises upon effective leadership performance.[30] And in any case, Communist China is a neighbor which constantly challenges India on all fronts. For this challenge India needs an answer which must include an impressive rate of economic performance.

In addition, leadership now seems to recognize that it must find a solution to India's agricultural problem. The developments of the past few years make it impossible for leadership to continue to handle the matter with policy statements; a program of action is demanded by all groups. Foreign advice and guidance are seldom sought on matters of decisive importance in internal policy in India. Yet here foreign expert groups do present a reasonably solid front. And the work of the Ford Foundation, especially the recent report of a group of foreign experts, may well help in formulating new action programs.[31] Indeed, one should envisage the possibility that new international assistance programs in the years ahead will include joint research facilities. These would be directed toward discovering the true deterrents to economic progress.

Finally, the core of responsible leadership may itself change. Analysis reveals that the Congress leadership—still below the top levels—is being increasingly recruited from groups which differ from those presently in command. There is evidence of a shift toward greater representation from rural areas; there is evidence of the emergence of caste organizations as potent forces for political change; there certainly is a growing concern in India about problems below the national level. All of this means that the future may see a leadership which has different characteristics from those mentioned earlier.

[30] Thus see my "India and China: Contrasts in Development Performance," *American Economic Review*, XLIX (1959), 284-309; also Malenbaum and Stolper, *op. cit.*

[31] Government of India, Ministry of Food and Agriculture, *Report on India's Food Crisis and Steps to Meet It* (New Delhi, April 1959).

This may well mean less "rationality" in India's development effort.[32] But the effort might nonetheless be more pointedly directed toward actual deterrents to India's more rapid economic progress than was the action of India's leadership over the past decade.

[32] See above, n. 18.

6

Some Constitutional Aspects of Planning

S. P. Jagota

AMONG THE PRINCIPAL ACTIVITIES of free India has been the attempt to bring about rapid economic and social development by planned effort. Although an awareness of the importance of planning was manifest before independence in 1947, realistic and ambitious planning on an all-India basis could not be started effectively until India had become free and its major problems relating mainly to the partition of the country and the integration of the native Indian states had been resolved.

The Constitution framed by the Constituent Assembly between 1946 and 1949 enunciated the basic principles of the state and its structure and included a detailed description of the political and other institutions to be established. The preamble declared India to be a sovereign democratic republic insuring to its citizens justice, equality, and liberty in all their aspects. The directive principles of state policy[1] indicated, *inter alia*, that India must be a welfare state, whose economic, social, and welfare aspects were elaborated. The basic principles of economic policy were defined as follows:

(1) That the ownership and control of the material resources of the community are so distributed as best to subserve the common good; and

(2) That the operation of the economic system does not result in the concentration of wealth and means of production to the common detriment.[2]

Although these directives were described as fundamental in governing the country and it was the duty of the state to apply them in making laws, they were not the source of legislative powers but only their political justification. The legislative power had to be derived

[1] *The Constitution of India*, Part IV.
[2] *Ibid.*, Article 39 (b, c).

with reference to the structure of the state. Structurally, India was described as a union of states organized on federal lines, with powers divided between the Centre and the states. The subjects of jurisdiction were described in detail in the Seventh Schedule of the Constitution, and Articles 245 and 246 gave the requisite power to the appropriate legislatures to enact laws on the subjects in their jurisdiction. A law passed without or in excess of jurisdiction could to that extent be struck down by the judiciary as unconstitutional. The Constitution also contained detailed provisions governing Union-state relations which would promote harmonious functioning of the total political structure.

A basic principle of political organization was the adoption of a parliamentary type of executive both at the Centre and in the states. The real executive power of the government was to be exercised by the Council of Ministers comprising the leadership of the political party or parties holding a majority in the legislature and collectively responsible to it in its working. This system, it was believed, provided competent leadership to the legislature in all matters—legislation, finance, policy enunciation, and so forth—promoted harmonious functioning of the legislature and the executive, which is so desirable in a developing economy, and assured larger responsibility of the government to the legislature and to the people.

While the Constituent Assembly took approximately three years to finish its work and produced a bulky constitution comprising 395 articles and 8 schedules (now 9), surprisingly the Constitution did not contain any provisions regarding the planning institutions and procedures by which the effort for planning has been directed and streamlined, although the Constitution did contain some provisions giving the state the requisite authority to legislate on subjects relating to development.[3] Legislation on these subjects has been adopted

[3] Thus, for instance, Article 298 authorized the Union and the states to carry on trade or business, to acquire property, to enter into contracts, and so forth, under the regulatory authority of the appropriate legislature. The law could create state monopolies to the extent necessary (Article 19(6), as amended). Item 20 of the Concurrent List related to "Economic and Social Planning." Under Item 52, Union List, Parliament could legislate on "industries, the control of which by the Union is declared by Parliament by law to be expedient in the public interest." Similarly, under Item 54, Union List, Parliament could regulate by law the mines and mineral development to the extent "expedient in public interest." Under Item 56 it could regulate and develop interstate rivers and river valleys. Other items, more precise, relating to development subjects may be found in the appropriate lists of the Seventh Schedule.

by the appropriate legislature within the framework laid down by the Constitution. Nor has responsibility of the political institutions been undermined. Nevertheless, despite the formality of legislative competence and procedure and the responsibility of the executive to the legislature, the planning institutions and procedures have affected the constitutional framework within which the political institutions were expected to function. The extent to which this has happened will be described and examined in this essay. The essay is neither comprehensive nor exhaustive. Problems of constitutional significance arising *indirectly* from planning as a result of the increase in legislation and administrative power, such as the problems of delegated legislation, judicial review of administrative action, administrative tribunals, and so forth, have not been examined. Only the problems arising *directly* from planning have been selected for this study. The four aspects studied hereunder are organized in the following sections: (1) Planning and Parliamentary Democracy, (2) Planning and Union-State Relations, (3) the Planning Commission and the Finance Commission, and (4) Public Undertakings.

I. *Planning and Parliamentary Democracy*

As stated at the outset, although planning consciousness preceded the attainment of independence in 1947 and although efforts for planning started even with the interim government in 1946, the Constitution did not contain any provisions relating to the planning machinery, such as the Planning Commission and the National Development Council. Nor were these agencies established under a statute. Following the recommendations of the Advisory Planning Board of 1946, the Planning Commission was established by a Cabinet resolution of March 15, 1950. The National Development Council was established in 1952.

The terms of reference of the Planning Commission were the following:[4]

(1) to make an assessment of the material, capital and human resources of the country, including technical personnel, and investigate the

[4] For text of the Cabinet resolution and the terms of reference of the Planning Commission, see Estimates Committee, *Twenty-First Report* (*Planning Commission*), Second Lok Sabha, April, 1958, Appendix I, pp. 34-36.

possibilities of augmenting such of these resources as are found to be deficient in relation to the nation's requirements;

(2) to formulate a Plan for the most effective and balanced utilisation of the country's resources;

(3) on a determination of priorities, to define the stages in which the Plan should be carried out and propose the allocation of resources for the due completion of each stage;

(4) to indicate the factors which are tending to retard economic development and determine the conditions which, in view of the current social and political situation, should be established for the successful execution of the Plan;

(5) to determine the nature of the machinery which will be necessary for securing the successful implementation of each stage of the Plan in all its aspects;

(6) to appraise from time to time the progress achieved in the execution of each stage of the Plan and to recommend the adjustments of policy and measures that such appraisal might show to be necessary; and

(7) to make such interim or ancillary recommendations as might be appropriate on a consideration of the prevailing economic conditions, current policies, measures and development programmes, or on an examination of such specific problems as may be referred to it for advice by Central or State Governments for facilitating the discharge of the duties assigned to it.

It will thus be apparent that the Planning Commission was thought of as a staff agency to prepare national plans for economic development within the framework of a federal state, a parliamentary democracy, and a welfare state. The Commission was to suggest, co-ordinate, phase, and evaluate policies and programs, although the final responsibility to the people's representatives and to the people remained with the political institutions. Although the states had no planning commissions of similar status, they had special planning departments and mixed (official and non-official) advisory boards to do the planning work. Since 1957, the emerging *Panchāyatī Rāj* institutions in the villages, the blocks, and the districts are increasingly being associated with the formulation and implementation of plans within the range of responsibilities assigned to them.

The terms of reference of the National Development Council were the following:

(1) to review the working of the National Plan from time to time;

(2) to consider important questions of social and economic policy affecting national development; and

(3) to recommend measures for the achievement of the aims and targets set out in the National Plan, including measures to secure the active participation and cooperation of the people, improve the efficiency of the administrative services, ensure the fullest development of the less advanced regions and sections of the community, and, through sacrifice borne equally by all citizens, build up resources for national development.[5]

The Council consists of the Prime Minister, the chief ministers of the states, and the members of the Planning Commission and is thus intended to approve the plan and transmit it to the Centre and the states, which assume responsibility for implementing it. On occasion the National Development Council takes decisions on behalf of the states and the Government of India.

Constitutionally, two aspects of the planning machinery are significant: one, its impact on federalism, and two, its impact on parliamentary democracy. Since the former will be discussed in the next section, we shall here examine only the latter question.

As stated earlier, the Constitution established a parliamentary type of executive in India both at the Centre and in the states. Accordingly, although the executive power is vested in the president at the Centre and the governors in the states, it is actually exercised by a Council of Ministers drawn from the legislature and responsible to it. The Constitution did not elaborate the structure or the method of functioning of the Council, which have therefore developed by conventions. Thus at the Centre the executive power is not exercised by the Council of Ministers as a whole but by the Cabinet which is its core; the Council comprises ministers of different status and functions; the Cabinet functions mainly by committees which have affected the concept of collective responsibility of the Council as a whole; and so forth.[6] The functioning of the Cabinet has also been affected by its intimate relations with the Planning Commission; hence, the question whether the planning machinery established by an executive resolution has affected the constitutional responsibility of the executive. The following facts about the composition of the Planning Commission and its functioning may be noted before we refer to some criticisms which have been voiced on the subject.

[5] S. R. Sen, "Planning Machinery in India," *Indian Journal of Public Administration*, VII (1961), 233. This entire issue is a special volume on "Administration and the Third Five Year Plan."

[6] For details of the working of the Council of Ministers at the Centre, see Asok Chanda, *Indian Administration* (London, 1958), pp. 63-93.

Four of the nine members of the Planning Commission are ministers of the Central Cabinet—the Prime Minister, the Finance Minister, the Defence Minister and the Minister for Planning. Other ministers may be invited to attend the meeting of the Planning Commission when matters concerning their departments are being discussed. Conversely, the members of the Planning Commission attend all the meetings of the Economic Committee of the Cabinet and the Cabinet meetings when economic affairs are being discussed. Important economic proposals of the ministries are considered in the Planning Commission before they are put up to the Cabinet. The members of the Planning Commission also attend the meetings of the National Development Council. The Secretary of the Cabinet acts as secretary to the Planning Commission. The economic adviser to the Ministry of Finance is also the economic adviser to the Planning Commission.

The procedures of the formulation and the implementation of the plans also indicate the extent of the intimate relations between the Cabinet, the Planning Commission, and the ministries both at the Centre and in the states. These procedures may be summed up as follows: the Planning Commission prepares tentative long-term (15 to 20 years) goals for economic development, which after being approved by the Central Government are broken up into five-year targets. Working groups comprising representatives of the Planning Commission and the central and the state ministries are then set up in their respective spheres for each sector of economic and social development. They prepare long-term and five-year targets of sectoral development and also work out the details of policies and programs needed for achieving these targets. On the basis of their reports, the Planning Commission prepares a draft memorandum on the plan, which is considered by the Cabinet and the National Development Council. With their approval the draft plan is prepared and discussed extensively in Parliament and in the country. Within the targets set out in the draft, the central ministries and the states prepare detailed plans in their spheres which are modified after discussion with the Planning Commission. On the basis of these discussions and modifications, the final plan is prepared and then laid before the National Development Council for its general approval. The approved plan is transmitted to the appropriate governments for implementation of their respective programs of development.[7]

The plan is then broken up into annual plans which are approved by the Planning Commission before budget proposals for parliamentary authorization are prepared. The estimates of expenditure on Plan schemes are also cleared with the Planning Commission before they are included in the budget. Periodic progress reports on expenditures, after authorization by Parliament, are made to the Planning Commission to assist it in its evaluation work.

Let us now note some of the criticisms of the Planning Commission. The Estimates Committee of the Lok Sabha, while examining the Planning Commission, criticized its composition and made the following recommendations:

While the Prime Minister's formal association was absolutely necessary during the formative stages and while he would still have to provide the guidance and assistance to the Planning Commission so as to facilitate the success of planning, it is a matter for consideration whether it is still necessary for him to retain a formal connection with the Planning Commission. Similarly, it would also have to be considered whether it is necessary to continue the formal association of the Finance Minister and other Ministers of the Central Government with the Commission. The association of Ministers is justified mainly on the ground that it facilitates close consultation and co-ordination with the Ministries. This can, however, be effected by the Minister being invited to attend the meetings of the Commission when a subject with which he is concerned is discussed. The co-ordination with the Cabinet can also be maintained by a representative of the Commission attending the meeting of the Cabinet when a matter of interest to the Commission is considered. This practice is said to be followed even at present.[8]

The Committee also disapproved of having the Cabinet Secretary act as secretary to the Planning Commission, which they thought was neither necessary for any high level contacts nor conducive to efficiency.[9]

The criticism regarding the composition of the Planning Commission aroused controversy both as to the merits of the proposals and as to the competence or the desirability of having the Estimates Committee enter into policy questions.[10]

[7] For details, see S. R. Sen, *op. cit.*, pp. 219-20, and Government of India, Planning Commission, *Third Five Year Plan* (1961), Introduction, p. xv.

[8] Estimates Committee, *Twenty-First Report*, p. 8.

[9] *Ibid.*, pp. 9-10.

[10] The Estimates Committee is an important financial committee of the Lok

Asok Chanda, the former Comptroller and Auditor-General of India, regarded the Planning Commission as virtually the Economic Cabinet of the country and made the following comments on its position:

This undefined position of the commission and its wide terms of reference have gradually led to its growth as the Economic Cabinet, not merely for the Union but also for the States. The policies of a welfare state embarked on a programme of planned development of her industrial strength and social services have necessarily an economic orientation. The commission has seized upon this position and extended the scope of its activities to embrace functions and responsibilities which must both traditionally and otherwise belong to the constituted government. This has been facilitated by the inclusion of the Prime Minister, the Finance Minister, and two other Cabinet Ministers in the composition of the commission, by giving the other official members the status of Ministers of Cabinet rank, and by the appointment of the Cabinet Secretary as the Secretary of the commission. The *de facto* role of the commission as the Economic Cabinet is further stressed by the attendance of its members at all meetings of the Economic Committee of the Cabinet and also meetings of the Cabinet when economic questions come up for discussion.

. . . .

It would be only stating the obvious to say that the determination of policy and the objectives which it has to fulfil must necessarily be the primary function of the Cabinet accountable to Parliament. Equally, the unhampered execution of accepted plans and programmes must be the responsibility of the departments. These functions could hardly be shared with any other authority.

Sabha. Its terms of reference are defined in Rule 310 of the *Rules and Procedures of Lok Sabha* (1957 ed.) and include reporting on "what economy, improvements in organisation, efficiency, or administrative reform, consistent with the policy underlying the estimates, may be effected," and suggesting "alternative policies in order to bring about efficiency and economy in administration." This led to the controversy regarding the role of the Committee *vis-à-vis* the House. It was argued that by entering into policy questions, the Committee was "arrogating to itself a role which, constitutionally, is that of the House." (Asok Chanda, *op. cit.*, p. 193). The term "policy" has been defined by the Speaker in his Directions as relating only to "policies laid down by Parliament either by means of statutes or by specific resolutions passed by it from time to time," and that even regarding the latter, "when it is established on evidence that a particular policy is not leading to the expected or desired results or is leading to waste, it is the duty of the Committee to bring to the notice of the House that a change in policy is called for" (*Directions by the Speaker under the Rules and Procedure of Lok Sabha*, 1957 ed., Direction No. 98). Hence the claim that the Estimates Committee was perfectly within its jurisdiction when it criticized the composition of the Planning Commission, which had never been formally approved by Parliament. See S. L. Shakdher, "Two Estimates Committees," *Indian Journal of Public Administration*, V (1959), 391-92, nn. 9, 10.

The position of pre-eminence accorded to the Planning Commission is inconsistent with the conception of a Cabinet form of government.[11]

Hence, Chanda suggested that if the Commission were to be reorganized, comprising experts of vision and experience, "it should place the commission in its proper relationship with the Cabinet and the Ministries; it should also make it more effective in fulfilling its assigned task."[12]

In the same strain, while dealing with the effect of planning for Union-state relations, K. Santhanam, the former chairman of the Second Finance Commission, described the National Development Council as a "super-Cabinet of the entire Indian federation, a Cabinet functioning for the Government of India and the Governments of all the States."[13]

On the other hand, the constitution of the present planning machinery may be defended on the grounds that a statute might have made it more rigid, that a commission composed of experts totally detached from government might have been an ineffective body, for it would have thought in a vacuum, that the present membership promotes mutual respect between the government and the Commission and assures realistic planning, that the ministers constitute the membership of the Commission in their personal capacity, that anyhow they are capable of acting and in fact do act in a dual role, and so forth.[14]

S. R. Sen also emphasizes that since the main functions of the

[11] Asok Chanda, *op. cit.*, pp. 92-93. For identical criticisms, see K. V. Rao, "Centre-State Relations in Theory and Practice," *Indian Journal of Political Science*, XIV (1953), 347-355; and D. R. Gadgil, "The Role of the Planning Commission in Indian Planning," *Planning and Economic Policy in India* (Bombay, 1961), pp. 88-111, at 104, 106, and 108-110.

[12] Asok Chanda, *op. cit.*, p. 93.

[13] K. Santhanam, *Union-State Relations in India* (New Delhi, 1960), p. 47. Illustrating the working of the National Development Council, the author said: "The other day I referred to the surrender by the State Governments of their sales taxes on textiles, sugar and tobacco. Normally, this would be a major constitutional issue because they were taxes which have been assigned to the States. Under normal federal political conditions, there would have been discussions in every State legislature and in the press, as to whether the States should surrender or not. I believe the decision to surrender these taxes and substitute them by additional excise duties was taken at a single sitting (of the National Development Council) at which many of the Chief Ministers had not even fully consulted their own Cabinets. . . . I do not suggest that the States have suffered. It has already been pointed out that the States have gained 8 crores of rupees. Still, from the constitutional point of view, it was major decision to take" (pp. 46-47).

[14] These views in favor of the existing arrangements are cited in the Estimates Committee, *Twenty-First Report*, pp. 7-8.

Planning Commission are advisory and co-ordinating rather than executive, and in view of the constitutional, political, and economic situation that obtains in India, "it is as well that the Planning Commission should rely more on consultation and agreement than on sanction."[15] The necessary sanction operates through the constitutional framework; in other words, the responsibility is assumed by the Councils of Ministers at the Centre and in the states. Nor need it be forgotten that the plan is examined, discussed, and approved by Parliament[16] and thereafter adopted again in the annual budgets, with ample opportunities for debate and criticism. The Planning Commission's activities are also within the over-all scrutiny of Parliament and its various committees.

It is not known with certainty why no provisions were made in the Constitution or in statutory law regarding the establishment or functioning of the planning institutions. As noted above, the constitutional provisions relating to the Council of Ministers were also very meager, and hence conventions had to grow regarding its composition and the manner of its operation. Nor does the Constitution mention anything regarding political parties, which are the base determining the effective functioning of a parliamentary democracy. Thus there was ample scope for the emergence of suitable conventions regarding the working of the Council of Ministers, comprising a coalition of parties, and their relations with the constitutional head. Similarly, the conventional growth of institutions established under resolutions of the Cabinet would facilitate the formulation and implementation of effective plans and avoid the rigidity which would have necessarily arisen if the authority had been derived from a statute. The statute must remain strictly within the Constitution or its constitutionality will be questioned. Moreover, under a statute

[15] Op. cit., p. 221. The author concluded his study as follows: "The ultimate picture of the planning organisation in the country would be a network of planning units in the villages and enterprises co-ordinating at successive higher levels by appropriate planning organisations, which will all ultimately feed the planning at the Centre. It will, no doubt, take quite some time before this stage is reached, but considerable progress has already been made towards it" (p. 235). Such a flexible set of institutions would probably justify the absence of statutory authority for planning machinery. But in an identical situation, five Zonal Councils were established under the States Reorganisation Act 1956. These Councils are advisory bodies and their terms of reference were kept flexible but they were intended to consider matters of interstate interests and to promote interstate amity.

[16] For working of parliamentary committees on the draft Second Five Year Plan, see the *Journal of Parliamentary Information*, II, No. 2 (October, 1956) 200-204; on the draft Third Five Year Plan, VII, No. 1 (April, 1961), 29-39.

it would not be as easy as otherwise to modify the composition of the Planning Commission and its relations with the ministers. The significance of the outgrowth of these institutions should be tested on two grounds: (*a*) its effectiveness and success in planning and (*b*) its not disturbing or diffusing the line of responsibility of the constitutional institutions, namely, the Council of Ministers and the legislatures at the Centre and in the states. By and large, the present procedures have functioned effectively and the constitutional structure has not been crucially undermined. With modifications in the composition of the Planning Commission as suggested by the Estimates Committee, i.e., by not associating the ministers of the Central Cabinet with the Planning Commission as members but inviting them to attend their meetings to the extent necessary, and with the emergence of suitable procedures providing for an effective discussion and adoption of the plan in the state legislatures as well as in Parliament, the main constitutional objections to the position acquired by the Planning Commission may be cleared. The realism and effectiveness of planning, however, must not suffer, for they will themselves vitalize parliamentary democracy.

II. *Planning and Union-State Relations*

In the federal structure of India, the nation is divided into states and Union territories. The latter comprise only about 1.2 per cent of India's population and are administered as if they were parts of a unitary state. Predominantly, therefore, India is federal. In certain circumstances, particularly in war or other emergencies, federalism may be suspended by the declaration of President's Rule but it is assumed that it would be revived as soon as the emergency is over. In normal times, the Centre has more authority than the states, but the spheres of both are clearly demarcated in such matters as legislation, administration, finance, trade and commerce. This is provided for by the Constitution in some detail. Thus, the states have their own governmental machinery—legislature, executive, and services, functioning within the sphere guaranteed to them, in matters such as those relating to law and order, police, administration of justice, agriculture, land, forests, irrigation, fisheries, health, education, internal communication, mines and mineral development, industries, internal trade and commerce.

The impact of planning on this federal structure has taken place in the forms described below:

(1) Planning has been unified and is comprehensive, despite the federal structure of the Union. The plans deal not only with Central subjects but also with state subjects, such as agriculture, irrigation, land reform, community development, social welfare, and so forth. In fact, the outlay on state subjects has been approximately 70 per cent of the First Plan, 65 per cent of the Second Plan, and is expected to be over 65 per cent in the Third Plan.[17]

(2) The responsibility for the formulation of the Five Year Plans has been given to the Planning Commission, which, although it includes members of the Central Cabinet, has no members from the states. The states do not have any planning commissions of their own and their role in the formulation of plans, even in their own sphere, is subject to the targets set out by the Planning Commission and subject to their general approval.[18] This gives the Planning Commission and the Central Cabinet greater control over the formulation of policy in the state sphere than the Constitution warranted. Hence the establishment of the National Development Council in 1952. The National Development Council, which includes the chief ministers of the states, approves the plan, reviews its working, and recommends to the Centre and the states measures for the achievement of the aims and targets set out in the plan. The Council is, however, neither a constitutional nor a statutory body. Again, the plans are discussed and approved by Parliament, but not by the state legislatures, although the bulk of the matters in the plan relates to state subjects.

(3) In the implementation of the plan in the state sphere, the autonomy of the state has been affected by the fact that the Five Year Plan has been broken up into annual plans in the interests of flexibility, more effective management, and necessary adjustment to changed situations; and the states have to approach the Planning Commission every November or December for the approval of the next year's plan. Since the states are dependent for about 70 per cent of their development expenditure on revenue account and almost the whole of it on capital account on the grants and loans from the

[17] *Third Five Year Plan;* see tables on pp. 33, 58 and 59.
[18] The procedures of the formulation of plans have been described on pp. 178-179, above.

central government,[19] their functional autonomy is affected by their financial dependence. This enables the central government to sponsor policies or schemes on state subjects in addition to assisting state schemes, and with the financial carrot in hand, the Centre can affect state autonomy in a manner not warranted by the Constitution. Thus, the Central Ministries concerned with state matters, such as education, food and agriculture, irrigation and power, health, and so forth, could not only initiate schemes of development in these subjects and offer financial assistance to the states on the basis of matching grants, but the state schemes in the same or allied subjects had to be scrutinized and approved before financial assistance was promised and released. The system was criticized by the Comptroller and Auditor-General of India and the Public Accounts Committee of Parliament and by other critics, such as Santhanam, who expressed the opinion that the formulation procedures had superseded or by-passed federalism, whereas implementation procedures had at best converted the federation into a vertical one.[20]

Before referring to the criticisms, the extent of the financial dependence of the states on the Centre should be noted. The total outlay in the Third Five Year Plan in the public and private sectors is of the order of Rs. 104,000 million, out of which the public sector accounts for Rs. 75,000 million. The states' share is Rs. 37,250 million, which does not include outlays on centrally sponsored schemes of economic and social development relating to state subjects. The states' resources, however, are limited to Rs. 14,620 million, which includes additional taxes;[21] the rest will have to come from the Centre. Thus, over 60 per cent of the state outlays will have to be financed by the Centre. To this, however, must be added the assistance for centrally sponsored schemes. Assistance by the Central Government will be in the form of shared taxes, grants, and loans.[22]

[19] Santhanam, *Union-State Relations in India*, pp. 53 and 59.
[20] *Ibid.*, pp. 47 and 54.
[21] *Third Five Year Plan*, pp. 100-101.
[22] It might be noted here that the grants are of two types: one, statutory grants given under Article 275 of the Constitution, the principles and the quantum of which are recommended by a Finance Commission appointed once in five years, and two, discretionary grants given by the Central Ministries to the state governments. The latter has been done under Art. 282, which reads: "The Union or a State may make any grants for any public purpose, notwithstanding that the purpose is not one with respect to which Parliament or the Legislature of the State, as the case may be, may make laws." This exceptional provision has therefore been utilized to finance state plans and has affected Union-state relations.

Taking the budgetary position of the states as a whole for the year 1961-62, including expenditures on development and non-development subjects, both plan and non-plan, the states were estimated to spend Rs. 10,574 million on revenue account and Rs. 5,232 million on capital account, totalling Rs. 15,806 million. The Central assistance in this total figure amounts to Rs. 8,009 million, comprising Rs. 1,600 million in shared taxes, Rs. 2,317 million in grants, and Rs. 4,092 million in loans. This amounts to 50.7 per cent of the total state budgets.[23]

This has been made possible by the elaborate division of sources of revenue between the Union and the states as laid down in the Constitution. The sources for the Centre comprise the corporation tax and custom duties and excises. The sources for the states comprise a long list, including land revenue, sales tax, and taxes on professions, entertainments, and vehicles. In addition, the Centre was to levy some taxes which were to be appropriated or shared by the states. Thus the tax on incomes was to be levied and collected by the Centre but shared between the Centre and the states.[24] But in spite of the elaborate provisions, the division of resources was such that the Central taxes were bound to yield more with the increase in economic activity, whereas the states' taxes were bound to be more or less static, except for sales taxes. The Constitution recognized this and provided for grants-in-aid of the revenues of the states.[25] With the increase in the international credit of India, generous assistance has been offered for India's plans,[26] and this further improved the finances at the disposal of the Centre and facilitated implementation of ambitious plans. The financial surplus with the Centre might also be desirable for rapid economic development on a unified basis all over the country. Shortfalls in state resources due to reluctant or ineffective efforts to raise taxes and inadequate discharge of their loan

[23] For details, see "Finances of State Governments," *Reserve Bank of India Bulletin*, June, 1961, pp. 856, 858, 860-62, 868-69. For detailed analysis of the resources transferred from the Centre to the states, see "Budget of Government of India for 1961-62," *ibid.*, April, 1961, pp. 506-7. The resources transferred in the First and the Second Plans totaled Rs. 14,129 million and Rs. 28,907 million respectively. The percentage will obviously be much higher for developmental and still more on plan expenditure.

[24] For details, see Santhanam, *op. cit.*, chap. iii, entitled "Financial Relations."

[25] Articles 275 and 282. See n. 22 above.

[26] Foreign assistance counted for 10 per cent in the First Plan, 24 per cent in the Second, and is expected to amount to 30 per cent in the Third Plan. See *Third Five Year Plan*, pp. 33 and 94.

obligations[27] to the Centre have further strengthened the Centre in relation to the states.

We might now refer to the criticisms of the Comptroller and Auditor-General and the Public Accounts Committee of Parliament relating mainly to the system of grants-in-aid in India.

The Comptroller and Auditor-General in a note on "Estimates and Financial Control" appended to the *Audit Report (Civil), 1955*[28] examined Union-state financial relations, particularly those arising out of the administration of the Central financial assistance to the states on the basis of matching grants, that is, where the Centre contributes a fixed percentage of the total expenditure on the state schemes or the centrally sponsored schemes. The Comptroller and Auditor-General observed that since the states did not have adequate resources to contribute their share, the implementation of the schemes suffered and there were heavy shortfalls in expenditure. He also criticized the system of the release of Central assistance which was done on a recoupment or reimbursement basis. In other words, the expenditure on the schemes had first to be incurred by the states, and if the states did not have the resources available, the projects got held up. He therefore made the following proposals:

(1) In lieu of the Centre rendering financial aid to the States for a proportion of the expenditure on all the approved schemes, they should accept full financial responsibility for a specified number of such schemes, up to an equivalent amount. Programme Advisers should be required to report that the remaining schemes have been undertaken by the States out of their own resources.

(2) Detailed scrutiny of States' schemes should be discarded. The examination by the Centre should be confined to—

(i) a broad administrative scrutiny by the Ministry concerned and the Planning Commission, to ensure that they fall within the framework of the Plan, and

(ii) A broad financial review based, mainly, on the certificate of the States Finance Department, that the schemes have been drawn up in accordance with standards, schedule of rates, etc., prevailing in the States and as are applicable to States' schemes.[29]

[27] The amount of total loans against various States on March 31, 1960, amounted to Rs. 17,612 million. For analysis of loans made to states, see Lok Sabha *Debates*, 12th Session, Appendix I, p. 96.

[28] For text, see Public Accounts Committee, Second Lok Sabha, *Eighth Report* (April, 1958), Annexure I.

[29] *Ibid.*, p. 23.

These proposals were commented on by the Government of India (Ministry of Finance) and by the Planning Commission. The Government of India said the following:

With regard to No. (1)

It is felt that acceptance of the suggestion that the Centre should take the responsibility for meeting the cost of selected individual schemes rather than a share of expenditure on all the schemes of an agreed type might result in the blurring of the State Government's responsibility for execution and might create problems in the matter of selection of individual schemes to be financed by the Centre.

With regard to No. (2)

This recommendation has been made with a view to avoiding an excessive concentration of Central control in regard to States' schemes which are assisted by the Government of India. The Planning Commission at present exercise only a broad scrutiny of schemes submitted by State Governments, mainly from the point of view of principles set out in the Plan and the physical targets to be achieved. Any further scrutiny of State Governments' schemes in the Central Ministries is done in a broad way and is mainly directed to ensure the best utilisation of the funds available for the purpose. There is no interference in matters of detail.[30]

In its memorandum the Planning Commission wrote the following:

With regard to No. (1)

In view of the methods of planning which have developed and the scope of each State's plan, it is more convenient and appropriate to deal with the entire plan rather than to single out certain schemes for which full financial responsibility is accepted, leaving others to be financed from State resources alone. In relation to each State a view has to be taken of its resources as a whole as well as its outlays as a whole, both plan and non-plan. The size of Central assistance in any year has to be adjudged in terms of a State's total programme, made up of a large number of schemes, rather than in terms of certain selected schemes alone.

With regard to No. (2)

For schemes included in the plans of States, it is intended to dispense with detailed financial and administrative scrutiny and sanction at the Centre, and to leave them to the administrative departments and the Finance Departments. This follows the suggestion made by the Comptroller and Auditor-General.[31]

[30] *Ibid.*, p. 30.
[31] *Ibid.*, p. 36.

The Public Accounts Committee, examining the question of Budget Estimates and Financial Control in its Eighth Report, addressed itself to the above proposals, and the comments thereon, and recommended: (*a*) that the procedures for the allocation of Central grants to the states should be made flexible so that their utilization by the states may be improved; (*b*) that the detailed scrutiny of state schemes for approval by the Planning Commission and the Central Ministries was not necessary, since the schemes had already been approved in the course of formulating the plan and determining the pattern of assistance. "In their opinion, as the States are the executors of those schemes, the Finance Departments of the States will certainly ensure that the schemes are executed efficiently and economically. This will fasten responsibility on the Finance Departments in the States and will result in greater cooperation and speedy execution of the Plan Projects";[32] and (*c*) that to promote effective implementation of state schemes, "in the first year the Central grants towards schemes approved for matching grants should be placed at the disposal of the State Governments in advance at the commencement of the financial year with the condition that they should be utilized only on the schemes accepted for assistance. In subsequent years the grants to be made should be regulated with reference to the State's performance in the previous year in fulfilling its own part of the programme as contemplated while making the grant."[33]

The system of administering Central assistance to the states has been modified since 1958, in line with recommendations of the State Ministers' Conference held in November, 1957. Although the matching grants continue and are not replaced by block grants for specified projects, the state schemes approved for Central assistance are now grouped under suitable heads of development. Once the quantum of Central assistance to the state schemes has been determined (for which the schemes may be examined individually), the states are free to regulate the expenditure on the schemes without reference to the Central Government. However, "where the total expenditure under one group is proposed to be covered by reduction of expenditure in another group under the same head of development, the concurrence of the Central Ministry concerned should be obtained and the Plan-

[32] *Ibid.*, p. 11.
[33] *Ibid.*, p. 12.

ning Commission kept informed.   Similarly, where the same Central Ministry is concerned with more than one head of development, adjustments between them may be made in consultation with the Ministry under advice to the Planning Commission.   Where such adjustments are considered necessary as between one Ministry and another, the concurrence of the Planning Commission should be obtained, and a copy of the proposal sent simultaneously to the Ministries concerned."[34]

This system does not apply to the centrally sponsored schemes on state subjects.   They will continue to require specific approval from the administrative ministry concerned before expenditure is incurred.

Again, the Central assistance for both the state schemes and the centrally sponsored schemes is now released to the states in advance as a lump-sum ways and means by the Ministry of Finance in nine monthly instalments, these and the balance being cleared in February each year.[35]

To sum up, planning has affected Union-state relations by bringing about the evolution of over-all or comprehensive policies of development, by the establishment of new institutions, such as the Planning Commission and the National Development Council, neither of which derives its authority from the Constitution or a statute, and by evolving the procedures for the formulation and implementation of the plans on state subjects which have been described above. Nor is the plan prepared by the Commission laid before the state legislatures for their discussion and approval.   The annual plans of the states have also to be approved by the Planning Commission; the states are dependent on the Centre for financial assistance which has affected state autonomy and developed Central supervision over the administration of state subjects; and so forth.

The impact of planning on states' rights, however, is certainly not entirely adverse.   It may be argued that comprehensive planning will be desirable and justified for rapid over-all and uniform economic development throughout the country, that this has been recognized and agreed to by the political leadership of the country both at the Centre and in the states.   This has been promoted by the

[34] P. P. Agarwal, *The System of Grants-in-Aid in India* (New Delhi, 1959), pp. 22-23.
[35] For details, see P. P. Agarwal, *op. cit.*, pp. 21-23; Public Accounts Committee, *Eighth Report*, pp. 37-38.

fact that the same political party held authority in the Union and most states and that over the Planning Commission there were institutions like the National Development Council which safeguarded the interests of the states. Further it should not be forgotten that the implementation of the state plans, whether by legislation or by administrative action, is still in the hands of the states. This fact led Appleby to lament that the Centre was in fact only a large staff agency and that the states had far more money and personnel than in any other federation.[36] Nor is the scope for varying the programs by the states insignificant. Thus, for instance, there has been considerable variety in land reform legislation, whether in regard to the elimination of intermediaries, or tenancy reform, or the fixing of ceilings, or the consolidation of holdings.[37] The organization of the *Panchāyatī Rāj* institutions also varies from state to state. Ultimately, the states have not been losers in the process. Left to their own resources, the states would not be growing so rapidly. The jurisdiction of the states is still intact, despite the fact that planning has grafted new institutions and procedures. The Centre-state relations in matters of finance and administration have been modified to keep to the constitutional position guaranteed to the states. In the resulting balance, the structure of the state, though affected by planning, basically remains federal.

III. *The Planning Commission and the Finance Commission*

As will be apparent from the above section, the most significant impact of planning has been on Union-state financial relations. After making provisions for the transfer of resources from the Union to the states in the form of shared taxes and the grants, the Constitution provided for the establishment of a Finance Commission[38] to suggest the principles and the amount of such sharing. Other similar matters could also be referred to such a commission by presidential order.[39]

[36] Paul A. Appleby, *Report on Public Administration in India* (Government of India, 1953), pp. 2, 45, and 56.
[37] For details of variation in state legislation on land reform, see *Third Five Year Plan*, pp. 236-38; also Lok Sabha *Debates*, 13th Session, 1961, Appendix I, pp. 179-83.
[38] Article 280.
[39] The terms of reference of the Second Finance Commission comprised (1) the division of the proceeds of the taxes to be shared by the Union and the states, (2) the determination of the principles and the quantum of Central grants-in-aid of the

As a commission is to be appointed every five years, three commissions have so far been appointed: the first reported in 1952, the second in 1957, and the third on December 14, 1961. The last report was placed before Parliament in March, 1962.

Because the Planning Commission has established the maximum financial outlays in the state plans and has indicated the states' own resources and available Central grants, by and large, the function of the Finance Commission has been reduced to filling the gaps between the two sums. In other words, the Commission, taking into consideration the needs and revenue capacity of the states, must recommend the amount of shared taxes and statutory grants required by the states to carry out the Plan.[40] As a consequence, a curious phenomenon is noted: the constitutional commission has been subordinated in its functioning to an extra-constitutional commission.[41] Nor should it be forgotten that because of the increasing dependence of the states on the Centre for loans, the states are less dependent on the shared taxes and statutory grants, although their quantum is not insignificant.

We might quote here the views of the Second Finance Commission with regard to its relations with the Planning Commission:

Some anomalies inevitably arise where the functions of the two Commissions, the Finance Commission and the Planning Commission, overlap. The former is a statutory body with limited functions, while the latter has to deal comprehensively with the finances of the Union and the States in the widest sense of the term. So long as both these Commissions have to function, there appears to be a real need for effectively coordinating

revenues of the states having regard, among other considerations, to (a) the requirements of the Second Five Year Plan, and (b) the efforts made by those states to raise additional revenue from the sources available to them, (3) the determination of principles by which the proceeds of Central taxes and duties will be given over to the states, and (4) the suggestion of modification, if any, in the rates of interest and the terms of repayment of Central loans to the states.

[40] Thus, for instance, the Second Finance Commission assessed the total developmental (Plan) expenditure on revenue account of the states as Rs. 7,090 million, which was to be financed by Rs. 2,060 million by additional taxation and Rs. 2,750 million from Central grants under Article 282, thus leaving a balance of Rs. 2,280 million, which the Commission had to provide to the states out of Central revenues to enable them to implement the Plan. See *Report of the Finance Commission*, 1957, p. 47.

[41] The basic limitation in the competence of the Finance Commission in regard to the grants-in-aid may, however, be noted: the Commission is concerned only with the principles which should govern the giving of Central grants-in-aid of the *revenues* of the state. It does not deal with the financing of state developmental expenditure on capital account.

their work. It will be an advantage if, in future, the period covered by the recommendations of a Finance Commission coincides with that of a five year plan. Further, it is desirable to eliminate the necessity of making two separate assessments of the needs of the States.[42]

Asok Chanda, chairman of the Third Finance Commission, addressing a Rotary Club meeting at Jaipur, Rajasthan, on September 12, 1961, is reported to have suggested that some demarcation should be made between the authority and functions of the Planning Commission and the Finance Commission; the Planning Commission could be given a place in the Constitution or the two could even be fused.[43]

A little later, commenting on the Madras Government's Memorandum to the Third Finance Commission, K. Santhanam, chairman of the Second Finance Commission, wrote the following:

Chapter I of Part XII of the Constitution which regulates the financial relations between the Union and the States is based on two major assumptions. The first is that the main assistance required from the Centre would be in the nature of shares in taxes and grants towards the recurring revenue expenditure of the States. Though under Article 293, the Government of India is empowered to make loans to States or give guarantees in respect of loans raised by them, it was contemplated that normally the capital needs of a State would be met by its own borrowing. The second assumption is that the Finance Commission would be the chief instrument for determining the subventions and grants and the discretionary power under Article 282 would be used only for special emergencies like famines and floods or other natural calamities.

Both these assumptions have now broken down on account of the adoption of the policy of planned development under the guidance of a Central Planning Commission.[44]

The Third Finance Commission in its report discussed by Parliament on March 13, 1962, made proposals for adjustments in the functioning of the Finance Commission and the Planning Commission.[45]

The Commission's recommendations of constitutional significance relate mainly to the grants-in-aid under article 275. The Commission

[42] Report of the Finance Commission, 1957, p. 13.
[43] Hindustan Times (Delhi ed.), Sept. 14, 1961, p. 5. See also ibid., Sept. 15, 1961, p. 7 (editorial), and Sept. 16, 1961, p. 5.
[44] The Hindu, Oct. 17, 1961, p. 6. See also Santhanam, Union-State Relations in India, pp. 51-52.
[45] Government of India, Report of the (Third) Finance Commission, 1961 (New Delhi, 1961). See esp. par. 71, 81-83, 93-94.

examined the question of the impact of planning on Union-state financial relations and noted the increasing dependence of states on Central discretionary grants made under article 282, the constitutional validity of which the Commission seemed to challenge. The report mentioned that although the assistance given under this article was 48.7 per cent of the total Central grant in 1952-53, it was 80.2 per cent in 1961-62. Since the Constitution did not anticipate the bifurcation between the plan and non-plan needs of a state, the Commission suggested that the budgetary gap of a state on both these accounts should be filled by statutory grants under article 275. However, recognizing the need for flexibility in planning and for adequate promotion of national policies by the Centre, the Commission recommended that 75 per cent of the revenue component of a state plan should be given to the state as statutory grants under article 275. A note of dissent was written by the member-secretary of the Commission who indicated how plan financing under article 282 was necessary to promote uniformity of policy throughout the country and to enforce responsibility on the part of the states. The government accepted the dissenting note and rejected this majority recommendation of the Commission.

The Commission made the following additional recommendations:

(1) It expressed concern at its status vis-à-vis the Planning Commission and suggested that to avoid unnecessary duplication and consequent frustration in its functioning, either the jurisdiction of the Finance Commission should be increased and the Commission should be authorized to examine the total financial needs of the states both on revenue account and on capital account, or else the Planning Commission might be constituted as the Finance Commission at the appropriate time.

(2) An independent commission should be established to make a comprehensive examination of the tax potential of each state, to review its tax structure and to recommend rates under different heads of levies in the state list. This commission should also review the impact of planning on Union-state financial relations in general and make appropriate recommendations regarding the redistribution of resources between the Union and the states, so as to ensure the adequacy of states' resources to meet their development needs.

Shri K. Santhanam, Chairman of the Second Finance Commission, in reviews[46] of the report of the Third Finance Commission has congratulated the majority of the Commission in making the bold recommendation for the financing of state plans under article 275 and also for the recommendation regarding the establishment of a high power Commission to rationalize Union-state financial relations in the new context of large-scale planning. He, however, did not approve of the appointment of a special commission to examine the tax potential of a state which was the function of the Planning Commission itself, and which could more effectively be done by a special department within the Planning Commission.

IV. *Public Undertakings*[47]

An attendant problem of the decision to industrialize the country rapidly by government initiative, as contemplated in the Industrial Policy Resolutions of 1948 and 1956 and provided in the Plans, was the manner of establishing the host of business, manufacturing, financial, promotional, and other undertakings. The number has been increasing rapidly since 1950. At present there are over a hundred such public bodies under the Central Government, organized either departmentally, or under a statute, or in company form, or as boards, authorities, or commissions.[48] In almost all cases the

---

[46] *The Hindu,* March 16, 1962, p. 4 and March 24, 1962, p. 6.

[47] The literature on public undertakings is extensive. The following materials will give a fairly comprehensive picture: Public Accounts Committee, First Lok Sabha, *Third Report* (Dec., 1952); Estimates Committee, First Lok Sabha, *Ninth Report* (May, 1954), *Sixteenth Report* (June, 1955), Second Lok Sabha, *Seventy-Third Report* (Feb., 1960) and *Eightieth Report* (April, 1960); Asok Chanda, *Indian Administration,* pp. 194-203; S. S. Khera, "Government and Public Enterprises—Problems in Communication and Control," *Indian Journal of Public Administration,* VII (July-Sept., 1961), pp. 331-44; N. C. Srivastava, "Management of State Industrial Undertakings," *ibid.,* pp. 345-52; Krishna Menon Committee Report on *Parliamentary Supervision over State Undertakings,* 1959; Indian Institute of Public Administration, *The Question of Parliamentary Committee for Public Enterprises,* Oct., 1960; H. C. Dasappa, "Parliamentary Control and Accountability of Public Undertakings," *Indian Journal of Public Administration,* VII (April-June, 1961), 136-44; *Third Five Year Plan,* chap. xvi; a comprehensive bibliography can be found in "Problems and Prospects of Public Enterprise in India—A Syndicate Study," *Journal of the National Academy of Administration,* July, 1961, pp. 86-180.

[48] For a list of these undertakings, see Estimates Committee, Second Lok Sabha, *Seventy-Third Report,* Appendix I, pp. 14-16. The list comprises 14 statutory corporations, 45 government companies, 8 committees, 7 boards, 1 commission, 3 councils and 3 miscellaneous. A list of 34 industrial undertakings is also given in *Third Five Year Plan,* pp. 274-75.

undertakings were started from scratch by the Central Government. Hence the financing of their share capital or loans has been done from the Consolidated Fund of India. It is estimated that the total Central investment in these undertakings at the beginning of 1960 was of the order of Rs. 7,650 million.[49] By 1965-66 the investment on industries and minerals alone will have reached Rs. 24,000 million.[50] The public undertakings are expected to contribute Rs. 4,500 million, excluding another Rs. 1,000 million from railways, to the resources of the Third Plan.[51]

The principal constitutional problems raised by public undertakings are those relating to their organization, their relations with the Central Government, the role of the Comptroller and Auditor-General, and their accountability to Parliament.

By and large, the type of organization of an undertaking determines its relations with the government, the Comptroller and Auditor-General, and Parliament. The public undertakings are mainly organized into three types: (1) departmental, such as railways and related manufacturing units for locomotives and coaches, (2) statutory corporations, comprising mainly public utility undertakings, enterprises which not being commercially self-supporting have to be financed by regular grants from government, and enterprises which involve exercise of powers which can be conferred only by legislation, and (3) government companies comprising enterprises for the manufacture and sale of articles. The departmental undertakings are by and large under the over-all supervision and control of the government and are subjected to full scrutiny of Parliament. Their accounts are audited by the Comptroller and Auditor-General in the same way as those of other government departments. The statutes creating corporations prescribe the relations between the undertaking and the government, such as in matters of financing, expenditure control beyond a specified limit, allocation of profits, and submission of reports. They generally provide for audit either by the Comptroller and Auditor-General exclusively, as in the case of the Damodar Valley Corporation, or by professional auditors including an appointee of the Comptroller and Auditor-General, as in the case of the Industrial Finance Corporation and the Central Ware-

[49] Estimates Committee, *Seventy-Third Report*, p. 1.
[50] N. C. Srivastava, *op. cit.*, p. 345.
[51] *Third Five Year Plan*, p. 95.

housing Corporation, although audit by the Comptroller and Auditor-General is excluded in the case of the Life Insurance Corporation and the State Bank of India. The statutes also require the submission of budgets, or annual reports, or audited accounts to Parliament. The government companies,[52] which have been proliferating, have been rather suspect from the viewpoint of audit and parliamentary control, and informed parliamentary and other attention has been concentrated on the question of their responsible administration. Initially, they were not only established and financed by the government but were staffed by government officials, who constituted the boards of directors. The managing directors were mostly officials. In fact, they functioned like any other department, which for a business or an industrial enterprise led to serious complaints, irregularities, delays, and inefficiency and affected production adversely.[53] On the other hand, they escaped parliamentary accountability on the ground that they were autonomous and functioned under the company law. This prompted the Comptroller and Auditor-General to initiate an intensive attack on this aspect of the government's activity. In a statement before a subcommittee of the Public Accounts Committee (December 13, 1952) he said:

These 'Private Ltd.' Companies are, in my opinion a fraud on the Companies Act and also on the Constitution, because money cannot be taken away from the Consolidated Fund for the establishment and transformation of certain concerns into Private Companies in the name of the President and Secretary to Government. Under the Companies Act, a Company can be formed by a group of persons. The President or the Secretary to Government is not a person. These officers do not have any personal financial interest in the Company, and their joining together cannot constitute a Company in the correct sense of the term. Further to convert a Government concern into a Private Company solely by executive action is unconstitutional. While recognising that the management of industrial and business concerns differs from normal day to day activities of administration and that special organisation and delegation of authority more in accordance with the speedier business practices may be necessary,

[52] A government company is defined under section 617 of the Indian Companies Act, 1956, as amended in 1960, as a company "in which no less than fifty-one per cent of the paid-up share capital is held by the Central Government or by any State Government or Governments, or partly by the Central Government and partly by one or more State Governments, and includes a company which is a subsidiary of a Government company as thus defined."

[53] See Estimates Committee, First Lok Sabha, *Ninth Report*, p. 16; *Sixteenth Report*, pp. 4-5.

the Government should have the backing of suitable Parliamentary enactment for the setting up of Corporations.

There is another important point involved in this procedure of creating a Private Company under the Indian Companies Act. Private Companies are to be audited by Auditors nominated by the Board of Directors. The Comptroller and Auditor-General will not, therefore, have any automatic right to audit such a Company. It is likely to be argued that his audit control is thus ousted. It is true that the Company may request him to be the Auditor if necessary by incorporating suitable provisions in its Articles of Association, but this would be neither proper nor binding as the Comptroller and Auditor-General's duties and functions are prescribed by Parliament, and cannot be regulated by the Articles of Association of a Company. Furthermore, even if he undertakes audit on a 'consent' basis, on payment of fees, he can only submit his Audit Report to the Company, and not to Parliament through the President. Parliament cannot watch through the Public Accounts Committee the regularity of the operations and the financial results of any such Company. These observations also apply to concerns in the form of Private Companies in which Government take substantial share capital or guarantee against losses.

I regard the entire procedure adopted in these cases as unconstitutional and invalid, and hold that I have a right to exercise audit on the accounts of the Company on the basis that by an improper diversion of funds they should not escape my audit scrutiny.[54]

This and other criticisms of the Public Accounts Committee and the Estimates Committee led to the amendment of the Indian Companies Act in 1956, bringing the companies within the audit scrutiny of the Comptroller and Auditor-General. The Act was further amended in 1960. The Act now requires that the auditor of a government company shall be appointed or re-appointed by the Central Government on the advice of the Comptroller and Auditor-General. He may give instructions to the auditor regarding the manner in which the company's accounts shall be audited and conduct a supplementary or test audit of the company's accounts. The audited report may also be supplemented by the Comptroller and Auditor-General and, in this form, placed before the annual general meeting of the company and also before Parliament.[55]

The relations between the government and the companies are

[54] Public Accounts Committee, First Lok Sabha, *Third Report* (Dec., 1952), pp. 12-13.

[55] Sections 619 and 619A of the Indian Companies Act I of 1956 as amended by the Amendment Act LXV of 1960. See also Asok Chanda, *Indian Administration*, pp. 201-2.

generally regulated by the articles of association of the companies, which provide, *inter alia*, for the appointment of directors, managing director, and chairmen by the President, the approval by the government of all appointments carrying a salary of Rs. 2,500 per month and the approval of capital expenditure beyond a specified limit. The President may also be authorized to give general directions to the company regarding finance and the conduct of the business, while the chairman may be authorized to reserve any important issue for the consideration of the President. These provisions have been modified since 1958, giving in effect more financial responsibility to the boards of directors. For the past two or three years the government has been issuing Instruments of Instructions containing the general directions of the government to the Companies.[56]

The Companies Act also requires the companies to prepare annual reports within three months of the holding of their general meeting. The report, along with the audit report and the comments of the Comptroller and Auditor-General, shall be laid before both Houses of Parliament in the case of Central Government companies and the state legislatures in the case of state government companies.[57] Parliament has become increasingly eager to bring within the pale of accountability all government companies and other institutions, on which monies from the Consolidated Fund of India have been spent. The present opportunities for Parliament to review arise in the question hour, during the debates on the budget and the demands for grants, the consideration motions relating to the reports of the undertakings, and in the reports of the Public Accounts Committee and the Estimates Committee. Since July, 1957, a subcommittee on Public Undertakings of the Estimates Committee has been established. Apart from the detailed examination of the working of some public undertakings, the subcommittee has issued a number of reports of a general nature.[58] However, these parliamentary procedures have not been considered adequate.

[56] S. S. Khera, *op. cit.*, pp. 333-34.
[57] Section 639 of the Indian Companies Act, 1956. This section has now been made 619A by the Amendment Act LXV of 1960.
Sections 617-620 of the Indian Companies Act, as amended in 1960, relate to the Government companies. For text and notes on these provisions, see A. Ramaiya, *A Guide to the Companies Act* (2nd ed., Madras, 1961), pp. 546-548.
[58] See, for example, the *Seventy-Third Report* and the *Eightieth Report* in February and April 1960 respectively. For a history of the establishment of the subcommittee and a review of its working, see Dasappa, *op. cit.*, pp. 136-44.

The subject of the legitimate degree of autonomy for the companies has been examined since 1958 by a committee of the Congress party in the Parliament under the chairmanship of V. K. Krishna Menon. The committee reported in 1959, and the report has been debated extensively since then. Reportedly, the government has, by and large, agreed to its main recommendations, in particular to the suggestion for establishing a parliamentary committee to review or oversee the working of these undertakings. A controversy has arisen as to whether this committee should consist of members from both Houses of Parliament or whether its membership should be restricted to the Lok Sabha. The committee's competence will combine the functions performed now by the Public Accounts Committee and the Estimates Committee's Subcommittee on Public Undertakings.[59]

Thus, even in regard to government companies, institutions and procedures affecting their relations with the government and Parliament are in the process of evolution. In due course Parliament will be able to approve the formation of companies, secure regular and timely reports from them, and through the Committee on Public Undertakings, review their over-all functioning. The parliamentary review, while assuring complete accountability and responsibility of the undertakings to the people's representatives, should encourage the undertakings to be productive and fulfil, if not exceed, expectations.

* * *

To conclude, it may be observed that planning, which has been done in the context of a federal state and a parliamentary democracy, has modified both in the interests of a rapid economic and social development. Planning machinery and procedures, established neither under the Constitution nor under a statute, have grafted new institutions which have affected the functioning of political institutions, the governmental machinery, the budgeting procedures, the Union-state financial relations, the role of the Finance Commission, and so forth. Planning has also raised problems of the organization of public undertakings and their relations to the government and to Parliament. The approach to these problems has, by and large, been pragmatic, and suitable institutions and procedures have been

[59] *Hindustan Times* (Delhi edition), Nov. 22, 1961, p. 9, and Nov. 25, 1961, p. 6; *Indian Institute of Public Administration Newsletter*, Dec., 1961.

emerging. Notwithstanding these extensive influences, planning has not, it must be noted, disrupted the constitutional framework in its vitals. Structurally, the country remains basically federal, even to the extent of eliciting comments that it impedes national integration and that what the country needs for an efficient administration and rapid economic development is a unitary government. Parliamentary democracy has also grown roots in the country and, with the changes suggested in the composition and functioning of the Planning Commission so as to continue it as an effective staff agency, will be further strengthened.

The harmonious functioning of responsible governments at the Centre and in the states and their interrelationships have been facilitated by the fact that the same political party is in power throughout the country, which might not continue forever. The other factor promoting this harmony has been the financial power wielded by the Centre. Although the Union-state financial relations should be rationalized, as suggested by the Third Finance Commission in its report (1961) so as to support that states' functional autonomy with adequate financial resources, the interests of national growth on a uniform basis, which require extra resources at the disposal of the Centre to promote them, must not be affected adversely. In other words, both the Union and the states should increase in strength.

7

The Influence of Caste on Indian
Economic Development

Robert O. Tilman

> Transformation of an underdeveloped society into a developed
> one entails transformation of the contents of the minds of the elite
> who direct and of the men who man such underdeveloped society.
> Above all it entails transformation of the contents of the minds of
> individuals who are interacting in ways significant for politico-
> economic development.[1]

THIS ESSAY IS BASED on the assumptions that social mobility is a
condition necessary for economic modernization,[2] that the value
system basic to the traditional idea of caste is inimical to social mobility, and that the success of Indian economic development is therefore dependent in part upon the outcome of the interaction between
the inertia of tradition and the forces of change.

Beginning with this postulate, I shall attempt in this essay to
appraise the hold of traditional caste ideas on the minds of present-
day Indians. To make this appraisal I shall survey available writings
to determine the reaction of the traditional caste system to environmental conditions dissimilar to those in which caste developed and
crystallized throughout Indian history.[3] A change in the environmental setting surrounding caste is seen to take place in two ways:
villagers may move to urban centers, thus transferring their caste

[1] Joseph J. Spengler, "Theory, Ideology, Non-Economic Values, and Politico-
Economic Development," in Ralph Braibanti and Joseph J. Spengler, eds., *Tradition,
Values, and Socio-Economic Development* (Durham, 1961), pp. 3-56 at 5.
[2] This assumption is examined in greater detail in a later section. See *infra*,
pp. 211-13.
[3] This study represents an analysis of published and unpublished research. It
is not based on the author's personal observations in the field.

attitudes and practices into an alien environment;[4] or the forces of modernization may be injected into the villages by increased economic intercourse across village lines, by community development projects, by increased movements of people in and out of the villages, and by mass media of communications that penetrate to the village level. Several, or all, of these factors may of course be in operation at the same time.

After surveying these writings I shall point out certain apparent trends growing out of the interaction between the old and the new. I shall conclude with certain extrapolations based on the *a priori* assumption that the reaction of caste-oriented Indians in an environment foreign to the traditional caste idea provides a reliable measure of the response of the indigenous social system to the intrusive forces of change.[5]

The Meaning of Caste

Careless use of the English word "caste" has been the source of considerable confusion.[6] On the one hand, the term is used to describe in the broadest sense the total system of social stratification peculiar to India; on the other hand, it is used to denote three, per-

[4] For a discussion of the character of the population that is likely to migrate from the villages to the urban centers, see Morris D. Morris, "Caste and the Evolution of the Industrial Work Force in India," *Proceedings of the American Philosophical Society*, CIV (April, 1960), 125-27. Morris concludes that with a lack of reliable statistical information it is impossible at this time to form generalizations about the caste composition and income levels of these migrants. A related point must also be mentioned. As at least one author has shown, care must be exercised in defining a "rural" and an "urban" setting. See Richard Dewey, "The Rural-Urban Continuum: Real but Relatively Unimportant," *American Journal of Sociology*, LXVI (July, 1960), 60-66. While it may be true that it is growing increasingly difficult in advanced societies to draw a sharp distinction between the terms "rural" and "urban," the contrast seems to be sufficiently marked in India at this time to permit the use of the terms as a tool of analysis.

[5] However, cf. Morris, *op. cit.*, p. 124. Morris, citing a previous study by Bert F. Hoselitz ("The City, the Factory, and Economic Growth," *American Economic Review*, XLV [May, 1955], 166-84), begins his essay with the assumption that "unfortunately, the effects of urbanization are not necessarily the same as the effects of the industrial environment."

[6] "Caste" derives from the Portuguese word *casta*, "breed, race or kind." The Portuguese of the sixteenth century applied the term indiscriminately to the various social and occupational groups found in the subcontinent, and the confusion has continued to the present time. For the probable evolution of the meaning as it is used today, see J. H. Hutton, *Caste in India* (Cambridge, 1946), p. 42. For an illuminating discussion illustrating the complexity of defining "caste," see Adrian C. Mayer, *Caste and Kinship in Central India* (Berkeley, 1960), pp. 3-10.

204 ADMINISTRATION AND ECONOMIC DEVELOPMENT IN INDIA

haps four, more or less distinct aspects of this total system. In this essay the term will be used in the first sense; when more particular aspects of the total system are intended, transliterations of Indic words will be employed.

The four great divisions of Hindu society (*brāhman, kṣatriya, vaiśya*, and *śūdra*), usually referred to as the four *varṇa*, are probably historically the earliest classifications.[7] Superimposed upon these endogamous social strata are two additional systems of stratification, the *jāti* and the *gōtra*. The *jāti*, which is usually endogamous and craft-exclusive, is often referred to as a "sub-caste," for these strata rarely if ever cut across the lines of the four *varṇa*. By contrast, the *gōtra*, or clan, described by Hutton as "an exogamous unit of individuals theoretically descended from a single ancestor,"[8] cuts freely across *jāti* lines and possibly across *varṇa* lines (though it exists primarily in the *brāhman varṇa*). To this confusion of interlocking hierarchies we must add yet a fourth division when dealing with South India, where by the time of the *Cōla* period (*ca.* 850-1267) there had occurred a great and still unexplained bisection of the *śūdra varṇa* into the "*jātis* of the left hand" and the "*jātis* of the right hand," a division that still exists today and is reflected in the continuing rivalry between *jātis* of opposing hands.[9]

Varṇa in its broadest meaning denotes color, and from this many writers have placed great emphasis on racial characteristics as social determinants.[10] Traditionally, according to the literature of Hindu-

[7] While this is the generally accepted view, it has been disputed in some detail by Iravati Karve. Professor Karve argues that the *jāti* system existed in India prior to the arrival of the Aryans. The invaders also brought with them a class system, and the two systems then had to become accommodated to each other, usually on a local basis. For the most thorough treatment of this thesis, see "The Hindu Society—A New Interpretation," a series of three papers presented before the South Asia Colloquium, University of California, 1959-60 (Berkeley, 1959-60, mimeographed). Also see Professor Karve's essay dealing with this and related subjects in less detail, "Some Aspects of the Organisation of the Caste-Society of the Hindus," in N. V. Sovani and V. M. Dandekar, eds., *Changing India* (Bombay, 1961), pp. 143-66.
[8] Hutton, *op. cit.*, p. 48. According to Indian tradition, all *brāhmans* are descended from one of a number of legendary seers, after whom *gōtra* names are derived. *Gōtras* are not strictly a part of the caste stratification since they are exogamous, are not craft-exclusive, and are to be found across *varṇa* lines. We shall therefore not be directly concerned with the *gōtra* in this essay.
[9] A. L. Basham, *The Wonder That Was India* (London, 1954), p. 150.
[10] For a convenient summary of the views of earlier writers on the origins of caste, see Hutton, *op. cit.*, pp. 146-57. Iravati Karve does not accept the view that the original meaning of *varṇa* was "color." The author argues that in the early sacred literature and in grammatical works *varṇa* meant "class." Professor Karve

ism, each *varṇa* was assigned a broad occupational field within which its members were theoretically confined.[11] Thus, members of the *brāhman varṇa* were to study, teach, and offer sacrifices, generally fulfilling the role of a priestly and intellectual elite. The *kṣatriya* consisted of the warrior class and the governing nobility, while mundane but necessary matters such as trading, sheepherding, and land management fell to the *vaiśya*. These three classes constituted the wearers of the sacred thread, or the "twice born"; beneath them fell the *śūdra*, low in the hierarchy but still within the pale of Hinduism. For the *śūdras*, or serfs, "the Lord has prescribed only one occupation. . . , namely, service without malice of . . . these other classes."[12] These traditional duties were fixed, and it was better to "do one's duty badly than another's well."[13]

The stratification system that most directly affects the daily lives of the Indian people, and the system with which I shall be chiefly concerned in this essay, is the *jāti*. It is difficult to date the origins of this social institution. Hints of such stratifications occur early in Indian history, yet there is considerable evidence pointing to a much later date for the origin of the system as it exists today. Later *Vedic* literature (*ca.* 900-500 B.C.), in cataloguing the various trades and professions, perhaps contains the germ that was eventually to grow into the *jāti* system. There is further evidence that there existed at least an occupational consciousness as early as *ca.* 300 B.C., when the Macedonian ambassador Megasthenes, in a report from the Mauryan court at Pataliputra, noted the existence of seven endogamous, craft-exclusive classes: (1) philosophers, (2) husbandmen, (3) herdsmen and hunters, (4) artisans, laborers and tradespeople, (5) soldiers, (6) overseers, and (7) councillors and assessors.[14]

continues that "at a later time the word . . . came to mean 'color' and the fourfold division of the ancients was then taken to be based on a physical feature, namely, color." See "The Hindu Society—A New Interpretation," Part I, pp. 22-24.

[11] On the writings of traditional Hinduism delineating *varṇas*, see William T. de Bary, ed., *Sources of Indian Tradition* (New York, 1958), pp. 224-26.

[12] *Manu Smṛti*, 1.87-98, translated in de Bary, *op. cit.*, p. 225. In this selection the *varṇa dharma*, or class duties, are defined. The *Manu Smṛti*, or *Code of Manu*, dating from about the second century B.C., was traditionally regarded as one of the authoritative sources of orthodox Hinduism.

[13] *Manu Smṛti*, 10.97, quoted in Basham, *op. cit.*, p. 138.

[14] There is no extant manuscript of Megasthenes' report, but it has been reconstructed from Greek and Latin sources. See J. W. McCrindle, *Ancient India as Described by Megasthenes and Arrian* (rev. ed.; Calcutta, 1926), pp. 1-178 at 83-86. According to this translation, the duties of "overseers" seem more akin to those of the ancient Chinese censors than to the duties of supervisors or foremen.

The importance of occupational considerations in the *jāti* system led some early writers to regard occupation or craft as the sole basis of the institution. Nesfield, for example, regards the *jāti* as the logical extension of guild-like organizations, the more difficult of which have taken progressive precedence over those considered to require less skill.[15] Sir Edward Blunt, although hesitant to accept a single factor to the exclusion of others, nevertheless places great emphasis upon an occupational basis for the evolution of the *jāti* system and goes so far as to attempt a twelvefold hierarchical classification of occupational duties, listing the various *jātis* that constitute each of the functional classifications.[16] Most scholars today consider occupation of great importance but only one of the many factors that contributed to the origin and development of the caste system in general and the *jāti* system in particular.[17]

We do not know when the *jāti* crystallized into the institution that exists today. Blunt, noting a legend of the twelfth century that first mentions the word *jāti* in its modern meaning, fixes the date of the "last stage in the evolution of the caste system . . . between the second half of the seventh, and the end of the twelfth century, A.D."[18] Basham prefers a slightly later date. In his view, after the conquest of India by the Muslim invaders—and, though some writers would disagree, throughout the period of British rule—the caste system fulfilled a definite social function, for, whatever might have been its inherent disadvantages,

the organization of the castes, independent of the government, and with social ostracism as its most severe sanction, was a powerful factor in the survival of Hinduism. The Hindu, living under an alien political order

---

Present-day scholarship questions the accuracy of Megasthenes' account. For example, see Basham, *op. cit.*, pp. 147-48.

[15] J. C. Nesfield, *Brief View of the Caste System of the North-West Provinces* (Allahabad, 1885), cited in Hutton, *op. cit.*, pp. 146-47.

[16] Blunt, *op. cit.*, chap. xii, esp. pp. 247-50.

[17] Hutton, *op. cit.*, pp. 164-65, for example, lists fifteen possible factors. Ramkrishna Mukherjee begins his discussion of caste on the assumption that "it is likely that several factors working conjointly led in course of time to the emergence of the Indian caste system; its social, economic, and ideological facets being specifically influenced by several factors." See *The Dynamics of a Rural Society* (Berlin, 1957), p. 61. The *jāti*, however, Mukherjee regards as the unique feature of Indian caste that sets it apart from other systems of social stratification, and he places primary emphasis on the economic origins of the total Indian caste system. See esp. pp. 62-67.

[18] Blunt, *op. cit.*, p. 19.

. . . retained his cultural individuality largely through his caste, which received most of the loyalty elsewhere felt toward king, nation and city.[19]

One last point remains to be considered: the relation of *jāti* to *varṇa*. Unhappily, the relationship is not altogether clear. The classical interpretation has been that the *varṇas* constituted the primary system and that growing out of these were the sub-castes, or *jāti*. This view, however, is no longer accepted, except in a most general sense. Most writers agree that *jāti* and *varṇa* emerged more or less separately but simultaneously as a result of different sets of historic influences, and that each "developed as an organic response to the requirements of the particular case."[20] *Varṇa*, on the one hand, probably represents a broad scale of distinctions between the immigrants and the indigenous population, while, on the other hand, *jātis* arose as a logical compartmentalization of society in response to the parochialism and localism of traditional Indian life. Whatever the specific origins, it seems evident that the complex structure "did not develop out of the four Aryan *varṇas*" and that "the two systems have never been thoroughly harmonized."[21]

The Characteristics of Caste

I shall next consider several general characteristics of the caste system that are important to the present study. No attempt need be made to distinguish between characteristics peculiar to a particular stratification system and those common to the total caste system. Moreover, when dealing with caste characteristics I shall be speaking of the system as it is ideally envisioned; the actualities of caste will be considered later.

First, as we have seen, the caste system is ideally composed of rigidly endogamous units. Intermarriage is frequently governed not only by the *varṇa* and the *jāti* but also by the sub-*jāti* and, in many cases, by limitations imposed by the extended kinship system. Thus, it usually happens that no village bachelor is considered eligible or

[19] Basham, *op. cit.*, p. 151. Karve, "The Hindu Society—A New Interpretation," *passim*, holds the view that *jātis* existed in India at the time of the Aryan invasions.

[20] Hutton, *op. cit.*, p. 1. Cf. Basham, *op. cit.*, p. 149. In the writings of traditional Hinduism sub-castes were seen to arise as a result of inter-marriages among different *varṇas*. See de Bary, *op. cit.*, pp. 226-28.

[21] Basham, *op. cit.*, pp. 149-50.

attractive for marriage and the girl's family must therefore extend its search for a suitable mate to neighboring villages. Under such strict conditions of endogamy the search for a mate can be lengthy and tedious.[22]

Second, as a means of guaranteeing ritual purity, the caste system prescribes rules of commensality and food-handling in very specific detail. The upper strata of the hierarchy must interdine only with certain other levels—frequently only their own equals or superiors— and this rule extends in turn to each of the levels from top to bottom. Moreover, there are many groups that cannot take food from the lowest members of the fourth *varṇa*, the "unclean" *śūdras*, and some in the higher levels who accept food only from equals or superiors.[23] Similar rules apply to the drawing of water. As a means of guaranteeing symbolic purity, each village usually has separate wells for higher and lower castes, with water-drawing privileges informally but rigidly assigned according to social status.[24]

Third, craft-exclusiveness is maintained by strict hereditary succession of the male offspring to the occupation of the father. Theoretically, at least, this perpetuates an unchanging division of labor and establishes the social immobility so necessary to the effective operation of the *jajmānī* system.[25]

---

[22] The "search for a bridegroom" in the village of "Rampur" (the name is fictitious) is well described in Oscar Lewis, *Village Life in Northern India* (Urbana, 1958), pp. 163-69.

[23] It is impossible to generalize on the subject of food handling without greatly oversimplifying the relationships. There is, for example, a sharp distinction drawn between *kaccā* (food cooked in water) and *pakkā* (food cooked in ghee). Rules regarding the handling of the latter are generally more liberal than rules governing *kaccā*.

[24] For example, see Lewis, *op. cit.*, p. 8, and Mayer, *op. cit.*, pp. 52-53.

[25] Literally, *jajmān* means "sacrifice," or, later, "gift." In the traditional village economy there existed (and to a lesser extent continues to exist) a complicated hereditary system of bartering, including both goods and services. To quote from the pioneer study of the *jajmānī* system as it functioned in North India: "Each individual has a fixed economic and social status, established by his birth in any given caste. If he is born into a carpenter family, he finds himself related by blood to carpenters exclusively. . . . The men folk in all of these families earn their livelihood through the carpentry trade, sometimes supplemented by agriculture. Each carpenter has his own clientele, which has become established through custom, and which continues from generation to generation. . . . The relationship fixes responsibilities both on the carpenter and the one whom he serves. The carpenter during the sowing season must remove and sharpen the plough point once or twice a week. During the harvest he must keep sickles sharp and renew handles as often as demanded. He must be ready to repair a cart whenever called upon by a customer, or to make minor repairs on the customer's house. In exchange he receives at each harvest, twenty-eight pounds of grain, for every plough owned by

A last general practice that must be mentioned is, in truth, a con-comitant rather than an integral characteristic of the caste system. The practice of untouchability[26] exists not within the caste system but outside it; the untouchables are those who by birth (or, in some cases, by outcasting) fall outside the major classifications. Un-touchability itself is graduated; the touch of upper untouchables may not necessarily be defiling, while lower levels of this general stratum may be considered so ritually impure that their presence alone is sufficient to require ceremonial ablutions and they are therefore re-quired to warn caste Hindus of their impending arrival on the scene by producing some warning noise. Moreover, the classification of "untouchable" is not consistent throughout India except in the case of a few groups. Exterior castes, to use Hutton's term, in one area are not necessarily considered as untouchables elsewhere in India.

Broadly speaking then, the Hindu caste system is a scheme of rigid social and economic stratification that would appear to render the individual and the group hopelessly immobile. However, given human nature as it is, theory and practice in such matters frequently fail to coincide perfectly.

The caste laws probably best kept over a long period of time were those regarding endogamy and commensality. To be sure, there were occasional eccentrics, romantic couples, and ambitious non-conformists, but the severity of the social sanctions that were applied to them kept their imitators few.[27]

Craft-exclusiveness was another matter, for fertility is no re-spector of the *jajmānī* system. In a small village, should several sons be born into a family occupation already overcrowded, it is clear that

his client." See William H. Wiser, *The Hindu Jajmani System* (2nd ed.; Lucknow, 1958), pp. xvii-xviii. Wiser's study was first published in 1936 and remains a definitive analysis of the system. Also see Thomas O. Beidelman, *A Comparative Analysis of the Jajmani System* (Locust Valley, 1959); and Lewis, *op. cit.*, pp. 55-84.

[26] "Untouchables," as a general descriptive term for all who fall without the four *varṇa*, is actually a misnomer. There are many terms also applied to the group: for example, underprivileged, depressed, or backward classes, scheduled or exterior castes, or, a term coined by their champion Gandhi, which has gained wide acceptance, *harijans* (literally, God's people).

[27] The most severe sanction might be outcasting by the caste *panchāyat* and ostracism by the village *panchāyat*. Two examples of threatened village ostracism are described in F. G. Bailey, *Caste and the Economic Frontier* (Manchester, 1957), pp. 107, 222. For a description of the punishment imposed by several caste *panchāyats*, see G. S. Ghurye, *Caste and Class in India* (Bombay, 1957), pp. 3-4. Village and caste ostracism together are not unlike the Japanese village sanction, *mura hachibu*.

one or more of these must move to another village or change occupations. If there are similarly no vacancies for the son's trade in surrounding villages, there is thus no choice. Early Hindu literature recognized that such hardships might arise, and there emerged the practice of alternative "duties when in distress" (*āpad-dharma*), the means by which limited horizontal mobility might take place.[28]

Although upward mobility is far more difficult, a number of aspiring Hindus have accomplished it. For the most part vertical social movement seems limited to groups rather than individuals, although many an Indian, upon arriving in a new village, must have successfully emulated the customs and rituals of a higher caste and thus gained acceptance not due him by birthright. As an example of this group mobility, in Bengal, the Yogi (a weaver *jāti*) succeeded in moving into the *brāhman varṇa* in the space of just twenty years (1911-31) thanks to the concerted efforts of the caste *panchāyats*, which undertook to rewrite the caste history—thereby discovering the true noble origins of the *jāti*—and then to enlighten members on the duties and privileges of the newly acquired status.[29]

Although most writers are agreed that the caste system over a long period of time has proved considerably more flexible in terms of social mobility than the orthodox literature would seem to suggest, in the last analysis examples of its flexibility in the past have been limited almost exclusively to group efforts. An individual may rise in the social scale, but to do so he often must carry his group with him.[30] Moreover, the climb necessitates rigid group discipline and

[28] See Basham, *op. cit.*, pp. 140-42.

[29] Nirmal K. Bose, "Some Aspects of Caste in Bengal," *Journal of American Folklore*, LXXI (July-Sept., 1958), 405-6. For other examples, see Basham, *op. cit.*, pp. 145-46, 148; Blunt, *op. cit.*, p. 210; M. N. Srinivas, "A Note on Sanskritization and Westernization," *Far Eastern Quarterly*, XV (Aug., 1953), 481-96; Mayer, *op. cit.*, pp. 47-49; and Eric J. Miller, "Caste and Territory in Malabar," *American Anthropologist*, LVI (June, 1954), 410-20, esp. 418. Anthropological literature contains many descriptive studies illustrating successful and unsuccessful attempts of groups to move upwards. Bernard Barber, "Social Mobility in Hindu India" (unpublished MS), challenging the "old" interpretation of caste "derived from the official religious and ideological literature of Indian society," presents an incisive analysis of social mobility in light of modern field research. Barber, citing the work of E. Kathleen Gough Aberle, McKim Marriott, James Silverberg and others, makes the important point that, contrary to the traditional interpretation, caste status over a long period of time tends to seek the level of the economic and power position of the group.

[30] "In seeking to improve his position in the ritual system of rank in his own community, the rich man cannot throw off his poorer caste fellows: he must carry them along with him." Bailey, *op. cit.*, p. 270. The same point is made in a more

can be accomplished only over a long period of time. Understandably, in the eyes of many present-day Indians, social mobility within the traditional caste system is too limited to satisfy the needs of modern society.

The official view of caste in India today is perfectly straightforward. According to the Constitution of India there can be no discrimination exhibited toward citizens "on grounds only of religion, race, caste, sex, [or] place of birth . . . [in] access to shops, public restaurants, hotels and places of public entertainment; or . . . [in] the use of wells, tanks, bathing ghats, roads and places of public resort maintained wholly or partly out of State funds or dedicated to the use of the general public."[31] In addition, untouchability "is abolished and its practice in any form is forbidden."[32] Legally, then, the caste system can no longer serve as a basis for regulating social relationships. Legal fictions, however, often do not agree with hard facts, for no discerning observer could argue that the effects of the caste system have in fact disappeared. In fact, while abolishing discrimination, the Constitution itself has contributed to a new caste awareness, though perhaps on a broader geographic scale than has been known in the past.[33]

Caste and Mobility in Industrial Life

According to official Indian sources 6.5 million new non-agricultural workers entered the industrial labor force in India between 1955 and 1961, and an additional 10.5 million are expected to enter by the close of the Third Five Year Plan in March, 1966.[34] Each of these 17 million presumably will have been conditioned to a considerable extent by the omnipresent restrictions and privileges of caste. It therefore seems necessary at this point to investigate further the extent to which caste ideas and the requirements of industrialization are theoretically compatible.

general application by Selig S. Harrison, *India, the Most Dangerous Decades* (Princeton, 1960), pp. 102-3.

[31] Part III, Article 15, Section (2), Paragraphs (a) and (b).

[32] Part III, Article 17.

[33] The emergence of "casteism"—that is, the cohesive ties of caste on a broader geographic basis—is discussed in more detail, *infra*, pp. 219-20.

[34] See the *Hindustan Times* (Delhi), July 5, 1960, p. 1; and *ibid.*, July 6, 1960, p. 9.

Economists seem in general agreement that social mobility is a precondition necessary for economic development. A committee appointed by the United Nations concluded in 1951 that in some underdeveloped countries "it may not be possible to recruit labour, because it is tied to the soil by law, or because caste restrictions prevent labour from moving to new occupations. . . ."[35] Kingsley Davis has written that at least six preconditions seem essential for economic modernization: "(1) nationalism, (2) secularization, (3) a universal ethical and legal discipline, (4) vertical social mobility, (5) widespread education, (6) technological training and research."[36]

An Indian observer has commented that

it is well known that the caste system creates a powerful obstacle to moving from one occupation to another. . . . Under this system, birth rather than education or talent determines eligibility for particular occupations. . . . Along with the caste system there developed certain social attitudes influenced by religious beliefs which gave rise to occupational taboos. Some professions came to be thought of as "superior," some less "high," and some "inferior". . . . It was adjudged below the dignity of the highest castes—whose role was essentially to spread knowledge—to enter industry or trade. Thus, a great chasm developed between educational competence and occupational skill.[37]

It has been said that "it is typical of the industrial way of life that in a large measure the participant's position in the system, and his daily contacts with other persons, are related to what he does rather than who he is."[38] It is of course true that in the *jāti* system an individual's position in society is based on the factors of birth and occupation, but the latter of these is determined in traditional thought by the former. Theoretically, there can be no significant difference between "what he does" and "who he is." As opposed to this tradi-

[35] United Nations Organization, Department of Economic Affairs, *Measures for the Economic Development of Under-Developed Countries* (New York, 1951), pp. 13-16.

[36] Kingsley Davis, "Social and Demographic Aspects of Economic Development in India," in Simon Kuznets, Wilbert E. Moore, and Joseph J. Spengler, eds., *Economic Growth: Brazil, India, Japan* (Durham, 1955), p. 293.

[37] Chandulal N. Vakil, "Business and Leadership in the Under-developed Countries," in United Nations Organization, Department of Economic and Social Affairs, *Industrialization and Productivity*, Bulletin 2 (New York, 1959), pp. 46-51 at 47-48. For a discussion of related problems on the American scene, see Gary S. Becker, *The Economics of Discrimination* (Chicago, 1957). In his introduction Becker points out that "in most underdeveloped countries there is so much discrimination against women and persons of lowly origins . . . that this is uniformly agreed to be a major obstacle to rapid economic progress," pp. 1-2.

38. Wilbert E. Moore, *Industrialization and Labor* (Ithaca, 1951), p. 98.

tional ideal of acute immobility, the needs of an industrial society demand a high degree of social mobility, both horizontally and vertically, if the constantly changing needs of a developing economy are to be satisfied. Thus, the caste system seems totally incompatible with India's plans for economic development. Practically, however, some *modus vivendi* must have been reached since ten years have passed during the two five-year plans without notable bloodshed in the industrial centers of the nation. What accommodations, if any, have both forces made and what is the future likely to produce?

It is readily apparent that one of three results must emerge from the collision of social forces occasioned by the impact of economic development upon the traditional Hindu caste system.[39] At one extreme, the labor force might conceivably remain so dedicated to its caste norms that no worker would be able to accept a promotion, or a new assignment, or a co-worker from another caste, and thus all development schemes would be doomed to failure. At the opposite extreme, there is a hypothetical possibility that upon contact all caste barriers might immediately fall, that a new set of social values might promptly emerge, and that India could thus progress toward the goal of industrialization (assuming countless other obstacles were also overcome). If history is any guide, however, the emerging social pattern will be neither of these extremes, but rather a synthesis of the old and the new. The total synthesis may be far in the future, but certain trends already apparent seem to indicate its general nature.

The Emerging Synthesis

The attempt here will be to predict the emerging synthesis by determining the reaction of the caste system under environmental conditions different from those in which caste developed and flourished. It is of course readily apparent that an infinite number of variables are at play and that to each conclusion many exceptions may be cited, but, based on evidence pointed out below, the following tentative generalizations are suggested.

[39] Here I am considering only the impact of modern industrialization. The development of cottage industries is excluded primarily because such industries could conceivably function effectively within the limitations imposed by the traditional caste system.

1. *Social mobility has increased; craft-exclusiveness has declined; and these changes may be expected to continue.*

It has already been noted that through the practice of *āpad-dharma* some occupational mobility existed for the individual even in the traditional system. In addition, for the group, society in India has not been so static as it is often supposed. Sir Denzil Ibbetson, who was responsible for carrying out the census of the Punjab in 1881, noted that

the whole theory of society is that occupation and caste are hereditary; and the presumption that caste passes unchanged to the descendants is exceedingly strong. But the presumption is one which can be defeated, and has already been and is now in process of being defeated in numberless instances. As in all other countries and among all other nations, the graduations of the social scale are fixed; but society is not solid but liquid, and portions of it are continually rising and sinking and changing their position as measured by that scale; and the only real difference in this respect is, that the liquid is much more viscous, the friction and inertia to be overcome infinitely greater, and the movement therefore far slower and more difficult in the former than in the latter.[40]

As the impact of the British on the subcontinent became felt, the process of change was accelerated. It was the West that introduced influences that were ultimately to disrupt craft-exclusiveness and shake the very foundations of the existing economic order. When the Indian economy became linked to the expanding world economy, new occupations were introduced and old trades attracted new workers by promises of greater financial rewards. Thus, Buchanan observed in 1934 that the *camārs* (leatherworkers), a caste extremely low in the Hindu hierarchy, had gained considerable prestige because the sale of hides to European countries had produced a new source of wealth out of all proportion to their traditional income. Similarly, the *tēlī* (oil pressers) of Bengal had profited greatly from the new markets, and many of their numbers had become wealthy bankers and merchants.[41]

In a more recent study (1947) of twenty-eight *jāti* in a rural Bengal village, it was found that only twelve were still performing

[40] Sir Denzil Ibbetson, *Panjab Castes* (Lahore, 1916), p. 9. For a recent statement pointing out the same conclusion, see D. N. Majumdar, *Caste and Communication in an Indian Village* (Bombay, 1958), pp. 330 ff.

[41] Daniel H. Buchanan, *The Development of Capitalist Enterprises in India* (New York, 1934), p. 24.

their traditional occupations exclusively; five were in a state of transition between traditional occupations and new functions; and eleven no longer performed any part of their traditional roles.[42]

Kingsley Davis, in his study of the Indian census reports of 1921 and 1941, furnishes the following table showing the percentages of Indians (including the areas of the subcontinent that are now Pakistan) still engaged in their traditional occupations:[43]

	Per cent
Dealers in food and drink	37
Agricultural	21
Laborers and village menials	14
Pastoral	20
Learned professions	20
Boating and fishing	9
Trade and industry	
Unspecified	70
Specified	51

Similarly, N. K. Sharma, basing his conclusions on the study of a village about ten miles from Kanpur, shows statistically that a large percentage of the membership of each caste has forsaken its traditional occupation.[44] Clearly, craft-exclusiveness has yielded to the pressures of changing times. As Davis concludes, mobility can be seen up and down the hierarchy, and with the mobility there is emerging a new middle class that draws from all castes, "some more than others to be sure, but certainly from no particular caste."[45]

[42] These figures were compiled from the tables appearing in Bose, *op. cit.*, pp. 398-99. It might also be pointed out that, according to one report, "the untouchable castes . . . represent the majority of the labor force at Ahmedabad and Nagpur." See Radhakamal Mukerjee, *The Indian Working Class* (3rd ed.; Bombay, 1951), pp. 8-9. Since the two centers mentioned are involved in the manufacture of textiles, it is not surprising, therefore, that a large percentage of the labor force should be of the lowest strata. Many tasks in textile mills are considered defiling to caste Hindus. Nevertheless, the untouchables are provided with jobs providing incomes out of proportion to those of their traditional roles. Also see Bernard S. Cohn, "The Changing Status of a Depressed Caste," in McKim Marriott, ed., *Village India: Studies in the Little Community* (Chicago, 1955), pp. 53-77.

[43] Kingsley Davis, *The Population of India and Pakistan* (Princeton, 1951), p. 170.

[44] Sharma presents detailed charts summarizing his findings in the field. See "Occupational Mobility of Castes in a North Indian Village," *Southwestern Journal of Anthropology*, XVII (Summer, 1961), 146-64 at 148-49.

[45] *The Population of India and Pakistan*, p. 176. The transformation from

2. *Other major characteristics of the caste system are proving increasingly vulnerable to mutation and rationalization.*

As we have noted, endogamy and commensality have shown the greatest resistance to change in traditional Hindu society, but there is ample evidence today that these barriers are rapidly weakening. The informal atmosphere of rapidly expanding urban centers has placed a great strain on traditional endogamous rules, and, in addition, economic factors are increasingly rendering endogamy impractical. For example, in one of many interviews in the industrial center of Kanpur, it was found that a *brāhman* was prepared to permit the marriage of his daughter to a member of a lower *varṇa*, not out of sympathy for the lot of the young couple, but because the *brāhman*, now working as a clerk in a factory, could not provide the necessary dowry for a *brāhman-varṇa* marriage.[46]

Commensality and taboos related to the handling of food and water are also undergoing many changes, especially in the urban industrial areas. It has been shown that Hindus who observe rules of commensality at home in the villages often do not hesitate to break the same rules when visiting the cities.[47] For the permanent residents of the cities, Mukerjee has pointed out that the water taps (which are usually very scarce, especially in the slum areas) have become great social levelers. All classes frequently must draw water from the same source, and, although in queueing up for water much discrimination still exists at some taps, at other taps a late-comer, regardless of caste, puts his vessels near the fountain and awaits his chance.[48]

Rituals and taboos associated with the preparation and consumption of food have also felt the pressures of present-day life. As in any other country, urbanization has given rise to hotels and restaurants, and as it was said even several decades ago,

---

caste-consciousness to class-consciousness has been noted by several authors. See, for example, Ghurye, *Caste and Class in India;* Humayun Kabir, *The Indian Heritage* (3rd ed.; New York, 1955), pp. 140-42; and K. M. Panikkar, *Hindu Society at the Crossroads* (Bombay, 1955), pp. 6-26.

[46] Basuder Narayan, "Changing Caste Distances in the Urban Industrial Community," in Radhakamal Mukerjee, *Inter-Caste Tensions* (Lucknow, 1951), p. 94. A similarity might be pointed out in the experience of nineteenth-century France, where the nobility intermarried with the new commercial aristocracy for much the same reason.

[47] Mayer, *op. cit.*, pp. 47-49.

[48] Mukerjee, *Inter-Caste Tensions*, pp. 27, 84.

the exigencies of office work have forced city people to put aside the old ideas of purity. Caste-Hindus have to eat articles of food prepared by Christians, Musalmans, or Persians, because Hindu restaurants have not been easily or equally accessible during office hours. In Hindu hotels, they have to take their meals in the company of people of almost any caste —as the hotel keeper cannot manage to reserve accommodations for members of different castes. What was originally done under pressure of necessity has become a matter of routine with many in their city life.[49]

When old taboos come in conflict with new patterns of life there is the tendency initially to seek rationalizations that might render the old and the new more compatible. For example, when caste-Hindus are compelled to use the same tap from which untouchables also draw water, a supply of clay may be kept close at hand by which the tap may be ceremonially cleansed before use.[50] Another interesting example of this process of rationalization is related by M. N. Srinivas. According to the author, brāhmans exposed to Western influence soon discovered the advantages of bicycle riding, but there was a serious religious difficulty involved. Bicycle seats were covered with the hide of the sacred cow and were therefore defiling to the touch. This taboo was at first rationalized by concealing the leather beneath a protective cover of pure deerskin, but later this deerskin disappeared and the exposed leather seat was used. Similarly, Srinivas notes that running water in homes was at first rejected even by those who could afford the luxury because the water had to pass through a leather washer on the valve. Soon, however, the temptation became too great and ritual gave way to convenience.[51]

3. *While caste debilitations are diminishing, the lingering effects of caste remain.*

Although the observance of caste prejudices and rituals seems to be on the wane, the ties of caste, on a much broader scale, are becoming increasingly important in Indian life. The Indian Constitution undoubtedly gave some support to this trend by reserving seats for the "backward classes" in the House of the People, in the legislative assemblies of the states, and in the public services (con-

[49] G. S. Ghurye, *Caste and Race in India* (London, 1932), p. 173.
[50] Mukerjee, *Inter-Caste Tensions*, pp. 27, 84.
[51] Srinivas, "A Note on Sanskritization and Westernization," p. 489.

sistent "with the maintenance of efficiency of administration").[52] While the definition of "backward classes" may be vague,[53] the agitation for increased benefits is not.

Recent debates in the Lok Sabha have pointed up well the demands of the scheduled castes and tribes for a better-than-even break for the backward classes. One member was critical of admission policies to colleges based on merit, arguing that these procedures discriminated against the backward groups. To this another member added that those of the depressed classes satisfying matriculation requirements should automatically receive scholarships. Several members criticized Government for not doing more for the depressed classes in government service; one suggested the holding of a special examination for these groups for recruitment into the all-India services, and further suggested that special reservations should be made for them in promotions.[54]

This broadening emphasis on the ties of caste has given new life to India's caste associations. Caste associations, in addition to fulfilling a number of fraternal purposes, originally served as centralized bodies for directing the attempts of their castes to achieve higher status in the caste hierarchy. With the coming of popular elections, however, their value as political organizations soon came to be recognized. Although reliable statistics on caste voting are difficult to obtain, it seems to be accepted by most political observers that caste associations play a primary role in most local and state elections.[55]

---

[52] Articles 330-36. The Constitution provided that these special reservations should end on January 26, 1960, but by the *Constitution (Eighth Amendment) Act, 1959* these provisions were extended for an additional ten years. Provision has also been made for the reservation of scholarships for the backward classes.

[53] The appropriate provisions of the Constitution (Articles 15, 46, 335, and the Fifth and Sixth Schedules) do not define "backward classes of citizens." In *Venkataramana v. State of Madras* (A. I. R. 1951, S.C. 229), the Supreme Court, without defining backward classes, found it impossible to include groups other than *harijans* and backward Hindus in this category.

[54] This debate is fully reported in the *Statesman* (Delhi), Aug. 10, 1961, p. 9.

[55] For the most thorough treatment of this point, see Harrison, *op. cit.*, pp. 96-136. Also see Lloyd I. and Susanne H. Rudolph, "The Political Role of India's Caste Associations," *Pacific Affairs*, XXXIII (March, 1960), 5-22. For an illuminating insight into the political sophistication of some representative villagers, see Majumdar, *op. cit.*, pp. 297-300. Viewing Majumdar's findings, it is easy to understand how voting could be influenced by traditional ties. For an incisive analysis of the conflicts of local issues in state elections in Orissa, see the series of nine articles by F. G. Bailey in the *Economic Weekly* (Bombay, Aug. 29, Sept. 12, 19, 26, Oct. 3, 10, 17, 24, and Nov. 7, 1959).

Whatever may be the long-range disadvantages of this political use of caste, this very trend itself is increasing social mobility by breaking down the debilitating restrictions traditionally imposed on the lower castes. Commenting on a recent village election in which an *ahīr* defeated a *brāhman* and a *ṭhākur*, it has been pointed out that it "was a revolution for the village—one that demonstrated most eloquently the decline of the caste hierarchy and the rise of casteism." The writer concludes that "what is dying is caste hierarchy, [that is,] that acceptance of superior and inferior status with concomitant social ·obligations and restrictions."[56] Two Western political observers, perhaps too optimistically, have recently reached similar conclusions.

> The caste associations bring political democracy to Indian villages through the familiar and accepted institutions of caste. In the process it is changing the meaning of caste. By creating conditions in which a caste's significance and power is beginning to depend on its numbers, rather than its ritual and social status, and by encouraging egalitarian aspirations among its members, the caste association is exerting a liberating influence.[57]

Upward social movement, crucial for economic modernization, has been made easier, although possibly at the expense of long-range political stability.[58]

Although the political implications of caste deserve increased attention by social scientists, of more immediate concern to this essay must be the continuing influence of caste restrictions in the Indian economic sphere. It has often been observed that in Indian industry high-caste workers are frequently employed in supervisory, skilled, or semi-skilled positions, while lower-caste laborers usually gravitate toward unskilled tasks, often finding roles similar to their traditional occupations.[59] For example, in the factories of Kanpur, Mukerjee's UNESCO research group found that 90 per cent of all the workers performing duties classified as unskilled were drawn from the four lowest classes; the same classes filled 24 per cent of the semi-skilled

---

[56] This paragraph is based on an excellent analysis of several *panchāyat* elections contained in the *Statesman* (Delhi), June 20, 1961, p. 6.

[57] Rudolph and Rudolph, *op. cit.*, p. 9.

[58] The long-range consequences of the political manipulation of caste associations is one of the objects of Harrison's scrutiny. *Op. cit., passim.*

[59] There are of course the two factors of education and caste to consider here, and one feeds upon the other. High-caste Hindus are the best educated and thus qualify for the best jobs. Having the best jobs they are then able to provide their children with the best education. The continuation of this cycle will undoubtedly be observed for many years to come.

jobs and only 13 per cent of the skilled jobs.[60] It has also been pointed out that entrepreneurial as well as managerial personnel are drawn chiefly from only certain castes and groups. In Indian business and industry, one will most often find these positions filled by *Marwaris, Gujeratis, Chettiars, Sindhis,* and *Parsis.*[61]

Outside the factories of Kanpur, there are many evidences of a social leveling. To be sure, the residential areas still show the marks of caste consciousness: the better housing is usually occupied by the upper castes, inferior quarters are taken by the lower castes, and the untouchables are frequently found living in squalor some distance from all caste-Hindus. The situation is especially true of slum areas, where, the UNESCO report adds, "caste distance and segregation are writ large." But in general the signs are encouraging for the proponents of social change. Averaging the figures for all residential areas, for example, we find that approximately 30 per cent of the members of the lowest three castes now reside in common wards with the upper castes.[62]

The lingering effects of the traditional caste system will undoubtedly remain in Indian society for an indefinite time. But the question remains: What effect will these have on attempted economic modernization in India?

Conclusion

Almost every sociological, economic, and political study of India today takes note of at least some degree of social unrest. In the south, along the historic Malabar coast, the area first touched by European merchants and adventurers, changes have occurred more rapidly than probably even the Indian Government would have desired:

[Industry] threw open not only many avenues of getting a living but also made necessary certain adjustments on the part of old ways of getting a living. The wider dissemination of technical knowledge was to a great extent responsible for breaking the spell of the hereditary nature of occupation. . . . The industrial economy has brought with it the working class

[60] Mukerjee, *Inter-Caste Tensions,* p. 23. Cf. *ibid.,* p. 82. Actually, the figure 13 per cent indicates a hopeful degree of vertical mobility.
[61] Vakil, *op. cit.,* pp. 47-48. Also see Oscar A. Ornati, *Jobs and Workers in India* (Ithaca, 1955), pp. 40-41.
[62] Mukerjee, *Inter-Caste Tensions,* p. 25.

and the capitalists. . . . The emergence of these classes modifying the caste system is a dominant strain in the changing pattern of society. . . . With the contact of a foreign culture, mainly the Western, there is a great shifting of values in the older and new modes of thinking and behavior. The pattern of culture receiving the traits acts, reacts and operates like a sieve in the process of assimilation. . . . Malabar . . . has grown sensitive to change.[63]

To be sure, the primary areas of change are the large urban centers,[64] but the villages are not immune. For the first time in India's history large numbers of restless laborers are moving back and forth between city and village, in search of work in the cities but still impelled to return to the villages by strong familial and cultural ties. As has been succinctly written:

in the city the villager is free to live as suits him. Thus the city acts as a center of new ideas and of new experiences as well as of a new freedom from customary controls and beliefs. Going back to the village, the peasant carries elements of an "urban" intellectual ferment and disseminates this ferment among those who have remained tied to the soil.[65]

Humayun Kabir, discussing the conflict of social inertia and social progress, has similarly observed the importance of increased intercourse between villages and cities:

the tendency toward change and progress was accelerated. . . , not only in the circulation of goods, but also in that of ideas. Towns were brought nearer the villages. . . . The impact of the towns on the villages has shaken the complacence of traditional modes of life.[66]

The result of this transplanted social ferment has been felt to some degree in almost every aspect of village life. Writing in 1952 of a rural village of about 1,800 population in southeastern Uttar Pradesh, Morris Opler noted that significant changes had occurred since 1947 in modes of transportation, the use of agricultural implements, farming methods, the diet, the household, communications,

[63] M. S. A. Rao, *Social Change in Malabar* (Bombay, 1957), pp. 201-6.

[64] However, cf. McKim Marriott, "Some Comments on William L. Kolb's 'The Structure and Functions of Cities' in the Light of India's Urbanization," *Economic Development and Cultural Change*, III (Oct., 1954), 50-52. According to Marriott, citing several field studies, "that a kind of extended primary group organization has in fact remained strong—perhaps grown stronger—along with the growth of cities in India is attested by the lively existence of urban caste councils and associations," p. 51.

[65] Robert I. Crane, "Strata Disruption and Social Change in South Asia," *United Asia*, VI (Nov., 1954), 233.

[66] *Op. cit.*, p. 142.

and education. An observation of particular relevance to this study is that

with the coming of independence two trends developed. The first was an organization of the low castes in opposition to the Brahmans, Thakurs, and Kayasthas; the second trend was an alignment on a political basis regardless of caste. Both kinds of groupings are present still but grouping on a caste basis is growing weaker while alignment on a wider political basis is growing stronger.[67]

According to Opler, the village he observed is typical of its region, and in a general sense typical of rural India.[68]

Seeking to discover the most significant changes in Indian village life, Opler finds them not in technology but in the field of political and social relations:[69]

The mass education of "untouchable" children, the introduction of co-education, the toleration of widow re-marriage, the wresting of political power from the land owners and high-caste groups—these are momentous changes that penetrate to the core of village life. They bespeak the end of an era and a reorganization of intellectual and social energy.

While casteism may be on the rise, there seems to be no reason to assume that this can seriously impede economic development so long as the new ideas associated with casteism do not include an emphasis on acute social immobility. In fact, there seems to be mounting evidence that caste might be reinterpreted to fit in with the needs of industrialism. In a brilliant field study of the Seetaa-Raam Sugar Mill, located in a village of almost one thousand in Uttar Pradesh, Joseph W. Elder has illustrated that Hinduism is sufficiently elastic to include within its fold the intrusion of Western technology.

There was evidence to indicate that the ease with which village Hindus became Mill laborers . . . indicated more than mere accommodation or compartmentalization and more than simply the pressure of financial necessity to support their families. They seemed to be able to fit their

[67] Morris E. Opler and Rudra Datt Singh, "Economic, Political and Social Change in a Village in North Central India," *Human Organization*, XI (Summer, 1952), 5-12 at 11. The momentous changes occurring in India's villages have occasioned one anthropologist to conclude pessimistically that "in perhaps ten years . . . it is questionable whether the village will any longer be a useful isolate for study." See E. Kathleen Gough, "The Social Structure of a Tanjore Village," in Marriott, *op. cit.*, pp. 36-52 at 52.

[68] *Op. cit.*, p. 12. However, for a contrary view expressing the continuing rigidity of caste restrictions in the village, cf. Lewis, *op. cit.*, pp. 83-84.

[69] *Op. cit.*, p. 12.

participation in the Mill meaningfully into their total world view. In other words, as Hindus they could have a certain type of commitment to their jobs in the Mill. This commitment was not absolute. . . . But, given the fact that these laborers were employed by the Mill, they seemed able to fit their jobs in the Mill into a larger religious frame of reference. . . .[70]

Almost all writers would agree that "the old order still has a good deal of life in it,"[71] in the sense that India is no more likely than Meji Japan to abandon its own traditions completely for those of the invading culture. It may be all but certain, however, that one of the most significant casualties in the struggle between inertia and change will be social restrictions associated with the traditional Hindu-caste stratification. It may appear unduly optimistic to predict that "if industrialization proceeds rapidly in . . . [India], the caste system will have essentially disappeared by the end of the century,"[72] but there is impressive evidence that its religious-ritualistic hold is rapidly loosening on the minds of men. It is this hold that was likely to pose the most serious threat to economic modernization.

[70] Joseph W. Elder, "Industrialism in Hindu Society: A Case Study in Social Change" (Harvard University, unpublished Ph.D. thesis, 1959), p. 151, by permission. Also see *ibid.*, p. 308.

[71] W. Norman Brown, "Class and Cultural Tradition in India," *Journal of American Folklore*, LXXI (July-Sept. 1958), 245. For a less hopeful appraisal of the viability of the caste system, see M. N. Srinivas, "Castes: Can They Exist in India of Tomorrow?," *Economic Weekly* (Bombay), Oct. 14, 1955, pp. 1230-32. Srinivas concludes, however, that modernization "should remove the more obnoxious features of the caste system gradually," p. 1232. Also see Elder, *op. cit.*, pp. 152-53, 167, 304-7.

[72] Davis, *The Population of India and Pakistan*, p. 176.

8

Arthaśāstra Economics

Joseph J. Spengler*

A clever servant shows his master
The gleam of triumph or disaster
From good or evil courses springing,
And shows him wit, decision bringing.
                              Panchatantra

MEN WERE SLOW in every society to give explicit analytical expression to what they knew of economic phenomena. Those best informed either were not able to set down their knowledge in organized form, or they preferred to write of less mundane matters. One is compelled, therefore, to infer ancient economic thought from the contents of philosophical, legal, political, and closely related literature. Of the forms of literature in which implicit economic thought is to be found, one of the more important is the manual of statecraft designed to guide the ruler of a state and perhaps others engaged in the governance of its people. This essay has to do with the economic content of one of the most complete of these manuals extant in any language, the *Arthaśāstra* attributed to Kauṭilya, minister to the founder of the vast Mauryan empire at the close of the fourth century B.C. In it we find much of economic practice, something of the importance of economic values and institutions, and traces of economic theory.

I. *Importance of* Arthaśāstra

Kauṭilya's *Arthaśāstra*, though not chronologically the first work of its genre, is of great significance for several reasons. It is a major

* This paper, a component of a larger research project, was completed while I held a Guggenheim Fellowship. The research has also been aided by the Ford Foundation.

work of reference to the ancient past. "To the student of Indian Sociology, the year 1909 is memorable. It saw the publication of the *Arthaśāstra* of Kauṭilya, the most remarkable work on social polity now available in Sanskrit."[1] In consequence it has since become the chief literary source of information respecting economic and political practice and thought in and sometime before and after the period of the Mauryan, "greatest of India's ancient empires," whose sway over most of the country lasted for some 130 years after the empire's establishment about 320 B.C.[2] In fact, the *Arthaśāstra*, together with Aśoka's inscriptions and Megasthenes's observations, provides "us with a large volume of information calculated to give a more complete picture of this epoch" than we have "of any other till we reach the time of Akbar and the *Āin-i-Akbarī*."[3] Even after the collapse of the Mauryan empire, Kauṭilya's manual apparently continued to serve as a guide to both rulers and later writers, much of its content still being reflected as many as fifteen centuries later in the *Sukranīti*, "the last summing up of Hindu political thought."[4] For, as Aiyangar remarks, "In India more than in many parts of the world the past persists in the present."[5] Finally, some of the values and the princi-

[1] K. V. Rangaswami Aiyangar, *Indian Cameralism* (The Adyar Library) (Madras, 1949), p. 5. See also *idem, Aspects of Ancient Indian Economic Thought* (Benares, 1934). I have made use of the sixth edition (Mysore, 1960) of the translation of the *Arthaśāstra* by R. Shamasastry, based on the text published by him in 1909, as volume 37 of the *Bibliotheca Sanskrita* of Mysore, a few years after a manuscript of the text, together with some commentary, came into the hands of the Mysore Government Oriental Library. The first edition of the English translation appeared in 1915. I have also used Johann Jakob Meyer's annotated translation, *Das Altindische Buch vom Welt-und Staatsleben* (2 vols.; Leipzig, 1926).

[2] A. L. Basham, *The Wonder That Was India* (New York, 1954), pp. 50-57; K. A. N. Sastri, ed., *A Comprehensive History of India*, II (Calcutta, 1957), chaps. i-ii. Economic conditions did not change substantially for several or more centuries after the close of Mauryan ascendance (*ibid.*, chap. xiv). See also Romila Thapar, *Aśoka and the Decline of the Mauryas* (Oxford, 1961), chap. 3, esp. pp. 92-93.

[3] Sastri, *op. cit.*, p. 50.

[4] See Beni Prased, *The State of Ancient India* (Allahabad, 1928), p. 245. Sukra's work is assignable to a period "not later than the thirteenth century," concludes U. N. Ghoshal, *A History of Indian Political Ideas* (London, 1959), p. 495. See also *ibid.*, chap. xxviii, in which Ghoshal discusses the place of Sukra's treatise in the development of Indian political thought. In the twelfth century the minister of the King of Benares classed the *Arthaśāstra* as a sixth Vēda, the *Mahābhārata* having been declared the fifth. See Aiyangar, *Indian Cameralism*, p. 30. Kauṭilya's influence is illustrated here and there by Ghoshal in *op. cit.* and in his *Contributions to the History of the Indian Revenue System* (Calcutta, 1929). *Arthaśāstra* influence is manifest even in the famous Indian collection of fables, *Panchatantra*, originally composed in Kashmir about 200 B.C.

[5] *Ancient Indian Economic Thought*, p. 6. On this persistence, see P. V. Kane, *History of Dharmaśāstra* (5 vols.; Poona, 1930 ff.).

ples described in the *Arthaśāstra* help to explain why India's economy failed to supply the mass of its inhabitants with at least a slowly rising level of living instead of with one that sometimes fell short of minimal requirements.

Scholars still dispute regarding the authorship and the date of composition of Kauṭilya's *Arthaśāstra*. For example, Basham believes that the current version is of a vintage falling between Mauryan and Guptan times. "It is certainly pre-Guptan, and is, we believe, the elaboration of a Mauryan original which was perhaps the work of Kauṭilya himself."[6] A. Bose supposes that the *Arthaśāstra* dates from the first century A.D., and some scholars even assert that the work may possibly not have been composed until A.D. 300.[7] Kauṭilya's authorship as well as the date of about 300 B.C. is supported by the translator, Shamasastry, and by others.[8] It is likely that some interpolations were introduced after the original work was composed. It is questionable, however, that many changes were made, or that they rendered the original author's principles less applicable to the governance of a vast empire of the sort first ruled by the Maurya and, not again, until five centuries later, by the Gupta.[9]

In the Mauryan period as at other times much of the population of productive age was unproductively employed, in that the second most numerous class, the *kṣatriyas* or warriors, had principally military duties to perform. Agriculture was overwhelmingly predominant, and land was the main source of income and revenue, even though over half of the land seems not to have been cultivated. Industry and trade were better organized than in preceding periods, with the state playing a major role in the determination of the use to which productive agents were put. The population was occupa-

[6] *Op. cit.*, p. 79. The Gupta Empire lasted from A.D. 320 to A.D. 467.
[7] See A. Bose, *Social and Rural Economy of Northern India*, II (Calcutta, 1945), 494-507, and views of M. A. Mehendale and H. C. Raychaudhuri expressed in R. C. Majumdar, ed., *The History and Culture of the Indian People*, II (Bombay, 1953), 274-75, 285-87.
[8] See Shamasastry's introductions to editions 1-3 of his translation, pp. vii-xxxii of the sixth or 1960 edition; also Majumdar, ed., *op. cit.*, p. 274; Sastri, ed., *op. cit.*, pp. 50-53; Narayan Chandra Bandyopadhyaya, *Economic Life and Progress in Ancient India*, I (Calcutta, 1945), 28-30; F. J. Monahan, *The Early History of Bengal* (Oxford, 1925), p. 30; Thapar, *op. cit.*, pp. 218-25.
[9] E. W. Hopkins states that while Kauṭilya's *Arthaśāstra* "may date from about 300 B.C.," it does include some rules which agree with those found in later law books instead of with those of 300 B.C. or earlier. See E. J. Rapson, ed., *The Cambridge History of India*, I (New York, 1922), 294-95.

tionally differentiated and output was quite varied. Transport conditions were fairly good and foreign as well as domestic trade could flourish, though production seems to have been adjusted mainly to local demands. While guilds continued to enjoy privileges, much use was made also of hired and servile labor, especially in the public sector. Undoubtedly, the distinguishing organizational feature of the Mauryan economy was the magnitude of the public sector and the extent of bureaucratic paternalism.[10]

Although we do not know how well India's population lived at this time, data suggest that while there was much poverty, many people may have been better off then than at times in recent centuries.[11] Our information regarding population growth is similarly defective. It has been inferred, however, that India's population grew very little if at all between 300 B.C. and A.D. 1800. Accordingly, if, as sometimes happens, average income and numbers tended to move together, it is unlikely that average income rose over the long run and probable that it eventually declined.[12] According to Pran Nath, there was about one acre of cultivated land per inhabitant (i.e., enough to support an adult); yet he finds that laborers were about as badly off in the fifth century A.D. as in Akbar's time.[13] Colin Clark estimates that in the nineteenth century, when India's long stationary population was again growing, and at a relatively

[10] See Sastri, ed., *op cit.*, pp. 66-80; Rapson, ed., *op. cit.*, chap. xix; Majumdar, ed., *op. cit.*, chap. xxiii.

[11] According to S. K. Das, the lot of the poor was unusually hard in pre-Mauryan times. See *The Economic History of Ancient India* (2nd ed.; 1937), I, 278-80.

[12] Pran Nath, on the basis of slight evidence, estimated India's population at 100-140 millions about 300 B.C. while W. H. Moreland put it at about 100 millions about A.D. 1600, again on the basis of very limited evidence. Nath estimates that ancient India numbered about 7 million *grāmas* (estates), averaging about 80 acres per estate, of which 15-25 were cultivated by the 4-5 tenant families which, together with the landlord family, were sustained by the estate. With families averaging 5 persons, an estate would support 25-30 people. Even if it supported only 15-20, India's population would approximate 105-140 millions. Kingsley Davis endorses the former figure, increases to 125 million the figure for A.D. 1600, and reports the population as numbering 120, 175, and 282 millions, respectively, in 1800, 1855, and 1891. See his *The Population of India and Pakistan* (Princeton, 1951), pp. 23-27; Pran Nath, *A Study in the Economic Condition of Ancient India* (London, 1929), pp. 39-41, 117-18, and 118-23 on supplementary estimates; Moreland, *India at the Death of Akbar* (London, 1920), p. 22.

[13] *Op. cit.*, pp. 39-40, 82-85, 118, 148, 152-53. In the sixteenth century, according to Moreland, "the mass of the nobles were steeped in luxury and . . . the mass of the people were miserably poor, poorer even than they are today" (*op. cit.*, p. 254).

high long-time rate of about 1 per cent per year, real wages were decidedly lower than they had been in the seventeenth or even in the sixteenth century, and that in the eleventh century real wages were substantially higher than in the early seventeenth.[14] Misuse of the nation's investible surplus and of some of its population of working-age was primarily responsible for the absence of growth.[15] At times typical of this misuse must have been the hoarding of appreciable portions of the considerable importation of gold in exchange for exports to the West, a practice attributable in part to widespread insecurity and to the cupidity of government officials.[16]

While Kauṭilya's manual is a rich repository of factual information, economic and otherwise, its orientation is descriptive, prescriptive, and didactic rather than analytical, and its content is predominantly political. Moreover, what is said is often obscure and sometimes subject to quite varied interpretation. The economic matter is found largely in the first, second, and fifth books and, in lesser measure, in the third and fourth books. Yet even in these there is much non-economic matter. For example, the first book is concerned primarily with how the king must proceed if he is to choose reliable ministers, set up and operate effective internal and external spy systems, and generally guard his internal and external security. The second deals with political as well as with economic regulatory agencies, and the next three with family regulations, criminal justice, and public service as well as with various economic issues. The more important of these economic matters we deal with below. The ten remaining books have to do with bases of sovereignty, international relations, sources of national distress, invasion, war and the conduct of military operations, and international intrigue.

[14] *The Conditions of Economic Progress* (3rd ed.; London, 1957), pp. 204-8.

[15] Of such misuse in Akbar's time Moreland writes: "The upper classes, small in numbers . . . , enjoyed incomes which were very great relatively to reasonable needs, and as a rule they spent these incomes lavishly on objects of luxury and display. They did practically nothing towards promoting the economic development of the country, and such part of their income as was not spent was hoarded in unproductive forms" (*op. cit.*, p. 279).

[16] Tenney Frank believes that Pliny was well informed when he indicated that about half of the 100 million sesterces flowing annually from Rome to India, China, and Arabia went to India. See Frank, *An Economic Survey of Ancient Rome*, V (Baltimore, 1940), pp. 282-83. See also Sastri, ed., *op. cit.*, pp. 439-50. On hoarding see Pran Nath, *op. cit.*, pp. 59, 66, 130-33.

II. *Pre*-Arthaśāstra *Literature*

Pre-*Arthaśāstra* literature is of importance for the study of later Indian writings touching upon economic matters.[17] For Kauṭilya drew upon some of this literature, and what he had to say respecting various empirical matters may be compared with what appeared in earlier works. Of these earlier works the most important seem to have been the technical works of polity prepared by Kauṭilya's fourth-century B.C. intellectual forebears, above all those representing the three *Arthaśāstra* schools of Manu (Manava), Brihaspati, and Uśanas, whose main concern was "the means of gaining success in the material world."[18] Kauṭilya's manual, probably the last of these works to be composed and the only one now extant, incorporated, greatly modified, augmented, and effectively organized the diverse ideas which had appeared in earlier technical treatises. It included many prevailing customs and rules, among them those characteristic of a *Brāhman* society, Kauṭilya being the first to attempt to codify Indian laws and customs.[19] It also reflected Brahmanical ethics and earlier Smṛti "ideas about the authority and sources of law of the social order,"[20] in part perhaps because

[17] E.g., passages relating to statecraft were inserted in the epic, *Mahābhārata*, especially in the form of the twelfth book, "in the early centuries of the Christian era." About this time similar matter was inserted in section seven of the law book attributed to the primeval sage Manu. See Basham, *op. cit.*, p. 80; Ghoshal, *A History*, chaps. viii-xiii.

[18] Narayan Chandra Bandyopadhyaya, *Kauṭilya* (Calcutta, 1927), p. 18. See also *idem, Economic Life and Progress in Ancient India*, pp. 13-14, where it is indicated that the study of the "Artha-Vēda" (the Upavēda of the Rig-Vēda), a work devoted to the means of acquiring wealth, "gave rise to systematic treatises dealing with practical politics and the ways of acquiring wealth." There were also treatises on agriculture, cattle-rearing, the conduct of business and trade, town-planning, architecture, etc. (*ibid.*, pp. 14-17; also Aiyangar, *Ancient Indian Economic Thought*, pp. 38-39). Few of these works have been preserved.

[19] On these various sources of Kauṭilya's ideas see Ghoshal, *A History*, chaps. v-vi; Bandyopadhyaya, *Kauṭilya*, p. 71. While Kauṭilya's manual is said to describe a "purely Brāhman society" (Rapson, ed., *op. cit.*, p. 166), its translator, R. Shamasastry, states that "caste distinctions and undue partiality to Brāhmans" are assigned "no prominence in the Arthaśāstra." See *Arthaśāstra*, p. 220 n. See also M. V. Krishna Rao, "who describes Kauṭilya as "the interpreter of Neo-Aryanism against the nihilistic anarchy of Buddhism," but who characterizes passages derogatory to *Śūdras* as later interpolations. *Studies in Kauṭilya* (Delhi, 1958), pp. 186, 229. In what may be an interpolation, Kauṭilya lumped Buddhists with Śūdras (III, 20, pp. 223-24).

[20] Ghoshal, *A History*, p. 113; Bandyopadhyaya, *Kauṭilya*, p. 39. *Smṛti*, a branch of Brahmanical sacred literature dealing with civil and religious law, was a source of both the law of the social order and of state law (*ibid.*, pp. 22-23, 43-48; 73, 582). The *Arthaśāstra* was not recognized as being an independent source of

Kauṭilya, aware of the value of propaganda and of the extent of belief in the infallibility of the Vēda, found in these ideas a powerful source of social stability.[21] It should be noted, however, that the world for which Kauṭilya's statecraft was intended differed from that in which earlier authors had found themselves. The Mauryan Empire at its height embraced much of India and her population of perhaps 100 million people (about as many as lived in Europe in A.D. 1600). Its dimensions, much greater than those of its predecessor Magadha Empire, reflected both the unifying influence generated by foreign invasions of India and the Persian (if not also the Hellenistic) demonstration that vast empires could be administered.[22] Kauṭilya was concerned, therefore, to devise a statecraft that would keep this large empire unified, guard its integrity against the intrigues of power-seeking nobles and attack from abroad, and prevent a dissolution of the sort that took place less than 150 years later. Hence he found it necessary to dismiss unrealistic and world-rejecting values and practices which were unfavorable to the functioning of a great empire and to strengthen those conducive thereto. He may be said to have subordinated ethics to politics, though he did not endorse principles that ran counter to the Vēda on which the teachings of the *Dharmaśāstra* rested.[23]

There is economic matter, though little of it of a theoretical sort, in early non-Arthaśāstra literature, perhaps because the authors of

state law, along with *Dharmaśāstra*, until the second or third century A.D. in the *Smṛti* work of Yajñavalkya. See Ghoshal, *A History*, p. 161. In time the maxims of the *Arthaśāstra* and the *Dharmaśāstra* came to be looked upon as being in harmony. See Aiyangar, *Indian Cameralism*, pp. 38-39.

[21] Aiyangar emphasizes the importance of sanctifying an institution or a principle by associating it with the Vēda. See *Ancient Indian Economic Thought*, pp. 40-41; also Bandyopadhyaya, *Kauṭilya*, p. 46. For evidence of Kauṭilya's skill as a propagandist, see his *Arthaśāstra*, I, 13; X, 3; XIII, 1.

[22] E.g., see Majumdar, ed., *op. cit.*, chaps. ii, iv; Sastri, ed., *op. cit.*, chap. i; Rapson, ed. *op. cit.*, pp. 385-86, 467-73. Monahan expressed the opinion that Kauṭilya's government was intended for "a relatively small state" (*op. cit.*, p. 31).

[23] Aiyangar, *Indian Cameralism*, pp. 32-33. On the world-rejecting view current in and before Kauṭilya's time and his reaction thereto, see Bandyopadhyaya, *Kauṭilya*, pp. 22-27, 37-40, 87-88; also M. V. Krishna Rao, *op. cit.*, pp. 246, 252. In his *The Discovery of India* (Garden City, 1959, Bk. III, chap. xiii) Jawaharlal Nehru observes that "there was hardly anything Chanakya [i.e., Kauṭilya] would have refrained from doing to achieve his purpose; . . . yet he was also wise enough to know that this very purpose may be defeated by means unsuited to the end." On the power-seeking nobles, see Pran Nath, *op. cit.*, pp. 65, 131-38. George Modelski says that Kauṭilya's "remarkable concept of the Circle of States is as close to that of an international system as we could wish." See "Comparative International Systems," *World Politics*, XIV (1962), 665.

these works were not concerned with analysis or with prevalent analytical notions.[24]   In this literature society is pictured as much less complex and politically organized than that which Kauṭilya envisaged. In the Rig-Vēda, portions of which antedated his work more than five centuries, one encounters private property, absence of city life, some democratic political organization, occupational specialization, the beginnings of the caste system, some slavery, bare references to price-bargaining, interest-bearing loans, an emerging theory of kingship, and a developing conception of a social order subject to social law (*dharma*) and sustained by coercive authority (*daṇḍa*).[25] In the Sūtras (manuals of aphoristic instruction adapted to an age in which easily memorized phrases had to substitute for written instructions) life is described as village-centered and parochial, landholdings usually are small, and inheritance laws are unsystematized and vary with locality.   Property is protected and false weights and measures are forbidden.   The king's taxes are generally fixed at between one-tenth and one-sixth of (net?) farm produce, at smaller rates on other activities, and at one day's work per month for artisans.   Trading is permissible to most individuals, and moneylending can be carried on by all but the highest caste members, with the basic interest maximum fixed at about 1.25 per cent per month.[26]

[24] Mrs. C. A. F. Rhys David, writing of economic conditions as represented in early Buddhist literature, remarks: "If during, say, the seventh to the fourth century B.C. it had been the vogue, in India, to write treatises on economic institutions, there might have come down to us the record both of conventions and of theories as orderly and as relatively acceptable to the peoples as anything of the kind in, say, the latter Middle Ages was to the peoples of Western Europe" (in Rapson, ed., *op. cit.*, p. 219).   According to Bandyopadhyaya, however, "We have nothing which can help us in showing whether the ancients knew, or cared to know the laws governing demand and supply or production and distribution."   See *Economic Life and Progress in Ancient India*, p. 308.   See also Bose (*op. cit.*, II, 471-89), who argues that India's economic history was quite different from that portrayed in Brahmanical and Buddhist literature.

[25] Rapson, ed., *op. cit.*, pp. 88-101; S. K. Das, *The Economic History of Ancient India*, chap. iv, esp. pp. 23-24, 58-62, 65-66; Ghoshal, *A History*, chaps. ii, xxx, and *The Agrarian System in Ancient India*, Calcutta, 1930, chaps. i, v; Aiyangar, *Ancient Indian Economic Thought*, pp. 56-57.

[26] Rapson, ed., *op. cit.*, pp. 227-48.   See also *ibid.*, pp. 267-70, on the epic poems in which local government, light taxes, merchant guilds, and minimum wages for herdsmen are endorsed.   In the law-book of Manu the old Sūtra rule permitting interest at 1.25 per cent per month is confirmed, though a monthly rate as high as 5 per cent is allowed for low-caste debtors (*ibid.*, p. 287).   In Manu's and other legal works what amount to minimum wages are specified for various kinds of workers (*ibid.*).   The tax rates specified in the early Sūtras are declared just: between one-twelfth and one-sixth of crops, lower rates on merchandise, one-fiftieth of the taxpayer's cattle and gold (or increment therein), and one day's work

In other Brahmanical writings antedating or appearing contemporaneously with *Arthaśāstra* literature we find developed the concept of *dharma* as the sum total of duties incident upon members of castes and other social categories, together with observance-enforcing sanctions. Administrative machinery is discussed; the theory of Brahmanical immunities and privileges is further developed; and the king, in exchange for his share of the produce, is duty-bound to protect his subjects. State relief for the weak and indigent is indicated.[27]

In the early Buddhist writings the Indian economy is described as overwhelmingly rural and the landholdings as usually small. Pricing is little regulated other than by custom, except in the public sector, though price increases are frowned upon. Money mediates most trade, and money-lending forms (with tillage, trade, and harvesting) one of the four honest callings. Occupations are numerous, sometimes carried on under guild auspices, and often pursued in particular localities. The lot of the poor is hard and that of the wage-earner is described as often little if any better than that of the slave. States are represented as republican, oligarchic, or monarchial in form, and the economic role of the state as increasing. The king's share of his subjects' output is reported fixed at between one-twelfth and one-sixth, with mining as a royal undertaking.[28]   Politics and political behavior are subordinated to ethical principles, wisdom is described as superior to wealth, and *dharma* is made to signify political righteousness and universal ethical principles rather than an enforceable hierarchical order.[29]

Accounts of the economy of the Mauryan Empire are somewhat confusing, for the purposes of this essay, since they are based in part

per month for artisans (*ibid.*, p. 289). For detailed summaries of various aspects of the early economy of Northern India as described in contemporary writings see Bose, *op. cit.*, especially Bk. I, chap. ix on land taxation, Bk. III on trade and commerce and the roles of competitive markets and state controls, and Bk. IV on money, money-lending, etc. Bose develops the argument that taxes were usually in kind, based on net rather than on gross output, and assessed in light of quite good estimates of the tax base (*ibid.*, I, 116-127). See also N. Bandyopadhyaya, *Economic Life and Progress in Ancient India*, I, 288-90, 306-8, and S. K. Das, *op. cit.*, chaps. v-vi; Ghoshal, *The Agrarian System*, chap. i.

[27] Ghoshal, *A History*, chap. iii, also chap. xxx, and *Contributions*, pp. 17-18. On the king's obligation under *dharma* to protect his subjects, see Ghoshal, *A History*, pp. 50, 165, 202, 317, and *passim*.

[28] Rapson, ed., *op. cit.*, pp. 198-219; Das, *op. cit.*, chap. vi; Ghoshal, *The Agrarian System*, pp. 7-8, 27-28.

[29] Ghoshal, *A History*, chap. iv; also *ibid.*, chap. xiv.

upon Kauṭilya's own work. The government was monarchial, with the royal power upheld by the sacerdotal power. The king enjoyed ownership of much of the soil and subsoil though not quite so absolutely as in the contemporary Hellenistic world, and he also had the right of eminent domain. He may have commanded as much as one-fourth of the farm produce.[30] He could subject economic life to quite complete administrative control, though traditionally the Indian state had not interfered with the activities of the people except to prevent "hindrances to their lawful pursuits." Even so, villages retained considerable autonomy, and paternalistic and related tendencies were tempered by respect for religion and custom and by the somewhat weakened privileges of guilds and corporations. In sum, the state played a much greater role than formerly in industry and trade. It was able to provide greater security than in the past. It was also more inclined to restrict competition, to participate directly in industry, trade, and mining, and to tax more heavily than had been customary.[31] During the post-Mauryan period (say 184 B.C. to A.D. 200) economic conditions remained much as in the Mauryan period, though fluctuating with political circumstances and with the extent of external trade. The castes may have become more differentiated in terms of occupational constraints and privileges, however, with the result that factor mobility probably was reduced.[32]

III. Arthaśāstra *Objectives and Orientation*

Kauṭilya's *Arthaśāstra* has as its primary purpose instruction of the king in the business of extending and preserving his dominion,

[30] See Ghoshal, *The Agrarian System*, pp. 29-34, 93-98, and *Contributions*, pp. 169-70, 278. Taxes on cattle amounted to one-fiftieth. There were also taxes on workmen and merchants (*ibid.*, pp. 176-80). There was much private ownership of land in and before Mauryan times. See L. Gopal, "Ownership of Agricultural Land in Ancient India," *Journal of the Economic and the Social History of the Orient*, IV, Part 3 (1961), pp. 242-43, 262.

[31] K. A. N. Sastri, ed., *op. cit.*, chap. iii; Rapson, ed., *op. cit.*, chap. xix. Aiyangar maintains that Indian tradition favored a strong economic role on the part of the state. See *Ancient Indian Economic Thought*, pp. 44-50.

[32] See K. A. N. Sastri, ed., *op. cit.*, chaps. xii, xiv-xv, all by U. N. Ghoshal. See especially pp. 450-451, 459-468, on the progress-retarding aspects of Brahmanical, Buddhist, and Jaina canon law and of the caste system. On the revenue system in the Mauryan period, see Ghoshal, *Contributions*, pp. 165-85. Shamasastry uses the term "caste" to translate *varṇa*, or social order (I, 3; notes 38-39 below). Hence I have so used it as well as in the sense of *jāti*, later the legal term for

by whatever means, political or economic, that seem suitable to this end. The term *artha* signifies "wealth," "the subsistence of mankind," "the earth which contains mankind"; the term *śāstra* (science), when affixed to *artha*, designates the "Science of Polity" which "treats of the means of acquiring and maintaining the earth."[33] Wealth is conceived of largely in territorial terms, given that population is available to exploit the land. Moreover, even though primary emphasis is placed upon politics, or the "science of government" (*daṇḍanīti*), the importance of this science is said to derive in considerable measure from the dependence of three other crucial sciences "for their well-being on the science of government." These sciences are philosophy, theology, and economics, the last of which plays a major role in the generation of wealth (I, 4-5) and, as Kauṭilya's later discussion suggests, in the achievement of that welfare which the king is duty-bound to seek for his subjects (I, 19).

How successful a king will be depends not only upon his possessing required personal attributes but also upon his having become well versed in philosophy, theology, economics, and, above all, in the science of government. Numerous personal attributes requisite in kings are listed by Kauṭilya (VI, 1; VIII, 2). Yet, even given that the king possesses many of these attributes (Kauṭilya's argument suggests), he must understand science (which presumably includes economic matter) if he would administer well and strengthen his sovereignty.[34] As it is essential also that the king's councillors and ministers be proficient in the sciences,[35] Kauṭilya implied that persons

caste, defined as an essentially hereditary, etc., occupational group. See Tilman's essay in this volume.

[33] *Arthaśāstra*, Bk. XV, chap. 1, also Bk. I, chap 1. Hereinafter I shall use roman numerals to designate the Book referred to and Arabic numerals to designate the chapter. References are to the translation by R. Shamasastry, cited in note 1. At times Kauṭilya defines "wealth" broadly and loosely: "wealth, virtue, and enjoyment form the aggregate of the three kinds of wealth" (IX, 7). *Artha* may also denote aims of life, or (especially when *Dhanam* is used to signify "wealth") "goods." See Aiyangar, *Ancient Indian Economic Thought*, pp. 21-22.

[34] VIII, 2; also I, 4-5. A king who hates "the science of polity" cannot "maintain his sovereignty" (V, 4; also VI, 1). "A wise king, trained in politics, will, though he possesses a small territory, conquer the whole earth with the help of the best fitted elements of his sovereignty, and will never be defeated" (VI, 1). "The king who is well educated and disciplined in sciences, devoted to good government of his subjects, and bent on doing good to all people will enjoy the earth unopposed" (I, 5). See also I, 19, where it is said that the "duties of the king" require that at night he shall spend something like ninety minutes recalling "to his mind the injunctions of sciences as well as the day's duties."

[35] "Whoever is not well versed in the sciences shall be unfit to hear of council

chosen for these posts must have not only suitable personal attributes but also some knowledge of the relevant sciences (I, 8-10; V, 5-6; VIII, 1-2).[36]

Insisting that there are four and not more or fewer sciences crucial for the king's (and presumably the people's) well-being, Kauṭilya proceeds to identify each and prescribe its role.[37] The first "Ānvīkṣhakī," dealing with philosophical matter, "is most beneficial to the world, keeps the mind steady and firm in weal and woe alike, and bestows excellence of foresight, speech and action" (I, 2). It inculcates both knowledge and virtue. The second, and "triple Vēdas," "are the most useful" in that they "determine the respective duties of the four castes (*brāhman, kṣatriya, vaiśya,* and *śūdra*)[38] and of the four orders of religious life" (I, 3);[39] for observance of these duties assures happiness "here and hereafter" to him who also follows the "customs of the Āryas" and "the rules of caste division of religious life" (I, 3).[40] The third science, "economics" or "Vārtā," comprises "agriculture, cattle-breeding and trade." It

deliberations" (I, 15; also I, 19). A courtier seeking the king's favor should, when admitted to his presence, "give the king instructions in sciences" (V, 4).

[36] The attributes of persons suited to be spies are described in greater detail than those of councillors in I, 11-14, 16. See also Bks. XII-XIII on the use of spies. Kauṭilya's treatment of the selection and use of spies is more elaborate than that found in chap. xiii of the famous Chinese classic, *Sun Tzu on the Art of War*, written about 500 B.C. See translation by Lionel Giles, London, 1910.

[37] "Four, and only four, are the sciences; wherefore it is from these sciences that all that concerns righteousness and wealth is learnt" (I, 2). "Righteousness" here seems to refer to *dharma*, or the law of the social order. On the place of the four sciences in Hindu thought, see Ghoshal, *A History*, pp. 83-84. On *dharma* see *ibid.*, pp. 23, 27, 69, 83.

[38] Concerning the duties of the castes the author writes:
"The duty of the Brāhman is study, teaching, performance of sacrifice, officiating in others' sacrificial performance and the giving and receiving of gifts.

"That of a Kṣatriya is study, performance of sacrifice, giving gifts, military occupation, and protection of life.

"That of a Vaiśya is study, performance of sacrifice, giving gifts, agriculture, cattle-breeding, and trade.

"That of a Śūdra is the serving of the twice-born (dvijāti), agriculture, cattle-breeding, and trade (vārtā), the profession of artizans and court-bards (kārukuśī-lavakarma)" (I, 3). The term "twice-born" refers to those who have undergone initiation into one of the three foregoing classes.

[39] These orders include besides three ascetic orders (student, forest-recluse, and ascetic), the householder whose duties are defined (I, 3): "The duty of a householder is earning livelihood by his own profession, marriage among his equals of different ancestral Rishis, intercourse with his wedded wife after her monthly ablution, gifts to gods, ancestors, guests, and servants, and the eating of the remainder."

[40] "The world, when maintained in accordance with injunctions of the triple Vēdas, will surely progress, but never perish" (I, 3). Hence, the "king shall never allow people to swerve from their duties" (*ibid.*).

is "most useful in that it brings in grains, cattle, gold, forest-produce (*kupya*), and free labor (*viṣṭi*). It is by means of the treasury and the army obtained solely through Vārtā that the king can hold under his control both his and his enemy's party" (I, 4). Vārtā is thus represented as the science dealing with occupations that supply the king with the sinews of war and power. The fourth science is that which treats of "daṇḍa" (punishment) on which "the well-being and progress" of the first three sciences depend. This, the "science of government (*daṇḍanīti*)," has to do with coercion and the appropriate use of "punishment" as a means of keeping people in "their respective duties and occupations" (I, 4).[41] Daṇḍa is further described as "dependent on discipline," acquired through instruction and training in the precepts of the sciences (I, 5; also I, 6-7 and VIII, 3).

Kauṭilya's insistence on the importance of *daṇḍa* indicates that he conceived of the politico-economic world (as did many ancient authors) in essentially Hobbesian terms. It indicates also that he greatly underestimated the self-adjusting or homeostatic character of social systems, together with the mechanisms governing their behavior. He did not infer from such higgling (of which he was aware) as took place in markets that analogous processes of adjustment might be operative elsewhere in society; or perhaps he supposed that the results flowing from such an unconstrained process of adjustment would be incompatible with what he took to be the proper objectives of policy and of the king's welfare.

Arthaśāstra contributes also to resolution of the problem of justice, a subject dealt with at length by Kauṭilya, though not quite after

[41] Kauṭilya observes of "punishment": "It is a means to make acquisitions, to keep them secure, to improve them, and to distribute among the deserved the profits of improvement. It is on this science of government that the course of the progress of the world depends" (I, 4). He observes further (I, 4):

"For punishment (daṇḍa), when awarded with due consideration, makes the people devoted to righteousness and to works productive of wealth and enjoyment; while punishment, when ill-awarded under the influence of greed and anger owing to ignorance, excites fury even among hermits and ascetics adwelling in forests, not to speak of householders.

"But when the law of punishment is kept in abeyance, it gives rise to such disorder as is implied in the proverb of fishes (mātsyanyāyamudbhāvayati); for in the absence of a magistrate (daṇḍadharābhāve), the strong will swallow the weak; but under his protection the weak resist the strong."

Kauṭilya apparently supposed, as did many Indian authors, that in the absence of a strong state anarchy would prevail. See Bandyopadhyaya, *Kauṭilya*, p. 71; Aiyangar, *Indian Cameralism*, p. 96.

the manner of Plato and Aristotle.[42] Kauṭilya's concern was with rules intended to produce sufficient certainty in various interpersonal relations to preserve social stability; even his treatment of price regulation and of weights and measures (II, 15-16, 19) serves this purpose. His conception of law, though not wholly free of metaphysical content, was essentially empirical, and his conception of justice consisted in compliance with what the law sanctioned, on the ground that it promoted the common good.[43] This conception of justice presumably embraced the realization of the four accepted ends of existence: virtue, wealth, pleasure, and salvation.[44]

Most of Book III, on "Law," is devoted to listing or outlining a variety of regulations, which gave expression largely to established customs. The regulations include, among others, those relating to the marital contract and associated property rights; to conditions of purchase and sale and rules governing boundary disputes and inheritance; to the construction and sale of buildings, sanitation, roads and waterways; to non-compliance with contracts or agreements and to the recovery of debts and deposited property; to the conduct of gambling and the punishment of offenses against person or property. The rights as well as the obligations of both slaves (who were comparatively well treated in India) and laborers are dwelt upon (II, 1; III, 13).[45] In Book IV regal rather than customary laws are described. Herein, for example, one finds described various regulations relating to the work of weavers, washermen, goldsmiths, scavengers, physicians, musicians, and merchants (IV, 1-2). The punishment of various types of crime is dealt with particularly in Book IV, though touched upon in other books. Some three hundred offenses, together with the fines to be imposed, are indicated, principally in Books II-IV. Here and there considerable attention is given to both determinants of the validity of transactions and indices of the

[42] M. V. Krishna Rao holds, however, that Kauṭilya, being an exponent of the rule of aristocracy and an opponent of what made for anarchy, had much in common with Aristotle. See *Studies in Kauṭilya*, 2d ed., pp. 62, 172, 186. The supreme value of Kauṭilya's work consisted in "its giving a badly wanted corrective to the otherworldly bias of the Indian temperament and character" (*ibid.*, p. 252).

[43] On this point see Radha Krishna Choudhary, "Kauṭilya's Conception of Law and Justice," *Bihar Research Society Journal*, XXXVII, pts. 1-2 (1951), 284, 286, 288.

[44] Ghoshal, *A History*, p. 10; Aiyangar, *Ancient Indian Economic Thought*, pp. 18, 70-71; Basham, *op. cit.*, pp. 158-59, 215-16.

[45] According to Rao, Kauṭilya accepted the Śūdras as Āryas. Passages derogatory to Śūdras are said to be later interpolations (*op. cit.*, p. 229).

adequacy of evidence (III, 1, 11, 13, 19; IV, 6, 8, 9). It is declared that a fine should not always be an arbitrary multiple of the loss occasioned by an offense, but should "be proportioned to the guilt" (II, 7); but in discussions of fines stress is put upon deterrence from crime rather than upon the nature and degree of guilt. Kauṭilya thus seems to have assumed that fines, when heavy enough, tended to discourage most offenses by making the ratio of prospective cost to gain very high. He thus counted heavily upon individual self-interest, a force he took into account a number of times.[46]

The king was said to be the fountain of justice and one of the four sources of rules and regulations with which individuals must comply if they would enjoy well-being (at least in the next stage of existence); and his heavenly reward was said to depend upon his "protecting his subjects with justice." In a sense, however, the king's role resembled that of the Physiocrats' "despot"; for his function consisted in carrying out the maxims of the cosmic order whence flowed the authority which the king embodied.[47] Thus:

In virtue of his power to uphold the observance of the respective duties of the four castes and of the four divisions of religious life, and in virtue of his power to guard against the violation of the Dharmas, the king is the fountain of justice (dharmapravartaka).

Sacred law (dharma), evidence (vyavahāra), history (caritra), and edicts of kings (rājaśāsana) are the four legs of Law. Of these four in order, the latter is superior to the one previously named.

Dharma is eternal truth holding its sway over the world; vyavahāra, evidence, is in witnesses; caritra, history, is to be found in the tradition (sangraha) of the people; and the order of kings is what is called śāsana.

As the duty of the king consists in protecting his subjects with justice, its observance leads him to heaven. He who does not protect his people or upsets the social order wields his royal sceptre (daṇḍa) in vain.[48]

[46] Kauṭilya's recognition of the importance of self-interest could have had several sources. Bhraspati, author of an earlier work on polity, had formulated a crude hedonism. A sense of responsibility for one's actions had been generated by the belief that the lot of the immortal soul in any given stage of its many stages of diverse existence depended upon its conduct in the previous stage. This belief, however, also generated a strong disposition on the part of the representative individual to accept his station in life and discharge the duties associated with it. See Aiyangar, *Ancient Indian Economic Thought*, pp. 39-44.

[47] See *ibid.*, pp. 48-49; Basham, *op. cit.*, p. 100; Bandyopadhyaya, *Kauṭilya*, p. 67; Kane, *op. cit.*, III, pp. 98-101.

[48] Bk. III, chap. 1. See also n. 49. When the king punished an innocent man, he was required to distribute thirty times the unjust imposition to the Brāhmans (IV, 13). Inasmuch as there was no constitutional check on royal absolutism, Indian writers sought to implant checks in the king's "conscience." See Aiyangar,

It was through kingly power (*daṇḍa*) that the monarch accomplished his duty; supposedly, it was not very difficult for him to discover wherein duty and justice consisted. For sacred law was both known and, as a rule, overriding; it was considered ascendant even over the king's edicts unless it came into conflict with rational law expressed in these edicts. Of course, with the extension of the scope of rational law, uncertainty regarding the content of justice must have increased, particularly in the economic realm wherein the limits on the king's power were not very clear. For example:

It is power and power (daṇḍa) alone which, only when exercised by the king with impartiality and in proportion to guilt, either over his son or his enemy, maintains both this world and the next.

The king who administers justice in accordance with sacred law (dharma), evidence (vyavahāra), history [or usage] (samsthā), and edicts of kings (nyāya), which is the fourth, will be able to conquer the whole world bounded by the four quarters (chaturantām mahīm).

Whenever there is disagreement between history and sacred law or between evidence and sacred law, then the matter shall be settled in accordance with sacred law.

But whenever sacred law (śāstra) is in conflict with rational law (dharmanyāya = king's law), then reason shall be held authoritative; for there the original text (on which the sacred law has been based) is not available.[49]

IV. *The Economic and Demographic Bases of Power*

According to Kauṭilya political power is greatly dependent upon economic power, even though political power may be employed and should be employed to augment economic power, so long as the prospect of gain from such an undertaking sufficiently outweighs the associated risk of loss. This argument, bearing some similarity to

Indian Cameralism, pp. 99-102. See also Kane, *op. cit.*, III, pp. 96-102; and on "the king's judicial sovereignty," Ghoshal, *A History*, pp. 113-15.
[49] Bk. III, chap. 1. The term *dharma* signifies the Sacred Canon; *vyavahāra*, current law; *samsthā*, usage; and *nyāya*, reasoning. Kauṭilya was the first to emphasize the importance of secular law and to make reasoning a source of state law, along with the Sacred Canon, current law, and usage. In or shortly after the first century A.D. it was recognized that the *Arthaśāstra* as well as the *Dharmaśāstra* was a source of state law. See Ghoshal, *A History*, pp. 113-14, 161; Choudhary, *op. cit.*, pp. 288-89. The weight allowed traditional usages permitted the settling of inheritance and some other matters in accordance with local custom (III, 7; also II, 7), unless these customs ran counter to the king's interest or were deemed "unrighteous" (XIII, 5). Guild, caste, and comparable usages usually had royal sanction (III, 1, 14; XIII, 5).

that encountered in European mercantilist literature, had the support of various subsequent Hindu political writers.[50] Moreover, it led Kauṭilya to urge the king to extend the territory under his control and to amass other forms of wealth as well. For he believed that realization of "charity and desire," which along with wealth formed the "three pursuits of life," depended largely upon the prior possession of "wealth" (I, 7); and he went so far as to describe wealth as superior to "virtue" and "enjoyment."[51] It was essential, therefore, that the king be active; after all, activity gave rise to wealth, and (presumably) wealth made for the welfare and happiness of his people (I, 19)[52] and for the progress of virtue.[53]

It was the revenue yielded by wealth that was of major concern, in Kauṭilya's opinion. Revenue was of general importance:

All undertakings depend upon finance. Hence foremost attention shall be paid to the treasury.

Public prosperity (pracārasamṛddhih), rewards for good conduct (charitrānugrahah), capture of thieves, dispensing with (the service of too many) government servants, abundance of harvest, prosperity of commerce, absence of troubles and calamities (upasargapramokṣhah), diminution or remission of taxes, and income in gold (hiranyōpāyanam) are all conducive to financial prosperity.

[50] E.g., see Ghoshal, *A History*, chaps. xxi, xxvii; Aiyangar, *Indian Cameralism*, *passim*.

[51] See IX, 7, where doubt is expressed respecting some modes of acquiring wealth through international strife. He said (*ibid.*):

"Wealth, virtue, and enjoyment form the aggregate of the three kinds of wealth. Of these, it is better to secure that which is mentioned first than that which is subsequently mentioned in the order of enumeration.

"Harm, sin and grief form the aggregate of the three kinds of harm. Of these, it is better to provide against that which is mentioned first than that which is subsequently mentioned in order of enumeration.

"Wealth or harm, virtue or sin, and enjoyment or grief, are the aggregate of the three kinds of doubts. Of these, it is better to try that which is mentioned first than that which is mentioned later in the order of enumeration, and which it is certain to shake off. Thus the determination of opportunities."

[52] "In the happiness of his subjects lies his happiness; in their welfare his welfare; whatever pleases himself he shall not consider as good, but whatever pleases his subjects he shall consider as good.

"Hence the king shall ever be active and discharge his duties; the root of wealth is activity, and of evil its reverse.

"In the absence of activity acquisitions present and to come will perish; by activity he can achieve both his desired ends and abundance of wealth" (I, 19). At least a fourth of the king's daily duties consisted in economic administration. See also VIII, 1, on the interdependence of the king's and his subjects' welfare.

[53] "As virtue is the basis of wealth and as enjoyment is the end of wealth, success in achieving that kind of wealth which promotes virtue, wealth and enjoyment is termed success in all (sarvārthasiddhi). Thus varieties of success" (IX, 7). On the importance attached to wealth, see Basham, *op. cit.*, pp. 215-16.

Obstruction (pratibandha), loan (prayōga), trading (vyavahāra), fabrication of accounts (avastāra), causing the loss of revenue (parihāpaṇa), self-enjoyment (upabhōga), barter (parivartana), and defalcation (apahāra) are the causes that tend to deplete (the treasury).[54]

Revenue was also of particular importance. It served to retain the support of the king's army and prevent its going over to the enemy (VIII, 1). It thus made for "strength of sovereignty" which depended on the ruler's possessing "a prosperous treasury and a strong army" (VI, 2). For this reason apparently Kauṭilya sometimes described gold as preferable to population, since gold could attract population (VII, 5, 9). As a rule, however, he emphasized the importance of population, even though he considered territory the most significant form of wealth since it attracted both gold and population (VII, 5, 9, 10). Whence he described "command of plenty of men and wealth" as a major subject of "every" deliberation of the king's council and a main means to the accomplishment of the king's concerns (I, 15). Mineral wealth was sometimes distinguished from territorial wealth, inasmuch as mines yielded gold. "Mines are the source of treasury; from treasury comes the power of government; and the earth whose ornament is treasury is acquired by means of treasury and army."[55]

While peace and industry made for wealth,[56] it could be won also through military undertakings. But such undertakings were indicated only if what the king stood to gain sufficiently outweighed the loss of men and materials that an invasion might entail, together with any other adverse effects.[57] It was essential also that the "wealth" in prospect not constitute a source of potential difficulties. Thus (IX, 7):

[54] II, 8. On the prevention of peculation, a problem then as now, see II, 9.

[55] II, 12; see also VII, 9. "Uneconomical transactions" were to be avoided (I, 7).

[56] See VI, 2, where it is said that "acquisition and security (of property) are dependent upon peace and industry."

[57] "When profits (from two sources) are equal, he should consider the place and time, the strength and means (required to acquire it), affection and disaffection (caused by it), intrigue and absence of intrigue (involving it), its nearness and distance, its present and future effects, its constant worth or worthlessness, and its plentifulness and usefulness; and he should accept only that profit which is possessed of most of the above good characteristics.

"Obstructions to profit are: passion, anger, timidity, mercy, bashfulness, living like one who is not an Ārya, haughtiness, pity, desire for the other world, strict adherence to virtuous life, deception, neediness, envy, negligence of what is at hand, generosity, want of faith, fear, negligence, inability to endure cold, heat, and rain, and faith in the auspiciousness of lunar days and stars" (IX, 4).

Wealth which, when obtained, increases the enemy's prosperity, or which, though obtained, is repayable to the enemy, or which causes loss of men and money, is dangerous wealth; for example, wealth which is enjoyed in common by neighbouring kings and which is acquired at their expense; or wealth which is asked for by an enemy; or wealth which is seized like one's own property; or wealth which is acquired in the front and which causes future troubles or provokes an enemy in the rear; or wealth which is obtained by destroying a friend or by breaking a treaty which is therefore detested by the Circle of States—all these are the varieties of dangerous wealth.

Wealth which causes fear from one's own people or from an enemy is provocative wealth.

Having been acquired, wealth could be preserved by avoiding the causes of wealth-destroying "troubles" and by correcting such troubles if they arose (VIII, 4).

Population was important for two main reasons: it was the source of military manpower; and, being the essential complement to territory and mines, it made possible both the colonization of territory and wasteland and the exploitation of land and mines. Whence population constituted one of the two main sources of political and military strength; physical wealth, above all land and mines, was the other.[58]

Kauṭilya, therefore, devoted considerable attention to the comparative value of different kinds of land under given conditions and to the business of selecting the land of most value under prevailing circumstances (see Book VII, which has to do with the acquisition of territory and with international relations and foreign policy). For example, he declared it better to colonize fertile, well-watered land than land not so endowed, since the former was more productive and hence (presumably) capable of supporting more people; but of two landed areas which differed little, the larger one was to be preferred. Land containing mines was to be preferred to land that was merely fertile, since precious metals could be used to purchase additional land. Thickly populated land was to be preferred to sparsely populated land, for it was more productive; and this was particularly true when the lowest of the four castes predominated, since its members were most serviceable and permanent.[59] When a king lacked people

[58] E.g., see I, 15; VII, 9, 11.
[59] This paragraph is based on VII, 11. In VIII, 4, Kauṭilya suggests that it "is possible to recruit vulgar men," and much more easily than "noble" men. The military aspects of land being considered for acquisition from foreign countries are evaluated and compared in VII, 10; see also VIII, 1, 4-5.

to settle waste land (VII, 11, 13-14), he might, if possible, Kauṭilya seems to imply, draw upon external sources. While a king profited most when he acquired land and people in combination, it usually was advisable to acquire territory even though it was little-peopled at the time (VII, 11, 14; VIII, 1). For such territory could be used to attract gold and population (VII, 9).

While Kauṭilya did not deal directly with checks to population or with its qualitative composition, he did refer to these matters indirectly. He approved remarriage of women under various circumstances (III, 4). He noted several times that war might reduce population (e.g., IX, 4) and he observed that famine, being widespread as a rule, was more destructive of numbers than pestilence, which usually was incident only in local areas (VIII, 4). He noted that while "vulgar" people were useful (VII, 1), it was essential also to recruit able and noble men, who were very rare (VIII, 4). He enjoined revenue-collectors "to find out causes of emigration and immigration of persons of migratory habit" (II, 35) and he limited the right to become an "ascetic" largely to persons who had "passed the age of copulation" (II, 1). His references to checks, however, are little more than isolated *obiter dicta*. Procurement of abortion was declared punishable only when the subject was a female slave (III, 20).

Kauṭilya dealt with the colonization and settlement of newly acquired and underpopulated areas and with the means whereby either population pressure or population shortage might be relieved. The king was to facilitate the construction of certain kinds of overhead capital (II, 1), to avoid "overtaxation" and other causes of "impoverishment" which caused people to emigrate (VII, 5), to grant remission of taxes for several years and thereby encourage improvement of the land (III, 9; V, 2; XIII, 5), and to make a country (especially one recently conquered) more attractive than it had been (XIII, 5).

Either by inducing foreigners to immigrate (paradeśāpavāhanena) or by causing the thickly-populated centres of his own kingdom to send forth the excessive population (svadeśābhishyandavamanēna vā), the king may construct villages either on new sites or on old ruins (bhūtapūrvama-bhūtapūrvam vā).

Villages consisting of not less than a hundred families and of not more than five hundred families of agricultural people of Śūdra caste,* with boundaries extending as far as a krōśá (2,250 yards) or two, and capable of protecting each other, shall be formed. Boundaries shall be denoted by a river, a mountain, forests, bulbous plants (gṛṣṭi), caves, artificial buildings (sētubandha), or by trees such as śālmali (silk cotton tree), śamī (Acacia Suma), and kṣīravṛkṣa (milky trees).[60]

Villages were not to be constructed in parts of the country exposed to "the inroads of enemies and wild tribes"[61] or subject to "frequent visitations of famine and pestilence" (II, 1), but provision was to be made "for pasture grounds on uncultivable tracts" and for elephant "forests" (II, 2).[62] Villages usually were surrounded by a fence or stockade (III, 10). Provision was also to be made for fortification of the kingdom's frontiers and for protection within the interior. A fortress city was to be set up "in the centre of each eight hundred villages," and smaller cities at the center of smaller collections of villages (II, 1); and strong and productive "capital cities" were to be situated "in the centre and the extremities of the kingdom" (VI, 1).[63] The king was to provide, or to assist the inhabitants in providing, various types of overhead capital and keeping it "in good repair" (II, 1), as well as to supply with money (V, 3) or with grain and cattle those who colonized waste land (V, 2).[64] He was also to carry on activities more or less for his own

[60] II, 1, p. 45. According to Meyer, the phrase marked by an asterisk should be translated as "Śūdras and agricultural people" (op. cit., I, 58).

[61] Elsewhere he compares "wild tribes," together with their power, to enemy countries (VIII, 4).

[62] See also II, 31-32 on elephant raising and training. Elephant forests and elephants were so highly prized because they were deemed essential to victory in war (II, 2).

[63] "There shall be set up a sthānīya (a fortress of that name) in the centre of eight hundred villages, a drōṇemukha in the centre of four hundred villages, a khārvāṭika in the centre of two hundred villages, and a saṅgrahaṇa in the midst of a collection of ten villages." (II, 1). Kauṭilya thus envisages a network of places of different sizes, a large town in the center of 800 villages, a smaller one in the center of 400, a still smaller one in the center of 200, and a large village at the center of each 10 small villages. What amounts to a discussion of town planning and the location of activities in large capital cities is presented in II, 3-4, concerned with the construction, peopling, and provisioning of forts. The king's treasury was to be located in the centrally located and fortified capital city (II, 3-4; V, 6) or at the boundary of the kingdom (II, 5; V, 6). See also III, 1.

[64] "He shall also construct reservoirs (sētu), filled with water either perennial or drawn from some other source. Or he may provide with sites, roads, timber, and other necessary things those who construct reservoirs of their own accord. Likewise in the construction of places of pilgrimage (puṇyasthāna) and of groves.

"Whoever stays away from any kind of cooperative construction (sambhūya sētubandhāt) shall send his servants and bullocks to carry on his work, shall have a share in the expenditure, but shall have no claim to the profit" (II, 1).

"He shall protect agriculture from the molestation of oppressive fines, free

account, presumably for profit and to foster settlement (II, 1).[65] Kauṭilya referred particularly to setting up "manufactories to prepare commodities from forest produce and forests productive of commodities."

Kauṭilya did not suggest the existence of an optimum population or economy, though he believed a considerable density of population was economically advantageous (VII, 1). He did, however, identify (VI, 1) what he called the "elements of sovereignty" (i.e., "the king, the country, the fort, the treasury, the army and the friend, and the enemy") and indicate the qualities whereon depended the strength of these elements, among them the qualities of a good king (VI, 1; VIII, 2) and of a "good country." He described "a good country" or territorial division thus:

Possessed of capital cities both in the centre and the extremities of the kingdom, productive of subsistence not only to its own people, but also to outsiders on occasions of calamities, repulsive to enemies, powerful enough to put down neighbouring kings, free from miry, rocky, uneven, and desert tracts, as well as from conspirators, tigers, wild beasts and large tracts of wilderness, beautiful to look at, containing fertile lands, mines, timber and elephant forests, and pasture grounds, artistic, containing hidden passages, full of cattle, not depending upon rain for water, possessed of land and waterways, rich in various kinds of commercial articles, capable of bearing the burden of a vast army and heavy taxation, inhabited by agriculturists of good and active character, full of intelligent masters and servants and with a population noted for its loyalty and good character—these are the qualities of a good country.[67]

labour, and taxes (daṇḍaviṣṭikarābādhaih); herds of cattle from thieves, tigers, poisonous creatures and cattle disease.

"He shall not only clear roads of traffic from the molestations of courtiers (vallabha), of workmen (kārmika), of robbers, and of boundary guards, but also keep them from being destroyed by herds of cattle.

"Thus the king shall not only keep in good repair timber and elephant forests, buildings, and mines created in the past, but also set up new ones" (II, 1).

[65] "He shall carry on mining operations and manufactures, exploit timber and elephant forests, offer facilities for cattle breeding and commerce, construct roads for traffic both by land and water, and set up market towns (paṇyapattana)" (II, 1).

"The king shall exercise his right to ownership (swāmyam) with regard to fishing, ferrying and trading in vegetables (haritapaṇya), in reservoirs or lakes (sētushu)" (II, 1).

[66] See II, 2; also II, 17, for list of forest products.

[67] VI, 1. See also VIII, 1, where the importance of *both* cultivators and potential warriors is stressed. Pran Nath rejects Shamasastry's translation of *janapada* as "kingdom," saying it indicates a territorial division sufficiently large and varied to constitute a self-supporting independent state, though much smaller than a country (*deśa*) of which there were eighty-four in India in the seventh

246 ADMINISTRATION AND ECONOMIC DEVELOPMENT IN INDIA

The seven elements of sovereignty were interrelated in that weakness in one might be compensated by the relatively greater strength of others (VIII, 1). It was possible, above all, for a wise and well-trained king to overcome weaknesses in elements of sovereignty and in time to strengthen them (VI, 1). It was essential, however, to identify which elements were critical and to strengthen them accordingly.[68]

V. *Revenue and Expenditure*

It is not surprising, given Kauṭilya's emphasis upon the political importance of wealth and income, that he had much to say of the collection of revenue from both the subjects and the properties of the king and something to say of the disposition of this revenue. He devoted more attention, in fact, to administrative aspects of public finance than to any other economic subject. For he looked upon adequacy of revenue as fundamental to the continuity of the state (i.e., the king and his bureaucracy), and he believed taxation justifiable on the ground that kings prevented anarchy and maintained "the safety and security of their subjects" in what, if kingless, would have been a strife-ridden, Hobbesian world.[69] His discussion, however, reflected the essentially Brāhman character of the society for which he was prescribing in that the priestcraft enjoyed tax exemption and other privileges.[70]

---

century A.D. (*op. cit.*, pp. 14, 45-50). Such a division might number several thousand square miles, though its average size may have been only about a thousand (*ibid.*, pp. 35, 50-52, 56). Among the king's problems was that of preventing the nobility from obtaining control of such self-sufficient territories (*ibid.*, pp. 130-38). On the adequacy of countries and the meaning of Sanskrit terms, see Kane, *op. cit.*, III, pp. 132-38.

[68] This subject is dealt with in Book VIII and also in Books VII and IX, where alternative courses of action are contrasted and assessed.

[69] See I, 13. This argument in support of taxation was anticipated by earlier writers, the Indo-Aryan polity having become sufficiently organized already in "the early Vedic period . . . to make it possible for the king to collect regular taxes (usually called *bali*) from the subjects" and from conquered enemies. See Ghoshal, *A History*, pp. 50-53, and *Contributions*, pp. 9-10, 17-19. Also Aiyangar, *Ancient Indian Economic Thought*, pp. 44-50, 146-47, on the importance Indian writers attached to the state and its protective role.

[70] "Brahmadeya lands yielding sufficient produce and exempted from taxes and fines" were granted to those who performed sacrifices, spiritual guides, priests, and persons learned in the Vēdas (II, 1). Some forest land was set aside for Brāhmans (II, 2). Men learned in the Vēdas were allowed salt toll-free as were persons engaged in penance and some laborers (II, 12). Brāhmans, along with mes-

Kauṭilya's treatment of revenue collection embodied almost no economic analysis, being confined largely to describing the duties of collectors of revenue, the level and character of the imposts, tolls, etc., quite elaborate methods of account-keeping, the prevention of fraud and embezzlement (of which there were some forty forms), and the penalties to be imposed upon officials and tax-liable persons found guilty of violating rules relating to payments of money, goods, and services due the state.[71] Nor is much attention given to the economic effects of tolls, imposts, etc., in chapters on tolls and on the king's share in the output of various industries; only in discussions of tax rates does implicit theory emerge in the form of maxims.[72] Chapters concerned with the duties of the superintendents of some twenty governmental departments (Bk. II) are devoted almost entirely to the police and regulatory duties of these superintendents and to descriptions of attributes of the activities subject to regulation. Even in Kauṭilya's account of modes of discovering individuals suited to be collectors of revenue, his emphasis is upon their personal attributes (e.g., honesty) and not upon their economic knowledge.[73]

---

sengers, relatively helpless people, and specified productive workers could freely cross rivers (II, 28). Unclaimed property that had belonged to a Brāhman learned in the Vēdas was made over to similar persons instead of to the king (III, 5). Other tax-exempt classes were much smaller than the Brāhman. See Ghoshal, *Contributions*, pp. 136-41.

[71] Book II (chaps. 6-9, 15-16, 35) deals with the collection of revenue, the keeping of governmental accounts, the detection of embezzlement, and the prevention of undesirable fiscal conduct; other chapters (II, 15, 24) deal with the production and use of agricultural products, taxes thereon, and the administration of crown lands; another (II, 17) deals with forest produce. The duties of a city superintendent, seemingly confined to the police of the city, included ascertaining the income and expenditure of households, as did the duties of parallel officials responsible for districts and villages (II, 35-36). The prevention of false weighing is treated in II, 14, 19.

[72] Chapters are devoted to tolls and their collection (II, 21-22), mining and manufacture (II, 12), the production and sale of liquor (II, 25), commerce and forest produce (II, 16-17), navigation and fishing (II, 28), dairy husbandry (II, 29), and the duties of prostitutes (II, 27). The role of the state goldsmith is treated in II, 13-14.

[73] "Native, born of high family, influential, well trained in arts, possessed of foresight, wise, of strong memory, bold, eloquent, skillful, intelligent, possessed of enthusiasm, dignity and endurance, pure in character, affable, firm in loyal devotion, endowed with excellent conduct, strength, health and bravery, free from procrastination and ficklemindedness, affectionate, and free from such qualities as excite hatred and enmity—these are the qualifications of a ministerial officer (amātyasampat)" (I, 9). See also V, 5-6 on the attributes of ministers. "Capacity shown in work" is also stressed (I, 8; II, 9). Further tests, accomplished with the aid of spies, are suggested. "Those whose purity has been tested under monetary allurements shall be employed in the work of a revenue collector and

Kauṭilya classified the sources of revenue in various ways, but always on administrative rather than on economic grounds. He distinguished between revenue collection under ordinary circumstances and revenue collection when the king was in extraordinary need (V, 2). He distinguished between what the king collected through taxation and fines and what he got from the operation or the leasing (for rents and shares in the output) of his mining and manufacturing properties, crown land, etc.[74] He listed sixty-six or sixty-seven sources of the king's revenue, based predominantly on land, and grouped them under seven heads resting essentially upon the geographical location of the activities and individuals subject to taxation, tolls, etc.: those found in fortified and urban areas and those found in rural situations; those found at sites of mineral exploitation, or in pastoral, forest, or intensely cultivated (e.g., horticultural) areas; and those situated along traffic-carrying roads and waterways (II, 6). He also distinguished seven forms of revenue by type (II, 6). Finally, for purposes of administration he divided the kingdom into four districts, distinguished the urban centers from the villages, and classified the villages according to size and nature of tax liability.[75]

While Kauṭilya listed a variety of taxes and tolls, together with tax rates, it is difficult in many instances to discover the resulting tax liability, in part because the bases to which the rates applied are

chamberlain" (I, 10). Government officers may lose revenue if they are careless or insufficiently active (II, 7). The importance of memory is implied in a chapter (II, 5) on the duties of the chamberlain respecting revenue collection. "He shall have so thorough a knowledge of both external and internal incomes running even for a hundred years that, when questioned, he can point out without hesitation the exact amount of net balance that remains after expenditure has been met with." Elsewhere (II, 9) it is indicated that a minister should not employ "prodigal, spendthrift" persons, or "niggardly" persons who hoard money and thereby inflict hardship on their servants, and that, if such persons lack "support of a strong party," they shall be deprived of their property.

[74] II, 12. The king collected ten kinds of revenue from mines as well as tolls on mineral imports (e.g., one-sixth on salt). He could derive other advantages from his state monopoly in mining and commerce in mineral products. See II, 12, 22. He also derived revenue from his participation in the distribution of merchandise (II, 16) and from coinage (II, 12). According to K. T. Shah, Kauṭilya when serving as prime minister debased the coinage in order to raise money for the state. See *Ancient Foundations of Economics in India* (Bombay, 1954), p. 156.

[75] II, 35. Some villages were exempted from cash taxation; some supplied soldiers; some furnished labor or dairy produce; and some paid taxes in the form of grain, cattle, gold, or raw material (*ibid.*, also III, 10). An accountant was made responsible for each five or ten villages and charged with registering the population, estimating income and expenditure by family, collecting taxes, etc., though under the surveillance of inspectors and spies (II, 35).

imperfectly specified. Similarly, it is difficult to determine what proportion of the income originating in mining, manufacturing, agricultural, and commercial activities undertaken in the king's name finally passed into the king's hands.[76] Under ordinary circumstances taxes on agriculturalists were fixed at one-sixth of the produce, a rate become traditional even before Kauṭilya wrote, but this burden was accentuated by various other taxes.[77] The king's share of catches of animals, fish, and birds ranged between one-tenth and one-sixth (II, 26, 28). Import rates, intended for revenue rather than for trade-limitation, generally ranged between 4 per cent and 20 per cent ad valorem; for trade apparently was forbidden or highly restricted only in military equipment, precious stones, grains, and cattle (II, 16, 21, 22, 28). Various other charges were imposed on merchants (II, 16, 19, 21, 22, 28). Prostitutes were taxed two day's earnings per month (II, 26). The state collected 5 per cent on liquor sales (II, 25) and gambling stakes (III, 20).[78] There were taxes in terms of labor and soldiers as well as in money and kind (II, 35).

In times of emergency the king could make greater demands upon his subjects, but supposedly "only once," and then only on some and in rough proportion to their capacity to pay.[79] He might take one-fourth of grain; one-sixth of forest and farm products; one-tenth to one-sixth of the stock of those raising various animals; one-half of ivory, animal skins, and the stock of those raising cocks and pigs; all the property of goldsmiths; half the wages of prostitutes and dramatists; and cash payments from merchants, artisans, and traders (V, 2). He might require the peasantry to raise an extra crop

---

[76] Some of these obscurities are clarified by Ghoshal in his *Contributions to the History of the Hindu Revenue System* and in his *Agrarian System in Ancient India*. See also Bose, *op. cit.*, I, chap. ix.

[77] II, 15, also I, 13. See Ghoshal, *Contributions*, pp. 9, 17, 27-29, 34-42, 58.

[78] For detailed accounts of these various taxes, see Ghoshal, *Contributions, passim*.

[79] "The king who finds himself in a great financial trouble and needs money, may collect (revenue by demand). In such parts of his country as depend solely upon rain for water and are rich in grain, he may demand of his subjects one-third or one-fourth of their grain, according to their capacity. He shall never demand of such of his subjects as live in tracts of middle or low quality; nor of people who are of great help in the construction of fortifications, gardens, buildings, roads for traffic, colonisation of waste lands, exploitation of mines, and formation of forest preserves for timber and elephants; nor of people who live on the border of his kingdom or who have not enough subsistence." Colonizers of waste lands, forest tribes, and Brāhmans were exempt from these taxes, though they might sell the king produce at satisfactory prices in gold. See V, 2, entitled, "Replenishment of the Treasury."

(V, 2). Should all these methods prove inadequate, deceitful means might be employed to induce benevolences and voluntary donations (V, 2).[80]

The king derived revenue also from various undertakings in his name. When agriculture was conducted entirely by employees of the king, he got all the produce. When crown lands were cultivated by tenants, however, the latter got one-fifth to one-half or more of the harvest and apparently, if the land was irrigated, paid specified water rates (II, 24). Revenue was collected from the state goldsmith (II, 13-14), from mining and manufacturing operations (II, 12), from those handling the king's merchandise (II, 16), from forest products (II, 17), from state weaving establishments (II, 23), and from activities in several other branches of the government (II, 6).

Public expenditure, of which there were many forms,[81] prompted a number of Kauṭilya's observations. First, it was essential that expenditure on staff be limited. "In accordance with the requirements of his forts and country parts, the king should fix under one-fourth of the total revenue the charges of maintaining his servants" (V, 3). This entailed "dispensing with (the service of too many) government servants" (II, 8). It is not quite clear, however, if this limitation extended to profitable employment on behalf of the king, that is, to the employment of persons to carry on his mining and manufacturing operations and his commercial, agricultural, trading, forest-product, and other undertakings (II, 1, 12, 16-17, 24). Presumably, it did not. It was essential, second, as noted below, that wasteful and unnecessary expenditures be avoided by the king and his servants.[82] Third, while Kauṭilya was opposed to indiscriminate mendicancy and idleness (II, 1, 23), he stated it was essential to keep on hand a reserve of food, clothing, munitions of war, etc., sufficient to support

---

[80] See also Ghoshal, *Contributions*, pp. 125-35.

[81] Bandyopadhyaya identifies eleven objects of public expenditure in Kauṭilya's work: royal household; religious establishments; magistracy, judiciary, spies, and menial staff; military personnel and establishment, together with pensions; government factories; hired labor; loans to cultivators, colonization costs, irrigation expense; widows, orphans, indigents; teachers and teaching establishments; pensions to widows and children of those killed in the king's service; public works, roads, canals, embankments. See *Kauṭilya*, pp. 167-68; also Ghoshal, *Contributions*, pp. 153-59.

[82] Kauṭilya urged the king to avoid "expensive sports" and advocated that villagers not be diverted by sports, plays, etc. (II, 1). "A sporting king causes oppression by showing indulgence to his courtiers, by seizing and begging, and by obstructing work in the manufactories" (VIII, 4). Prodigals, spendthrifts, etc., are criticized in I, 9; II, 36; and IV. 1.

the population in times of calamity, for years if necessary, and to be able at all times to sustain the currently needy, the helpless, the orphans, and so on.[83] Fourth, the king had to undertake various kinds of overhead capital and other improvement expenditures, on irrigation, roads, highways, buildings, fire protection, and so on (II, 1, 5-6, 34, 36; III, 8, 10). Fifth, it was desirable that the king undertake profitable forms of expenditure, such as those upon objects which yielded income periodically (II, 6, 9). "The king will have to suffer in the end if he curtails the fixed amount of expenditure on profitable works" (II, 7).[84] Sixth, it was important that the king's stewards manage his properties, together with expenditure upon them, so as to render them profitable (e.g., II, 12, 17, 23, 24).

Kauṭilya's principal concern apparently was to conduct the assembly and the distribution of the king's (or the state's) income in such wise as to strengthen the state. His aim was to increase current if not also "accidental" revenue (i.e., fines, treasure troves, escheated property, etc.), to avoid wasteful outlays while also undertaking profitable or socially necessary expenditure, and to enlarge the cumulating balance of past receipts over past expenditures. "A wise collector-general shall conduct the work of revenue-collection, increasing the income and decreasing the expenditure."[85] Wasteful expenditure apparently assumed the form both of excessive outlay when gathering in revenue and of waste or misuse of funds, a practice that seems to have been common (though subject to heavy penalties) because difficult to detect.[86] Respecting revenue, Kauṭilya observed also that

[83] II, 1, 4, 15. The superintendent of the storehouse was instructed to treat half his store as a reserve and to keep it intact by replacing its contents as those on hand were consumed (II, 15). Apparently there was also local assistance for the needy. In time of famine the ruler might distribute seed and provisions from the hoards "of the rich" as well as from his own stores (IV, 3).

[84] See also II, 6, 12, 15 on the distinction between income and income-yielding instruments.

[85] II, 6. See also II, 7-8; and II, 9, where he says that "those who increase the king's revenue instead of eating it up, and are loyally devoted to him, shall be made permanent in service." Elsewhere (V, 3) he concludes that "when both the receipts and expenditures are properly cared for, the king will never find himself in financial or military difficulties." Some hoarding was essential to guard against the heavy requirements of war, notes Aiyangar (*Ancient Indian Economic Thought*, p. 123).

[86] II, 9. "Just as it is impossible not to taste the honey or the poison that finds itself at the tip of the tongue, so it is impossible for a government servant not to eat up, at least, a bit of the king's revenue. Just as fish moving under the water cannot possibly be found out either as drinking or not drinking water, so government servants employed in the government work cannot be found out (while) taking money (for themselves)" (II, 9).

the king would suffer if either too little or too much revenue were collected. He who "lessens the revenue eats the king's wealth" while he who "doubles the revenue eats into the capital of the country" (II, 9; also II, 1). Kauṭilya thus implied that the king should adjust his demands to the "capacity" of various parts of the country to supply revenue, taking into account the effect of current taxation upon this capacity in the future (V, 2). If he did not, the revenue-yielding capacity of the economy could not expand as it otherwise might.[87] Kauṭilya indicated also that sometimes taxes had best be remitted temporarily or deferred until the source had become productive (II, 1, 16; III, 9-10; V, 2). It was inadvisable, however, to remit the taxes of leaders, neighboring kings, wild tribes, etc., since such action would merely cause loss of wealth and "stagnation of financial position" (VIII, 4). He took no notice of the possibility that the accumulation of gold and silver in the coffers of the king might have a depressive effect on prices and economic activity, perhaps because he considered a vast store of gold, silver, and gems the best offset to "calamities of long duration" (VI, 1).

V. Economic Organization

The economy which Kauṭilya envisaged and which therefore closely resembled that in which he lived was predominantly agricultural, with services, mineral extraction, and essentially handicraft activities predominating in the non-agricultural sector. Something like nine-tenths of the population lived in villages.[88] The working

[87] "Just as fruits are gathered from a garden as often as they become ripe, so revenue shall be collected as often as it becomes ripe. Collection of revenue or of fruits, when unripe, shall never be carried on, lest their sources may be injured, causing immense trouble" (V, 2).

[88] While villages, under Kauṭilya's plan, would number 200-500 families, made up of śūdras and agricultural people, it is not clear how many persons there would be per family, many of which would be joint, though 5 seems an acceptable average. Each 800 ordinary villages would have as centers 80 large villages, 4 small towns, 2 medium size towns, and one large town. The boundaries of a village being said to extend 2,250-4,500 yards, area per village probably would vary between 1.7 and 7.2 square miles, or 5-22 acres per family (II, 1). Assume that four-fifths of the population is non-urban, and that in the rural or village population one worker in each nine is engaged in non-agricultural activities. Assume also that the 880 villages average about 2,000 (given families of 4-6 members) persons per village, or 1,760,000 in all. Next assume that the 7 towns (or cities) have a population approximating one-ninth of the village population, or about 196,000 in all. The population per town (or city) would then average about 28,000, with

up if not also the extraction of minerals seems to have been conducted on a very small scale as was the exploitation of agricultural and forest products.[89] Responsibility for making decisions respecting production was vested in agents of the king who managed his agricultural, mining, manufacturing and commercial undertakings and in peasants, merchants, and others who were essentially independent though subject to various rules and regulations set down in the *Arthaśāstra*.[90] There was little restriction upon external trade other than that in arms, gems, grain, and some animals for reasons of military strength (II, 21).

The functioning of this economy was not subjected to explicit economic analysis though theoretical inferences are implied. Thus there is no discussion of division of labor as such, but it is frequently noted that specialists or experts should be employed (II, 10, 12, 18, 23, 24, 25, 32). It is also noted that the location of activities is or should be oriented to consumers or raw materials (II, 4, 12, 17, 24) and that it is affected by the condition of transport facilities (II, 6, 34). The importance of invention is noted only once, in a discussion of the national armory, which was well equipped.[91] The role of self-interest is recognized, but not that of the price system (though price regulation is advocated).

Kautilya did not hold trade, manufacture, or mining in disesteem or describe any of these activities as socially inferior to agriculture. The role of the merchant was an honorable one (II, 16, 28), and he

---

(perhaps) 4 averaging about 16,000, 2 about 33,000, and 1 about 66,000. This conjectural pattern, suggested by Kautilya's plan (II, 1), is compatible with Davis's estimate (*op. cit.*, pp. 127,200) that 90.7 per cent of India's population lived in places under 5,000 in 1881 and 88.9 per cent in 1931, at which time the corresponding percentages for Pakistan and East Pakistan were 89.5 and 92.6. Of those living in places of more than 5,000 in 1931 in India and West Pakistan, respectively, about two-thirds lived in places under 50,000. Pran Nath supposes 5 to be the average number of persons per family in ancient times and indicates a village of 100 estates (400-600 families) to be large (*op. cit.*, pp. 39-40, 57).

[89] His discussion of gems, the extraction and fabrication of mineral products (e.g., copper, lead, tin, mercury, brass, bronze, arsenic, iron), and the production and use of agricultural and forest products ran in technological rather than in economic terms, though not to the complete neglect of the economic and administrative rules deemed relevant. See in particular II, 11-15, 17, 23, 29-32.

[90] See also VIII, 4, where the importance of grains, cattle, gold, and raw products for the maintenance of the people is stressed. How well these rules were known and/or enforced is not inferable from Kautilya's observations. The heaviness of the penalties for non-compliance suggests, however, that the native propensity to comply was not very powerful and needed considerable reinforcement.

[91] The Superintendent of the Armoury is instructed to keep in stock "new inventions of expert workmen" (II, 12).

was guarded against theft (IV, 13).[92] Lending in money or kind at interest was not condemned, though subject to regulation in that limits were put on amounts to be repaid and that maximum rates were prescribed for various types of loans.[93] His discussion of private economic activities ran in terms of the regulations to which such activities were subject and of their taxation, whereas his discussion of the property of king (or state) ran in terms of its management by the various superintendents in charge of the king's agricultural, mining, manufacturing, and commercial undertakings (Book II).

Of price formation as such Kauṭilya had little explicit to say, though he was aware that changes in supply or demand might occasion price changes. He seems to have envisaged an economy in which sellers were licensed and products were distributed through sellers removed from places of manufacture (II, 16, 21; IV, 2). He noted that price depended upon what bidders stood ready to pay,[94] and he suggested that if sales were concentrated in the hands of one or few sellers, prices might become higher than they otherwise would have been.[95] He implied that the superintendent of com-

[92] It is suggested that a prince living under restraint might engage in mining or manufacturing (I, 18).

[93] II, 15; III, 11. "An interest of a paṇa and a quarter per cent per month is just. Five paṇas per month per cent is commercial interest (vyāvahāvrikī). Ten paṇas per month per cent prevails among forests. Twenty paṇas per month per cent prevails among sea traders (sāmudrānām). Persons exceeding, or causing to exceed, the above rate of interest shall be punished" with fines. Some obligations were further regulated and various legal conditions were stipulated.

"The nature of the transactions between creditors and debtors on which the welfare of the kingdom depends, shall always be scrutinized. Interest in grains in seasons of good harvest shall not exceed more than half when valued in money. Interest on stocks (prakṣhepa) shall be one-half of the profit, and be regularly paid as each year expires. . . . If it is allowed to accumulate . . . the amount payable shall be equal to twice the share or principal." Interest on debts due from certain persons (i.e., underprivileged, minors, etc.) "shall not accumulate." Sons and grandsons were liable for pledged debts not limited in respect of time or place. In respect of litigation involving debts, three "reliable, honest, and respected" witnesses were obligatory. See III, 11, which deals with interest and debts; also III, 12 on deposits, to which rules concerning debts also apply.

[94] "The enhancement of price due to bidding among buyers is another source of profit" (II, 6). See also II, 21, where he indicates that potential purchasers could bid prices above the level at which merchants were prepared to sell, or that merchants, foreseeing the prospect of such bidding, might elevate the price asked in anticipation of this bidding.

[95] See II, 16, where he indicates that what he calls centralization of selling serves to raise prices and IV, 2, where he indicates that such centralization may prevent price decline. See also II, 12, on the centralization of the sale of mineral products.

merce could influence prices by regulating the assembly, inventory, and resale of products (II, 16):

The superintendent of commerce shall ascertain demand or absence of demand for, and rise or fall in the price of various kinds of merchandise which may be the products either of land or of water, and which may have been brought in either by land or by water path. He shall also ascertain the time suitable for their distribution, centralization, purchase, and sale.

That merchandise which is widely distributed shall be centralized and its price enhanced. When the enhanced rate becomes popular, another rate shall be declared.

While Kautilya did not advocate complete price-fixing, he did advocate arrangements and regulations which would limit profit margins and insure the weight and quality of the goods offered for sale. He seems to have feared that in the absence of regulation, excessive profits would be made (VIII, 4). The superintendent of commerce might fix prices in the light of certain conditions.[96] The mark-ups and fees that might be earned were indicated by Kautilya (IV, 1-2; II, 12). Adulteration or misrepresentation of products, false weights and measures, and the sale of defective merchandise were prohibited (IV, 2; also III, 15). Sellers presumably were to make allowance for weight losses attributable to pouring, preparation of product, etc. (II, 15, 19). The significance of weights and measures for production and exchange was implied a number of times (II, 6, 12-16, 19, 21). Kautilya indicated that the king should not sell in local or foreign markets if a profit could not be realized, but he added that he should not sell his merchandise at prices yielding "such large profits as will harm the people" (II, 16). The superintendent of commerce was instructed to make detailed inquiries into the costs and other factors affecting the profitability of the king's merchandise (II, 16).

Wages and other modes of personal remuneration are referred to a number of times, but only in a prescriptive sense. There is no analysis of the forces that determine wages. A variety of members of the king's bureaucracy were "endowed with lands, which they shall have no right to alienate by sale or mortgage" (II, 1), whereas others were paid in cash, sometimes at very high rates to insure their

[96] "The superintendent shall, on consideration of the outlay, the quantity manufactured, the amount of toll, the interest on outlay, hire, and other kinds of accessory expenses, fix the price of such merchandise with due regard to its having been manufactured long ago or imported from a distant country" (IV, 2).

loyalty (V, 3).[97] The sons, wives, and possibly other relatives of (some if not all of) those who died while in the King's service "shall get subsistence and wages" (V, 3). Families of workmen living in fortified central cities (and presumably working for the king) were provided with gardens and paddy fields and an allowance of grains and merchandise (II, 4).[98] Those engaged in training elephants received part of their wages in kind (II, 32). The superintendent of agriculture was to supply his workmen with provisions and also pay them 1.25 paṇas per month when they worked (II, 24).[99] The superintendent of weaving was instructed to pay workers in accordance with the quantity and the quality of the work done (II, 23).[100] In general Kauṭilya stipulated that workers and servants were to be paid for work done but not for work not done and that contracts were to be kept (III, 13-14).

As has been indicated, Kauṭilya believed that those who managed the king's affairs must take into account the self-interest of affected individuals, by rewarding them in some proportion to the usefulness (to the king) of their activities. For example, in respect of the use of the king's land, he said (II, 1):

> Lands prepared for cultivation shall be given to taxpayers (karada) only for life (ekapuruṣikāni). Unprepared lands shall not be taken away from those who are preparing them for cultivation.

[97] The most-highly paid ministers received 48,000 paṇas per month whereas many received only 250-500. Trained soldiers, accountants, and writers got 500 paṇas per year; musicians, 250; artisans and carpenters, 120; persons engaged in spying, 250-1000 (V, 3). Pran Nath interprets Kauṭilya's statement regarding the ratio of fines to wages (III, 13) as indicating the minimum wage of a day laborer to be about 1 paṇa. See *op. cit.*, pp. 142-43. According to Kauṭilya (II, 7) 354 "days and nights is a working year." On the meaning of the rates reported by Kauṭilya, see Kane, *op. cit.*, III, pp. 120-26, 150-53.

[98] There was also a "water well for every ten houses" (II, 4). Elsewhere (V, 3) Kauṭilya states that "superintendents of a hundred or a thousand communities shall regulate the subsistence, wages, profits, appointment, and transference of the men under them," and that wages should reflect "learning and work."

[99] Inasmuch as the superintendent employed slaves and prisoners as well as workmen and artisans, and as artisans were to be paid in proportion to the work they did, varying rates of pay are indicated (II, 24). Elsewhere smaller rations are indicated for low castes than for Āryas and for women and children than for men (II, 15). The superintendent of agriculture could also engage share-croppers who would get between one-fifth and one-half the produce raised, or perhaps a larger share if essential to their health (II, 24).

[100] Severe punishment was provided for both non-payment of wages and non-delivery of work contracted for (II, 23). See also IV, 1 for penalties to which artisans become subject when they fail to fulfil their engagements. The rules which Kauṭilya lay down respecting the distribution of fees among priests performing a

Lands may be confiscated from those who do not cultivate them and given to others; or they may be cultivated by village labourers (grāma-bhṛtaka) and traders (vaidēhaka), lest those owners who do not properly cultivate them might pay less (to the government). If cultivators pay their taxes easily, they may be favorably supplied with grains, cattle, and money.

The king shall bestow on cultivators only such favour and remission (anugrahaparihārau) as will tend to swell the treasury, and shall avoid such as will deplete it.

A king with depleted treasury will eat into the very vitality of both citizens and country people. Either on the occasion of opening new settlements or on any other emergent occasions, remission of taxes shall be made.

Professional people, whether engaged in the supply of sacred or profane service to the king, were to be allotted the use of land (ownership of which remained vested in the king) by virtue of the services they rendered (II, 1). Admission to villages was to be denied to those who were not useful or who interfered with the villagers' work, most of it agricultural (II, 1). Rewards were to be given to those who performed services (e.g., brought in the tusks of an elephant dead of natural causes) (II, 2), carried out assignments with success (II, 9), and so on. Moreover, as has also been indicated, the king was to conduct his revenue collection in a fashion that did not interfere too markedly with the self-interest of the taxpayer, since it would not pay to strangle the goose that laid the golden eggs (V, 2). Ordinarily the king's demands were to be limited to a tolerable fraction of the tax-payer's income or stock (V, 2), and confiscatory or similar measures were to be resorted to only in respect of "seditious" or "wicked" persons (V, 2). In some instances, furthermore, as in that of subjects engaged in colonizing waste land or improving the king's property or augmenting the country's overhead social capital, payment of taxes (at least in full) was not to be required (V, 2), or it was to be deferred (II, 1; III, 9-10; V, 3), or the subjects were to "be shown favourable concessions" (III, 10).

Conclusion

This review of what Kauṭilya had to say respecting economic matters reveals very little economic analysis, and most of that

---

sacrifice (III, 1, 14) were subsequently applied in secular joint undertakings. See Kane, *op. cit.*, pp. 469-70.

touches only implicitly upon the behavior of prices and the supposed role of self-interest. Kauṭilya was content to lay down administrative rules based on past or current experience and apparently deemed adequate. He gave little attention to economic alternatives or to building economic policy upon the analysis of specific economic problems.

Kauṭilya was not devoid of analytical skill. This is evident in his game-theory-like approach to intrigue and to politico-military maneuvers in the international sphere. For, though he did not make use of the concept of "chance," he did distinguish between "providential" (i.e., "unforeseen") causes and "human" causes. Apparently only the latter fell within the realm of the rational, that is, within the realm where one could attempt so to design one's course of action as to realize a predetermined goal. "Desired" ends thus could usually be attained through "policy" (i.e., good policy as distinguished from "impolicy," which was bad policy), that is, through careful deliberation and the subsequent employment, as found necessary, of military and financial power (VI, 2). The evils flowing from "impolicy" could always be averted by proceeding rationally (VIII, 1-5). Presumably one could guard against the unfavorable impact of "unforeseen" events or causes only by setting up economic reserves, cushions of political power, etc.[101] Kauṭilya did not carry over his analytical approach to the economic realm.

Why did he not do so? He may have assumed that what we call the economy was impervious to radical manipulation. He probably looked upon the economy as a set of wealth-producing routines, stable enough except for the recurrence of unforeseeable "misfortunes," and against these protective action might be taken.[102] For in the world in which he lived the forces of economic change produced little if any movement; accordingly, having discovered the rules which permitted this economy to function, one needed only to insist upon their continued observance. So stable a system could be milked by whatever group got control of the apparatus of state, possibly for a long time provided that the interests of the underlying

[101] See Book VIII. Book XIV is loaded with superstition. Presumably Kauṭilya was taken in by this, though one might say that one could make use of some of the counsels laid down, given that the objects of these counsels were disposed to believe and act as the counsellor intended.

[102] Among these unforeseeable "providential visitations," he included not only fire, pestilence, flood, and famine, but also rats, snakes, tigers, and demons (IV, 3). Elsewhere (VIII, 4) only the first four are mentioned.

population were not too much disregarded. There was not much then that could be done to improve the functioning of the economy, given that economic conditions tended to change very little even when political control passed, as it frequently did, from one group to another. Kauṭilya's views respecting these matters may have been fed by the fact that the caste system, though not division of labor gone "to seed" (as some have averred), was unfavorable to social mobility and hence to economic development and that the values emphasized by members of the two top castes were not conducive to such development.

Kauṭilya had a very imperfect understanding of the forces making for economic growth. He recognized the importance of the members of the third and fourth castes, but he insisted upon their control, perhaps because he was so alert to the unbridledness with which self-interest, as conceived by him, operated in a world of political power free of constitutional restraints and subject only to such limitations as flowed from several *dharmas*. His conception of human nature, formed on the premise that the struggle for political power tended to be fierce, may have prompted him to infer that self-interest would operate similarly in the economic realm if the economic activities of merchants, lenders, artisans, and workmen were unregulated. Had he better comprehended the role of the price system, he might have allowed greater scope to the pursuit of individual advantage, at least in the cities where economic life had become quite monetized. He did, of course, recognize in some degree the importance of public and private capital, but he gave little attention to its sources and he disregarded the productive role of technology and education almost entirely.[103] Above all, he had no vision of a gradually rising level of living; for many if not most, his economy would always be a "pain economy."

[103] It is interesting to note that in his discussion of functions of the "superintendent of cows" (II, 29) and the raising and feeding of cattle he was oblivious to the need to screen herds of animals rendered unproductive by age, disease, etc.

9

Non-economic Aspects of India's Economic Development

N. V. Sovani

This essay concerns the non-economic aspects of India's economic development in the recent past and the future. Since independence was attained in 1947 India has made significant economic progress. A three-year moving average of the national income over the last decade shows that the real national income has increased at an average annual rate of about 3 per cent. Productive capacity in the Indian economy has increased through increasing investment and the rate of economic performance has been quickened. There is little doubt that the Indian economy is moving away from dead center and cannot be characterized as "stagnant," a term which could have been applied to it with some justification during the earlier decades.

It is, however, clear that this rate of growth is small relative to the rate of population increase, which has been estimated to be 1.5 per cent per annum. The rate of increase of per capita income, there-fore, comes to 1.5 per cent per annum. If the rate of increase of population accelerates in the future, as some experts forecast on very good grounds, the present rate of increase of national income will be found to be completely inadequate and India will have to run faster and faster even to keep herself at the same level of per capita income.

Could India have done better than she has during this period? If so, why did she not? And if we know why, can she be made to perform better in the future and by what means? These are big questions, and no student of Indian problems can be expected to have all the correct answers. I am here trying to indicate in a tentative way some of the answers to these questions.

There is considerable evidence, both official and nonofficial, from Indian and foreign observers, to indicate that the development effort in India during the last decade has been characterized by much inefficiency and waste; that the available economic resources have not been as productively used under the given conditions as they could have been. And when one begins to consider and analyze this, he soon comes up with the fact that the causes lie deep in the whole Indian cultural and social setup and that it involves the whole problem of the social efficiency of the Indian society. But this is to anticipate. Let me first substantiate the opening gambit that the Indian development effort during the fifties was inefficient.

Perhaps I can begin by noting the observations of the latest Indian delegation to China, which visited that country early in 1959 to study the Chinese achievements in the conservation and maximum utilization of water, including rain water. What the delegation found most impressive, it is reported, was the type of organization employed for achieving the remarkable results in this field rather than the use of any new techniques which were being used in China and which were not known or used in India.[1]

This is an important observation because in India irrigation is not a new problem, and a failure in this respect cannot be explained away by pleading lack of know-how or inexperience. Yet the failure in this field is glaring and extensive. At the end of the First Five Year Plan the irrigation potential created by major irrigation works was 559,000 acres in Bihar and 465,000 acres in West Bengal, of which only 265,000 and 223,000 acres respectively were actually irrigated, thus leaving about half of the potential unutilized.[2] In many of the irrigated areas water is available for more than one crop per year. Yet a recent survey showed that only about 12 per cent of the land under irrigation has more than one irrigated crop per year.[3]

[1] *Economic Weekly* (Bombay), June 20, 1959, p. 796.
[2] Government of India, *Report of the Foodgrains Inquiry Committee*, Nov., 1957, p. 107.
[3] *Report on India's Food Crisis and Steps to Meet It*, by the Agricultural Production Team sponsored by the Ford Foundation, Government of India, April, 1959, p. 146. Professor René Dumont, who visited India as a member of the U.N. team to study India's efforts at agricultural development, has observed that in the case of many large scale irrigation projects water flows down only the various big and small canals constructed by government; no network of subsidiary canals has

This failure of organizational effort is by no means unique or solitary. Many others can be easily met with in India today. Take the program of Community Development Projects launched in 1952 with the express purpose "to set free the creative energies of the people so that they may build up through their own effort and through their own institutions a richer and improving social life."[4] The recent appraisals, both official and non-official, of the achievements of this program have indicated that this objective has not been reached; that there has been more concentration on welfare aspects than on productivity aspects; that the program has settled down to a dead administrative routine so as to smother the growth of local leadership and initiative.[5] It is again very largely an organizational failure.

This list of failures need not be added to except to note that the same kind of failure is evident, in more or less degree, in regard to land reforms, population control, education, social legislation, etc. The failures are too widespread and blatant to be explained away by such factors as inexperience or expediency. We should try to probe deeper, if we can.

An interesting aspect of the situation is that there is consciousness in the country regarding these failures. In the examples here given the appraisals and observations of responsible Indians have been principally cited. Many Indian leaders have drawn attention to them from time to time, have deplored them, and have emphasized the need for their speedy removal. If one mentions these failures in India today, there would be no reluctance to admit them. There would also be almost unanimous agreement regarding the desirability of removing their causes. But this candor will not be in evidence as

---

been dug by the cultivators, nor have lands been elevated to hold back on the fields a large part of the water received from rains. Of the acreage officially brought under irrigation, he estimates that not more than a sixth gets actual benefits (in *Le Monde*, as reported in *Economic Weekly*, July 4, 1959, p. 860).

[4] Government of India, Programmes Evaluation Organization, *Evaluation Report on the Second Year's Working of the Community Projects*, Summary, April, 1955, p. 51.

[5] Albert Mayer and Associates, *Pilot Project, India—The Story of Rural Development at Etawah (Uttar Pradesh)* (Berkeley, 1958); S. C. Dube, *India's Changing Villages* (Ithaca, 1957); *Reports* of the Programmes Evaluation Organization, Planning Commission, Government of India, 1954-1958; Balvantray Mehta (Chairman), *Report of the Team for the Study of Community Projects and National Extension Service* (New Delhi: Government of India, 1957); Carl Taylor, "Two Major Evils," *Kurukshetra*, Jan. 26, 1959.

soon as one goes on to discuss the reasons underlying them. A common view would be that these defects and failures are not abiding but passing and that they require only like remedies. A variation of the argument would be to take a historical view and attribute them to the long period of foreign rule in India. Self-rule, given time, will almost automatically cure them.[6] No wonder there is complete apathy or reluctance to undertake a deeper appraisal of the situation.

The causes of the present *malaise* in Indian society lie deeper and cannot be explained by the superficial arguments listed above. My reflections on this theme were sparked a few years ago when I began to assess the success of economic planning in independent India. I have since been struck again and again by the repetition of similar mistakes in government policy with similar consequences. The failure to learn from experience was everywhere patent in the economic sphere. For some time I attributed this to the political element that dominates everything in India today. Politicians are notoriously shortsighted, and I thought that this was the main reason for repeated failures in the economic sphere. But later I realized that the same kind of failure was also evident in the political sphere in India, and in many other spheres also. I was forced to the conclusion that the causes were more pervading and deeply embedded in the whole society than I had suspected.

An analysis of these causes, however, is not easy. First, my own limitations as a social scientist are, to say the least, overwhelming. Secondly, it involves introspection, a difficult art to practice anywhere. Being a part of the Indian society and having been born and brought up in it, I am not sure of my ability to look at it from outside from a critical angle. I decided, however, to make the effort, perhaps in a foolhardy way, because I thought somebody must begin to do this sometime, and if I am wrong at least it would provoke abler minds to attempt the task sadly neglected so far.

We have to examine for this purpose the social efficiency of the Indian society as a whole in relation to economic and social development. But as Davis observes:

. . . in the matter of societal efficiency we have a concept but little else. In practice it is hedged about by the preconceptions and institutions of a going

[6] Echoes of these lines of thinking would be found in ample measure in most of the writings of nationalists in the earlier periods also. Discussions in social sciences in India were also very much suffused by nationalistic emotions which

society; in social science it is handicapped by the unreality of ignoring these practical limitations and by the lack of an adequate set of measuring devices. The concept says: Given a certain quantum of natural resources and human population, there exist numerous ways of bringing the two together for the production of goods and services, some of these ways being more effective than others. But it does not tell us how to measure effectiveness with respect to the non-economic parts of the social system. We can make use of such makeshift indices as exist, but in the last analysis we are thrown back on speculation and general theory.[7]

Davis goes on to warn: "Depending on verbal description and intuitive judgment, one tends to see causal relationships *in principle* and then to assume erroneously that they exist in fact. The case of India is particularly difficult because of the country's extreme cultural diversity."[8] The analysis that I am attempting here is of course subject to all these limitations and should be understood as such.

One must, I think, begin by analyzing the basic ways and *mores* of the traditional Indian or Hindu society, note the changes that have taken place in them in modern times under British rule, and then try to see if these in principle and in fact give some clues to the analysis of the complex problem.

Max Weber's analysis of the sociology of Hinduism is perhaps the best point of departure for this purpose from many points of view. Weber found that in religion, cultural values, personality, motivation, and social structure come together, and he discussed Hinduism from that point of view. In summarizing his analysis, I quote the able summary given by Dr. Bellah:

> Weber finds the notion of *dharma*, religiously prescribed obligation, to be the core of Hinduism, especially in its deep inner connection with the idea of *karma*, the endless chain of causation working itself out in successive rebirths. The orthodox view is that whatever position one finds oneself in, in this life, is due to the force of *karma* in previous existences, and one's obligation is to fulfill the *dharma* of one's position so that one will improve one's chances in the next incarnation. The intellectuals, revolting against this notion, always sought escape from the wheel of rebirth through some sort of individualistic salvation. Weber shows how these conceptions hindered cultural rationalisation beyond a certain point.

often vitiated scientific analysis. A typical example is the writing on the population problem in India.

[7] Kingsley Davis, "Social and Demographic Aspects of Economic Development in India," in Simon Kuznets, Wilbert E. Moore, and Joseph J. Spengler, eds., *Economic Growth: Brazil, India, Japan* (Durham, 1955), p. 266.

[8] *Ibid.*, p. 292.

On the one hand they contributed to the development of special technologies appropriate to the *dharma* of each profession—from construction technique to logic as the technology of proof and disproof to the technology of eroticism—but at the same time they hindered the development of levels of generalisation above the technological because of the fragmentation involved in the notion of occupational *dharma*. On the other hand, the intellectuals were so completely preoccupied with the problem of salvation that all philosophy was made subservient to this end.

With respect to the social structure, it is the *dharma* concept as integrated with the idea of caste, which is the key to the situation. In spite of the remarkable achievements of certain castes, there is always a limit imposed by the traditionalistic definition of the caste *dharma* itself. Further, the division of society into innumerable watertight compartments, while engendering a very stable integration of sorts allows a minimum of flexibility and especially limits the generalisation of political power making the society an easy prey to foreign conquest. The major religious movements which reject this mode of social organisation either fall back into it in the form of a new caste, or, as in the case of Buddhism, remain an individualistic and socially negative group existing symbolically in relation to traditional society and unable to generate any really different mode of social organization.

In terms of personality, the *dharma* idea results in the fragmentation of response directed to the external demands of ritual obligation on the one hand, or a passive withdrawal into mysticism on the other. There is no basis of inner unification of personality for action in response to the command of a transcendental God. The Indian alternatives tend to be action without unification and unification without action.[9]

Theoretically, nobody would disagree that this kind of socio-religious framework is not very suitable to modern economic development. But many have denied its relevance to the day-to-day life of the people as actually lived in India in the past and the present. Some have stressed the tradition of practical values in India which, it is said, is evident throughout her history. Others have insisted there exists an ethic in Indian life which can "sanction" the materialistic values of an industrial society.[10]

Whether the main beliefs and ideals embodied in Hinduism shape and influence the actual *mores* of Hindu society today is a question that can be answered on the basis of such reliable and well-

[9] Robert N. Bellah, review of *Religion of India: The Sociology of Hinduism*, by Max Weber (Glencoe, 1958), in *American Sociological Review*, XXIV, No. 5 (1959), 731-33.
[10] Cf. the interesting discussion on "India's Cultural Values and Economic Development: A Discussion," in *Economic Development and Cultural Change*, VII, No. 1 (Oct., 1958), 1-13, and other writings cited there.

tested information as may be available on this point. So far as I know, the available information is not very ample; nevertheless what is available is, in my opinion, significant. O'Malley has discussed such information in his *Popular Hinduism, the Religion of the Masses*. He cites the work of Miriam Young, in 1931 in the Punjab, who after a three-year study concluded that *karma* was a practical philosophy coloring the villager's whole outlook on life. He also refers to Crooke's study in the same region in 1897, which takes an opposite stand. O'Malley also refers to several inquiries bearing on this carried out in different regions in India at the 1891 and 1901 censuses. He refers to these discussions and to his own extensive experiences in India and arrives at the following, I think, balanced judgment:

> Materialistic, however, as the villagers may be in their relations to the outside world and in the conduct of their everyday life, there can be no question that their general trend of thought is strongly devotional and that religion is deeply ingrained in thought and feeling and is a very real thing to them. One impelling force is undoubtedly the desire to accumulate merit in the expectation of a higher or better life in the next existence, and of eventually obtaining release from the burden of individual existence, though it is doubtful how far the attainment of such a distant goal as the latter is actually a motive idea among the masses. . . . Another factor is the absence of a nationalistic spirit and lack of scientific knowledge. Natural phenomena and the vicissitudes of human life are ascribed to the working of supernatural powers, and the possibility of divine intervention in human affairs is an article of faith which is held with simple sincerity.[11]

Two recent studies using modern anthropological and psycho-analytical methods broadly confirm the importance and influence of the Hindu belief systems in the day-to-day life of the people. These recent studies focus on the cumulative effect of attitudes towards each other, towards the social order, and towards the supernatural on the formation of adult personality. W. S. Taylor, who worked and lived in Madhya Pradesh, concluded that Orthodox Hinduism is

> able to create a basic personality pattern in which personal initiative is replaced by the sense of conformity, in which responsibility is exercised without personal authority, in which security is associated with the sense of dependence and self-respect with a sense of helplessness, and in which opportunities for frustration and acute anxiety are minimized. It is a

[11] L. S. S. O'Malley, *Popular Hinduism: The Religion of the Masses* (Cambridge, 1935), pp. 51-52, chaps. i and ii.

basic personality whose integration and stability are primarily a function of the cultural system to which it belongs and are not organized around any system of personal choices.[12]

G. Morris Carstairs, who intensively studied a village in Rajastan, confirmed generally Taylor's findings and tried to take the analysis further in psychoanalytic terms.[13] These two recent studies in fact go deeper than the two cited before, because they delve into the personality formation process which governs the conduct of individuals throughout life, and both of them show the great influence of the basic values embodied in Hindu culture. They also show how the institutions of joint family and caste play a dominant role in this set up. I submit that an analysis accepting this, at least as a hypothesis, is likely to be more fruitful than one which loses itself either in arguing away its significance or rejecting it altogether. I proceed by accepting the hypothesis that the institutional structure and functioning of Hindu society was and continues to be inimical to the development of a community. This together with its *mores* gives rise to a widely common personality pattern devoid of personal initiative, purposefulness, involvement, etc.

To attribute all the evils resulting in social inefficiency in India today to British rule is surely to ignore realities. The basic framework of Hindu society was complete and in full operation before the British and also before the Mohammedan conquest of India. The lack of social and political cohesion in the Indian society made it, as Weber notes, an easy prey to foreign conquest. So far as the basic attitudes, personality patterns, motivations, etc. are concerned, they were independent of the British and the Mohammedan rulers. It is, of course, true that they were influenced by foreign rule. So far as the Mohammedan rule is concerned, the Mohammedans seemed to have been themselves influenced by Hindu social institutions, as witness the development of castes among Mohammedans in India. So far as British rule is concerned, it is possible to note more specifically what it did to Hindu society.

This is neither the occasion nor the place to dilate at length on the whole theme of British impact on India. Its ramifications are

[12] W. S. Taylor, "Basic Personality in Orthodox Hindu Culture Pattern," *Journal of Abnormal and Social Psychology*, XLIII (Jan., 1948), 3-12, and other writings of Taylor and others cited there.
[13] G. Morris Carstairs, *The Twice-born: A Study of a Community of Highcaste Hindus* (London, 1957).

too wide and too numerous to deal with in this paper. I shall confine myself here to the influence of British rule on the caste structure, the pivotal structural parameter of the Hindu social system.[14]

Under the British many things happened to weaken as well as to strengthen the caste system but on balance the latter outweighed the former.

The British, in contradistinction to their predecessors, progressively refused to perform certain social functions, perhaps the most important of which were those connected with the regulation of a caste society involving the functioning and relative status of castes. The pre-British rulers, including the Muslims, by performing these functions helped maintain, even in a caste society, a degree of social integration. Thereby the process of continuous adjustment and wider integration was always at work. This process of over-all social regulation and integration could no longer be maintained when the British refused to perform these functions; as a result the social structure lost its adaptability and integration. In the pre-British days caste loyalty was tempered by the sense of loyalty to the Hindu society as a whole which was maintained by the secular authority. The loyalty to one's own caste increased under the British as occasions and opportunities for emphasizing or exhibiting the over-all sense of Hindu loyalties decreased. It is in this manner that the institution of caste became more rigid than before in the period of British rule.[15]

Under the British also economic and social dividing lines in society became parallel, which they were not before.

J. S. Furnivall has observed that the impact of the West on India has been less violent than, for instance, on Burma, because of the caste system in India which afforded considerable protection to the social system in India.[16] It is true that it prevented social disintegration, so characteristic of other societies, but it also left the Indian society loose and weak and hampered its transformation into a modern social and industrial community.

British rule also brought to India new ideas from the West— bureaucracy, the judiciary, and an effective system of laws. It also gave rise to nationalism. I will try to assess their effects, briefly in the reverse order. The development of nationalism in India was sparked by British rule and, though it began as a movement allied

[14] An extensive and more detailed treatment of the subject can be found in N. V. Sovani, "British Impact on India before 1850-57," *Journal of World History*, I (1954), 857-882, and "British Impact on India after 1850-57," *ibid.*, II (1954), 77-105.

[15] N. V. Sovani, *Journal of World History*, II (1954), 101.

[16] J. S. Furnivall, *Colonial Policy and Practice* (London, 1948), p. 9.

with social reformism, it gradually lost this aspect and became more and more a purely political movement. Only the negative aspects of nationalism developed in India, i.e., its aim was the negative one of driving away the foreign ruler, but the positive aspects of nationalism did not appear. In 1947 India acquired nationhood but has not been able to develop as yet sufficient unity and emotional integration for the effective functioning of a modern society.

The judiciary and the law system developed by the British brought about far-reaching changes in the concepts of private property. Together with the bureaucracy, they smothered village self-rule and helped to bring about a malfunctioning of the social system.

The bureaucracy developed by the British effectively killed whatever little self-rule there was and furthered the demise of most vestiges of initiative. Perhaps the bureaucracy as an impersonal machine, with its impersonal character, its hierarchical order, its prescriptions of definite action in definite contexts, etc., was well suited to the general social structure of caste society. I suspect that this is one of the reasons the bureaucracy developed so well in India as compared to other underdeveloped countries and still continues to flourish. It finds a social background that is very favorable to the growth of its formal structure, though not necessarily to its working efficiency.

With British rule came English education, and this opened up the whole world of Western knowledge to educated Indians.

This knowledge was and has been absorbed more at the theoretical than at the practical level. The intellectual tradition in India, which is mainly the Brahmin tradition, has that characteristic. It is singularly free from restrictions or inhibitions regarding intellectual speculation. In India there has rarely been a persecution for holding certain opinions, even heretical opinions. This was partly because, though intellectual speculation was free, the translation of any new ideas into practice was hidebound by the prevailing ethics and modes of behavior. The Brahmins themselves had laid down the rule that though many things might be rationally obvious and good, they should not be brought into practice if they were not in tune with the traditional behavior pattern and against popular folkways. Such a tradition would naturally be much more ready to absorb ideas on the philosophical plane than in actual life. Today, therefore, the intellectual climate in India appears to be much more pronouncedly Western than in Japan or China.[17]

[17] N. V. Sovani, *Journal of World History*, II (1954), 105. See also Kingsley Davis, *op. cit.*, p. 297, and references cited there.

Taking everything into account, it would be fair to say that British rule did introduce some bad kinks into the old social structure and its functioning, but it cannot be held responsible for all the evils. It would be perhaps better to say that the Indian social structure responded to the British impact in a way in which some of the bad characteristics were scored deeper while some of the good characteristics could not develop much further than they perhaps would have done in the absence of British rule. But the basic cultural and institutional patterns have very largely remained unchanged. As a result, in India today we find in the people a widespread lack of personal initiative, involvement, and purposefulness in life, a tendency towards empty ritual, general apathy, casteism, communalism, indifference, and absence of a feeling of participation in national endeavor. This has often been noted and deplored by Indians themselves with reference to the two plans of economic development undertaken by the Government of India in recent years. It represents a position of confusion and social ambivalence not conducive to social or economic efficiency.[18]

[18] The view that Indian society has failed to progress economically in the modern age because of the presence of the caste, the joint family and the other-worldly or spiritual outlook is old and was propounded by many Westerners. It was equally hotly contested by Indian writers whose writings had pronounced nationalistic overtones. They argued, firstly, that India had a glorious past and the achievements of Hindus in various fields were quite notable and comparable with those of any other people and nations that could be described as progressive. These achievements were possible even with caste, joint family, and a spiritual outlook and as such these were irrelevant to the whole argument. Secondly, caste and joint family, it was argued, were now breaking down and can be expected to fade out. Some also argued that there is nothing inherently wrong in the caste system but that British rule had made it more rigid, vitiated its proper functioning, and that it will disappear with the end of British rule. The fatalistic and spiritual attitude of the people was also attributed to British rule because people were so powerless against the all powerful alien government and could only look up to it for favors.

As in all such arguments, there was a steady refusal to see the real issue or to argue it away by reference to foreign rule. The achievements of the past are surely inspiring, but it takes only a little reflection to realize that the achievements required for modern development are of a completely different order and quality and that the drawbacks noted may be very relevant and crucial in that context. Whereas the older attainments could take place within the old structural social setting the new ones require a thorough change in the structure itself. It is also patent that caste and joint family are not breaking as fast as is often made out. Available evidence shows that they have been affected only at the fringes and continue to function vigorously even today. The fatalistic and passive attitude of the masses was a reality even before British rule, though it might have increased considerably under the British. That Tilak felt the necessity to write a commentary on the *Gita* and expound the doctrine of selfless and disinterested action as the central teaching of the great book itself testifies to the fact and presence of the passive and fatalistic attitude among the Indian people. Tilak's other writings also draw attention to

A critical and historical examination of the Hindu social organization brings out the fact that Hinduism is not a religion in the Western sense of the word. It is really a social system, a method of organizing society. In its earlier stages it proved a powerful instrument of absorbing diverse kinds of peoples and tribes into the Hindu fold without disturbing their individual rituals and practices. It is conceivable that if this process had gone on, perhaps caste rigidity would not have developed and the social and occupational mobility would have been maintained so as to weld all the Hindu people into an integrated community. This grand process, however, did not go on but stagnated. The Hindu society today is an unfinished social experiment that has rigidified the social institutions into a mold. In understanding this it is necessary to realize that the doctrines of *karma, dharma,* etc. in their philosophic context would not have mattered much had they not had in Hindu society their social institutional counterparts in terms of the caste system and the joint family. Weber has referred to the developments in China and Japan, where this did not happen to the same extent as in India.[19]

As a matter of historical fact, the growth and development of nationalism should have accomplished many of the things that are needed for the rejuvenation of Hindu society. But the growth of nationalism in India has not done this. The Hindu social institu-

what he called the "age old idleness" of the people and in a specific reference to the progress of Japan and the absence of it in China in the latter part of the nineteenth century, he stated that India can progress only if the people shed their age-old slumber in the way Japan did. B. G. Tilak, "China and Japan," *Kesari* (Poona, 14 May, 1895, in Marathi). Tilak's commentary on the *Gita,* however, did not make much headway against the age-old slumber. Hindu Pandits always regarded his thesis as not proved and it hardly percolated to the masses. Though he is remembered today as a great national leader, his book is scarcely remembered and is known only to certain sections of the Indian intellectuals. Books entitled *Indian Economics* by V. G. Kale, S. V. Ketkar, Jathar and Beri, refer to these discussions in a summary way. See also: B. G. Tilak, *Shrimad Bhagvadgita Rahasya,* trans. by B. S. Sukthankar (2 vols.; Poona, 1935-36); M. N. Srinivas, "Caste in Modern India," *Journal of Asian Studies,* XVI (1957), 529-48; "India's Cultural Values and Economic Development: A Discussion," *Economic Development and Cultural Change,* VII, No. 1 (Oct., 1958), 1-12, and other writings cited there.

[19] "These intellectual soteriologies now found themselves confronted by the practice in the life experiences of Asiatic strata. An innerconnection of performance in the world with the extra-worldly soteriology was not possible. The single inwardly consistent form was the caste soteriology of Vedanta Brahmanism in India. Its conception of calling had to operate politically, socially, economically in an extremely traditionalistic manner. However, it is the single, logically closed form of 'organismic' holy and societal teaching which could occur" (Max Weber, *Religion of India: the Sociology of Hinduism,* p. 333).

tions have subdivided the social organism in such a way as to make the units (caste and family) smaller and smaller and unrelated to the general society. *"Thus it denies the entire theory of community* and bases the organization of Hindu life on the opposite principle of disintegration and division."[20]   Nationalism in India has not been able to reverse this process.   In fact, it bent the nationalist movement in its own direction rather than the other way round.   I have described this elsewhere as follows:

Nationalism struck flame on foreign rule.   The first generation of the English educated Indians was completely bowled over by Western culture as brought to India by the British.   The effective suppression of the Mutiny in 1858 impressed on them the superiority of the British.   Fired by the ideas imbibed through English literature they came to the view that the old Indian ways had to be remodelled on Western lines.   They came to regard British connexion with India as a providential dispensation for the good of India.   They visualized political and social development to go hand in hand and believed that social reform was of basic importance even for political advancement.   The Brāhma Samāj in Bengal and the Prārthana Samāj in Bombay (founded in 1865) which bore the stamp of Christian ideas were manifestations of this tendency in the social and religious field.   The Indian National Congress was founded in 1885.

The next generation that came of age around the 1880's developed a more virile strain of nationalism.   It was backward-looking and appealed to India's past glory.   The ideology of resurgent Hinduism as put forth by Vivekananda, provided the social and religious basis for this school of nationalists.   While acknowledging the benefits of British rule, this school refused to recognise it as a providential dispensation.   It further maintained that these benefits will be nullified if they were not followed by home rule which was their logical culmination.   The demand for self rule cannot be satisfied by good rule by a foreign bureaucracy.   Political advancement was primary to all social reform.   The latter will automatically follow political independence and therefore the national movement must not dissipate its strength in fighting for social reform but must concentrate on the struggle for liberation from the British yoke.   For that, all means, whether constitutional or otherwise, should be used.

This stand was more nationalistic than that of their predecessors.   If the first generation suffered from an inferiority complex with regard to the West this generation was overcompensating for it.   The neglect of social reform further underlined their backward looking orientation and made them line up with socially reactionary elements.   It inevitably took a Hindu colour and ensured in time the development of a separate Muslim nationalism as a reaction.   The Muslim League was founded in 1906. The more direct type of action in the struggle for independence assumed

[20] K. M. Pannikar, *Hindu Society at Cross Roads* (Bombay, 1955), p. 23.

the form of the Swadeshi movement, which included the use of Indian goods and the boycott of British and foreign goods. This suited the newly rising class of industrialists and brought them into the fold of the national movement.

Gandhian orientation of the nationalist movement in the 'twenties of this century was pronouncedly Hindu, anti-intellectual and more backward-looking than that of the generation that had gone before. It condemned Western science and technique and advocated revival of cottage industries, village uplift, etc. It gave to some of the religious terms of Hinduism, like satyāgraha, ahiṅsa, ṣwaraj, etc., a political meaning, and political doctrines were clothed in spiritual terms. Its intellectual content was very much inferior but its emotional appeal was great as was evidenced by the various mass movements that were conducted under the leadership of the Indian National Congress in the period after 1914. It can perhaps be said that without a watering down of the severe intellectualism of the earlier movement, it could not have appealed to the masses. It also became progressively more political, and its already declining social content gradually dwindled into insignificance. It only came to the surface when political exigencies required it, as for example, in the case of the untouchables in the 1930's.[21]

Nationalism in India has been oriented much more towards the negative goal of ending foreign rule and much less towards evolving the positive content of what was to be done after achieving that goal. This I have called the lack of positive aspects of nationalism.[22] The social content of positive nationalism therefore remains to be developed in India, and that is the task facing the present national leadership.

The immensity of the task of bringing about the necessary extent of social change in India can be gauged from the fact that it is nothing short of the whole problem of the remaking of a nation. History affords examples of such problems being solved by violent as well as peaceful methods, and perhaps the examples of the former kind are more numerous than those of the latter kind. India has chosen the latter and, perhaps, the harder path of change, but possibly has not yet appreciated the wide ramifications of the problems and the all-sided and clear-sighted effort that is necessary for accomplishing the difficult task. Attention and effort have been focused primarily on economic development and change. The other fields have not received as much attention.

[21] N. V. Sovani, *Journal of World History*, II (1954), 99-101.
[22] Cf. Rupert Emerson, "Progress of Nationalism," in *Nationalism and Progress in Free Asia* (Baltimore, 1959), p. 72.

Surely the problem cannot be solved by economic change alone, though it can be an instrument of considerable force in this connection. Yet social structures are found to be much more resistant and persisting than economic structures. Social development is known to lag considerably behind economic and technological development. If planning for economic change is hard, planning for social change is harder, even hardest. Knowledge regarding economic planning is relatively much more ample than regarding social planning. No wonder we get more of economic planning and only talk about social planning. In India today "organizational inputs" is the new fashionable term bandied about without much thought being given to its content and still less to how to increase its supply. Very few have realized that they are the kinds of inputs that cannot be bought by money or imported from abroad. They must arise from within the Hindu society.

The previous discussion has underlined the deadening efficiency of Hindu society in maintaining the *status quo*, and in that context one can hardly expect the right type of social change to arise naturally from within the Hindu society. As in the economic sphere so also in the social sphere, deliberate and designed action to bring it about becomes necessary.

But this is neither here nor there. We must go further and indicate what kind of action is needed, who should take it and in what way. This is the province of sociology, and one would naturally turn to students in that field for guidance. Unfortunately, the available sociological writings and analyses of the Hindu social structure are not very helpful in the matter. An economist cannot presume to supply what sociologists have not supplied. And yet he cannot just pass the buck to the sociologists because it can equally well be passed back to him. So at the risk of rushing in where angels fear to tread I shall, in all humility, outline a policy for social reconstruction of the Hindu society according to my judgment. Let me emphasize that there is no clear-cut, valid sociological analysis behind it, but only a mass of ideas, inchoate, hazy and ill-assorted. In the interest of fruitful debate I should like to state them as clearly as I can. I do that first and then turn to policy measures.

Taking such guidance as I have been able to derive from the sociological writings that I have been able to lay my hands on, it seems to me that the mechanism of social control mediates between the personality structures and the specific environment in any society.[23] If personality structure is left out as changing slowly and in response to changes in the other two, and if changes in external environment are taking place, it is the mechanism of social control that is the key variable in the picture. Social change induced by changes in the external environment and reinforcing those changes in its turn can take place only if the mechanism of social control is catalytic rather than refractory. Social control mechanisms work through small and intimate groups, and status seeking within them is one of the most common motives that enter the making of human conduct. The Hindu society has an irrevocable group and status system in the institution of the caste, and the deadly efficiency of social control in Hindu society derives mainly from this. As a result of political independence, the setting up of the formal democratic political structure and the planned effort undertaken by the national government for economic development, the environment in India is changing as never before. We see, however, evidence all around us today that the mechanism of social control is grinding as efficiently and as truly as before, so as to smother most of the required social changes and to slow down and perhaps ultimately stop the change in the environment also. Action therefore must be taken to break this vicious circle by an attack on the caste system and all that is associated with it. This can be done by deliberately creating new loyalties across caste lines, new status systems and power structures that are not based on or dependent on caste. This can be done only by a national leadership that is not merely popular but also dedicated and regarded as such by the people at large, because in an effort to break the power of the caste, which offers many advantages today to its members in the absence of anything else on which they can fall back in times of need, the national leadership will have to ask the people to make present individual sacrifices for future social and national gains, and this can be done only on the moral plane. In effect the national leadership will have to be a moral leadership.[24]

The present national leadership in India comes mainly from the urban educated elites and is largely one that has won its spurs in

[23] I am broadly accepting in this the analysis developed by Richard La Piere, *A Theory of Social Control* (McGraw Hill Series in Sociology and Anthropology; New York, 1954).

[24] See La Piere's discussion in *ibid.*, pp. 197-98.

the struggle for independence. This is at once an advantage and a disadvantage. It is an advantage because it has been able to take up where the British left off and to carry on successfully in many respects without any violent break in the process of take-over. The disadvantage is that it has grown up with and adapted to negative nationalism and is not well equipped to give a far-reaching constructive lead to the people. Most of their ideas, such as the abolition of untouchability, the Hindu Code, the abolition of zamīndārī, etc., have been now put on the statute book. The expansion of the public sector, co-operative farming, and the socialist pattern of society have been accepted in principle. But most of these ideas are not new. In Nehru's case they were formed as far back as 1928, as his biographer Brecher shows.[25] One suspects that the present leadership has not only no new ideas about social reorganization but has also only vague notions about bringing the ideas that they have into actuality.

I can now proceed to discuss a few of the main problems of social reorganization and to indicate what can be done and what has not been done.

The first problem is that of the emotional integration of the Indian people, a problem that has been mentioned several times recently and has been underlined by the recent *debacle* in Kerala. In this respect it needs to be realized that India contains territories and regional societies that are not completely integrated and in many of these the suspicion of undue centralization at the national level, of differential treatment of ethnical, religious, and regional groups at the hands of the national leadership has persisted. The agitation for linguistic provinces during the last decade in India amply testifies to this. That the demand has now been conceded, though quite reluctantly and with much avoidable delay and bitterness, is, in my opinion, a good augury for the future. In a society where group loyalty is strong and overwhelming, the gap between it and national loyalty is too wide. A linguistic regional loyalty, which already exists and has triumphed recently, has a useful role to play in bridging this gap. In other words, this is the principle of concentric loyalties, very much necessary to temper the intolerance which usually is known to arise out of nationalism and national feeling.

The linguistic group loyalty has also shown itself as a positive

[25] Michael Brecher, *Nehru: A Political Biography* (London, 1959).

force cutting across community and caste loyalties, particularly during the last general elections in Maharashtra.[26]

In shaping this powerful instrument of national integration the present leadership lost a precious decade entirely from mistaken ideas of national unity and personal interests and prejudices, though the principle of the formation of linguistic provinces was adopted by the Indian National Congress leadership as far back as 1928. The present leadership has had to concede it (even in the case of Maharashtra and Gujarat lately) under pressure and on the whole it has not come out of it with great credit. Its failure in appreciating the power of this instrument of national and emotional integration was costly in terms of time and progress.

And this leads to the role of political and democratic processes and institutions in this effort at social change. It would be agreed without much controversy that the Indian social structure, values, and mores are not democratic and individualistic in spirit or actuality. Equality of every citizen before law was introduced into India by the British and it was, we know, resented very thoroughly. But it has come to be accepted in principle. The political equality of the citizens required and assumed in a democracy has come recently with adult franchise. The ideas about economic equality have also become accepted in principle in the official documents. These impulses have created tensions—social, economic, and political—in the present Indian society, the older and traditional form of which was noted for their absence. All these are essentially democratic impulses that must work their way through the social structure, altering it in the process through the continuous building up and relieving of tensions. The creative role of tensions, about which anthropologists speak, is very relevant in this context.

But these impulses will thrive only if the proper functioning of democratic institutions is insured in the country. The present leadership is perhaps the most blameworthy in this respect. Its actions and behavior have created a sense of unreality in the democratic processes in India. The small role that Parliament plays in really vital and important decisions, the way the intervention of the Prime Minister and the Congress Working Committee is sought to

[26] Cf. D. R. Gadgil, "Social Change and Liberal Democracy in New States," *Artha Vijnana: Journal of the Gokhale Institute of Politics and Economics*, I, No. 3 (Poona, Sept., 1959), 183.

influence such decisions, the obvious fact that power resides in persons and not in offices that they hold, the gap that exists between what the Indian Constitution lays down and what is done in practice, all go to make up this sense of unreality.

The most crucial question of reorganization is to break the hold of the institution of caste. As has been pointed out earlier, because of historical reasons the higher castes have also become the richer castes, and economic and social divisions have tended to become parallel. As a result social inequality and economic inequality have become welded together to form the hard core of vested interests in the country. The groups holding economic and political power in India today are partly vestiges of the older order belonging to the aristocratic, priestly, and other classes, based mainly on concentrations of property in land and partly new growth related to the growth of modern industry and business in India. It is generally agreed that the state must take an active part in breaking the power of the older groups, as is witnessed by the interest in land reform legislation in India, but the same is not agreed to in regard to modern business. There is, in fact, concerted opposition to it, the opposition to the so-called "socialistic pattern of society."

The programme called "socialistic" includes little which is not accepted in principle and practice in, say, the United States under the anti-cyclical or social security measures and nothing which is not part of accepted government policy in the United Kingdom. It usually includes some enlargement of the public sector, so that basic major investments are properly made and their fruits conserved for economic development and social progress, and aims at maintenance of stability, stopping further increase in the concentration of power and wealth, making a beginning with the humbler forms of social security, encouraging decentralisation, strengthening cooperatives, and making a beginning in the building of an open national educational system. Unless such a programme is rapidly pushed ahead, there is little hope of a peaceful social transition. In the face of the concentrated and growing strength of big business in these countries, the only possible counteravailing force is action by the state.[27]

This is where the present national leadership shows its greatest weakness. The rise of the modern business class in India was associated with the development of the national movement for independence. The protection of modern industry and business in Indian hands and its growth against the opposition of the vested

[27] *Ibid.*, pp. 185-86.

British interests in these fields was an important plank in the platform of the national movement throughout. The national movement was largely financially supported by these elements. The present leadership has grown up in an atmosphere where these elements have been its supporters and associates, and as such it is hard for it to take vigorous action against them. As a result this core problem is not energetically tackled.

Another crucial task that the present leadership faces is that of creating conditions in which new and good leaders will rise. This is the task of "planting men," to borrow a Chinese proverb. This essentially involves two types of action. In the first place, the youth of the country must have before them the types of leaders they have to supply. As a historian has recently stressed: "The young are creatures of contingency. They pattern their lives on the standards their society in fact (not in theory) exalts. They will adopt standards that are held up to them, but only on the condition that they are genuine standards, only on the condition that their elders do subscribe to them and live by them, in deed as in word."[28] Indian leadership sadly fails today in putting up before the youth of the country the image of the creative leadership of the future. Their precept and example are often wide apart. Their stress on democracy and its values would be more effective if they in practice allowed those values to govern their actions. Their advocacy of equality in social, economic, and political life would make a more abiding impression if their actions in many instances did not belie it. Their condemnation of political expediency can be taken more seriously if they themselves by action show that they also are not governed by it. If casteism is an evil, according to them, let their record show that it does not influence their choice of candidates for election. On these and several counts, the present leadership has not a proud record.

The other type of action necessary is to allow younger leadership to grow. The atmosphere in India is not at present very conducive for such a growth. As S. K. Patil, Minister for Food and Agriculture in the Nehru Cabinet, is reported to have said in an interview on the BBC, Mr. Nehru "is both an asset and a liability to India." He is the greatest asset we have had because "he is just like a banyan

[28] Henry S. Commager, "Urgent Query: Why Do We Lack Statesmen?," *New York Times Magazine*, Jan. 17, 1960, p. 21.

tree under whose shade millions take shelter.   Through no fault of his own, he is also a liability because under the shade of that banyan tree, biologically nothing grows."[29]   What applies to Nehru applies to all other leaders in more or less degree whether in the political, economic, or social fields.   The ruling and the dominant persons and groups have to show greater foresight and vision and have to stand ready to shed with good grace positions of prestige, privilege, and advantage—social, economic and political—if a young and vigorous leadership is to rise to take their place.

Finally, the present national leadership has to conceive its task on lines similar to those that the first generation of English-educated Indian national leaders chalked out for themselves.   They regarded the nationalist movement as an all-sided one for the rejuvenation of the Indian people and made social reform and education an equally important part of it along with political advancement.   By now there is enough experience of political independence to show that by itself nationalism does not work the miracle of economic or social progress, nor can it be legislated, as was once believed in nationalist circles.   It is time to take this lesson to heart and to begin in right earnest in those fields of social reform and education which have been neglected.   Here again the effort has to be by way of operational ideology rather than a purely theoretical one, of which perhaps we have more than enough.   Only such an active policy along a broad front can succeed against the powerful block of social inefficiency in India.

Perhaps many other desirable lines of action can or will be suggested.   I have put down some that according to my light are important.   But the supreme need is to recognize the problem that exists and to try to face it and solve it.   I feel that its very existence has tended to be ignored or argued away in the past.   This obscurantism must be given up.   The problem is undoubtedly difficult but not intractable.   The first prerequisite of its successful solution must be its recognition.   I hope that this paper will contribute in a humble way to such a recognition.

[29] *Eastern Economist* (New Delhi), Nov. 27, 1959, p. 842.

10

Tax Burden for Indian Agriculture

Ashok Mitra

I

DESPITE THE TWO Five Year Plans, the outlook for Indian agriculture continues to be uncertain, and this state of affairs has been widely commented upon in recent discussions.[1] The advances in agricultural productivity during the First Plan are now being regarded with some circumspection, and even the record output reported for 1958-59 has failed to generate much optimism, since the harvest in 1959-60 again showed a decline. Although one can read an upward trend in the index of agricultural production since 1950-51, the influence of the climatic cycle obviously still remains preponderant (Table 1). It therefore needs some daring to try to isolate the genuine elements in India's agricultural progress—that is, those induced by fresh capital formation and improved organization —from the fortuitous ones. A rate of advance of 2.5 per cent per annum since 1950-51 is now considered to be a "realistic" estimate. Since the country's population is growing annually at 2 per cent,

Table 1. Index of Agricultural Production
(Agricultural year ended June 1950=100)

	1950-51	51-52	52-53	53-54	54-55	55-56	56-57	57-58	58-59
Food grains	90.5	91.1	101.1	119.1	114.0	114.9	119.9	108.3	128.0
Non-food grains	105.9	110.5	103.8	104.7	120.4	120.0	130.4	125.7	137.1
All commodities	95.6	97.5	102.0	114.3	116.4	116.9	123.8	114.6	131.0

Source: Ministry of Food and Agriculture, Government of India, *Agricultural Situation in India.*

[1] See, for example, Wilfred Malenbaum, "India and China: Contrasts in Development," *American Economic Review*, XLIX (1959), 284-309; The Ford Foundation, *India's Food Crisis and Steps to Meet It* (New Delhi, 1959); René Dumont, "India's Agricultural Defeat," *New Statesman*, December 19, 1959.

it can hardly be claimed that Indian agriculture has started to break out, even in a modest way, from the groove of subsistence.

What ails agriculture has in recent months become the subject of acute debate, and much of the discussion of the formulation of the Third Plan has concentrated on the possible alternative strategies for transforming Indian farm output. In analyzing the factors which would explain the lag in agriculture, some adverse comments have been made with respect to the amount of public sector outlay on agriculture and ancillary activities in the five-year plans and, more specifically, in the Second Plan.

Table 2. Pattern of Allocation in Indian Plans, Public Sector[a]

	First Plan		Second Plan	
	Rs. Crores	*Per Cent*	*Rs. Crores*	*Per Cent*
Agriculture and commu- nity development	299	14.8	510	11.3
Irrigation	311	15.5	330	7.2
Power	274	13.6	490	11.0
Industries and mining	100	5.0	950	21.1
Transport and commu- nications	532	26.4	1,340	29.8
Social services	423	21.0	810	18.0
Miscellaneous	74	3.7	70	1.6
	2,013	100.0	4,500	100.0

Sources: Government of India, Planning Commission, *Review of the First Five Year Plan*, 1957, and *Appraisal and Prospects of the Second Five Year Plan*, 1958.
  [a] The outlays on multi-purpose projects have been equally distributed between irrigation and power. The figures for the First Plan represent final outlay; for the Second, they represent revised estimates. (1 crore = 10 million.) Actually, total outlay in the public sector under the First Plan was about Rs. 1960 crores, according to final accounts. No breakdown of the latter figure is, however, available.

The reduction in the proportion of total outlay from above 30 per cent in the First Plan to a meager 18 per cent has been frowned upon: this pattern of allocation, it has been argued, does justice neither to the fact that nearly half of the country's output originates in agriculture nor to the operational reality that significant industrial expansion is not possible without corresponding progress in agriculture, which must provide the additional labor for the industrial sector, additional wage-goods to feed this additional labor transferred from agriculture to industry, and, finally, the raw materials needed for industrial processing. Through the neglect of agriculture, investment allocation in the Second Plan is supposed to have vitiated the most elementary of developmental strategies.

Dissent has also been entered regarding the Second Plan assumption of the capital-output ratio in agriculture. Private investment in agriculture was never expected to exceed Rs. 200 crores, and therefore developmental outlay of Rs. 820 crores in the public sector in agriculture implied an aggregate investment in the order of Rs. 800 crores, for at least a quarter of the public sector outlay was, from the beginning, intended for non-investment operations.[2] Since agricultural output was expected to increase by 18 per cent over the Plan period, the *ex ante* capital-output ratio would appear to have been slightly less than unity.[3] Given the presence of a large number of irrigation projects with long gestation in the Plan, such a rate of return was unlikely and has not come about. The lack of investment funds has allegedly slowed down the construction of field channels and other ancillary works, and has prevented the adequate provision of fertilizers and seeds; in short, through its policy of stint, the government has unnecessarily delayed the revolution in agricultural productivity.

It is being urged that the government, as the leading entrepreneurial entity in the country, ought to shift the emphasis in investment allocation to agriculture, because here the autonomous elements are unlikely to work out the pre-conditions for growth. Indian agriculture presents a qualitatively different case from Indian industry, which already possesses an articulate and rapidly expanding private sector. Economic planning, being a program for action at the margin, should therefore mean a relatively larger government effort in the field of agriculture. To correct the "sector lag," the state must act as the instrument for greater capital formation—on its own and through a program of subsidies—in agriculture. Also, since most of the agricultural sector is on the verge of subsistence, the wherewithal for agricultural development has to come from outside, and it should be the government's role to draw resources from the other sectors and turn them over to agriculture. That is to say, the state must not only look favorably upon, but also bring in operational instruments to influence, the inflow of investible funds from the industrial and commercial sectors to agriculture.

[2] These were, of course, mostly extension services.

[3] Agricultural output in 1955-56, the last year of the First Plan, was Rs. 4,390 crores.

Although cutting across classical notions with respect to the realization of surplus for economic development, the above opinion has gained considerable ground. The purely economic plea for improving backward agriculture through a draft on the "affluent" non-agricultural sectors often also gets mixed with extra-economic motivations. The biggest supporters of such assistance programs for agriculture, apart from the substantial agricultural blocs in Parliament and outside, are, for example, those idealists who dislike industrial development, equate agriculture with egalitarianism, and who would therefore rejoice at any arrangement which would make industry and commerce pay for the uplift of agriculture.

The common argument for subsidizing agriculture through a program of taxation of the other sectors is based on the fact that per capita income outside agriculture is nearly two-and-a-half times higher than the per capita income in agriculture. Given this wide disparity in earnings, it is considered only fair that the additional sacrifice developmental efforts call for should come, if not exclusively, at least overwhelmingly from the more advanced sectors. The relative burdens of sacrifice under the existing tax structure are scarcely referred to, and it is taken as self-evident that the present balance of advantage is against agriculture.[4] Little sympathy is shown for the point of view that, in a period of rapid development, the sectors of transport, commerce, and industry may not afford to launch an operation of net lending, that frequently the foreign exchange needed in these sectors is not to correct a particular technological deficiency but reflects a genuine resource gap; or that, while taxation of these sectors may be in order for a re-allocation of resources *within* subsectors, a policy of further taxation to enable a net transfer of resources *outside* may vitally affect growth.

Can one claim categorically that limits to tax effort have been reached in agriculture, and that there is no scope for further maneuverability? Does the level of per capita income convey adequately the taxable capacity of the different population groups constituting the total agricultural community? Is it established that government budgetary operations are, in the net, at present benefiting industry, transport, and commerce, if not exactly at the expense of, at least relative to the benefits accruing in, agriculture?

[4] This argument does not take into account the fact that urban living probably requires a higher money income, so that this type of straight comparison exaggerates the real differences in economic conditions.

Much of the discussion on these and related issues is carried on without reference to concrete data. It is the object of this paper to develop some estimates which might indicate the existing tax burdens on agriculture and the other sectors in the Indian economy. These estimates will be based on an assessment of what the government as a whole has taken out of and, as against that, has put into the agricultural sector in recent years.

II

We will start with an examination of the yield from direct taxes. By and large, the Indian Constitution gives the individual states the privilege to collect direct taxes from agriculture. Except for the areas directly administered by the Union Government, the proceeds from land revenue flow to the exchequer of the states. Similarly, the Constitution excludes incomes from agriculture from the purview of the general income tax, and the states are granted the prerogative to impose taxes on earnings from agriculture within their respective areas, as well as to levy estate duties in respect to agricultural land. These taxes between them nearly exhaust the category of direct levies on agriculture.[5]

The complicated pattern of the land revenue system in the different systems is described in detail in the *Report of the Taxation Enquiry Commission.*[6] The basis of collection varies from state to state, and the criteria used include, among others, net assets or economic rents, net produce or annual value, rental value, capital value, the amount of gross produce, and other empirical considerations. The Commission recommended the adoption of some form of standard assessment for the entire country, but hardly any progress has been achieved in this direction. Taxation of agricultural income is of very recent origin in India. The exemption limits and the rates of tax vary considerably, and in many states the tax is either non-existent or nominal. The estate duties on agricultural land have shown yields only since 1954-55, and the volume of collection is

[5] The *panchāyats* at the village level are empowered to levy certain minor taxes, but the existing yields are so insignificant that we can ignore them.

[6] Vol. III, p. 181 ff. See also Daniel Thorner, *Agrarian Prospect in India* (New Delhi, 1956).

scarcely significant.[7]   The aggregate revenue yield since 1950-51 under the various direct tax heads is presented in Table 3.

Table 3.   Direct Taxation of Agriculture

(Rs. Crores)

	1950-51	51-52	52-53	53-54	54-55	55-56	56-57	57-58	58-59	59-60
Land revenue (states)	49.58	47.99	57.41	70.73	72.58	80.33	92.66	87.33	92.81	100.45
Agricultural income tax	4.09	4.03	4.06	3.77	4.77	5.74	5.73	7.80	7.97	8.11
Estate duty (states)	—	—	—	—	0.52	1.94	2.38	2.43	2.51	2.52
Land revenue (Centre)	2.00	2.88	0.43	0.76	0.45	0.88	0.54	0.35	0.57	0.54
	55.67	55.20	61.90	75.26	78.32	88.89	101.31	97.91	103.86	111.62

Source: Report on Currency and Finance, 1957-58 and 1958-59. The estimates for 1958-59 and 1959-60 are provisional.

What about the incidence of indirect taxes on agricultural income? The most important basis for estimating the indirect tax burden is still the findings of the sample survey on tax incidence conducted by the Indian Statistical Institute at the instance of the Taxation Enquiry Commission.   This survey, which was made with reference to the fiscal year 1953-54, considered the incidence of the following taxes: central excise, transport duties, opium excise, liquor excise, general sales tax, sales tax on motor spirits, entertainment tax, interstate transit duties, sugar cane cess, and motor vehicles tax.

Although the results of the survey, summarized in Table 4, relate to 1953-54, in the aggregate both the structure and the rates of indirect taxes, at the Centre as well as in the states, have not changed appreciably since 1950-51.   Indirect taxes as a proportion of total tax revenue have oscillated around 60 to 65 per cent during this period.   The importance of certain individual taxes—such as the general sales tax—has increased significantly, but this has been compensated for by downward movements in yields from other indirect taxes, so that the absolute increase in the revenue earnings from this category has merely kept pace with the increase in national income

[7] A summary of the tax effort in the states during 1951-56 is given in the Planning Commission's Review of the First Five Year Plan, May, 1957, pp. 26-28.

since the beginning of the Plan era.[8]   It will thus not be farfetched to assume that the proportion of indirect taxes in aggregate expenditure has continued to maintain the level of 2.9 per cent in the rural parts of the country.

Table 4. Indirect Tax as Percentage of Total Expenditure

| | Monthly Household Expenditure Level (in rupees) | | | | | |
	1-50	51-100	101-150	151-300	Above 300	All Levels
Rural	2.2	2.3	2.7	2.8	4.4	2.9
Urban	3.3	4.4	5.1	5.1	8.3	5.9
Rural and urban combined	2.4	2.7	3.1	3.3	5.6	3.6

Source: Government of India, *Report of the Taxation Enquiry Commission*, I, 69.

A further assumption now becomes necessary.   The rural sector is wider than the agricultural sector as such and, in addition to the latter, will embrace segments of small enterprises, commerce, trade, and transport.[9]   Since it is likely that the level of earnings in the non-agricultural rural sector is higher than that in agriculture, the proportion of the tax burden should also be higher in the former case.   This burden therefore ought to be somewhat less than 2.9 per cent of total expenditure for agriculture.   Besides, we have to take into account the probability that, for the total agricultural population, expenditure incurred must be slightly less than income originating, despite the low level of capital formation.   We may conclude that approximately 2 per cent of agricultural income in the aggregate is being paid out in the form of indirect taxes.

The 1953-54 survey of indirect taxes was incomplete in one respect.   It excluded the incidence of export duties (Table 5).[10]   The three main categories of agricultural produce subject to export duties are tea, raw cotton and waste, and oil seeds.   The duties are subject

[8] For a detailed review, see "Indirect Taxes—Retrospect and Prospects," *Tata Quarterly*, Oct., 1959, pp. 95-116.

[9] ". . . the whole of the income from agriculture, ⅔ of the income from 'small enterprises,' ½ of the income from 'domestic services' and 'house property,' and ⅓ of the income from 'other commerce and transport' are assumed to constitute rural income" (K. N. Raj, "Resources for the Third Plan," *Economic Weekly*, Annual Number, 1959, p. 204).

[10] It is of course open to debate whether export duties should be considered as an indirect tax.

Table 5.   Export Receipts and Export Duties

(Rs. Crores)

	1950-51	51-52	52-53	53-54	54-55	55-56	56-57	57-58	58-59
Exports	596	729	572	526	588	604	607	631	565
Revenue from export duties	47	91	56	39	41	38	29	27	22

Source: "Indirect Taxes—Retrospect and Prospects," p. 101. The estimates for 1958-59 are provisional.

to continuous review, and with the exception of tea the importance of the duty content in total export earnings from these commodities has gradually dwindled over the years. Although a precise judgment is difficult, as a working hypothesis it can be taken that about 20 per cent of the aggregate revenue from export duties impinges on agriculture.[11]

We can thus arrive at estimates of the total burden of indirect taxes in the agricultural sector in recent years (Table 6).[12]

Table 6.   Impact of Indirect Taxation on Indian Agriculture

(Rs. Crores)

	1950-51	51-52	52-53	53-54	54-55	55-56	56-57	57-58	58-59
Levies other than export duties	95	98	94	104	85	88	107	103	120
Export duties	8	18	11	8	8	8	6	5	4
Total	103	116	105	112	93	96	113	108	124

It is now possible to develop a composite picture of the relative tax burdens in the agricultural sector and outside. Table 7 does this by bringing together the relevant elements in the Indian tax structure; Table 8, which is a derived table, presents the same facts in the form of percentages.

III

Certain features of the Indian tax structure immediately become evident. Agriculture accounts for nearly half of the country's

[11] Even a 100 per cent margin of error in this assumption will not seriously affect our argument.

[12] In Table 6, figures in the first row represent 2 per cent of aggregate income in the agricultural sector at current prices.

Table 7. Tax Burden in the Indian Economy

(Rs. Crores)

	1950-51	51-52	52-53	53-54	54-55	55-56	56-57	57-58	58-59
1. Direct taxes on agriculture	56	55	62	75	78	89	101	98	104
2. Indirect taxes on agriculture	103	116	105	112	93	96	113	108	124
3. Total tax on agriculture (1+2)	159	171	167	187	171	185	214	206	228
4. Total tax revenue	628	740	670	668	713	751	857	1,046	1,047
5. Tax on nonagriculture (4−3)	469	569	473	481	542	566	643	840	819
6. Income from agriculture	4,780	4,910	4,710	5,200	4,230	4,390	5,380	5,170	6,060
7. Total national income	9,530	9,970	9,820	10,480	9,610	9,980	11,310	11,360	12,480
8. Income from non-agriculture (7−6)	4,750	5,060	5,110	5,280	5,380	5,590	5,930	6,190	6,42

Sources: The figures for national income are official estimates by the National Income Unit, Central Statistical Organization, Government of India. The tax revenue estimates are from an unpublished document prepared by the Economic Division of the Planning Commission; the figure for 1958-59 is provisional.

Table 8. Tax Burden in the Indian Economy

(Percentages)

	1950-51	51-52	52-53	53-54	54-55	55-56	56-57	57-58	58-59
1. Direct tax burden in agriculture	1.2	1.1	1.4	1.4	1.8	2.0	1.8	1.8	1.7
2. Indirect tax burden in agriculture	2.2	2.4	2.3	2.2	2.2	2.2	2.1	2.1	2.0
3. Total tax burden in agriculture (1+2)	3.4	3.5	3.7	3.6	4.0	4.2	3.9	3.9	3.7
4. Tax burden in non-agriculture	9.9	11.2	9.3	9.1	10.1	10.2	10.9	13.4	12.8
5. Tax on agriculture in total tax revenue	25.3	23.1	24.9	28.0	24.0	24.4	24.5	19.2	21.8
6. Agricultural income in national income	50.2	49.2	48.0	49.6	44.0	44.0	47.6	45.5	48.6
7. Tax element in national income	6.6	7.4	6.8	6.4	7.4	7.5	7.6	9.2	8.4

aggregate output; the tax yield from agriculture, however, has accounted for between only one-fifth and one-fourth of the total tax revenue in recent years. In fact, the tax complex of the country is made up of two disparate fiscal systems. In the agricultural sector, barely 4 per cent of the aggregate income flows out to the state in the form of taxation. Outside agriculture, on the other hand, the government's tax claims are in the neighborhood of 10 per cent. The current average tax revenue for the nation as a whole—about 8 per cent of national income—tells only part of the story and conceals the significant reality of two parallel tax structures.

Table 8 brings out something else as well. The tax burden on the non-agricultural segments of the economy has increased somewhat in recent years. The rate of increase may not be regarded as sufficient in many quarters, but at least the stagnant pool of inelastic tax revenue has been disturbed. But this change has not affected the tax yield from agriculture at all. Since the initiation of the Five Year Plans in 1951-52, therefore, the relative tax burden has moved in favor of agriculture.

Of course, where per capita income levels are very wide, a comparison of the tax burden on aggregate incomes cannot adequately reflect the relative real sacrifices undergone by two sectors or communities. In Table 9 we have therefore tried to work out the per capita income levels in agriculture and in the rest of the economy on certain assumptions and have compared them with the per capita tax levels in the two sectors. This will provide some idea of the tax-income spreads in and outside of agriculture.

Per capita income in agriculture has thus been between one-third and two-fifths of the level of per capita income in the rest of the

Table 9. Per Capita Tax Burden in the Indian Economy
(in Rupees)

	1950-51	51-52	52-53	53-54	54-55	55-56	56-57	57-58	58-59
1. Per capita income in agriculture	126	127	185	201	160	163	195	184	213
2. Per capita income in non-agriculture	451	471	466	472	472	480	500	511	533
3. Per capita tax in agriculture	6.5	6.9	6.6	7.2	6.5	6.8	7.7	7.3	7.7
4. Per capita tax in non-agriculture	44.5	52.9	43.1	43.0	47.5	48.8	54.3	69.4	66.8
5. (1) as percentage of (2)	43.7	41.8	39.7	42.6	34.0	34.0	39.0	36.1	40.1
6. (3) as percentage of (4)	14.6	13.0	15.3	16.7	13.7	13.9	14.2	10.4	11.7

Note: The Census of 1951 estimates of the agricultural and non-agricultural populations form the basis of the per capita derivations; it has been assumed that, both inside and outside agriculture, population has increased by 2 per cent per annum.

economy over the years; per capita tax in the former case, in contrast, has been only between 10 to 15 per cent of the per capita tax level in the non-agricultural sectors.

There are two ways of looking at this phenomenon. It can be argued that the stiffer rates of tax assessment in the non-agricultural sectors are but a manifestation of the operation of a system of progressive taxation. If the income level of one community is two-and-a-half times that of another, under certain circumstances a tax rate differential of the order of even 600 to 700 per cent could be justified. It has also been suggested that the actual burden of taxation in the sectors outside agriculture is much less than one would think from a comparison of total tax revenue and total income. Once the revenue collected from the big firms and corporations is taken out of the tax receipts from non-agriculture, the "tax-income" spread between agriculture and the rest of the economy, we are told, is likely to come down appreciably.

But it is as easy to present a contrary point of view. An aggregate is an aggregate, and if there is any plea to leave out the taxes paid by the big corporations and business firms for making the estimate of the tax burden in non-agriculture more realistic, it can then be urged that, at the other end, the tax collected from the big plantations be also excluded while working out the arithmetic of tax burden in agriculture.[13] Considering both points of view, it seems permissible at least to ask whether agriculture is not relatively undertaxed in India.

This question has to be raised not for the sake of any abstract equity in taxation, nor for the sake of correcting in an exact degree the imbalance between the respective burdens borne by agriculture and non-agriculture. Where a considerable proportion of the agricultural population is close to the subsistence level, the pursuit of any precise balance between the taxation burdens inside and outside agriculture is beyond a point bound to be futile. At that point it becomes a matter of dealing with two separate economic realities, and, in consequence, of two distinct tax climates. Any thought of raising the rate structure in agriculture in order to lessen the tax burden in industry and commerce must therefore be discarded. Even if the case for such

---

[13] There can be no doubt, given the slab system in agricultural income tax, that an element of progressiveness, however mild, inheres in the agricultural tax structure too.

a realignment of burdens could be built, it would be impossible to put into operation such a scheme, given the political and social factors involved in the process of decision-making.

Another consideration, on a slightly different plane, can, however, be put forward. Can it not be that while a unilateral increase in the tax burden on agriculture would meet with fierce opposition, agriculturists might still be persuaded to acquiesce in contributing a larger share of income toward tax revenue, provided the non-agricultural sectors are also asked simultaneously to raise their rate of contribution?[14] One of the major problems for the country over the next several years will continue to be the problem of raising the tax yield as much as possible. A policy which best furthers this object should be considered to be the most desirable, irrespective of what it might do at the margin to the relative tax burdens of the different sectors. Thus, if it is found that further tapping of agricultural income is feasible only if accompanied by parallel taxation of the other sectors, it would be unwise not to do so for fear of further distorting the relative tax burden. The correct approach in such a situation would be to proceed with imposing further taxes in the non-agricultural sectors—assuming that this can be done within fair limits, thus facilitating the raising of tax rates in agriculture as well.

This strategy of simultaneous approach actually has other advantages. Much has been heard of late of the desirability of lowering the exemption limit for general income tax from the current level of Rs. 3,000 per annum. This exemption level is more than ten times the level of per capita income in the country and contrasts sharply to the practice in a large number of countries, where the spread is much narrower and hardly ever more than five times. A strong case no doubt exists for bringing down the income tax exemption level so that the relatively less affluent sections of the community would also contribute toward the country's rapid economic development. However, in the absence of any overt measures to increase the tax burden on agricultural incomes, it will be politically difficult to push down this level, the more so because of the strong union elements among the white-collar workers who would be most affected by any such lowering of the limit.

[14] Dr. A. K. Sen calls this phenomenon the "Isolation Paradox." See his paper "On Optimising the Rate of Saving," *Economic Journal*, LXXI (Sept., 1961), 479-96.

IV

Some ambivalence may appear to have crept into this discussion on the question of balance between the imposts on agriculture and the rest of the economy. When we suggest that, during the next few years, efforts should be directed to increasing the absolute burden in all sectors of the economy, that need not be read as a plea for retaining the current relative tax position between the different sectors. The issue is partly one of over-all priority and partly one of strategy. Since it is agreed that limits to taxable capacity have not yet been reached in either agriculture or non-agriculture, the task should be to introduce stiffer tax measures all around. While, given the existing political complex, an increase in the absolute volume of taxation in any sector would be difficult to enforce unless accompanied by corresponding measures in the "rival" sectors, it is not essential that the marginal increases in the burden must be the same everywhere. So long as particular groups are convinced that they are not being called upon to make a unilateral sacrifice, they are unlikely to examine too closely the relative shifts which follow from the new measures of taxation. It would therefore even be possible for the authorities to get away with a new tax structure which would move the relative taxation burden against agriculture.

Inter-country comparisons would fail to convince anybody that an increase in the tax burden on Indian agriculture would be grossly inequitable. In Japan the spread between per capita incomes in primary and secondary industries during 1893-97 was about the same as in India at present, and primary production also contributed between 45 and 50 per cent of national output.[15] But while India collects only about 20 per cent of the total tax revenue from agriculture, land tax made up more than 45 per cent of the government's revenue in Japan in 1893-94 (38.8 billion yen out of 85.8 billion yen).[16] This provides some indication of the lag in the Indian tax effort.[17]

---

[15] See Shigeto Tsuru and Kazushi Ohkawa, "Long-Term Changes in the National Income of Japan since 1878," *Income and Wealth*, Series III (Cambridge, 1953), pp. 19-44.

[16] G. C. Allen, *A Short Economic History of Modern Japan* (London, 1946), p. 44.

[17] It may also be useful, in the light of recent developments in China commented upon by both Wilfred Malenbaum (*op. cit.*) and René Dumont (*op. cit.*), to take a look at the following table on distribution of government receipts by

Can we say anything regarding the extent of subsidies which agriculture receives from the rest of the economy through budgetary operations? Let us consider this flow for the five years of the First Plan. During 1951-56, the aggregate non-Plan expenditure on the part of the Union and state governments was of the order of Rs. 1,939 crores and Rs. 1,927 crores, respectively.[18] On the very modest assumption that 20 per cent of the total non-Plan expenditure was spent on the agricultural sector, we get the figure of Rs. 773 crores as representing public non-Plan expenditure on agriculture. Since the Plan outlay on agriculture and irrigation amounted to Rs. 619 crores,[19] aggregate public expenditure in the field of agriculture must have been in the neighborhood of Rs. 1,400 crores over the First Plan period.

The total tax revenue from agriculture during 1951-56 was on

---

sectors in that country and also read the accompanying comment of the Economic Commission for Asia and the Far East:

Mainland China: Distribution of
Government Receipts by Sectors, 1953-57

(percentages)

Year	State enterprises	State-private enterprises	Co-operatives	Private enterprises	Peasants	Other	Total
1953	62.9	1.2	2.3	16.9	13.4	3.1	100.0
1954	65.2	1.7	3.7	13.3	14.2	1.9	100.0
1955	71.1	2.2	4.4	7.7	13.2	1.4	100.0
1956	73.6	5.5	5.4	2.8	11.2	1.5	100.0
1957	72.0	7.0	8.0	1.0	11.0	1.0	100.0

"The declining importance of agricultural taxes and land subscriptions from peasants is shown by the fall in their combined total from 13.4 per cent of aggregate state receipts to 11 per cent during this period. However, *peasants undoubtedly made a growing contribution to the receipts of state enterprises. These receipts were obtained largely from transactions with the peasants, from whom the state enterprises, through the medium of cooperatives and collectives, buy agricultural products and to whom they sell foodgrains (in the case of peasants, growing industrial crops), agricultural requisites and essential consumer goods.*" *Economic Survey of Asia and the Far East* (Bangkok, 1957), p. 101, italics supplied. Although the *modus operandi* of taxation is quite different in China, there can be little doubt that at present at least 50 per cent of the total revenue receipts of the state is coming from agriculture. This is also the conclusion of Malenbaum: "While direct taxes on agriculture (land and income) have been increasing [in India], they still account for less than 10 per cent of the total tax revenues in 1956/57. Rough estimates of the total tax burden for agriculture suggest an order of magnitude of about 20 per cent of all taxes, as compared with a ratio of at least three times as great in China." (Malenbaum, *op. cit.*, p. 305.)

[18] These figures are from the unpublished document prepared by the Economic Division of the Planning Commission referred to above.

[19] See Table 2 above.

the order of Rs. 880 crores, to which it is necessary to add the non-tax revenue receipts. The only item under this head, for the period under consideration, is the net receipts from irrigation, which add up to Rs. 47 crores for 1951-56.[20] Public receipts from agriculture during the First Plan therefore work out at about Rs. 925 crores in the aggregate.

This still leaves out any possible flow of funds on capital account from the agricultural sector to the public exchequer. The volume of total capital receipts involved in the First Plan outlay amounted to Rs. 600 crores, made up of market borrowings (Rs. 205 crores) and small savings and unfunded debt (Rs. 304 crores). Out of these the only category that might have drawn from agriculture would be small savings. It is hardly likely that anything more than 10 per cent of the total collection under small savings would have come from agriculture.

It would thus seem not unreasonable to conclude that a total sum of Rs. 950 crores represents the upper limit of the possible flow from agriculture to the government during 1951-56, while the government's disbursements to agriculture over the same period were at least Rs. 1,400.

V

Let us examine the several possible courses in terms of the magnitudes involved. If agriculture is to yield a surplus of even nominal size, the tax revenue from the sector must increase about 150 per cent above the present level. On the other hand, if it is intended that the current proportions of external subsidies be continued for agriculture, the authorities would have to raise the tax burden on the rest of the economy. The absolute quantity of subsidy claimed by agriculture would go up,[21] and since the public sector is likely to expand steadily in the rest of the economy, the rate of taxation outside agriculture must be adjusted upwards. This would call for a further

---

[20] The receipts from irrigation (net) have been estimated to have been Rs. 7 crores, Rs. 8 crores, Rs. 9 crores, Rs. 11 crores, Rs. 10 crores, Rs. 9 crores, Rs. 11 crores, Rs. 7 crores and Rs. 9 crores respectively for the fiscal years 1950-51 through 1958-59. Source: Reserve Bank of India, *Report on Currency and Finance*, 1957-58 and 1958-59.

[21] This would be so since a given proportion of resource gap would represent a larger sum as the economy moves forward.

increase of the tax rate above the 12 to 13 per cent already reached in non-agriculture. It is an open question whether such a policy of tax increase in the latter sector could be combined with a program of non-intervention in agriculture.

A compromise could be worked into a short-period program of action. A doubling of tax revenue from within would more or less close the resource gap in agriculture, and this target could be spread over a period of five to seven years. This limited program of action is likely to avoid the strains of more violent tax reforms, could be gradually worked into the existing system and would, as we have seen, allow the creation of a favorable climate for further taxation outside agriculture as well.

Here we come face to face with another issue. Granted the need for raising the revenue yield from agriculture, should this additional revenue be derived through the medium of fresh taxation, or should this be linked to the provision of certain basic services in agriculture? There is a powerful group of egalitarians who are convinced that any general raising of land taxes would do more harm than good to the prospects of economic development. An increase in the level of agricultural taxation across the board, they argue, would scarcely be able to differentiate between the different income ranges, would hurt people with inferior qualities of land to the same extent as those with better land, and would therefore be featured by a built-in inequity. Since the object is to transfer to the state a certain proportion of the *marginal* increase in income in agriculture, the best approach, according to this view, is to charge farmers at a high rate for the provision of irrigation facilities, to collect betterment levies from improved lands, and to levy prices which leave a sufficient margin of profit for chemical fertilizers supplied. In this way a definite *quid pro quo* could be introduced between the charges imposed and the services rendered to the farmers—an arrangement which would be not only much more politically acceptable but also economically justifiable. The element of discrimination would be removed from taxation; only those who are going to reap an extra benefit would be called upon to part with a portion of their marginal earnings.

This suggestion for transforming agricultural taxation into a system of service charges may appear tantalizing. The results obtained from the major experiment in this direction during the Second Plan are, however, discouraging. Since 1956 several states have tried to introduce betterment levies, somewhere at the level of Rs. 150 per acre, payable over a period of fifteen years. But although the additional irrigation potential created by the various major and medium projects since the beginning of the First Plan must have gone up by about 9 million acres by 1958-59, the yield from betterment levies up till now is hardly worth mentioning. The following comments of the Planning Commission, made in May 1958, are revealing:

The yield from betterment levies was expected to be Rs. 47 crores (Rs. 31 crores to be made available to the Centre by way of repayment of loans and Rs. 16 crores to be utilized for the States' own plans). As against this, the estimates of the likely yield over the Plan period given by the States in the course of their discussion with the Commission in December-January last, add up to Rs. 6 crores. In fact, from the measures taken so far, a yield of only Rs. 2 crores is expected.[22]

The yield from irrigation rates too has shown little improvement. The major problems involved in attempting to secure fresh revenue from such service charges are administrative. By their very nature, such charges call for separate and somewhat complicated organizational apparatus for purposes of collection, and this multiplicity of rates and modes of collection further adds to the burden of the shaky administrative hierarchy at the village level. Farming populations affected by such levies assert that since it is one of the essential functions of the state to insure, for example, an adequate supply of water, a special levy is unjustified and even discriminatory. Other groups of egalitarians are not lacking who would argue that it is immoral on the part of the state to try to make a profit from the sale of essential seeds, fertilizers, and water.

There is another consideration which suggests that such special charges, in the balance, might retard rather than encourage the rapid improvement of agricultural productivity. The crux of the Indian agricultural problem is to induce a breakthrough in the traditional attitudes of the farmer, so that on his own volition he takes to better farming practices, including increased utilization of water, seeds, and fertilizers. Once a high price tag is attached to the use of these services, it is possible that all passion for development would be quickly spent, and the farmer would fall back to his subsistence habits. If, however, he is encouraged to make use of these facilities

[22] *Appraisal and Prospects of the Second Five Year Plan*, p. 21.

and services at normal, or, in some special cases, even subsidized rates, he might not be averse to handing over to the state a part of the increased income resulting from the spurt in agricultural productivity. This debate can be interminable, and it can even be argued that raising the levels of land tax is one of the best ways to force lethargic farmer groups into adopting better techniques.

When the other issues are resolved, the stock argument remains that aired with respect to the proposal for raising direct taxes in agriculture: it would prove excessively harsh on smallholders. It thus becomes a question of the operational feasibility of evolving a series of new tax measures incorporating a set of protective clauses which would safeguard the interests of cultivators in the lower income ranges.

VI

It is the extreme inequality of income distribution in Indian agriculture that offers the greatest hope of working out such a progressive tax structure. That a skewed distribution of income promotes a relatively higher volume of savings is, after all, one of the commonest of hypotheses in economic analysis. Since, in India, despite the presence of acute income inequality, the system does not by itself turn the savings over to capital formation outside the agricultural sector, the catalytic role of the state and of rising levels of taxation assume much importance. The First Report on Land Holdings, conducted under the National Sample Survey,[23] has thrown fresh light on the pattern of distributional inequalities in Indian agriculture. The Survey indicates that of the 66 million rural households in the country, nearly 15 million, or 22 per cent, do not own any land at all, another 25 per cent hold less than one acre each, while, at the other end, 13 per cent of the total households exercise permanent ownership rights over almost 65 per cent of the total area. These data refer to the agricultural year 1953-54, but since the process of elimination of intermediaries was almost completed by that year, it is unlikely that the pattern has been substantially altered in the meanwhile. The basic findings of the Survey with respect to land ownership are reproduced in Table 10.

[23] *Sankhyā, The Indian Journal of Statistics,* XIX, Pts. 1 and 2 (Feb., 1958), 29-180.

Table 10. Distribution of Land Ownership in India

Size of holdings (acres)	Cumulative percentage of rural households	Cumulative percentage of total area
0.00	22.00	—
Less than 1.00	46.89	1.38
Less than 2.50	60.76	6.31
Less than 5.00	74.42	16.77
Less than 10.00	87.29	35.99
Less than 15.00	92.41	49.16
Less than 20.00	95.07	58.94
Less than 25.00	96.50	65.73
Less than 30.00	97.57	71.95
Less than 40.00	98.67	79.72
Less than 50.00	99.14	84.40
Less than 75.00	99.69	91.27
Less than 100.00	99.81	93.34
Less than 250.00	99.97	98.13
Less than 500.00	99.99	99.32
Above 500.00	100.00	100.00

Source: First Report on Land Holdings, *loc. cit.*, p. 90.

Since the Report includes information on the average size of the household for each size group of ownership holdings as well as on the average household size for the rural area as a whole,[24] it is possible to work out the ownership distribution of aggregate land area among various strata of the population. Table 11 shows roughly the manner in which holdings above 15 acres, constituting 50.84 per cent of total area, are held by less than 12 per cent of the agri-

Table 11. Land ownership in Rural India

Size of holdings (acres)	Percentage of agricultural population	Percentage of total area
More than 15	11.9	50.84
More than 20	8.2	41.06
More than 25	6.3	39.27
More than 30	4.7	28.05
More than 40	3.1	20.28
More than 50	2.4	15.60
More than 75	9.6	8.73
More than 100	0.4	6.66
More than 250	0.03	1.87
More than 500	0.01	0.68

[24] *Ibid.*, p. 167.

cultural population. The nature of the land problem becomes obvious from this pattern of ownership distribution.

Intense discussion has taken place in recent years on setting a ceiling to land ownership per family. At the urging of the Planning Commission, legislation regulating the size of holdings has been passed in a number of states, and similar measures are on the anvil in other states. Debate is still continuing on the economic advantages and disadvantages of imposing a ceiling and also, at a somewhat more concrete level, on the "correct" magnitude of the ceiling in different parts of the country, given qualitative differences in the soil, differences in crop pattern, variations in the availability of water, etc. The issue has obvious political implications. Despite the isolated pieces of legislation, the position by and large is still very confused, and it is unlikely that any definite pattern of decisions will take shape within the next few years.[25] Whatever way the controversy is resolved, it appears certain that some degree of inequality of land distribution will continue to be a feature of Indian agriculture.

While we may expect a gradual moving away from the gross inequalities in the land system, the case for evolving a differential system of taxation affecting cultivators owning holdings above a certain size will therefore continue to be strong. In the immediate short period, the case for such additional tax measures is indeed overwhelming, given the facts illustrated by Table 11.

Although it is not the intention of the present paper to explore all the ramifications of such a tax proposal,[26] it is our belief that the short-period target of doubling the revenue from agriculture can be achieved through the levy of a revenue surcharge on all household holdings in excess of 15 acres, the surcharge rising progressively for larger holdings.

Of course, ownership of holdings by itself does not imply that the entire income from the holdings flows exclusively to the owners. In the first place, there is an appreciable amount of leasing to tenants, so that it is not self-evident that the 11.9 per cent of the agricultural population who owned 50.84 per cent of the total cultivated area

[25] For a summary of the controversy, see Raj Krishna, "Agrarian Reform in India: The Debate on Ceilings," *Economic Development and Cultural Change*, VII, No. 3 (April, 1959), 302-317.

[26] Since the Census of Land Holdings includes particulars on the pattern of distribution of holdings in individual states, it should be possible to work out variations in the tax measures which would take into account local conditions.

obtained the same proportion of the aggregate income from agriculture in that year. The Report on Land Holdings[27] suggests the following pattern of leasing out of owned area for the upper agricultural groups:

Area Owned per Household (acres)	Percentage Leased Out
18.75	7.40
24.37	8.22
29.38	6.65
41.13	8.23
88.40	7.46

If we assume that on the average roughly 7.5 per cent of the area is owned by all households owning more than 15 acres of land, not more than 20 to 25 per cent of the income originating in these holdings would have accrued to the owners in 1953-54.

In the second place, even in the case of self-operated land, it is necessary to make allowance for hired agricultural workers, who share in the net income from cultivation. In the absence of direct estimates, we can but hazard a guess about the proportion of involvement of outside labor in owner-operated holdings. It is entirely possible that 10 to 15 per cent of the income from such holdings flows out as wages of hired labor.

At the other end of the scale, it is necessary to recognize that, as a rule, larger holdings are characterized by superior productivity per acre compared to holdings of less than fifteen acres. Apart from the fact that bigger family holdings imply larger cultivating units which allow for the familiar economies of scale, the ability to invest superior input also makes for a great difference. It is easy to see that output from the 51 per cent of the total agricultural land belonging to the more affluent 12 per cent of the cultivating community would form a substantially higher proportion of aggregate agricultural output.[28]

Let us make the courageous—but not very unrealistic—assumption that the "bonus" from superior productivity of land is more or less balanced by the claims on output from tenants and outside workers, so that, in the net, the several population groups owning

[27] Loc. cit., p. 59.
[28] Since the order of magnitude involved is small, we are here ignoring the fact that a part of the total agricultural output originates in non-rural holdings.

land in excess of 15 acres shared the total agricultural income in 1953-54 in the same proportion in which the total land area was distributed between them.   Granted this hypothesis, we can derive the agricultural income distribution in 1953-54 shown in Table 12.

Table 12.   Distribution of Agricultural Income Among Populations Owning More Than 15 Acres 1953-54

Size of Land Ownership (acres)	Population (crores)	Total Income (Rs. crores)	Per Capita Income (rupees)
More than 15	3.08	2,644	858
20	2.13	2,135	1,002
25	1.63	1,782	1,093
30	1.22	1,460	1,197
40	0.80	1,054	1,318
50	0.62	811	1,308
75	0.16	453	2,831
100	0.10	346	3,460
250	0.008	97	12,125
500	0.0026	32	12,308

Note: The assumption about total agricultural population is the same as in Table 9.

In 1953-54, therefore, of the total estimated agricultural population of 25.93 crores, 3.08 crores apparently earned Rs. 2,644 crores, enjoying a per capita income of Rs. 858, while the residual vast mass of 22.85 crores managed with only Rs. 2,556 crores, that is, with a per capita income of Rs. 112.   This pattern of income distribution is unlikely to have changed significantly in recent years.

These estimates again indicate that generalized observations about such categories as income or tax burden are not very meaningful; the components of the aggregate should always be looked into.   The statement that per capita income in agriculture is barely Rs. 200 per annum assumes a new operational reality when accompanied by the valuable additional comment that for at least one-tenth of the agricultural population the level of per capita earnings is at least four times as much.   The task of further taxation in agriculture should be relatively easy, given this highly skewed income distribution. Doubling the revenue yield from agriculture involves an additional claim, on the part of the state, of Rs. 200 crores per annum, which is equivalent to 6 or 7 per cent of the earnings of the agricultural population holding more than 15 acres.   There is no economic reason why this group, with an apparent per capita income of the order of Rs. 850 per annum, should not be compelled to undergo this marginal sacrifice, which is certainly moderate compared to what would be implied in some of the more radical proposals.[29]

VII

Despite the several crudities in our estimates, the margin of error is unlikely to be so high as to blur the one outstanding conclusion. About 10 per cent of the agricultural population in India constitutes a privileged minority: they own land which is more than half the total cultivated area, their per capita income is significantly higher than even in the major segments of organized industry and commerce, yet they are among the least taxed groups in the country. Even assuming that this minority contributes as much as four-fifths of the total revenue at present collected from agriculture, the tax burden is merely 5 per cent of their income. With a per capita income which is apparently 40 per cent lower, the non-agricultural population is carrying a tax burden which is twice this proportion.

The draft outline of the Third Five Year Plan suggests an additional taxation target of Rs. 1650 crores over the five-year period, and considers the fulfilment of this target as "vital for the successful implementation of the Plan."[30] Even if the program of doubling the tax yield from agriculture is phased over the Third Plan period, a minimum aggregate yield of Rs. 600 crores is not impossible to contemplate for the five years 1961-66, and this could go a long way to close the gap in the financing of the Plan. Can India afford the luxury of foregoing to claim, for purposes of the state, a slightly larger proportion out of the income of what appears to be the most affluent economic group in the nation? Given the will, working out the technical details of such a scheme of taxation, impinging on the prosperous peasantry, should not prove difficult. It is primarily a question of decision-making at the political level.

[29] See in this connection K. N. Raj's suggestions in "Resources for the Third Plan," *Economic Weekly*, Annual Number, 1959. They include: "(i) doubling of land tax on holdings above five acres; (ii) a tax on agricultural rent (deducted at source from tenants), the incidence of which falls on the rent-receivers, and fixed at, say, one-tenth of the gross produce of the tenants; and (iii) a surcharge on holdings, above five acres, under commercial crops (with adjustments, of course, for different kinds of commercial crops)," p. 206.

[30] Government of India, *Third Five Year Plan: A Draft Outline*, p. 49.